THE SYNTAX OF BEOWULF

WORD ORDER, POETIC METER, AND FORMULAIC TECHNIQUE IN THE OLD ENGLISH VERSE CLAUSE

THE SYNTAX OF BEOWULF

WORD ORDER, POETIC METER, AND FORMULAIC TECHNIQUE IN THE OLD ENGLISH VERSE CLAUSE

GEOFFREY RUSSOM

UPPSALA BOOKS
London

UPPSALA BOOKS

London, England

www.uppsalabooks.com

Copyright © Uppsala Books 2025

ISBN 978-1-961361-22-5 Hardback

ISBN 978-1-961361-23-2 Paperback

For Jacque

CONTENTS

1. Basic Principles of Language and Poetic Form   1

2. Formulaic Composition   67

3. SOV Clauses and Their Derivatives   103

4. SV Clauses and Their Derivatives   175

5. Existential and Predicate Adverbial Clauses   203

6. Predicate Adjective Clauses   219

7. Predicate Nominative Clauses   243

8. Participial Clauses   253

9. Clauses with Uninflected Infinitives   279

10. Remainders   343

11. Conclusions   369

Appendix   381

Glossary of Technical Terms   397

Bibliography   407

CHAPTER 1

BASIC PRINCIPLES OF LANGUAGE AND POETIC FORM

§1.0 Why *Beowulf?*

The oldest ancestor of English, called Proto-Indo-European, has been re-constructed from the earliest writings in languages descended from it, nota-bly Greek, Sanskrit, and Hittite. Proto-Indo-European is generally thought to have been spoken in an area east of Europe sometime between 4500 BCE and 2500 BCE. During the first millennium BCE speakers of an Indo-Eu-ropean language migrated to the Jutland peninsula of Denmark and adjacent territory to the south (Mallory 1989: 87, 197). By about 500 BCE their lan-guage, called Proto-Germanic, had differentiated from Indo-European lan-guages in the neighboring Baltic, Celtic, and Italic areas. As speakers of Proto-Germanic migrated to other parts of Europe their languages differen-tiated further. Gothic, an East Germanic language, provides the earliest sub-stantial corpus of written evidence, which dates from the fourth century CE. North Germanic languages like Danish, Swedish, Norwegian, and Icelandic developed among speakers who remained in Jutland or migrated farther north. West Germanic languages like English, Dutch, and German deve-loped among migrants who moved westward and southward. Germanic mi-grants settled among non–Indo-European peoples like the Finns and among early European peoples whose languages did not survive and whose ways of life could leave traces only as influences on cultures still accessible to inves-tigation.

Alliterative poetry survives in Old English, Old Norse, Old Saxon, and Old High German texts with remarkably similar features of style and meter. Some of these features are already present in a runic text inscribed around

1

300 CE, before North and West Germanic had differentiated (discussed below in §1.11). Kiparsky (1973: 321) observes that alliteration "seems to be found as an obligatory formal element only in languages where the stress regularly falls on the same syllable in the word, which then must be the alliterating syllable." The stimulus required for Germanic alliterative meters was a shift in late Proto-Germanic from the movable Indo-European accent to a strong expiratory stress on the first syllable of the word. A shift to initial stress also took place in neighboring Celtic and Italic languages and alliterative meters are also found in the oldest poetic texts from those language groups (Salmons 1992: 5; Russom 2017: 35–53).

In the late Proto-Germanic era poetic form was the main technique of preservation for history, mythology, customary law, and other indispensable fields of traditional culture. In order to perform that function poetry had to be accessible to a general audience and transmitted without the aid of writing. As in other pre-literate cultures, Germanic poets used formulaic techniques to compose long heroic narratives. Some archaic expressions were so memorable that they had survived the shift to alliterative meter. Watkins (1995: 374) reconstructs an Indo-European formula for the killing of a great serpent and identifies a descendant of this formula in epithets for famous Germanic dragon-slayers, including Sigurd Volsung, known as *Fáfnisbani* 'killer of the dragon Fafnir,' and the god Thor, known as *orms ein-bani* 'sole killer of the Midgard serpent,' a sea-dragon that encircles all of Middle Earth. Norse *bani* corresponds to Old English *bana,* which survives today as *bane.* This word is identifiable as poetic because it is derived from an Indo-European verb that became obsolete before the earliest surviving epics were composed and survived primarily in poetic texts. The defining plot of Indo-European heroic epic narrates a defense of society against chaos monsters, which include giants as well as dragons. According to Watkins (1995: 300), the chaos monster is a "figuration of all that is anti-social." That definition applies perfectly to the monsters of *Beowulf.* The man-eating giant Grendel is an *ān-genga* 'lone-walker' (165a, 449a), a sociopath who refuses to atone for his killings with compensation (154b–58b). The dragon killed by *Beowulf* hoards gold in a wasteland retreat, coming forth only to ravage his nearest neighbors. Beowulf, a giant-slayer, a dragon-slayer, the strongest warrior of his time (196a–97b), and the largest man his contemporaries have ever seen (247b–49b), bears a striking resemblance to Hercules, "the prototypical Greek hero" (Watkins 1995: 374).

Linguistic evidence dates *Beowulf* to around 700 CE (Fulk 1992; Neidorf 2014). It is by far the earliest long poem with traditional narrative content that survives to us in a Germanic language. It gives cultural historians their

2

best glimpse of what life was like in Germania before centralization of power in anything like a modern state. For literary critics *Beowulf* provides an instructive contrast with contemporary experimental poems in English, highlighting just what is experimental about them. The formulaic style that facilitated oral transmission in a pre-literate era stays close to basic clause structure, providing excellent statistical evidence for syntacticians. Rules of poetic meter provide information about the evolution of English that would otherwise be unavailable. Comparison with other poems in alliterative meter can provide explanations for divergent evolution in Germanic languages and syntactic innovations in later English (Russom 1998, 2017). These special opportunities for research make *Beowulf* an ideal candidate for comprehensive syntactic analysis.

§1.1 Evidence from related fields of study

Here I seek to explain the differences in word order that distinguish *Beowulf* from texts in Old English prose. Old English poets inherited an alliterative meter that had probably been used for a millennium before *Beowulf* was composed. Word order had changed significantly during that time but poets continued to use the original orders when newer alternatives would be metrically unacceptable. Archaic word order also plays a significant role in poetry of the English Renaissance. "Neither a borrower nor a lender be," a line uttered by Polonius in *Hamlet,* would have sounded quite old fashioned to people in the original audience of the play. Its verb-final word order was the predominant one in *Beowulf* but had become obsolescent by Shakespeare's time. We cannot interview the people in that audience, of course, but we know that Polonius's line would have sounded archaic because verb-final order is rarely used by Shakespeare when a modern alternative would be metrically acceptable. As Youmans (1983) showed, archaic order is required in this case because 'Be neither a borrower nor a lender' does not scan as a line of iambic pentameter. If the modernized alternative were recited by mistake during a performance of *Hamlet*, many lovers of poetry would know in a small fraction of a second that the line was metrically defective, though they could probably not say what was wrong with it. It would just *sound* wrong. In addition to purely syntactic topics, then, we will need to consider the prehistory of Old English, the rules of alliterative meter, and formulaic techniques for creating metrically acceptable verses, which include systematic use of archaic syntax. The first two topics are intimately related and will be explored in this chapter. Chapter two will be devoted to formulaic technique.

§1.2 The logical basis of syntactic terminology

A logical proposition consists of a PREDICATE, for example *races*, and one or more ARGUMENTS, for example *Frankie* and *Maseratis* in *Frankie races Maseratis*. In logical notation, this proposition can be expressed as *Rf,m,* with an upper-case abbreviation for the predicate followed by lower-case abbreviations for the subject and object arguments, in that order. Since *races* takes two arguments here, it is a two-place predicate. In *Frankie smiled, smiled* is a one-place predicate expressed as an intransitive verb with the subject *Frankie* as its only argument. This proposition can be notated as *Sf*. There are also three-place predicates like *Frankie gave a Maserati to Brett*, with the indirect object argument *Brett* in addition to the subject *Frankie* and the direct object *Maserati*. In a logical formula for this proposition, *Gf,m,b,* the order of arguments is subject, direct object, indirect object — an iconic representation of the fact that direct objects are more closely related to the verb than indirect objects. In an act of gift-giving, the subject performs the action of giving directly on the gift to transfer it to a recipient, who is more distant from the action.

Subject and object arguments are the major characters in the little story told by a sentence. They are distinct from ADJUNCTS, which provide additional information about a predicate or argument. Adjuncts do not affect the basic structure of a sentence (Crystal 1985: 8, 22). *Frankie gave a Maserati to Brett* has the same basic structure as *Acting on this generous impulse, Frankie gave a drop-dead gorgeous Maserati to an astonished and delighted Brett*. Though irrelevant to the basic structure of the larger sentence, each adjunct could express a proposition on its own, were it not for one defect: these adjuncts do not contain a FINITE VERB specifying the time within which a proposition is meant to be interpreted. The defect can often be repaired by a finite form of a 'be' verb, as for example in *Brett was astonished and delighted,* to be interpreted within past time. *Acting on a generous impulse* is not a proposition because its verb is a non-finite participial form that leaves the required time unspecified. For the same reason, *to act on a generous impulse* fails to qualify as a proposition because its verb is 'infinitive,' the familiar grammatical term for non-finite *act* as used in phrases like *to act*. With *act* used as a finite imperative form, on the other hand, we get *Act on this generous impulse!*, a proposition about what ought to happen right now.

Frankie told her to race the new Maserati expresses only one proposition because it has only one finite verb, *told*. *Frankie told her that she should race the new Maserati* expresses two propositions because *told* and *should* are both finite verbs. The difference between these sentences may seem trivial but it has a conspicuous effect on English word order, since the GRAMMATICAL PROPOSITION is the domain within which syntactic movement usually occurs. In both sentences the LOGICAL SUBJECT of *race* is a feminine pronoun. In the sentence expressing one proposition, the pronoun has been RAISED from the infinitive construction, moving leftward into a higher-level object position governed by the finite verb. In this position the pronoun has its appropriate object form, *her*. Native speakers of English have no trouble figuring out that the grammatical object of the finite verb is the logical subject of the infinitive, which is routinely unexpressed when the object is raised, as often happens with surplus information in human languages. The sentence expressing two propositions is like the more compact one with regard to meaning but *she* cannot be raised from the grammatical proposition introduced by *that*. If the subject of *should* were raised to object position after *told* we would have **Frankie told her that should race the new Maserati*, which is flagrantly unacceptable. The finite auxiliary *should,* which requires a grammatical subject, must have a separate pronoun of its own.

The concepts of predicate, argument, and adjunct can be very helpful when we consider important formulaic techniques such as use of adjunct modifiers and approximate paraphrases for their metrical value. We will not need to confront the very tricky problems that arise when theoreticians attempt a comprehensive integration of logic and syntax that accounts for the most remote structural possibilities. Quite the contrary: formulaic diction can be helpful to linguists because it maximizes use of the simplest, most effective, and most widely used structures, providing excellent statistical evidence for basic word order. In an important monograph on requirements for logical coherence, Nunes (2004: 81) must consider why *There arrived three men last night without identifying themselves* arguably conforms to rules of English grammar internalized by children but **I met three men last night without identifying themselves* is absolutely hopeless. No competent storyteller would use either of these constructions.

§1.3 Linguistic Typology

Our understanding of basic word orders has been enhanced by the typological approach introduced in Greenberg (1966), which is extended to an even wider variety of languages in Croft (2003) and Dryer (2007). See Traugott (1992: 168–289) for an application of typology to Old English prose syntax. At sentence level, rules of word order apply to verbs and arguments, the MAJOR CONSTITUENTS of the sentence. Adjuncts have no direct effect on the order of major sentence constituents and their placement is largely predictable from placement of the constituents they modify. The order of major constituents in many constructions can be predicted from the order of a sentence with a lexical subject, a lexical main verb, and a lexical object. The term LEXICAL refers to words that have low frequency and high information content, like the words in *Frankie likes Maseratis*. Lexical constituents contrast with FUNCTIONAL constituents like pronouns and auxiliary verbs, which have high frequency and low information content. The three most common orders in the world's languages are SOV, SVO, and VSO. These are the orders that have the subject before the object. SOV order is the most common of the three (Dryer 2007: 62, 72).

Smith (1971: 1–3) adopts the consensus view that Indo-European was an SOV language. His hypothesis is that Proto-Germanic, the prehistoric ancestor of Old English, retained its inherited SOV constructions and evolved gradually toward SVO syntax, with gradual loss of SOV constructions in the daughter languages after they differentiated. Smith surveys the evolution of Germanic syntax in chronologically stratified corpora of early texts, focusing on prose. The earlier strata include runic inscriptions, archaic laws, and manuscripts in Gothic. The Gothic manuscripts, dating from the fourth century CE, provide the earliest Germanic texts of significant length. To my knowledge, Smith's contribution to historical syntax is available only in his PhD dissertation, which may explain why so few subsequent publications on early Germanic word order mention it. Smith's dissertation director cites him in Antonsen (1971) but there is no citation in Antonsen (2002). Lehmann (1993) does not mention Smith in his study of Proto-Germanic but provides arguments that support Smith's SOV hypothesis. A few years after Smith wrote, Vennemann (1974: 368) hypothesized that Proto-Germanic had 'TVX' structure, with the verb in 'V2' position after the topic (T) and before everything else (X). Arguments in favor of verb-second order were also advanced by Hopper (1975: 68–71). Antonsen (2002: 295) identifies a serious problem with the evidence used by Vennemann and Hopper to support their claim: "This opinion," he observes, "is obviously based on the evidence of the later dialects, particularly Old English and Old High German. The older runic inscriptions, which are considerably closer to the parent language (often by some 500 years or more), still display XV order for the verb and its complements by a ratio of almost four to one, not counting those sentences consisting only of subject and verb." The misleading later evidence mentioned by Antonsen comes from Old English prose. As we shall see, *Beowulf* is more like the earliest runic inscriptions and provides evidence *against* the V2 hypothesis, not *for* it (Russom 2022a). The V2 hypothesis seems plausible only because the vast majority of runic texts come from the North Germanic area, in which verb-final order had become rare by about 600 CE, much earlier than in West Germanic languages (Smith 1971: 34, 97–99). Smith (1971: 82) observes a strikingly higher percentage of verb-final order in the East Germanic texts most likely to be in idiomatic Gothic, as compared with those most vulnerable to influence from a source language. I will adopt the SOV hypothesis here, partly for reasons explained in Russom (2022a). In this book, however, I will focus on the value of the SOV hypothesis as a necessary point of departure for analysis of word order in *Beowulf*. New metrical evidence for the hypothesis will be presented as the argument unfolds.

The relation of verbs to objects is called GOVERNMENT and transitive verbs are said to GOVERN their objects. As we shall see, the typology of government constructions plays a crucial role in the evolution of alliterative meter. Governors can assign special forms to the governed word. Verbs assign object case to their objects, as for example in *I like them* versus **I like they*. Auxiliary verbs govern other verbs and assign infinitive or participial form to them. Auxiliary *will* requires infinitive *melt* in *It will melt*. Without the auxiliary, we would have *it melts,* but **It will melts* is unacceptable. In the active form we have *I drove* but the passive auxiliary *was* requires *I was driven* rather than **I was drove* (except in dialects where *drove* is used systematically as a past participle). Other parts of speech can be governors as well. Like verbs, prepositions govern objects and assign objective case to them, as in *I'm suspicious of them* versus **I'm suspicious of they*.

Governors are generally less prominent than the words they govern. Auxiliaries and prepositions are usually unstressed in Modern English and their function is primarily grammatical, restricting the meaning of the governed word rather than expressing a meaning of their own. In *I will go*, the auxiliary functions as a grammatical marker of tense. It can become even less prominent by contraction, as in *I'll go*. When prominently stressed in *I wíll go*, *wíll* has the restricted sense of negating any assumption that the speaker will fail to go. Confinement to a restricted sense shows that a word is being used in an unusual way. A prominently stressed preposition has similarly restricted sense when placed before its object, as for example in *fly óver the bridge, not únder it, Wingnut!* Governors that are usually unstressed also bear stress in a restricted syntactic location: at the end of a phrase. The auxiliary has light but perceptible stress in *go now, if you wìll*. Since *wìll* has stress here, it cannot be contracted. Nobody says **go now, if you'll*. Main verbs have important meanings as well as grammatical functions. They are the most prominent governors. Though more prominent than other governors, main verbs are less prominent than the stressed nouns in a typologist's

SOV, SVO, or VSO sentence. In such sentences the verb is subordinated to a stressed argument (Gussenhoven 1992, Tuckenbrot 2006).

The placement of governors and their governed constituents tends to remain consistent in a given language (Dryer 2007: 42, 72). In a strict SVO language like Modern English, main verbs, auxiliaries and prepositions all come before the governed constituent. In a strict SOV language, main verbs and auxiliaries follow the constituents they govern and we find POST-POSITIONS rather than prepositions. Prepositions and postpositions are included in the more general category of ADPOSITIONS.

§1.4 Disruption of basic word order by leftward movement

As Nunes observes (2002: 1), "A fundamental property of human languages is that syntactic constituents are interpreted in positions different from the ones in which they are phonetically realized." A major factor in disruption of basic word order is a processing strategy that gets easy tasks out of the way before focusing effort on more difficult ones. There is a universal tendency toward placement of lighter, more easily processed constituents before heavier, more complex constituents (Croft 2003: 70–1; cf. Behaghel 1923–32: IV, 3–9). Object pronouns, for example, refer to entities that have already been introduced into the discourse. In Old English these pronouns often appear before heavier noun subjects that introduce something new with unpredictable characteristics. Case is more precisely marked on pronouns than on nouns in Old English and facilitates interpretation of a pronoun object fronted from its basic position after the subject. I will refer henceforth to the basic position of a constituent as its NORMATIVE position. I use 'normative' rather than 'normal' because movement from normative positions is too common to be called abnormal. As we shall see, constituents also have normative positions within the alliterative line. We will need to discuss relations between normative syntactic positions and normative metrical positions.

There is a tendency in human languages to perform similar grammatical functions in similar ways. The technical term for this is TYPOLOGICAL POLYSEMY (Croft 2003: 108–10). In Modern English, fronting of constituents to initial position performs two closely related grammatical functions: TOPICALIZATION and RELATIVIZATION. Consider an interchange between two speakers: *Do you like spaghetti and mushrooms? Spaghetti I like, mushrooms I don't.* The second speaker topicalizes the object nouns *spaghetti* and *mushrooms* by moving them from their usual locations after the verb to initial position before the subject. A similar function is performed by fronting

in *You're offering me spaghetti, which I like, and mushrooms, which I don't.*
Here the fronted objects are expressed as relative pronouns rather than repeated verbatim. In both kinds of construction fronting the object brings it
closer to the preceding clause, highlighting the semantic relation of the
fronted object to its antecedent. Emphatic fronting exploits the universal
principle of ICONICITY, whereby ordering of words tends to imitate ordering
of other entities in human experience (Croft 2003: 102–10). Closer syntactic
proximity is an effective way to emphasize close semantic relations. Emphatic fronting of objects has restricted frequency in Modern English, where
strict word order compensates for the decline of the inflectional system. It is
much more common in *Beowulf*.

The most conspicuous marker of linguistic prominence is stress but
there are also distinctions of prominence among unstressed syllables. In
Anttila, Dozat, Galbraith & Shapiro (2020), MEANINGFUL PROMINENCE in
unstressed constituents is distinguished from MECHANICAL PROMINENCE assigned by stress rules based on syntax. Greater meaningful prominence cor-
relates with lower frequency and higher information content. Unstressed
constituents with lower meaningful prominence are more vulnerable to reduction, omission, or loss from the language, all other things being equal.
Present-tense forms of *be,* the verb of highest frequency, can be reduced by
contraction in English (*I'm, you're, they're,* etc.). In these forms the verb
loses its vowel and becomes part of a larger phonological word. Third-person
present-tense 'be' verbs are often unexpressed in human languages, as for
example in the Latin motto *Dominus illuminatio mea* 'God (is) my light.'
Some varieties of English have the same kind of predicate nominative construction. Modal auxiliaries have high frequency and can be contracted with
a negative particle (*mightn't, shouldn't,* etc.). In these constructions the verb
retains its vowel and the vowel of the negative particle is lost. Auxiliary verbs
are less likely to be reduced than 'be' verbs because they supply important
information about probability and ethical values in addition to tense. A
somewhat different kind of prominence reduction occurs in unstressed constituents that are closely bound to stressed constituents. As Kiparsky (2018)
observes, inflections are less prominent than unstressed words because an
inflection contrasts with a stressed syllable in the smallest prosodic domain.
Rules of iambic pentameter are sensitive to such differences in prominence.
Unstressed pronoun subjects and objects are major sentence elements and
move rather freely within a sentence. As we shall see, rules of alliterative
meter are sensitive to a difference in prominence between unstressed arguments and unstressed words like adpositions, which are closely bound to
stressed constituents in smaller prosodic domains like postpositional or pre-

positional phrases (Kuhn 1933). Adpositions cannot be omitted but they are less prominent than major sentence constituents, including 'be' verbs. The effect of close binding is independent of information content.

The constituents with the lowest prominence are the ones most likely to be moved leftward and raised upward. This tendency becomes conspicuous when we look at the *Beowulf* poet's placement of Old English main verbs, modal auxiliary verbs, and 'be' verbs. Finite forms of these verbs often occur at the end of a phrase or clause, as in SOV languages. In this position they have mechanical prominence and are treated as stressed by the rules of Old English meter (OEG: 35–36). Finite forms of OE *wesan* 'be' and *weorðan* 'become' have the highest frequency and the lowest information content. In *Beowulf* 63% of these 'be' verbs have been moved leftward to positions where the metrical rules treat them as unstressed. Finite auxiliaries, with their low but significantly higher prominence, are moved leftward to unstressed positions in only 19% of total instances. Only 9% of main verbs are fronted to unstressed positions. As expected, the exceptional verbs have the highest frequency and the lowest prominence. They include verbs of motion like *cuman* 'come' or *gān* 'go,' verbs of perception like *sēon* 'see' or *cunnan* 'know,' and QUASI-AUXILIARIES like *onginnan* 'begin' or *lǣtan* 'let, cause.' Quasi-auxiliaries are so called because they often govern infinitive verbs as auxiliaries do, though not always. Modern English constructions with quasi-auxiliaries and infinitives are *let fly* and *begin to fly*. For detailed analysis of these prominence gradations see Russom (2017: 91–92, 118–23). Lexical nouns and adjectives are very rarely placed on unstressed positions. The handful of examples in alliterative verse are fronted predicate nominatives or adjectives, which appear to have undergone stress subordination when fronted to clause-initial position. A lexical adjective fails to alliterate in *tot ist **Hiltibrant*** 'dead is Hildebrand,' verse 44a in the Old High German *Hildebrandslied*; and a lexical noun fails to alliterate in *mál er mér at **ríða*** 'it is time for me to ride' in the Norse Eddic poem *Helgakviða Hundingsbana II*, stanza 49, first verse (Neckel 1983: 160). There is a single instance in *Beowulf* with a non-alliterating noun: *mǣl is mē tō **fēran*** 'it is time for me to go' (316a), which resembles the Norse example.

Major sentence constituents that move freely contrast with governors like adpositions, which are closely bound to nouns and are confined within phrases smaller than a clause. Like other governors, adpositions are postposed to the governed constituent in strict SOV languages. Postpositional phrases with typical SOV structure can still be found in *Beowulf*, e.g. *Scedelandum in* 'In South Swedish lands' (19b). The poet also employs postposed governors like the possessive pronoun in *hlāford þīnne* 'thy lord'

(267b) and the demonstrative adjective in *ūht-hlem þone* 'that morning-noise' (2007b). As closely bound constituents, these governors have lower prominence than pronouns or high-frequency verbs. The vast majority of adpositions are fronted and unstressed in *Beowulf*. Postpositional phrases are employed primarily when the corresponding prepositional phrase would be metrically unacceptable (Russom 2022a: 598).

§1.5 Fronting of verbs in Indo-European and Germanic

Although the verb usually occupies final position in the ancient IE languages surveyed by Luraghi (1995: 359), verb fronting is common under certain conditions. According to Luraghi, 'initial verbs tend to some extent to occur in clusters, in cases where a number of subsequent sentences can be singled out as constituting a textual sub-unit. Uniformity in word order highlights the coherence of the sub-unit.' Smith (1971: 64–5, 92) is aware of the IE linking function and discusses fronted Germanic verbs that perform the same function in early runic prose. Linkage is only one of the functions performed by fronted verbs. Luraghi (1995: 364) adds PRESENTATIVE sentences in which a fronted verb highlights a change of topic and subsequent sentences in the discourse unit use a different word order. According to Smith (1971: 64), verb fronting was usual in early Germanic clauses with "heavy emphasis on the verb." These include questions, imperatives, hortative subjunctives with imperative force, and clauses with dramatic or pathetic force (Smith 1971: 92). In *Beowulf* EMPHATIC FRONTING to a stressed position can occur with prominent finite verbs that are never fronted to an unstressed position before the first alliteration, e.g. in *stonc ðā æfter stāne* 'sniffed along the stones then' (2288a). Here and subsequently alliterating syllables are represented in boldface. The alliteration on *stonc* shows that it bears metrical stress (Russom 1998: 128–35). According to Griffith (2016: 108–11), many finite verbs that alliterate in initial position are rare or unattested in prose. With their low frequency and high prominence, these verbs are suitable for emphasis and unsuitable for unstressed usage. Some finite main verbs of high frequency can be fronted either to a stressed position or to an unstressed position. Compare for example *secge ic þē tō sōðe* 'I say to you in truth (590a), with alliteration on *s*, and *sægde him þæs lēanes þanc* 'said thanks to him for the loan' (1809b), with alliteration on *l*. Bliss (1967: 6–23) argued that such verbs were unstressed and that alliteration on them was 'ornamental' (cf. Kuhn 1933, Lucas 1987, Kendall 1991). However, as Griffith (2016: 105) observes, Bliss's only apparent reason for positing this kind of alliteration is "to explain away the inconvenient fact that many verbs alliterate where his view of the syntax predicts that they ought not to do so." Getty (2002: 47–48) finds Bliss's approach unacceptable because alliteration is biased toward robustly lexical verbs with rich information content.

As Kiparsky (1973: 231) observes, meters that govern alliteration by rule do not alliterate on unstressed syllables. Old English pronouns are governed by alliterative rules only when stressed. The demonstrative pronoun *þā*, for example, provides the required alliteration in *þonne **þā** dydon 'than **they** did'* (*Beowulf* 44b), where contrastive stress on *þā* 'they' distinguishes those who gave gifts at an earlier time from *hī* 'they,' the subject of the preceding clause, which refers to different people who have just given different gifts. When there is no independent evidence for stress on a pronoun, it appears where alliteration would be unacceptable. A typical example is line 43 of *Beowulf*: *nalæs hī hine **læ**ssan   **lā**cum tēodan* 'they by no means provided him with lesser gifts.' If *hī* had metrical stress in the first verse, placement of *nalæs* before it would be unacceptable (K4: 332).

Negation and interrogation perform similar functions and tend to be expressed similarly in the world's languages, in accord with the principle of typological polysemy (Croft 2003: 108–10). Modern English routinely fronts question markers like *why,* interrogative auxiliary verbs, and negative particles in obligatory instances of NEGATIVE ATTRACTION like *nobody goes.* Compare **anybody doesn't go,* an unacceptable construction with the negative particle incorporated into a later constituent (Labov 1972a). Fronting facilitates processing in these constructions by providing advance notice that the semantic content of the clause is being questioned or negated rather than asserted in the usual way. In Old English the same purpose is served by fronting negated verbs, something that occurs in most main clauses (OES: 661).

§1.6 Changes in placement of governors between Proto-Germanic and Old English

If we view gradations of prominence from a chronological perspective, a scenario for the prehistoric era can be constructed. It seems reasonable to suppose that postposed function words of very high frequency like adpositions, articles, and possessive pronouns — the constituents most likely to be fronted — were the first to disrupt SOV typology. If fronting of these constituents within small phrases acquired sufficient frequency it would set a pattern for fronting of slightly more prominent finite verbs within clauses, progressing gradually from 'be' verbs through auxiliaries to quasi-auxiliaries and high-frequency main verbs. The formulaic diction of *Beowulf* seems to represent a time when fronting of high-frequency function words was well on the way to completion but fronting of finite main verbs was just getting underway. Given the typically slow pace of change from one typology to another it is hard to date causes for a given change or even to distinguish causes from effects (Russom 2012). Sooner or later, though, an increasing disruption of SOV order by verb fronting must have accelerated the decline of SOV typology. SVO was a more likely choice for the new typology than VSO because VSO is less common among the world's languages and also because SVO required no change in the relative placement of subject and verb.

§1.7 Disruption of basic word order by heavy constituents

A proposition expressed as a that-clause can function as subject of a larger sentence. Consider two alternative placements for such clauses in sentences with comparable meanings. In both A and B the subject is defined by a that-clause. In placement A this clause stands before the verb in the position usually occupied by the subject. In placement B the clause follows the verb and *it* stands in subject position.

A. *That Frankie likes Maseratis is known.*

B. *It is known that Frankie likes Maseratis.*

Clauses stand at the other end of the complexity scale from unstressed pronouns, the most easily processed arguments and the ones most likely to be placed early in the clause. *That Frankie likes Maseratis* has a stressed main verb and two stressed argument nouns. This clausal constituent is very heavy indeed and the tendency toward rightward placement should accordingly be strong. As expected, placement B is by far the most common one. The pronoun *it* in B is appropriate for initial placement and provides advance notice that information about the subject will be provided later in the sentence. The short main clause sketches out the basic syntax. *It is known* could stand alone as a complete sentence. The decks are now well cleared for processing the information in the clause, which the hearer must accomplish in a small fraction of a second during normal conversation or normal recitation of narrative poetry.

A conspicuous stylistic feature of *Beowulf* is employment of verses like *bearn Ecgþeowes* 'son of Ecgþeow' and *sinces brytta* 'distributor of treasure,' with the noun modified by an adjective or by another noun in the genitive case. In chapter two we will focus on these modified-noun constructions, which frequently appear where a pronoun or single noun would be expected in prose (§2.4). Consider for example line 607 of the poem, *þā wæs on sālum sinces brytta* 'then the distributor of treasure was in a good mood.' If this were prose, we would expect *Hrōðgār* rather than *sinces brytta*, but then the line would be too short. Modified-noun constructions perform the important metrical function of transforming a single word that does not alliterate into a well-formed verse with the proper alliteration. Because modified-noun constructions are heavy, they are appropriate for placement after the verb, contrasting with unmodified noun arguments like *Hrōðgar*, which usually appear in pre-verbal position. Modified-noun constructions are also used as VARIATIONS that have the same referent as another expression in the sentence. The relation between a variation and its antecedent is called APPOSITION. Modern English variations often occur in expressions of contempt or outrage, for example *Heatherington tried to cheat me again, the rat!*, where *the rat!* has the same referent as *Heatherington*. Appositional phrases like *the rat!* can make for vivid dialogue but omission of *the rat!* would cause no problems of sense or grammar. Variations are used with high frequency in *Beowulf*. A conspicuous example appears in the b-verse of line 529, *Beowulf maþelode, bearn Ecgþeowes* 'Beowulf, the son of Ecgþeow, spoke.' Here the optional epithet completes the line and supplies the required alliteration on *b*. This line is repeated verbatim eight times in *Beowulf* when the main character is about to speak. An appositive phrase might convey necessary information in a sentence like *Chris, my sister's boy, just got married*. If the addressee has not met Chris and does not know why the speaker cares about his marriage, *my sister's boy* would provide the necessary introduction. The repetitions of *bearn Ecgþeowes* can have no such introductory function, however, and were evidently used for metrical reasons.

§1.8 Generative syntax

In the foundational era of Chomsky's universalist initiative, called transformational grammar, the starting point for derivation of word order was a DEEP STRUCTURE — a grammatically acceptable order of words with each constituent in the position where it is interpreted (Chomsky 1957). *Bees make honey* would have deep-structure syntax in an SVO language because *bees*, the logical subject, occupies its normative position before the verb and *honey*, the logical object, occupies its normative position after the verb. Alternative word orders were derived by applying transformational rules to deep structures. These rules could add or delete constituents, substitute one form of a constituent for another, and move constituents left or right. Consider placements A and B in §1.7, for example. To derive B from A it was necessary to move the that–clause rightward and insert *it* in subject position, a derivational process called EXTRAPOSITION. To derive the passive construction *honey is made by bees* required a transformation that performed several tasks in several ways: (1) moving the logical object leftward, (2) moving the logical subject rightward, (3) adding *by* before the logical subject, and (4) substituting a two–word predicate for the simple present-tense form *make*. Step (4) required two additional tasks, inflection of the 'be' verb in the singular to agree with the new grammatical subject and changing the finite verb form to a past participle.

Transformational rules sought to explain the kind of thing that happens when someone tries to polish an expression, starting with what comes to mind unbidden and exploring possible alternatives in search of the best one. It proved impossible, however, to represent all stylistic alternatives as transformations of fully formed sentences. In too many cases, even the most carefully formulated transformations generated constructions with the wrong form or the wrong meaning. Transformational grammar was a very productive first approximation. It identified previously unnoticed regularities and greatly clarified the problems to be faced. But words were just too idiosyncratic for that kind of theoretical approach. There was also the problem of explaining transformations as universal organizing principles of the human mind, the ultimate goal of generative syntax. In order to work at all well, transformations had to be implausibly complicated and varied too much from language to language. Although such transformations are no longer regarded as universal procedures that construct spontaneous conversational utterances, they offered precise descriptions of changes in word order used for rhetorical polishing and conformity to metrical rules. The sharp intuitions and analytical skills honed in the transformational era still have great value in metrics, stylistics, and oral-formulaic theory.

The current approach in generative syntax, called the MINIMALIST PROGRAM (Chomsky 1993), finds a way forward by representing all linguistic idiosyncrasies as features of particular word forms in a mental dictionary or LEXICON. Some of these features are syntactic, in the sense that they affect how the form can be placed in an acceptable syntactic structure. Some are purely semantic and have no effect on word placement. A lexical entry also contains phonological features relevant to pronunciation of the word. Factoring out semantic and phonological idiosyncrasies makes it possible to focus on the computational process that organizes words into intelligible orders. In a minimalist derivation a syntactic feature of a word is CHECKED when the word occupies a SYNTACTIC POSITION relevant to that feature. The word then becomes eligible for interpretation in the position where it is checked. Purely semantic or phonological features are carried along by a word during the computation. When a construction with all its syntactic features checked is presented to the faculty of understanding, the words can be interpreted if their semantic features are compatible. If not, the result is nonsense, as with *colorless green ideas sleep furiously,* a widely cited example of a sentence with acceptable syntax and unacceptable semantics (Chomsky 1971: 19). In a separate operation, a given order of words is presented to the faculty of articulation, which constructs an utterance if the phonological features are acceptable. Changes in word order that are not required for intelligibility can be performed on acceptable structures after they are interpretable and before they are pronounced (Chomsky 1993: 22). Such changes can be quite artificial. To show what does not happen in a language, a syntactician might scramble the order of words in a normal sentence. To satisfy the requirements of a strict meter, a poet might employ word orders that are not used in everyday speech. Internalized syntactic rules are required for spontaneous speech at the speed of conversation but we don't have to be satisfied with what first comes to mind and we can speak nonsense, too, if we want to make a point that way. The eminent logician Charles Dodgson, alias Lewis Carroll, made systematic use of nonsense in his fantasy narratives.

Minimalism does the work of transformations with one kind of movement: leftward and upward toward the beginning of a sentence. In §1.2 we encountered a typical example of this kind of movement: *Frankie told her to race the new Maserati,* where the subject of *race* in the infinitive construction has been moved leftward to object position in a higher-level main clause and has the appropriate object case. When a constituent is moved from a position where it has been interpreted it leaves a TRACE in that position. Traces facilitate analysis of complex sentences in which words are interpreted in more than one syntactic position. In *Frankie told her to race the new Maserati, her* leaves a trace in the infinitive construction, where it has been interpreted as subject of *race,* and is then interpreted as the mandatory object of the transitive verb form *told.* In minimalist theory movement rules no longer add or delete constituents. Rather than starting with a complete sentence, minimalism starts with word forms and assembles them into larger constituents with acceptable structures. Kayne (1994) provides a cogent argument for these radical simplifications and uses them to explain a variety of linguistic facts. The price to be paid for simplifying the computational process is a multiplication of abstract syntactic levels. This price is worth paying because it is now possible to formulate rules that could not be expressed with the earlier kinds of transformations.

Minimalist theory replaces the phrase structures of transformational grammar with a single, universal structure that has syntactic positions for a SPECIFIER, a HEAD, and a COMPLEMENT. In *Frankie races Maseratis*, the subject is the specifier, the verb is the head, and the object is the complement. In a prepositional phrase like *totally in ruins,* the adverb is the specifier, the preposition is the head, and the noun object is the complement. Every structure must have a head, and the head of the structure determines what syntactic positions the structure can occupy within a sentence. Specifiers and complements expand a head into a larger structure. The object complement *Maseratis* expands the verbal head *races* into a verb phrase. The subject specifier *Frankie* stands outside the verb phrase to its left and at a higher level of structure. It expands the verb phrase into a sentence. The structure of our Modern SVO example is represented in generative bracketing notation as below, where VP stands for 'verb phrase' and S stands for 'sentence.'

$$[\ [\ [\ \text{Frankie}\ ]_{\text{SPECIFIER}}\quad [\ [\ \text{races}\ ]_{\text{HEAD}}\quad [\ \text{Maseratis}\ ]_{\text{COMPLEMENT}}\ ]_{\text{VP}}\ ]\ ]_{\text{S}}$$

Since *Frankie* and *Maseratis* are logical arguments of *races,* the syntactic positions they occupy are called *argument positions*. Constituents occupying argument positions can enter into case relations with a verb. Each syntactic position in our representative SVO sentence is enclosed by labeled brackets identifying it as a specifier, head, or complement position. The constituents of the verb phrase are enclosed by the brackets labeled 'VP'. The whole sentence is enclosed by the brackets labeled 'S'. These brackets indicate that the sentence consists of a subject specifier followed by a verb phrase with a verbal head and an object complement. Below is a bracketing representation for the SOV construction in *Beowulf* 494b, *þegn nytte beheold* 'the thane performed his service.'

$$[\ [\ [\ \text{þegn}\ ]_{\text{SPECIFIER}}\quad [\ [\ \text{nytte}\ ]_{\text{COMPLEMENT}}\quad [\ \text{beheold}\ ]_{\text{HEAD}}\ ]_{\text{VP}}\quad]\ ]_{\text{S}}$$

The difference between the Modern English SVO structure and the Old English SOV structure is represented as a change in the order of head and complement within the verb phrase.

In our SVO example the transitive verbal head, *races,* has a case-assignment feature that requires a complement with an object-case feature. To be interpretable, the case-assignment feature on *races* must be checked against a complement with object case like *Maseratis*. In Modern English, case features are sometimes expressed as inflectional endings but are often marked by word order alone, with no overt case marking at word level, as with *Maseratis*. A syntactic case feature is present on Modern English object nouns whether or not it is pronounced as an inflectional ending and this feature must be checked against the corresponding verbal feature in a head-complement construction like *races Maseratis*. In such head-complement constructions the verb and object are adjacent at the relevant level of syntactic structure, satisfying a general requirement for checking. After checking, *races Maseratis* becomes interpretable as a verb phrase. In specifier position *Frankie* can have its syntactic features of nominative case, third person, and singular number checked against *races* and *races* can have its syntactic features of third person and singular number checked against *Frankie*. In a subordinate clause like *that Frankie races Maseratis, that* occupies a head position at a higher level of structure than the subject specifier *Frankie*. Conjunctions like *that* occupy a NON-ARGUMENT head position in which they cannot be checked against a verb and cannot receive case. These conjunctions are called COMPLEMENTIZERS because they transform a sentence into the complement of a verb in a main clause.

A minimalist approach to passive constructions can be illustrated with the complex sentence *Frankie is known to like Maseratis*. Some abstract minimalist structure can be ignored for our purposes here. We begin with a set of words in which each word has the form required in the completed expression: *Frankie, Maseratis, is, like, to, known*. The minimalist rules derive a sentence with interpretable word order from the set by merging words within permissible syntactic structures and moving words in such a way that all syntactic features can be checked. We begin by merging *Frankie, like,* and *Maseratis* within the same specifier-head-complement structure as the one discussed just previously, which had *likes* as the verb form. The relevant features are checked as before. Since *like* has infinitive form, it needs to be preceded by *to,* a complementizer that changes sentences into infinitive complements. *Frankie* must move upward and leftward to a higher-level position, leaving *to* and *like* in adjacent positions where their relevant syntactic features can be checked. When this structure has undergone checking it is merged with *known* in a higher-level structure that has a vacant specifier position, *known* as the head, and *Frankie to like Maseratis* as the complement. If the specifier position were occupied by *they* and the head position were occupied by *knew,* we would have *they knew Frankie to like Maseratis,* an infinitive equivalent of *they knew that Frankie likes Maseratis*. The derivation cannot stop here, however, because the past participle *known* must have its features checked in a head–complement construction headed by a finite form of *be* or *have*. What we have so far is accordingly merged into a higher-level structure with a vacant specifier position, *is* as head, and *known Frankie to like Maseratis* as complement. The relevant features on *is* and *known* can now be checked. If we had *it* in specifier position and *that* rather than *to* as the complementizer, the result at this stage would be *it is known that Frankie likes Maseratis* — placement B in §1.7 above. Since the specifier position is empty, however, *Frankie* must move to a specifier position before *is* so that their relevant features of person, number, and case can be cross-checked. The whole sentence now has interpretable word order. As the reader will have noticed, the semantic features of the words are compatible. Presentation to the faculty of understanding will be successful.

In minimalist derivation of a sentence movement follows an orderly upward and leftward pathway called a CHAIN. Chains must be orderly because the faculty of understanding must be able to identify the syntactic position of every trace that a constituent leaves behind when it moves (Radford 1997: 277). Within a chain, the phonological content of surplus traces is deleted before the sentence is presented to the faculty of articulation. In some cases the psychological presence of a trace that is not pronounced has phonological consequences, for example by blocking contraction across the position that it occupies (Postal and Pullum 1978). In English the highest link in the chain is the one pronounced. Other languages may require pronunciation of a lower trace or pronunciation of more than one trace (Nunes 2004: 22–50). Traces are not inherently inaudible and all of them seem to be perceived as normal linguistic constituents. It follows that the clausal sub-units of a sentence will be perceived as SYNTACTICALLY COMPLETE even when their traces are not pronounced. When appropriate, such sub-units can be distinguished as PSYCHOLOGICALLY COMPLETE. In this respect *Frankie is known to like Maseratis* is comparable to the sentences in a mirror-image PARATACTIC version: *Frankie likes Maseratis. People know this. This is known!* The complex sentence and the paratactic sequence of sentences have the same TRUTH VALUE, i.e. they would hold true under the same conditions.

Consider again placements A and B, repeated below for convenience.

A.   *That Frankie likes Maseratis is obvious.*
B.   *It is obvious that Frankie likes Maseratis.*

In transformational grammar the subordinate that-clause of placement B was moved rightward — EXTRAPOSED — to complement position. From the minimalist perspective, heavy constituents are simply hard to move — as the concept of weight would indeed suggest. When heavy constituents *are* moved, they are moved leftward and upward. Heavy lifting of this kind is typically employed for emphasis. What used to be explained as rightward movement of heavy constituents often occurs in Old English when a heavy subject phrase follows a light object, as for example when an object pronoun precedes a lexical subject modified by an adjective. It is now generally assumed that the light object moves upward and leftward to its position before the subject (Pintzuk and Kroch 1989). Stroik (1996) suggested that *it* originates as specifier of the heavy clause in B and that this light specifier then moves to subject position, with the heavy that-clause remaining in place. Though they have different derivational histories and may have different rhetorical effects, placements A and B have the same truth value and provide useful stylistic alternatives. An editor who changed A directly to B would be moving textual constituents from one location to another, somewhat as in transformational grammar, but would not be employing movement as defined in minimalist theory.

Generative grammar has achieved impressive results but much labor may be required to apply it usefully in other fields, as Chomsky was quick to emphasize (Chomsky 1971: 152–53). Minimalist syntax focuses on the many operations that come into play before a sentence becomes intelligible. As we speak and listen, these micro-operations take place with amazing speed and without perceptible effort or conscious thought. Studying them can take us a little farther on a very long journey toward understanding how the brain works, a journey that will not soon be completed, assuming that our species can complete it at all. Metrics and literary stylistics focus on choices among acceptable constructions with similar meaning that may have different minimalist derivations, starting more or less where minimalism leaves off. Ordinary conversation can be effortless but it requires hard work to create a novel in which every sentence has a laudably effective word order or a narrative poem in which effective word orders must be aligned with metrical patterns. In pre-literate cultures, to judge from available evidence, becoming an oral-formulaic poet required years of effort and advice from experienced practitioners (Watkins 1995: 77; Lord 1960: 78). This kind of apprenticeship contrasts sharply with the acquisition of ordinary language by children, who need no explicit instruction and require nothing but a responsive conversational partner (Gleitman and Wanner 1982). Art language is something quite different from ordinary conversation, whether it is composed with much deliberation by a literate writer or with automatic facility by a well-trained bard.

To explain poetic word order in *Beowulf*, clauses can be usefully divided into three domains: a CORE with normative positions for the major sentence constituents, a LEFT PERIPHERY before the normative position of the subject, and a RIGHT PERIPHERY after the core. I will reserve the term *movement* for leftward repositioning of lighter constituents and use DISPLACEMENT for rightward repositioning of heavier constituents. When a stressed finite verb is followed exclusively by heavy constituents in an SOV language a minimalist would say that the verb has been fronted from final position, stranding the heavy constituents in the right periphery. For assessment of choice among Old English word orders with varying derivational histories it is more convenient to assume that the poetic core ends with the normative position of the finite verb and that the core is followed by any heavy constituents in the right periphery. Observing a distinction between movement and displacement will keep the exposition consistent with current research on word order and at the same time allow for unburdened discussion of where a poet *chooses* to put words.

In contrast to rightward repositioning, leftward repositioning often corresponds to leftward syntactic movement in minimalist theory. An important choice in *Beowulf* is whether to leave a constituent in its normative core position or to move it leftward to a position near the beginning of the clause. One of these is the non-argument head position occupied by complementizers, abbreviated as COMP or C. The C position is filled by complementizers like *that* and *if* when they mark a clause as subordinate. In Modern English we can move auxiliary verbs to the C position in order to form direct questions like <u>*Will*</u> *you please express yourself more clearly?* In indirect questions, however, when the C position is filled by a complementizer like *if,* verb fronting is blocked, ruling out constructions like **I'm asking if* <u>*will*</u> *you express yourself more clearly.* Why complementizers and fronted auxiliaries should occupy the same position may become a little easier to understand if we reflect on subordinate clauses like *should you wish to go,* which is logically equivalent to *if you wish to go.* The fronted verb *should* performs the same subordinating function as *if.* For most speakers of English fronting is also blocked by interrogative adverbs when they head subordinate clauses, ruling out **I wonder whether* <u>*would*</u> *you do that* (Redford 1997: 287–94).

Old English makes much freer use of fronting with main verbs that are not interrogatives, imperatives, or hortative subjunctives. In *Beowulf* high-frequency verbs of this kind are fronted to unstressed positions in 115 clauses. Main verbs of lower frequency and higher prominence are fronted to stressed positions at the beginning of a clause in 81 instances. As in Modern English, however, verb fronting is blocked in indirect questions. In *Beowulf* this constraint applies in all clauses headed by *gif* 'if' and in indirect questions headed by *hū* 'how' (13X), *hwā* 'who, what' (3X), *hwā, hwæt* 'what' (8X), *hwǣr* 'where' (1X), *hwæt* 'what' (7X), *hwæþer* 'whether' (4X), *hwanan* 'whence' (2X), *hwyder* 'whither' (1X), and *hwylc* 'which' (2X). When they are used in indirect questions, fronting is also blocked by *þǣr* 'where, when' (35X), *þenden* 'while' (4X), and *þonne* 'when' (22X). *Beowulf* 2372b is a possible example of fronting after *þā* 'when' (30x), which seems to be used there as a subordinating conjunction. With rare exceptions, fronting is also blocked by the complementizer *þæt* 'that' (216X). Although negated verbs in main clauses are normally fronted to absolute initial position in Old English (OES: 661), there is no clear case in *Beowulf* of a negated verb fronted after *þæt*. The only possible example is verse 2657a, *þæt nǣron ealdgewyrht*, 'that they were not just rewards for former deeds,' in which the subject of a predicate nominative construction is unexpressed and the verb is not unambiguously fronted to pre-subject position within the subordinate clause. On the other hand, there are two very rare but unambiguous instances in which a non-negated verb is fronted before an expressed subject in a that–clause: 1593a–94a, *þæt wæs ȳðgeblond eal gemenged, brim, blōde fāh* 'that the tumult of waves, the sea, was all polluted, stained with blood'; and 2301a–2a, *ðæt hæfde gumena sum goldes gefandod, hēahgestrēona* 'that a certain one of men had meddled with the gold, the great treasure.' Both examples are participial constructions with unstressed auxiliary verbs of high frequency, which often undergo fronting to unstressed positions in the poem. These putative examples of 'doubly filled COMP' in West Germanic differ from those identified in Bacskai-Atkari (2020) and deserve further study in larger corpora of poetry and prose. They might be purely poetic constructions.

To the left of C is a higher-level non-argument specifier position occupied by interrogative and negative OPERATORS that trigger fronting of the auxiliary in Modern English direct questions like *why did you do that?* and exclamations like *never would I do such a thing!* Old English interrogative operators trigger verb fronting in the same way (OES 1: 683), but fronting is never triggered by the negative operators in *Beowulf*, which include *nǣfre* 'never' (8X), *nealles* 'by no means' (25X) and its shorter variant *næs* (3X), *nefne* 'if not, unless' (9X), *nō* 'by no means' (49X), and *nymþe* 'if not, unless' (2X).

In *Sir Gawain and the Green Knight,* a Middle English alliterative poem, a variety of constituents can be fronted before a C position occupied by a complementizer. A predicate nominative is fronted by the *Gawain* poet in line 131, *for vch **wyȝe** may wel **wit** <u>no **wont**</u> þat þer were* 'for each man may well know that there was <u>no lack</u>.' A prepositional phrase is fronted in line 903, *þat he **beknew** cortaysly <u>of the **court**</u> that he were* 'that he courteously made it known that he was <u>from the court</u> (of King Arthur).' A similar construction from *Beowulf* is *ðā ic <u>on hlǣwe</u> gefrægn hord rēafian, eald enta geweorc, ānne mannan* 'then I heard that a certain man plundered the hoard <u>in the barrow</u>, an ancient work of giants' (verses 2773a–74b). For further discussion of these and similar constructions with fronting before a relative pronoun see Russom (1976).

To discuss aspects of meaning relevant to word order we will need to consider what generative linguists call THEMATIC ROLES (also called *theta-roles* or *θ-roles*). Consider *Frankie races Maseratis* and *Frankie trusts Brett*, which are classified as MONOTRANSITIVE constructions because the verb governs a single direct object affected by the verbal action. In these constructions *Frankie* has the thematic role of AGENT. *Maseratis* and *Brett* have the role of PATIENT (the single entity that suffers or is otherwise affected by the verbal action). When a verb governs two objects in a DITRANSITIVE construction, the one affected indirectly by the action of the verb has the role of RECIPIENT and the one more directly affected has the role of THEME. In *Frankie gave Brett a Maserati*, *Frankie* has the role of AGENT, the direct object *Maserati* has the role of THEME, and the indirect object *Brett* has the role of RECIPIENT. Thematic roles are features assigned by verbs to their arguments and vary from verb to verb. Such features are are partly semantic and partly syntactic.

Bárány (2024) summarizes recent work that posits a universal underlying form for ditransitive constructions like those in *Beowulf*, which always realize indirect objects as nouns rather than as prepositional phrases governed by *to*. These DOUBLE-OBJECT constructions are defined in terms of thematic roles rather than in terms of case forms. In a double-object construction the verbal head forms a closely-bound constituent with the theme and the recipient stands outside this constituent in a higher-level specifier position. Below is the representation for the verb phrase in the Old English sentence *Hrōðgār Bēowulfe māðmas forgeaf* 'Hrothgar gave treasures to Beowulf.'

[[Beowulfe]_{RECIPIENT} [[māðmas]_{THEME} [forgeaf]_{HEAD}]]_{VP}

The special contribution of Bárány (2024) is to validate the closer relation of the verb to the theme in languages with agreement markers that link objects to verbs. As Bárány observes (2024: 389), prepositional objects have not been shown to control object agreement on verbs and would not be expected to obey the ordering constraints on double-object constructions. The verb phrases in Modern English sentences like *Frankie gave a Maserati to Brett* are distinguished from double-object constructions as PRE-POSITIONAL DATIVE constructions, which are subject to different syntactic constraints.

An important analytical technique in generative theory is construction of STARRED EXAMPLES to show precisely what word orders linguistic rules rule out. Starred examples have also been employed in generative work on poetic meter, as for example in Kiparsky (1977). We should not be satisfied with just any true statement about what occurs in a poem. The claim that no verse in *Beowulf* has more than thirty words is true but such claims are not helpful. A generative linguist would say that they have no EXPLANATORY POWER. We need to determine just what aspects of spontaneous language are restricted by metrical rules and just how they are restricted.

OPTIMALITY THEORY, an important trend in current generative research, formulates linguistic constraints not as rules specific to a given language, which often seem arbitrary and complex, but as universal micro-rules that facilitate the use of language in obvious ways (Prince and Smolensky 1993). These micro-rules are all potentially violable. Constraints are ranked in a hierarchy of influence that varies from language to language. A rule becomes CATEGORICAL when the language ranks it so high that it can never be violated by a more influential rule. The appearance of a categorical rule can also arise from additive effects when an expression violates more than one violable rule (Russom 2018). In OES Mitchell reaches similar conclusions about syntax, arguing that categorical rules for Old English proposed in earlier research are in fact tendencies, very important tendencies in many cases but not exceptionless. We will consider Mitchell's findings in detail as we review the constructions in the following chapters. The exceptionless 'laws' of language so highly valued in the late nineteenth and early twentieth centuries no longer have the same priority. Statistical frequency provides an indispensable way to identify violable rules with explanatory power, in poetic form as well as in ordinary speech. To understand how poetic composition works, we need to distinguish not only between what does and does not occur but also between what occurs routinely and what occurs seldom or rarely.

§1.9 Generative metrics

As with generative linguistics, the goal of generative metrics is to identify universal principles of construction (Kiparsky 1973, 1977; Hanson and Kiparsky 1996). The generative theory of Germanic meter employed here, initiated in Russom (1987), has since been elaborated in two book-length studies at progressively higher levels of generality (Russom 1998, Russom 2017). I have used the generative theory to explain important observations about English meters by linguists and textual critics, notably Sievers (1893), Kuhn (1933), Pope (1966), Bliss (1967), Kiparsky (1977), Youmans (1983), Duggan (1986), Cable (1991), Dresher & Lahiri (1991), Fulk (1992), Hutcheson (1995), Putter, Jefferson, & Stokes (2007), Griffith (2016), Duffell (2008), and Inoue (2009). In this book I introduce the most recent generalization of the theory, called the UNIVERSALIST THEORY, which integrates constraints on poetic syntax into the same rule system used for constraints on poetic phonology and morphology. The generative theory is justified in part by the fact that it explains what previous researchers have observed. Readers interested in that kind of justification should consult Russom (1987, 1998, 2017). I will not reiterate the argumentation, evidence, or bibliographical detail in earlier publications, focusing instead on an entirely different kind of justification: the ability of the universalist theory to explain departures from normative word order in *Beowulf* that have no purely linguistic explanations.

Sievers (1893) sorted Old English metrical patterns into verse types that were classified according to objective linguistic criteria. Sievers's classification system provided the foundation for research on Old English meter. Bliss (1967) identified additional objective criteria, provided important new statistical evidence, and refined Sievers's principles of classification. The problem that remained was to explain *why* the attested verse types were the only permissible ones and *why* a linguistic pattern acceptable as a verse should have its attested frequency. Sievers could not identify a metrical norm from which departure restricted frequency in a systematic way — what Jakobson (1960: 257) called a METRICAL CONSTANT. There was nothing like the iambic pentameter norm of ten metrical positions organized into five iambic feet with weak-strong prominence. Without a metrical constant it was impossible to formulate a generative rule system for Old English meter like the generative pentameter system in Kiparsky (1977).

Rules UM 1–7 are hypothesized principles of Universal Metrics, abbreviated as UM on the analogy of UG, the standard abbreviation for Universal Grammar.

UM 1. Metrical constituents are abstracted from linguistic constituents (metrical positions from syllables, metrical feet from words, metrical verses from phrases, metrical lines from sentences, etc.).

UM 2. Norms for a metrical constituent are abstracted from norms for the corresponding linguistic constituent. Departure from metrical norms causes METRICAL COMPLEXITY, restricting the frequency of a metrical constituent and its placement within a larger metrical constituent.

UM 3. Metrical complexity is additive. Each departure from a norm increases complexity.

UM 4. Metrical complexity is restricted with increasing severity toward the end of a metrical unit (the PRINCIPLE OF CLOSURE).

UM 5. When a metrical constituent contains sub-constituents of unequal weight, the lighter constituent normally precedes the heavier constituent. This constraint has been observed in other Indo-European meters and in Finnish alliterative poetry, where it is called WINNOWING (Behaghel 1923–32, vol. 4: 3–9; Leino 1986: 133–34). Winnowing is a metrical analogue of the ordering norm for linguistic constituents that differ in weight and complexity (§1.4).

UM 6. When metrical norms conflict, those at higher levels of metrical structure exert more influence than those at lower levels (Youmans 1989). This rule applies only when the conflicting norms are all violable and there is no conflict with a high-ranking norm that applies without exception at the relevant lower level.

UM 7. When smaller metrical constituents must occur some fixed number of times within a larger metrical constituent, it must be possible for the audience to enumerate the smaller constituents intuitively under normal conditions of reception. To make this possible, metrical constituents of different sizes must be kept distinct from one another and from EXTRAMETRICAL constituents.

Metrical norms cannot be defined arbitrarily in the universalist theory of Old English meter. Several norms are observed at several levels of structure in *Beowulf* and each one must correspond to a norm defined independently by linguists. These constraints make it impossibly awkward to fudge, waffle, or prevaricate when presented with contrary evidence. As we shall see, the many possible locations for syntactic constituents within the Old English line provide many ways to test the predictions made by UM 1–7. Given the number of norms and their fixed relation to linguistic norms, these predictions would be proved wrong with ludicrous frequency if there were serious

CHAPTER 1

problems with UM 1–7. The vulnerability to refutation of simple hypotheses that explain complex data has been observed in the most mature fields of scientific theory. If a hypothesis in physics makes correct predictions in a variety of clear cases, it is exploited as a valid approximation. Researchers generally assume that counterexamples will be explained by improvements that leave the heart of the theory intact (Feynman 1967: 170–72). A testable theory is foolproof in a concrete sense of the term. It cannot be tarnished by the theorist's human limitations. If a generative metrist is shown to miss a syntactic generalization, overlook relevant trends in formulaic theory, ignore an important publication in historical linguistics, propose an absurd literary interpretation, or get a citation wrong, the metrist may blush but the theory can shrug its metaphorical shoulders. The only valid reason for rejecting a testable theory is that it fails tests too often. When the birth of such theories is announced, the umbilical links are broken, and the offspring spring off on their own. If a theory is admired, the theorist may claim the glory of giving birth to it, as a proud mother would do. But ideally the theory will become independent. In their own special fields, researchers interested in a theory may be able to improve it more effectively than the theorist who first proposed it. If a universalist theory works, of course, an important question remains: how *much* work does it do? That is the question with which I am primarily concerned.

The line is the only metrical constituent required for the kind of verse form that flourishes when oral transmission is the guarantor of cultural continuity for law, ethics, ritual, mythology, history, medicine, hard-won practical wisdom, and nascent sciences related to food production. Biblical Hebrew poetry has no feet or metrical positions and its lines have patterns based on syntax and propositional semantics, the characteristic features of the sentence as distinct from the word and the syllable. Slavic heroic poetry has metrical positions but no feet. Some ancient Celtic meters have feet but no metrical positions. For further discussion of some representative world meters see Russom (2017: 7–44). Since the beginning of modernism, poets have experimented freely with verse form and not all of these experiments would be expected to conform to principles of UM. An experimental poet can scramble words in any imaginable way, without regard for ease of comprehension or ease of memorization. That kind of scrambling would be independent of UM in the same way that a linguist's scrambling of words to make a point is independent of UG (§1.7).

§1.10 A universalist theory of Old English meter

For a metrical theorist, Germanic alliterative poetry provides especially rich material for analysis because it employs so many kinds of metrical constituents. In addition to the verse and line there are nine foot patterns, two kinds of strong position, and three kinds of weak position. Applying UM 1–7 to *Beowulf,* we derive the following definitions for Old English metrical constituents.

OE 1. The normative OLD ENGLISH LINE is abstracted from a sentence with SOV typology (§1.3). The line is composed of two verses, the first called the A-VERSE and the second called the B-VERSE.

A syntactic constituent is said to have SOV typology if it has the normative order of major constituents for an SOV language. SV, for example, is the normative SOV order for a sentence with an intransitive verb. The prototypical Old English line is abstracted from a typologist's prototypical SOV sentence with prominent arguments and a less prominent finite verb. The line has two syntactic sub-constituents, the first abstracted from a subject specifier and the second abstracted from a verb phrase with an object complement preceding the verbal head (§1.7).

OE 2. The OLD ENGLISH VERSE is abstracted from a two-word phrase with normative word order. The normative verse consists of two words with the normative word pattern (see OE 3).

SOV order is normative for Old English verse phrases with two stressed constituents. At the stage of linguistic evolution represented by *Beowulf,* the change to SVO typology was nearing completion in phrases with high-frequency governors like prepositions, possessive adjectives, and demonstratives (§§1.4, 1.6). The normative placement of high-frequency governors in the poem is *before* rather than *after* the governed constituent, and in this position they are usually unstressed.

OE 3. The OLD ENGLISH FOOT is abstracted from an Old English word. There is an Old English foot pattern for every native word pattern, function words and compounds included, except for large compound words that fill an acceptable verse pattern. Each major sub-constituent in a whole-verse compound of this kind counts as a foot. The normative foot is abstracted from the normative Old English word, which has a trochaic pattern, with a stressed root syllable followed by an unstressed inflection (Dresher and Lahiri 1991).

CHAPTER 1

OE 4. Old English METRICAL POSITIONS are abstracted from syllables. Prominent positions abstracted from stressed syllables are called LIFTS. The *S position* is a PRIMARY LIFT abstracted from a LONG SYLLABLE with primary word stress. A syllable is long if it contains a long vowel, as with OE *sǣ* 'sea,' or a short vowel followed by a consonant, as with OE *scip* 'ship.' The *s position* is a SECONDARY LIFT abstracted from an Old English syllable with subordinate word stress, for example the subordinate root syllable *cyn-* in *mancynnes* 'of mankind.' Vowels are often shortened in syllables with subordinate stress, which vary in length (Bugge and Sievers 1890). Short stressed syllables can occur in subordinate linguistic constituents and an s position can be filled by a short syllable. The metrical *x position* is abstracted from an unstressed syllable. Long root vowels are normally shortened in unstressed syllables. The normative occupant of a metrical x position is an unstressed syllable with a short vowel. For further discussion of Germanic syllable structure see Russom (2001, 2002). Syllables with metrically significant stress are excluded from x positions. The most prominent metrical x positions are abstracted from unstressed words. Less prominent are x positions abstracted from unstressed syllables of stressed words.

OE 5. The VERSE CLAUSE is a metrical constituent abstracted from a grammatical proposition, as defined in §1.2. This rule captures important constraints imposed by Kuhn's laws within the same universalist metrical system that imposes constraints on phonology and morphology. See §1.19.

OE 6. Patterns of linguistic prominence normally match patterns of metrical prominence (UM 2). Prominence mismatches cause complexity. See §1.15.

OE 7. The rule for alliteration is abstracted from the rule for phrasal stress in an SOV language, which assigns the greater prominence to the first of two constituents in a given syntactic domain. See §1.15.

OE 8. The rule for RESOLUTION is abstracted from a rule of Old English phonology requiring a domain of one long syllable or two short syllables for prominent stress. Under certain conditions resolution makes two short syllables equivalent to one. See §1.15.

OE 9. Metrical x positions inherit their meaningful prominence from the corresponding unstressed linguistic constituent. Extrametrical x positions are not abstracted from words and have zero metrical prominence. See §1.18.

In this chapter we will introduce the reader to OE 1–9 and provide some examples of their effects on poetic word order. The rule summary in the appendix provides the full set of sub-rules derived from OE 1–9 as corollaries. Numerical designations for these sub-rules are provided to facilitate discussion of the many verses we will encounter in the following chapters.

§1.11 The oldest line of Germanic alliterative poetry

As a representative SOV construction from the earliest runic inscriptions, Antonsen (2002: 75) cites item (1), the first known line of alliterative poetry, dated ca. 300 CE, about four centuries before *Beowulf* was composed. Antonsen critiques earlier readings of the line that posit *ng* rather than *j* in the second stressed word. The relevant aspects of verse form are the same on either reading.

(1) *ek hlewagastiz holtijaz   horna tawido*

'I, Hlewagast, descendant of Holt, made the horn'

The stressed words in item (1) retain vowels and consonants that had been lost before the *Beowulf* poet was born. The longer word patterns in early runic inscriptions no longer appear in Old English texts. Since word patterns were different in 300 CE we would also expect constraints on foot patterns to differ in the lost poetry of that era, in accord with UM 1–7. In many respects, however, item (1) is a typical alliterative line. The a-verse is a modified subject specifier with two prominently stressed words that alliterate. The b-verse is a verb phrase with a non-alliterating finite verbal head preceded by an alliterating object complement. The midline caesura stands at the natural point of syntactic division, between the subject and the verb phrase. The unstressed pronoun *ek* looks like the earliest surviving instance of Germanic ANACRUSIS: placement of an extrametrical syllable before the first foot of a verse with two stressed feet — usually, as here, an a-verse (Russom 2017: 304).

§1.12 An inventory of foot patterns

The nine foot patterns in *Beowulf* correspond to OE words like *mid* 'with' (x), *ofer* 'over' (xx), *hār* 'old' (S), *rincas* 'men' (Sx), *tryddode* 'trod' (Sxx), *swāt-fāh* 'blood-stained' (Ss), *won-sǣlig* 'ill-fated' (Ssx), *hilde-rinc* 'fighting man' (Sxs), and *sibbe-ge-driht* 'band of friends' (Sxxs). There is considerable variation in FOOT LENGTH AND WEIGHT. The normative foot corresponds to trochaic SIMPLEX words like *rincas* (§1.10). Light feet correspond to unstressed words. Stressed feet include normative feet and heavy feet that correspond to compounds. Short feet correspond to monosyllabic words. Long feet correspond to words with more than two syllables. These foot-level features are marked by an 'X' on Table 1.

Table 1. Distinctive metrical features of acceptable foot patterns

	Light	Heavy	Long	Short	Stressed
x	X			X	
xx	X				
S				X	X
Sx					X
Sxx			X		X
Ss		X			X
Ssx		X	X		X
Sxs		X	X		X
Sxxs		X	X		X

Since feet correspond to words, they are subject to morphological norms as well as phonological ones. Morphological norms differentiate the three compound feet that are long and heavy. Most Old English compounds are like *won-sælig*, with adjacent stressed syllables and an inflectional ending. The normative compound pattern is Ssx. Compounds with the Sxs pattern depart from normative morphology in two ways, since they lack inflectional endings and have an unstressed syllable between the stresses. This word–internal syllable can be the second syllable of a trochaic constituent, as in *hilde-rinc*, or a prefixal constituent, as in *mōd-ge-mynd* 'mind-thought.' The Sxxs pattern of *sibbe-ge-driht* departs farther from normative compound morphology than the Sxs pattern, since it has both kinds of unstressed constituent between the stresses.

§1.13 Constraints on pairing of feet in verses

In addition to having normative syntax (in accord with OE 2), the normative verse has two feet with the normative trochaic pattern. This pattern is notated as Sx/Sx, with a slash marking the boundary between feet. The Sx/Sx pattern establishes a verse norm of two primary word stresses and four metrical positions. Old English meter provides the flexibility required for long narrative poetry, allowing considerable variation in VERSE LENGTH AND WEIGHT. There are long verses with five or six positions, heavy verses with more than two stresses, and light verses with only one stress. In accord with UM 2, however, departures from norms increase complexity and inhibit the frequency with which a verse pattern appears in *Beowulf*. There are strictly enforced limits on verse complexity, as we shall see. OE meter reconciles flexibility with strictness in a remarkably ingenious way.

A verse must have at least four metrical positions. A long foot is normally paired with a short foot and only one foot may be long. As with the order of words (§1.4), the order of feet is influenced by weight. Long heavy feet normally occupy verse-final position in Old English meter, in accord with the principle of winnowing (UM 4). Of the long heavy feet that correspond to compounds, only the morphologically regular Ssx foot can stand first in the verse. Sxs and Sxxs are restricted categorically to second position. All compound feet are restricted to second position in long verses, including Ss, the compound foot of normative length. In accord with UM 7, the poet avoids verses that could be confused with feet and feet that could be confused with verses (Russom 2022b: 55–57).

I will refer to each categorical restriction on foot pairing by a short title with an asterisk. Some of these restrictions are macro-constraints on violation of two or more micro-constraints. *HEAVY, for example, defines an unacceptable interaction between departure from normative verse length and departure from normative foot weight. These departures are acceptable in isolation but have unacceptable additive effects when they apply within the same verse. Micro-constraints can be derived directly from UM 1–7 and are more convenient for discussion of theoretical topics; macro-constraints are more concrete and more convenient for repeated use in scansion of individual verses.

*SHORT: A verse must not have fewer than four metrical positions.

*LONG: Verses with two long feet are unacceptable.

*HEAVY: Heavy foot patterns are excluded from first position in long verse patterns.

*MORPHOLOGY: The morphologically complex foot patterns Sxs and Sxxs are excluded from first position in all verse patterns.

*OVERLAP: A verse pattern overlaps a foot pattern if it has the same arrangement of x positions and lifts (S positions or s positions). Overlap is ruled out to keep foot patterns distinct from verse patterns, as required by UM 7.

The verse pattern Sxx/S is not used in *Beowulf* despite the fact that it has normative length and weight. In Old English poetry Sxx/S violates

*OVERLAP, a categorical constraint of the highest rank, since it has the same pattern of lifts and x positions as the foot pattern Sxxs. This universalist explanation for an odd metrical fact is confirmed by comparison with Eddic fornyrðislag, the Old Norse meter most like the meter of *Beowulf*. Old Norse lost its Sxxs word pattern due to loss of prefixes from the language (Kuhn 1929). When the Sxxs word pattern was lost, employment of an Sxxs foot would have violated UM 1. As predicted, the four-position Sxxs foot became obsolete, removing the obstacle to Sxx/S verses with normative length and weight. Verses with the new Sxx/S pattern are well attested in Eddic fornyrðislag (Russom 1998: 32). Middle English alliterative poets adjusted with equal facility to language change, abandoning OE metrical patterns that were no longer viable and adopting new patterns that were no longer problematic (Russom 2017). Patterning of metrical stresses is the most important factor that determines whether the foot pattern or the verse pattern will be acceptable in *Beowulf*, but normative morphology seems to play a role as well. Sxxs may have priority over Sxx/S in *Beowulf* because Sxxs words like *sibbe-ge-driht* are so much like Sxs words from a morphological point of view, combining the morphology of *hilde-rinc* with the morphology of *mōd-gemynd*.

§1.14 An inventory of verse patterns

Sievers organized the attested verse patterns into separate types and subtypes based on frequency of occurrence. The universalist theory represents Sx/Sx as the norm and analyzes all other types as departures from that norm. I must abandon Sievers's subtype designations, which are problematic in any case (Bliss 1967). The familiar types A–E provide useful groupings for two-word verse patterns, however, and I will redefine them rather than abandoning them. Subtypes of the redefined types are renumbered below according to the length and weight of their constituents. Two-word examples from *Beowulf* are used if they are available, as they usually are.

Types A1-8 show the acceptable combinations of word feet classified by Sievers as type A. I redefine type A as the set of verse patterns with a second foot of normative length.

A1. **Sx/Sx**   *mǣre / þēoden* 'famous chieftain' (129b)

A2. **Sx/Ss**   *fēondes / fōt-lāst* 'enemy's footprint' (2289a)

A3. **Ss/Sx**   *frum-sceaft / fīra* 'first creation of men' (91a)

A4. **Ss/Ss**   *gūð-rinc / gold-wlanc* 'gold-decked fighting man' (1881a)

A5. **Sxx/Sx**   *geōm*rode / *gidd*um 'sorrowed in songs' (1118a)

A6. **Sxx/Ss**   *beorht*ode / *benc*-*swēg* 'bench-talk increased' (1161a)

A7. **xx/Sx**   urðom / *síð*an 'happened afterwards' (HHv 5:5)

A8. **xx/Ss**   ganga / *fim*-tán '(there) go fifteen' (HH 50:1)

Type A patterns with two S positions are renumbered as A1–6. The two patterns with a single S position, classified by Sievers as type A3, are renumbered as A7 and A8. These subtypes are so complex that they are restricted categorically to the a-verse, the half-line most tolerant of complexity. Type A8 has very low frequency but there are about three hundred unambiguous instances of type A7 in *Beowulf* and a few ambiguous instances that might also be scanned as type A8. As we shall see in chapter two, the frequency of type A7 is elevated by its usefulness in formulaic composition. Two-word realizations of A7–8 are ruled out in OE meter to avoid confusion between the xx foot and extrametrical syllables in anacrusis (UM 7). Such two-word realizations do occur in Old Norse fornyrðislag, which abandoned anacrusis after the language lost the unstressed prefixes that made anacrusis necessary (Russom 1998: 49–52). The two-word Norse examples for A7 and A8 are cited from Neckel (1983), with abbreviated titles provided in the table of contents for this standard edition.

In types B, C, and D, the second foot is long. Type B is redefined as the set of verse patterns with a light first foot (x or xx) and a long second foot that departs from normative compound morphology.

B1. **x/Sxs**   on / *morgen*-tīd 'at morning-time' (484b)

B2. **x/Sxxs**   sum / *sāre* an-geald 'one paid dearly' (1251b)

B3. **xx/Sxs**   ofer / *eorm*en-grund 'over spacious-earth' (859a)

B4. **xx/Sxxs**   oðþæt / *ald*or-ge-dāl 'until end-of-life,' (GenA 1071b)

In the example for B2, the Sxxs foot is realized as a QUASI-COMPOUND with an alliterating adverb subordinating a prefixed verb (OEG: 36). The example for B4 comes from *Genesis A,* a Biblical narrative poem in traditional style that is similar in age and length to *Beowulf*.

Type C is redefined as the set of verse patterns in which the first foot is light and the long second foot has the simplex pattern Sxx or the normative compound pattern Ssx.

C1. **x/Sxx**   swā / *rīx*ode 'thus he prevailed' (144a)

34

C2. **x/Ssx**	*mid / ǣr-dæge* 'at day-break' (126b)
C3. **xx/Sxx**	*þenden / rēafode* 'meanwhile, he plundered' (2985a)
C4. **xx/Ssx**	*æfter / sǣ-sīðe* 'after the sea-journey' (1149a)

Type D is redefined as the set of verse patterns in which the first foot has normative weight and the second foot is long.

D1. **S/Sxx**	*secg / wīsade* 'the man led the way' (208b)
D2. **S/Ssx**	*lēof / land-fruma* 'dear land-ruler' (31a)
D3. **S/Sxs**	*flēat / fāmig-heals* 'foamy-neck [a ship] floated' (1909a)
D4. **S/Sxxs**	*sēon / sibbe-ge-driht* 'to see the band of friends' (387a)
D5. **Sx/Sxx**	*oftost / wīsode* 'most often showed the way' (1663b)
D6. **Sx/Ssx**	*wēoldon / wæl-stōwe* 'ruled the battlefield' (2051a)
D7. **Sx/Sxs**	*ēode / yrre-mōd* 'he strode with wrathful heart' (726a)
D8. **Sx/Sxxs**	*orðanc / enta-ge-weorc* 'skilled giant-work' (Mx2, 2a)

In types D1, D2, D5, and D6, the second foot has a pattern that is also used for the second foot in type C. In the remaining D types, the second foot has a pattern also used in B types. The heavy, very long, and very complex pattern D8 appears just once in *Beowulf* (verse 1420a). The two-word example for this subtype is from *Maxims II,* a collection of traditional gnomic observations. Type D5 is long and places Sxx, the most complex pattern with normal weight, after Sx, the simplest pattern, contravening the principle of closure as it applies within the verse. The complexity of type D5 restricts it to a total of 27 instances in *Beowulf.* The only b-verse example in *Beowulf* is the one provided. The note in K4 argues for emendation of this unique example to the uncontroversial b-verse pattern S/Sxx (D1). The same note refers the reader to a statement in the general introduction that the editors no longer agreed about this emendation after the book had gone to press (K4: cxc note 2). The statistical methods devised by Sievers to identify problematic verses are less than usually effective when the sample is small or skewed, and the D5 sample is both. All 26 a-verses have a personal name followed by *maðelode*. This is a useful formula for introducing speeches. It typically occurs in whole-line formulaic systems with the structure 'X spoke, Y's child.' X and Y are easily filled in lines like *Wīglāf maðelode, Wēohstānes sunu* (2862), where the child's name alliterates with the parent's, as often happens in early Germanic cultures. Traditional heroic poems in the cognate traditions employ the same kind of whole-line system.

There are many Norse examples, e.g. *þā qvað þat Brynhildr,   Buðla dōttir* 'then spoke Brynhild, daughter of Buðli' (*Guðrúnarqviða I,* 23/1). The only traditional heroic poetry that survives in Old High German is a 68–line fragment called *Hildebrandslied.* In this tiny sample we find two different whole-line formulas: *Hiltibrant gimahalta, Heribrantes suno* 'Hildebrand spoke, son of Heribrand' (line 45) and *Hadubrant gimahalta, Hiltibrantes suno* 'Hadubrand spoke, son of Hildebrand' (lines 14, 36). Variations and appositive phrases normally follow the constituent about which they supply additional information. The type D5 a-verses are a-verses for reasons peculiar to their formulaic structure, syntactic structure, and narrative utility. The discrepancy in numbers has no probative value. When confronted with the unique b-verse example of type D5 we should probably be content to say, "there are no other examples but this may be one" (cf. OES 1: lix).

There is only one type E pattern and it is the only pattern with a short second foot.

E. Ssx/S   *won-sǣlī / wer* 'ill-fated man' (105a)

Type E also stands apart as the only type with a first foot that is both long and heavy.

The coherence of the universalist system stands out on the matrix display in Table 2. The acceptable types, in boldface, are numbered according to the revised classification system. The foot patterns x and xx are excluded from the top row because function words bear stress in verse-final position, scanning as S or Sx rather than as x or xx. To assess the influence of metrical constraints on word order we will need compact notations for unacceptable verse patterns as well as for acceptable ones. In the notations for unacceptable patterns, "S" marks violations of *SHORT, "L" marks violations of *LONG, "H" marks violations of *HEAVY, "M" marks violations of *MORPHOLOGY, and "O" marks violations of *OVERLAP. Some unacceptable patterns violate more than one rule.

Table 2. First foot notated in left-hand column, second foot notated in top row.

	S	Sx	Ss	Sxx	Ssx	Sxs	Sxxs
x	S1	S2	S3	C1	C2	B1	B2
s	SO1	SO2	SO3	D1	D2	D3	D4
xx	S4	A7	A8	C3	C4	B3	B4
Sx	O4	A1	A2	A9	D6	D7	D8
Ss	O5	A3	A4	H1	H2	H3	H4
Sxx	O6	A5	A6	L1	L2	L3	L4
Ssx	E	H5	H6	HL1	HL2	HL3	HL4
Sxs	M1	MH1	MH2	MHL1	MHL2	MHL3	MHL4
Sxxs	M2	MH3	MH4	MHL5	MHL6	MHL7	MHL8

§1.15 Metrical prominence

In this section we will be concerned with constraints imposed on word order by OE 6, 7, and 8, repeated below for convenience. General principles of linguistic and metrical prominence are summarized in Appendix C.

OE 6. Patterns of linguistic prominence normally match patterns of metrical prominence (UM 2). Prominence mismatches cause complexity.

OE 7. The rule for alliteration is abstracted from the rule for phrasal stress in an SOV language, which assigns the greater prominence to the first of two constituents in a given syntactic domain.

OE 8. The rule for resolution is abstracted from a rule of Old English phonology requiring a domain of one long syllable or two short syllables for prominent stress.

In SOV languages, compound words, phrases, and clauses with two or more stressed constituents normally have the most prominent stress on the first constituent. OE 7 is abstracted from the rule for normative stress in SOV Proto-Germanic (§1.3), which subordinates the second constituent of a phrase or clause to the first one (Russom 1998: 64–96). At all levels of metrical structure within the line, the first lift subordinates any following lift, making it less acceptable for alliteration, which is universally associated with prominent stress. Alliteration is obligatory on the most prominent lift of each verse in the line. Alliteration is unacceptable on the subordinate lift of a subordinate metrical constituent.

Consider the following a-verses from *Beowulf*.

(2) (a) *lēof* / *land*-*fruma* 'beloved lord of the land' (31a)   S/Ssx (D2)

   (b) *se* / *scyn-scaþa* 'the demonic foe' (707a)   x/Ssx (C2)

   (c) *ond* / *orc-nêas* 'and evil spirits' (112b)   x/Ssx (C2)

   (d) *hringa* / *hyrde* 'guardian of rings' (2245a)   Sx/Sx (A1)

   (e) *mǣre* / *þēoden*, 'famous lord' (1046b)   Sx/Sx (A1)

In a compound foot with two lifts, the first lift subordinates the second. In item (2a) the secondary lift occupied by *-fruma* is subordinated twice, once within the foot and once within the verse. This verse would be unacceptable if *-fruma* were replaced by a constituent alliterating with *lēof* and *land*. In (2b) the secondary lift is subordinated only once and is eligible for alliteration. As (2c) shows, alliteration is not required on a secondary lift in this position. In a verse with two primary lifts, the first subordinates the second. In (2d) the second primary lift is subordinated once and may alliterate. As (2e) shows, alliteration is optional on a primary lift in this position. Since the b-verse is subordinated to the a-verse, a second stressed constituent in the b-verse will always be subordinated twice. Double alliteration is accordingly ruled out in the b-verse. Stress rules bind words into phrases and phrases into clauses, establishing a stress hierarchy that highlights relations between constituents and facilitates linguistic processing. Alliterative rules bind feet based on words into verses abstracted from phrases and lines abstracted from sentences, establishing a metrical hierarchy that highlights relations among metrical constituents and facilitates metrical processing.

Length is an absolute requirement for constituents of the highest prominence in Old English words. A short syllable with primary stress is always followed by an unstressed syllable, and the two syllables are resolved under prominent stress to provide the required stress domain (Dresher and Lahiri 1991). Two resolved syllables are equivalent to one long syllable and can occupy a single lift in Old English poetry. When stress is subordinated, the energy of articulation is reduced, a shorter stress domain may be sufficient, and vowel reduction can create short stressed syllables. Like alliteration, resolution is sensitive to metrical prominence as well as linguistic prominence. Constraints on resolution in *Beowulf* are quite similar to the constraints on alliteration. Where alliteration is obligatory, resolution is obligatory. Where alliteration is unacceptable, resolution is unacceptable or vanishingly rare.

We will often need to discuss the metrical prominence of lifts at various locations within the line. It will be useful to distinguish the following locations, which are numbered according to the prominence of the lifts that occupy them, with 1 being highest.

Location s1a: On the first S position of a verse with two lifts, where alliteration and resolution are obligatory. All verse patterns have two lifts except for A7 (xx/Sx), C1 (x/Sxx), and C3 (xx/Sxx)

Location s1b: On the first and only lift in type A7, C1, or C3, where alliteration is obligatory because no other lift is available and resolution is quasi-obligatory (or perhaps obligatory). Lifts in location s1b may be slightly less prominent than those in location s1a but the available evidence is difficult to interpret.

Location s2: On a subordinate S position in an a–verse of category II, where alliteration and resolution are sometimes optional and sometimes required. Category II includes type D, type E, and types A1–A6.

Location s3: On an s position in types B, C, and E, where alliteration is permissible in the a-verse but never required. In type B, resolution on the s position of the Sxs or Sxxs foot is required to avoid unacceptable verse patterns. In types C and E, where there is no interference from higher-ranking rules, resolution on the s position of the Ssx foot is dispreferred.

Location s4: On a subordinate lift in a subordinate metrical constituent, where alliteration is unacceptable and non–resolution is quasi-obligatory. Lifts of this kind include the s positions in type D verses and any lift after the first lift of the b-verse.

Complete summaries of rules for alliteration and resolution are provided in the Appendix.

§1.16 Relations between linguistic constituents and metrical constituents

It is possible to construct a line of iambic pentameter with perfect MATCHING of linguistic constituents to metrical constituents in Modern English. In the example below, stressed syllables are in boldface. The boundary between feet is represented by a slash. The double slash between positions four and five represents the normative location of the major syntactic boundary in the line, called the CAESURA (Kiparsky 1977: 230).

(3) *refined / gourmets // demand / superb / cuisine*

    xS / xS   //   xS / xS / xS

Each iambic foot in item (3) is REALIZED as an iambic word. In each iambic foot, the x position is matched by the unstressed syllable of the word and the following S position is matched by the stressed syllable. Stressed syllables in Modern English are normally long and each stressed syllable in the line has normative length. The caesura matches the major syntactic boundary, which falls between the subject, *refined gourmets*, and the verb phrase, *demand superb cuisine*. As Kiparsky observes (1977: 224), perfect matching is uncommon in the work of first-rate poets because too close an adherence to metrical norms creates metrical banality — the 'sing-song' effect. In the poems most widely admired for their craftsmanship, metrical interest is created by a disciplined counterpoint between language and meter that permits frequent departure from norms within limits defined by mismatch rules. A verse that mismatches the normative two-word expression of a verse type in one or more respects is a VARIANT of that type.

The mismatch rules of iambic pentameter can be rather permissive because there is only one line pattern. Since the line pattern is predictable, even extreme departures from norms can be tolerable, provided of course that the number of mismatches per line is kept within tolerable limits. In Shakespeare's plays, foot boundaries often fail to coincide with word boundaries and line boundaries often fail to coincide with the boundaries of a sentence or clause. Within limits, Shakespeare places stressed syllables on weak positions and unstressed syllables on strong positions. An important constraint on these mismatches is a categorical rule against stress mismatch and boundary mismatch in the same word. Shakespeare will place a trochaic word within an iambic foot, mismatching the iambic stress pattern, but will not place an iambic word across the foot boundary, since in that case the iambic word would have two stress mismatches and a boundary mismatch as well (Kiparsky 1977: 201–5). In *Beowulf*, metrical variety is provided in significant part by the many acceptable verse patterns, which can be combined in many ways to construct a line. To maintain a clear two-foot verse structure, less permissive mismatch rules must compensate for the more permissive verse-pattern rules. The *Beowulf* poet never places unstressed syllables on lifts and never places a foot boundary within a simplex word.

CHAPTER 1

§1.17 Mismatch rules for primary and secondary lifts

Rule OE 1 defines the Old English line as a metrical constituent abstracted from a clause with SOV typology. According to UM 2, departure from metrical norms in a realization of a metrical pattern increases complexity, restricting the frequency of the realization and restricting its employment toward the end of a larger metrical unit. A line is ideally realized as a verse clause. Placement of all major constituents in the same line reduces metrical complexity. The normative location for a line-internal caesura is at the major syntactic break. In a line that corresponds to a verse clause the major syntactic break lies between the subject and the verb phrase (the two major subconstituents of the clause). The normative metrical placement for a finite verb is in line-final position, the metrical equivalent of clause-final position (the normative syntactic position for a finite verb in an SOV language).

Rule OE 3 defines the foot as the metrical equivalent of a word. In some Old Irish alliterative meters the foot must always be realized as a word. These meters are extremely difficult to use for narrative poetry. Most examples consist of lists in asyndetic parataxis or minimal sentences with a noun and a verb (Travis 1973; Russom 2017: 39–44). In *Beowulf* a foot with a given stress pattern can be realized as a word group with the same pattern of lifts and x positions. This option provides much-needed flexibility but is not used with insouciance. The *Beowulf* poet takes special pains to clarify two-foot structure within the verse. When an initial foot with one lift is realized as a word group, for example, alliteration on the following S position is strongly preferred as a marker for the leftward boundary of the final foot. A typical instance is *gēar in / geardas* 'a year in the courtyards' (verse 1134a). As Bliss observed (1967: 37–38), the second alliterating syllable is 'quasi-compulsory' in type A1 when the first foot is realized as a word group, but when both feet are realized as words more than two-thirds of total instances have single alliteration. A typical instance is *mǣre / þēoden* 'famous chieftain' (1716a). When feet are perfectly matched with words a second alliteration is less urgently required as an aid to processing of verse form in real time.

Alliteration is also used to clarify the structure of compound feet. In a compound foot realized as a word group with a prominent lexical noun or adjective root on the s position, alliteration on the S position is obligatory (Russom 1987: 83–96). Typical instances are *frōd / folces weard* 'wise guardian of the people' (2513a) and *maga / māne fāh* 'a man stained with crime' (978a), both of type D3 (S/Sxs). These verses have the same pattern of lifts and dips as two-word realizations with an Sxs compound in the second foot

41

but they have a fully stressed noun or adjective on the s position. Obligatory alliteration on the S position of the compound foot enhances the relative prominence of the foot-initial constituent, re-establishing the strong-weak contour of the compound word from which the foot is abstracted.

According to OE 2, verse patterns are abstracted from two-word phrases. Additional constraints are imposed on verses like *frōd / folces weard* and *maga / māne fāh,* which have three-word phrases. The foot boundary must coincide with a well-marked boundary between constituents: with a word boundary, with the boundary between word-like constituents in a compound, or with the boundary between an unstressed prefix and the following stressed constituent (Russom 1987: 8–9). In a verse with three stressed words, moreover, the foot boundary must fall at the natural point of syntactic division and the compound foot must be occupied by a natural syntactic constituent. Items (4a–c) meet these requirements.

(4) (a) **fyrst / forð** *gewāt* 'time went on' (210a)   S/Sxs (D3)

   (b) **lēoht** / *ēastan cōm* 'light came from the east' (569b)   S/Sxs (D3)

   (c) **frōd** / **folces** *weard* 'old guardian of the people' (2513a)   S/Sxs (D3)

In (4a, b) the word group occupying the Sxs foot consists of an adverb immediately followed by a finite verb. In this closely-bound construction the adverb takes the main stress and the verb has subordinate stress. It is not entirely clear that adverb-verb constructions should be regarded as word groups. Campbell (1959: 36) refers to them as 'quasi-compounds.' What counts as a 'word' for the purposes of metrical rules is an interesting and largely unexplored question. Intuitive scansion is facilitated in (4a) by the second alliteration, which marks the leftward boundary of the second foot. As (4b) shows, however, alliteration on the first constituent of the quasi-compound is optional. Quasi-compounds are easy to identify as compound feet because they are closely bound and because the first constituent subordinates the second. In (4c), on the other hand, the second constituent of the word group is a prominent noun rather than a verb and alliteration on the S position of the compound foot is obligatory. If *frōd* in item (4c) were changed to *wīs* 'wise,' normal scansion would be impossible. A constructed example like **wīs folces weard* would not qualify as type E (Ssx/S), since the foot boundary would not coincide with the natural point of syntactic division, which lies between the adjective *wīs* and *folces weard,* the natural syntactic constituent modified by *wīs.* If scanned as S/Sxs, with the foot boundary placed correctly, the verse remains unacceptable, since alliteration would be required on *folces* rather than on *weard*. The three words in ***wis folces weard** are not organized into a proper metrical hierarchy with two constituents, one of which has two natural sub-constituents. These three stressed words would accordingly be interpreted as a sequence of three feet and the verse would be unacceptable for that reason.

As with the second lift at any level of metrical structure, a second S position in a verse is subordinated to the first S position. A subordinated S position is an appropriate site for a secondary nominal or adjectival constituent in a compound large enough to fill a whole verse.

(5) (a) **hilde-** / *bille* 'war-sword' (557a)   Sx/Sx (A1): 303X

   (b) **Sige-** / *Scyldinga* 'Victory-Scyldings' (597b)   S/Ssx (D2): 96X

   (c) **lēas-** / *scēaweras* 'deceitful surveyors' (spies) (253a)   S/Sxx (D1): 4X

   (d) **an**-*wīg*- / *gearwe* 'prepared against attack' (1247b)   Ss/Sx (A3)

   (e) **eafor**-*hēafod*- / *segn* 'boar-head banner' (2152b)   Ssx/S (E)

Verses like these occur with very significant frequency, about once every eight lines on average. Compounds like those in (5a–c) have far lower frequency in Old English prose. Many of them are restricted to alliterative poetry and some appear nowhere but in *Beowulf*. In the b-verse, where metrical complexity is restricted, verses like (5a) occur 74 times and verses like (5b) appear 47 times. Whole-verse compounds were clearly useful to the poet and the boundary between constituents is treated like a word boundary.

A verse with two stressed constituents and normative word order has the more prominent constituent first, as in SOV languages. Verses (6a, b) adhere to the SOV norm; verse (6c) has the object after the verb.

(6) (a) **gæstas** / **grētte** '(he) greeted the guests' (1893a)   Sx/Sx (A1)

   (b) **bēagas** / *dǣlde* '(he) distributed rings' (80b)   Sx/Sx (A1)

   (c) **miste** / **mercelses** '(he) missed the target' (2439)   Sx/Ssx (D6)

Item (6a) has normative OV order, with the more prominent object before the stressed verb. Alliteration on the verb is optional in this position, and instances like (6b), with single alliteration, occur more than twice as often as verses like (6a). In verses like (6c), however, alliteration on the most prominent constituent in the verse is quasi-obligatory (Russom 2017: 91, 117, 123, 283). Since alliteration is strongly associated with prominence, it is not surprising to find that the most prominent constituent in the verse normally alliterates.

In verses like (4c), as we saw, alliteration on the first constituent of the compound foot subordinates the prominent second noun in an Sxs word group, creating the required strong-weak prominence contour. Alliteration accomplishes a similar purpose in (6c), elevating the weak prominence of the finite verb to establish a strong-weak contour at the level of the verse. In Sx/Sx verses like (6a, b), reversing the order of feet leaves the verse pattern unchanged. Reversing the order of words in verses like (6b) would provide a convenient alternative with alliteration on *d-*, but that kind of reversal never happens in *Beowulf*. Although verses with two trochaic words have high frequency with single alliteration in the poem, we find nothing like **dǣlde / bēagas*. The most prominent word in such verses alliterates obligatorily. There would be no violation of OE 2.3 in an a-verse like **bǣdon / bēagas* '(they) asked for rings,' but such verses do not occur either. When OV order creates a normative verse of two-word type A1, the poet never chooses VO order. Normative OV order in (6c) would create **mercelses / miste*, with the unacceptable pattern *Ssx/Sx (H5). This is a more serious infraction than the departure from normative order in (6c) as it stands, since the rules for verse patterns have sufficiently high rank to be inviolable. VO order is tolerable when it avoids an unacceptable pattern. Here as in many other cases a complicated exceptionless constraint is best explained as an impermissible interaction of simpler constraints that serve obvious purposes and are violable in isolation. As we survey the syntactic structures employed by the poet, metrical interactions of this kind will provide decisive evidence for basic word orders.

§1.18 Mismatch rules for metrical and extrametrical x positions

A meter flexible enough for effective storytelling must allow for sequences of two or more unstressed function words. In iambic pentameter this flexibility is achieved by allowing unstressed constituents to occupy strong positions, as for example in *shall I / compare / thee to / a sum- / mer's day?* Here the unstressed pronoun *I* occupies the first strong position and the unstressed preposition *to* occupies the third strong position. Since Old English meter did not allow placement of unstressed syllables on strong positions, sequences of function words had to be accommodated in some other way. The solution adopted by alliterative poets was to permit employment of unstressed constituents outside metrical feet as extrametrical syllables that are literally 'outside the meter.' Since the meter also permitted employment of unstressed words as light feet, there was an obvious risk of confusion between light feet and extrametrical words. The matching constraints that prevented such METRICAL AMBIGUITY are among the most interesting features of Germanic alliterative verse, which differs in this and many other ways from the meters on which metrical research has largely been based.

To explain some important constraints we can consider just two categories of verse types: category I, for types with a single S position, and category II, for types with two S positions. Representative types in these classes are shown in (7a–f).

(7) (a) *in / **geār**-dagum* 'in days of yore' (1b) x/Ssx (C2: category I)

   (b) *ond þæt ge- / **æfn**don swā* 'and did it so' (538b) (x)x/Sxs (B1: category I)

   (c) *ic þæt ge- / **hȳre*** 'I hear that' (290a) (x)xx/Sx (A7: category I)

   (d) *(ge)**sægd** / **sōð**līce* 'stated truthfully' (141a) S/Ssx (D2: category II)

   (e) ***swǣ**se / (ge)**sī**þas* 'dear companions' (29a) Sx/Sx (A1: category II)

   (f) ***brūc** þenden / (þū) mōte* 'enjoy while you can' (1177b)

                                                             Sxx/Sx (A5: category II)

In (7a) the unstressed preposition *in* matches a light foot abstracted from an unstressed word. In (7b) the same location is occupied by a sequence of three unstressed syllables. It seems likely that the most prominent constituent in the sequence — in this case, the object *þæt* — was perceived as the light foot but this intuition is hard to validate because the only conspicuous metrical distinction is between anacruses and light feet. When it is relevant to do so I will use *(x)x* to represent any light foot accompanied by one or more extrametrical positions, as in the notation for (7b). The parenthesized constituents in (7d–f) are extrametrical. Scansions that placed them within the metrical pattern proper would create more complex variants or unacceptable ones.

Matching constraints on unstressed constituents explain many departures from normative SOV order in *Beowulf* and it will be convenient to have shorthand terms for metrical locations occupied by unstressed words with distinct levels of meaningful prominence. Five locations suffice, with location 1 for the most prominent constituents and location 5 for the least prominent.

Location x1: on an x position before the first alliteration in a category I verse.

Location x2: on an x position in a foot with normative weight.

Location x3: on an x position in a compound foot.

Location x4: on an extrametrical position before the second foot of a category II verse.

Location x5: on an extrametrical position before the first foot of a class II verse (in anacrusis).

Rule OE 9 (§1.10) states that metrical x positions inherit their meaningful prominence from the corresponding unstressed linguistic constituent. Since light feet are abstracted from unstressed words, they are normally occupied by such words, and unstressed Satzpartikeln normally occur as light feet in metrical location x1, the most appropriate location for unstressed words (see §1.19). Unstressed main verbs, the most prominent verb forms, are restricted absolutely to location x1. Finite 'be' verbs, the least prominent verb forms, are the only ones that occupy other metrical locations with significant frequency. Unstressed prefixes are situated at the other extreme of meaningful prominence, according to the criteria of binding, reduction, omission, and loss (§1.4). They are by far the most common occupants of extrametrical positions at metrical location x5. Unstressed prefixes are the most closely bound Old English constituents: nothing can intervene between an unstressed prefix and the stressed host to which it is bound. The unstressed negative particle *ne* is bound almost as closely as an unstressed prefix. Only an unstressed prefix can intervene between a negative particle and its stressed host. The low prominence of negative particles is shown by the fact that they undergo contraction, as in OE *næs* 'wasn't' (< *ne wæs*), and by the fact that pre-verbal *ne* has not survived as an independent constituent. *Ne* has now been replaced by post-verbal *not,* from OE *nāwiht* 'absolutely not in the least,' with prominent emphatic *nā* plus an intensifier that adds additional prominence. The low prominence of OE *ne* made it the second-most common occupant of extrametrical location x5.

Before the first alliterating word an unstressed constituent might be a light foot in a category I verse or an extrametrical anacrusis in a category II verse. If verse-initial unstressed constituents were wrongly interpreted, the verse would be perceived as unacceptable and a second round of intuitive processing would be required to arrive at a normal scansion. Unnecessary processing is avoided in part by maximizing the prominence of light feet and avoiding prominent anacruses. Unstressed verbs, the most prominent unstressed constituents, are never used for anacrusis. Any verb before the first alliterating word is immediately identifiable as a light foot. The anacrusis position is abstracted from an unstressed prefix and must not exceed two syllables, the maximum number of syllables in an Old English prefix. Any verse-initial sequence of three unstressed syllables is obviously a light foot. When extrametrical constituents are added to a light foot they create some complexity but this is outweighed by reduction of metrical ambiguity, which makes intuitive scansion easier at the speed of performance. Extrametrical constituents between the feet of a category II verse add to metrical complexity but do not create metrical ambiguity. Hence location x4 is preferable to location x5 for placement of extrametrical syllables.

For statistical analysis of the relations between x positions and linguistic constituents let us consider two extremes of prominence and a representative constituent with a level of prominence between them. At the high end of the scale are finite verbs and pronoun arguments, which are major constituents of verse clauses. At the low end of the scale are unstressed prefixes. The most common representatives of intermediate prominence are prepositions, which are confined within prepositional phrases but can be separated from their objects by other words, including stressed adjectives, as in *with a friendly smile*. Prepositions are more prominent than prefixes but less prominent than major sentence constituents.

Table 3. Placement of unstressed constituents before the first S position in class I verses as compared with placement of unstressed constituents in class II verses.

	in I before first S (location x1)	in II between S positions (locations x2 and x4)	in II before first S (location x5)
finite 'be' verbs	249	31	
finite auxiliaries	90	1	
finite main verbs	131		
personal pronouns	1049	40	1
prepositions	734	162	3
prefixes	230	433	72

What stands out at once is the preference for placement of prominent unstressed constituents in the most prominent location, location x1, where they serve as light feet or as extrametrical constituents that resolve metrical ambiguity. The most prominent unstressed constituents, finite main verbs, always occur at location x1. Personal pronoun arguments, our other major constituents, occur there 1049 of 1090 times (95%). The few major constituents that appear elsewhere are concentrated in the intermediate location. For the most prominent minor constituents, prepositions, frequency in the most prominent location falls to 82% (734/899), and the remaining instances are again concentrated in the intermediate location. For prefixes, the least prominent constituents, frequency in the most prominent location plummets to 31% (230/735). The highest frequency for prepositions is in the intermediate location, with 59% (433/735). In the least prominent location the frequency for prefixes jumps from a mere trace to 10% (72/735). The hypothesized correlation between linguistic and metrical prominence is confirmed by stark contrasts in statistical frequency.

By the criteria in §1.4, unstressed words are more prominent than unstressed word-internal syllables. We have lost most of the Old English inflections, for example, but relatively few unstressed words have been lost. From UM 1 it follows that the x positions in light feet, which are abstracted from unstressed words, are more prominent than foot-internal x positions, which are abstracted from unstressed word-internal syllables. When foot-internal x positions in stressed feet are mismatched by unstressed words or prefixes, prefixes create the smallest degree of mismatch.

Since metrical complexity is additive (UM 3), a verse with foot-internal mismatch to a more complex foot has greater total complexity than a verse with foot-internal mismatch to a less complex foot, all other things being equal. As we have seen (Table 1, §1.12), feet can depart from the Sx norm in more than one way and each departure makes the foot more complex. In order of increasing complexity, the stressed feet with internal x positions are Sx (normative), Sxx (long), Ssx (long, heavy), Sxs (long, heavy, morphologically complex), and Sxxs (ultralong, heavy, morphologically complex). Examples of mismatched x positions in these feet are shown between square brackets in items (8a–e).

(8) (a) **sinc** *[æt]* / **sym**le 'treasure at the feast' (81a)   Sx/Sx (A1)

  (b) **wan** *[under]* / **wolc**num 'dark under clouds' (651a)   Sxx/Sx (A5)

  (c) **up**lang *[ā-]* / stōd 'stood upright' (759b)   Ssx/S (E)

  (d) næs / **hearp***[an]*wyn 'there wasn't any joy from the harp' (2262b)   x/Sxs (B1)

  (e) **hond** / rond *[ge]*fēng 'hand seized shield' (2609b)   S/Sxs (D3)

  (f) hē mē / **mēd***[e]* *[ge]*hēt 'he promised me a reward' (2134b)   x/Sxxs (B2)

Prominent unstressed words add least complexity on the x position of the normative Sx foot, which has zero inherent complexity. Prepositions are often encountered on this position, as in (8a), and there are some instances with finite 'be' verbs, which never appear in anacrusis or within compound feet. Disyllabic prepositions with medial prominence occur with significant frequency on internal xx sequences in Sxx feet, as in (8b). In the more complex compound feet mismatch becomes increasingly more restricted. The most common mismatches to the x position of the Ssx foot are unstressed prefixes, which are just slightly more prominent than the inflectional endings from which foot-final x positions are abstracted. In the most complex compound patterns, Sxs and Sxxs, mismatches to the medial x positions stay even closer to the unstressed syllables in the corresponding compound words. In (8d) the unstressed final syllable in the first word of an Sxs word group stays as close as possible to the medial unstressed syllable in the first constituent of compounds like *morgen-tīd* 'morning-time.' In (8e) the unstressed prefix *ge-* stays as close as possible to the medial unstressed infix in compounds like *hand-ge-weorc* 'handiwork.' In (8f) the unstressed word-internal constituents stay as close as possible to the medial constituents of compounds like *sibbe-ge-driht* 'band of friends.'

Table 4 provides comprehensive frequencies for foot-internal x positions mismatched by finite verbs, pronoun arguments, prepositions, and prefixes.

Table 4. Placement of constituents before the first S position in class I as compared with foot-internal placement.

	in class I before first S (least complex)	x in Sx	xx in Sxx	x in Ssx	x in Sxs or Sxxs
		(less complex ————— > more complex)			
finite 'be' verbs	262	28	1	1	
finite auxiliaries	91	1			
other finite verbs	124				
personal pronouns	1049	19	3		2
prepositions	734	100	54	3	17
prefixes	230	147	5	69	296

As on Table 3, what stands out at once is the preference for placement of unstressed constituents before the first alliteration in category I, where they match light feet or reduce verse complexity by reducing metrical ambiguity. Most other placements of unstressed major constituents are concentrated in the least complex foot pattern, Sx. The complexity of Sxs and Sxxs relative to Sxx shows up clearly in the frequency for instances with disyllabic prepositions of intermediate prominence, which prefer the Sxx foot. The preference for near-perfect matching in Sxs and Sxxs is very strong indeed. Prefixes are more common on the medial x positions of these feet (296X) than before the first alliteration in category I (230X), the preferred location for unstressed constituents of all other kinds. In Sxs and Sxxs feet, where it is possible to mismatch the unstressed syllable of an Sx constituent in a compound, matching this syllable with the unstressed syllable of a trochaic word is strongly preferred, with 870 instances, as compared with the 296 instances for prefixes. As on Table 3, the hypothesized correlation between linguistic and metrical prominence is confirmed by gross statistical discrepancies. Here and in the following chapters we will encounter evidence of the strongest imaginable kind that would become invisible if we confined attention to what does and does not occur. In this case the evidence supports an explanation for *why* constituents of differing prominence are placed differently at verse level. Such differences follow straightforwardly from UM 1–3, which correctly predict that metrical constituents will have properties of linguistic constituents, that these properties will normally be matched by the same properties in language chosen by the poet, and that additive departures from matching norms will correlate with gradient decreases in frequency.

§1.19 The verse clause

Working on Germanic meters at a time when major advances had been made in phonological theory but syntactic theory was still in its infancy, Kuhn (1933) made some important discoveries about the evolution of Germanic languages. He began with the observation that unstressed constituents of small phrases — prepositions and definite articles, for example — were placed differently from unstressed constituents of clauses and sentences — constituents like unstressed pronouns, 'be' verbs, and sentential adverbs. Kuhn referred to the higher-level constituents as *Satzpartikeln* 'sentence particles' and to the lower-level constituents as *Satzteilpartikeln* 'sentence-part-particles.' Kuhn used *partikeln* to refer to unstressed words in general, not in the technical sense of English *particle,* which refers to "an invariable item with a grammatical function, especially one that does not readily fit into a standard classification of parts of speech" (Crystal 1985: 222). Kuhn's *partikeln* include familiar parts of speech like prepositions and words that vary in form like finite verbs. To preserve continuity while avoiding confusion I will refer to *Satzpartikeln* as SPs and to *Satzteilpartikeln* as STPs. Kuhn proposed two laws for SPs and tried to show that they applied without exception, like the famous sound laws of 19th-century historical linguistics. According to Kuhn's first law, called the *Satzpartikelgesetz,* unstressed SPs must be situated in the first verse of the clause, either before the first stress or between the first stress and the second. According to Kuhn's second law, called the *Satzspitzengesetz,* any unstressed syllables before the first stress of a clause must include an SP. Both the importance of Kuhn's observations and problems with the formulation of his laws have been widely acknow-ledged by later researchers (e.g. Kendall 1991, Getty 1997, Momma 1997, Orton 1999, Blockley and Cable 2000, Mines 2002, Griffith 2016, O'Neal 2018). These laws could not provide a plausible explanation for anacrusis, which rarely includes an SP and usually occurs at the beginning of a sentence. Nor could they explain why the location before the first stress (location x1) is over-whelmingly preferred to all other locations for placement of SPs in Old English. Mitchell (OES 2: 983–84) identifies serious problems with Kuhn's method of identifying clause boundaries, which avoids counterexamples by representing an offending clause as the rightward constituent of a larger verse clause. This device redefines clause-initial STPs that violate the second law as clause-medial. Kuhn speculated that the evolution of Germanic syntax began with a trend away from postpositions. This is a very important insight but Kuhn's proposed explanation for the trend would seem strange to a contemporary linguist. After the shift of stress to the first syllable in Germanic words, Kuhn suggested, postposed function words would create an unrelieved trochaic rhythm that was *unschöne und unbequeme* 'unlovely and unpleasant' (Kuhn 1933: 22). To my knowledge, aesthetic deficiency in sentence rhythm has not been identified as a precursor to syntactic change in any human language. For systematic critique of Kuhn's laws and a survey of relevant scholarship see Russom (2022a). Instead of reiterating this critique I will focus here on showing how the work done by Kuhn's laws can be accomplished by general principles that also explain many facts about word order not discussed by Kuhn. The operation of these principles will come into sharper focus if we replace Kuhn's controversial definition of the verse clause with OE 5, repeated for convenience below:

OE 5. The verse clause is a metrical constituent abstracted from a grammatical proposition, as defined in §1.2.

As understood for the purposes of this book, a verse clause includes one and only one finite verb and everything more closely related to that verb than to an adjacent finite verb. Some constructions in which a predictable finite verb is unexpressed will also be analyzed as verse clauses.

In formulating his second law, which requires that an unstressed SP be included among any unstressed syllables before the first stress of the clause, Kuhn made no distinction between major sentence constituents and SPs like clausal conjunctions, which normally appear between the clauses they join in human languages (Dryer 2007: 45). The joining function implicit in the term 'conjunction' is easily perceived by the hearer in part because clausal conjunctions are placed like links between two physical objects — tow-ropes, trailer hitches, couplings on railroad cars, and so forth. Placement of SP conjunctions is explained by the principle of iconicity (§1.4) and no special explanation is required for the fact that SP conjunctions precede the major constituents of a verse clause. In Germanic languages, relative pronouns also occupy a fixed position before the major constituents of the rela-tive clause. As formulated, Kuhn's laws would permit SP conjunctions and relative pro-nouns to stand after the first stress of their clause, which is obviously incor-rect. The rule for placement of these FIXED SPs is an ordinary-language constraint independent of Kuhn's laws. What does need to be considered is why the *Beowulf* poet places SPs like unstressed finite verbs and pronoun arguments with such remarkably high frequency in the first verse of a clause. The fact that such constituents are unstressed shows that they are easy to process and the universal tendency toward early placement of such constit-uents explains why they are often placed early in Old English prose. But we still need to explain why early placement of these constituents is quasi-ob-ligatory in poems like *Beowulf*.

I will refer to major sentence constituents as MOVABLE SPs. What needs to be explained, more precisely, is why movable SPs are attracted so strongly to unstressed positions in the opening verse of the clause. Within the uni-versalist theory of Old English meter this attraction is explained by rules and principles we have already discussed. According to UM 1, the verse is a metrical unit abstracted from a phrase. According to OE 2, the normative realization of a verse type is as a phrase with two words in normative order. According to UM 2, departure from metrical norms causes metrical com-plexity. Because fixed SPs precede all constituents of a following clause and stand outside those constituents in a higher-level syntactic position, they always complicate phrase structure in an opening verse, increasing metrical complexity. Because movable SPs introduce extraneous constituents when fronted into an earlier verse, they increase metrical complexity as well. Ac-cording to UM 4, the principle of closure, metrical complexity is restricted with increasing severity toward the end of a metrical unit. We would expect normative two-word verses to be highly favored toward the end of the clause and more complex verses to be disfavored there.

Consider a phrase with three stressed words, one of which is a stressed SP in archaic SOV position. If the two words provide an acceptable verse, the SP is metrically unnecessary and will increase metrical complexity if the whole phrase is used as a verse. When the poet wants to use such phrases toward the end of a verse clause, their metrical complexity can be appropriately reduced by fronting the SP to an earlier verse. Fronting of SPs to an unstressed position in the opening verse, which will contain any fixed SPs, puts both kinds of complexity in the verse least strictly regulated by the principle of closure. Complexity is kept to an absolute minimum when all unstressed SPs, movable as well as fixed, occupy normative location x1 in the opening verse. The universalist theory captures the effects of Kuhn's first law and also explains why the *Beowulf* poet strongly prefers placement of movable SPs before rather than after the first metrical stress. The universalist micro-constraints on SPs can be combined for convenience in a macro-constraint called the SP MOVEMENT RULE, abbreviated as SPMR.

Like lines, verse clauses are abstracted from grammatical propositions with SOV order. Principles applying within the line should also apply within clauses too long to fit within a line. The principle of closure (UM 4) predicts that more complex verse types will tend to appear earlier in the clause. UM 5 predicts that heavier verse types will tend to appear later in the clause. Table 5 shows the distribution of the most common verse types within the clause.

Table 5. Placement of representative verse types within the clause

	Initial Position	Non-initial in Core	In Right Periphery
A7 (xx/Sx)	293	1	---
A1 (Sx/Sx)	240	930	878
B1 (x/Sxs)	620	30	43
C2 (x/Ssx)	608	190	105
D2 (S/Ssx)	53	121	198
D3 (S/Sxs)	109	115	24
E (Ssx/S)	159	155	131

Type A7 is very complex because it departs farthest from normative weight, having just one lift. This complexity restricts type A7 categorically to the a-verse. Type A7 is also restricted to the first verse of the clause, with a single exception, *būton þone hafelan* 'except the head' (Beo 1614a). The normative verse pattern, type A1, has a dramatically different distribution, appearing most often where type A7 is avoided, with many instances in the right periphery. Types B and C are light but less anomalously so than type A7. B1 and C2 usually appear in the opening verse but have significant frequency in rightward verses. Its normative compound foot pattern Ssx makes C2 less complex than B1, with its morphologically complex Sxs foot, and this difference is reflected in the higher proportion of rightward placements for C2.

Types D and E are the heaviest patterns. As expected, they appear most often in non-initial position, contrasting sharply in this respect with the light B and C types. The least complex of these heavy patterns is type D2. Its normative compound foot is placed last in accord with UM 5 as it applies to foot complexity within the verse. The more complex type E has a normative compound foot but this heavy foot is placed in initial position, contravening UM 5. The difference in complexity is reflected in the larger proportion of type D2 verses in the right periphery, where metrical complexity is least acceptable. The morphological complexity of the Sxs foot explains why type D3 has the smallest proportion of instances in the right periphery.

§1.20 Alignment of syntactic constituents with verses and lines

A strong tendency to realize metrical constituents as syntactic constituents is recognized in traditional discussions of ENJAMBMENT, which occurs when words in close syntactic composition are split by the boundary of a verse or line (Russom 2017: 15–19, 33–34). Item (9a) is from Shakespeare's sonnet 18. Item (9b) is constructed to illustrate the surprising effect of enjambment. Item (9c) is from "The Tyger," by William Blake.

(9) (a) Shall I compare thee to a summer's day?

        Thou art more lovely and more temperate.

   (b) Shall I compare thee to this splendid new

        Morning, so lovely and so temperate?

   (c) What immortal hand or eye

        could frame thy fearful symmetry?

In (9a) both lines are realized as sentences. In (9b) the first sentence intrudes into the next line and the adjective-noun construction is split by the line boundary. Both (9a) and (9b) have stress patterns regularly employed by Shakespeare. The surprising effect in (9b) is a purely syntactic phenomenon. As lines become shorter, it becomes more difficult to say something interesting within them. Split sentences will become more common and less surprising. In (9c) Blake employs a two-line interrogative sentence but maintains syntactic coherence at line level by splitting the sentence at the natural point of syntactic division, between the subject and the verb phrase. The archaic line in item (1), *ek hlewagastiz holtijaz   horna tawido*, maintains syntactic integrity at verse level in the same way, with the subject in the a-verse and the verb phrase in the b-verse. As we shall see, this kind of line division is highly favored in *Beowulf.*

Tarlinskaja (1984: 2) observed that "the link between meter and grammar is only beginning to attract the attention of students of English verse." It was not until midway into the twentieth century that the metrical implications of enjambment began to be taken seriously. As an instance of the kind of work that had become possible Tarlinskaja cites the generative study of Youmans (1983), which shows that Shakespeare employs archaic verb-final syntax only when modern syntax would violate metrical rules. As this kind of work continues, the view of meter as a purely rhythmical phenomenon — expressed influentially by Jespersen (1933) and in early generative tradition by Halle & Keyser (1971) — seems less and less appropriate. Rhythm and meter may seem identical when we restrict attention to forms like iambic pentameter, which employs a line of five iambic feet with regular alternation of weak and strong metrical positions. When we turn to Old English meter, with its many distinct foot patterns, it becomes clear that rhythm and meter, though intimately related, employ different rule systems (Russom 2022c). As Wimsatt and Beardsley argued (1959), metrical rules that distinguish acceptable verses from unacceptable ones are most informatively expressed in purely linguistic terms. Since morphology and syntax are as important as phonology in linguistics, it is not at all clear why constraints on enjambment and word order should be excluded from rule systems that generate acceptable patterns of stress and syllable length.

The syntactic complexity caused by enjambment restricts its frequency in accord with UM 1. Consider the clearest and most frequent instances in *Beowulf,* which split a noun from its adjectival or participial modifier. Enjambment causes only moderate complexity in verses like (10a–e).

(10) (a) *nam þā mid / **handa** hige- / þīhtigne*

    ***rinc** on / ræste* (746a–47a)

    'with his hands he seized the stout-hearted man on the bed'

(b) *þæt ic on þone / **hafelan** heoro- / drēorigne*

    *ofer / **eald** gewin ēagum / starige!* (1780–81)

    'that I might gaze with my eyes on that sword-gory head after the old strife'

(c)   *Wīglāf / siteð*

    *ofer / **Bīowulfe**, byre / Wīhstānes,*

    ***eorl** ofer / ōðrum un- / lifigendum* (2906b–8b)

    'Wiglaf sits over Beowulf, one earl over the other dead one'

(d)   *þæt bið* / **driht**-*guman*

un- / *lifgendum* **æfter** / *sēlest* (1388b–89b)

'that is best for a dead warrior afterwards'

(e) *swylce ic* / **magu-þegnas** **mīne** / *hāte*

wið / **fēon**da gehw<u>one</u>   **flotan** / *ēowerne,*

nīw- / *tyrwydne* **nacan** *on* / *sande*

ārum / *healdan* (293a–96a)

'likewise, I will order my kindred thanes to respectfully guard your vessel — that newly tarred boat on the sand'

Kiparsky (1977) shows that poets disregard mismatch constraints when they make it difficult or impossible to use a native word. Audiences will learn to expect such mismatches. If an Old English poet wants to use a whole-verse compound like *higeþīhtigne* or *nīwtyrwydne* to modify nouns, something that happens with significant frequency in *Beowulf*, splitting the modifier from the noun will be unavoidable.

In clauses (11a–c) the enjambment is more conspicuous because the adjectives and nouns are smaller than a verse. Special constraints are imposed on such instances. For concision and readability only the first verse of the clause is included in the list of other examples like (11a, b).

(11) (a) *nalæs hī hine* **læs**san   **lā**cum *tēodan,*

    þēod-ge- / *strēonum* (43a–44a)

'they by no means provided him with lesser gifts, treasures'

(b) *ac hine se* / **mōdega** **mæg** / <u>Hygelā</u>ces

hæfde / *(be)* / **hon**da (813a–14a)

'but the brave kinsman of Hygelac had him by the hand'

(c)   *þæt hē* / **þrī**tiges

manna / **mægencræft** *on his* **mund**-gripe

heaþo-rōf / **hæbbe** (379b–81a)

'that he, bold in battle, had the physical strength of thirty men in his hand-grip'

(d) *þæt hīe ge-* / **sā**won   **swylce** / *twēgen[,]*

micle / **mearc**-stapan[,]   **mōras** / *healdan,*

ellor- / *gǣstas* (1347a–49a)

'that he saw two such (creatures) rule the moors — huge border-stalkers, alien spirits'

Opening verses in other instances like (11a): 293a, 418a, 533a, 965a, 1146a, 1344a, 2410a, 2479a, 2481a, 2522a, 2637a, 2683a; like (11b): 2011a, 2012a, 2587a, 2928a, 3120a.

The set of examples in item (11) differs in important ways from those in item (10). Of the five instances in (10), two have the enjambment after the b-verse (10a, d). Among 20 instances like (11a–c), the only such instance is (11c). Three of the five instances in item (10) have the enjambment after the second verse (10a, c, e). The instances like (11a–c) all have the enjambment after the first verse. Item (11d) would be an exception if *swylce* could modify *micle mearcstapan* to mean 'two such huge border-stalkers.' This seems very unlikely, however. Numerals are less closely bound to nouns than are adjectival forms. We say *two green apples* or *two such apples,* but not **green two apples* or **such two apples.* The same constraint applies in Old English (OES 1: 68, 71). Word order would be perfectly normal, on the other hand, if we interpret *swylce* as an adjectival pronoun and translate *swylce twēgen* as 'two such, two of this kind,' with *micle mearcstapan* following as a variation. Use of *twegen* as an archaic postposition is unproblematic (OES 1: 76). Most instances of *twēgen* in Old English poetry are postposed (see Bessinger & Smith 1978). As for *swylc,* when it means 'such' rather than 'which' or 'likewise' in *Beowulf,* it often functions as a pronoun meaning 'such a thing or person.' In this pronominal usage *swylc* occurs eight times (178b, 996b, 1328b, 1329b, 1940b, 2541b, 2708b, 2798b). 'Two such (creatures)' is the only plausible translation of 1347b. The bracketed commas are not present in K4 but should be added, since the editors normally set off appositive phrases with commas, as editors of a Modern English text would do. Kuhn's laws, as formulated, do not explain the intricate constraints to which enjambment is subject, but these constraints follow from the universal principle of closure as it applies to syntactic complexity.

§1.21 Purely poetic syntax

Enjambment splits closely bound constituents with a metrical boundary. In ancient Germanic poetry closely bound constituents can also be split by extraneous linguistic constituents, contravening the very strong tendency for modifiers to maintain their positions relative to the constituents they modify. In (12a–i) adjectival and possessive genitive modifiers are split from nouns. A variety of other split phrases will be identified in the chapters on particular constructions.

(12) (a) *habbað wē tō þǣm /* **mǣran** **micel** */ ǣrende*

      Deniga */ frêan* (270a–71a)

      'we have an important message for the famous lord of the Danes'

  (b)   *þæt ðū mē /* **ā** *wǣre*

      forð-*ge-* / <u>wite</u>num *on* / **fæder** *stæle* (1478b–79b)

      'that you would always be in the place of a father to dead me (after I died)'

  (c)   *nā þū /* **mīn**ne *þearft*

      hafalan */* **hȳdan** (445b–46a)

      'by no means need you hide my head (bury me)'

  (d)   *opðe /* **ende**-*dæg*

      on þisse / **meodu**-*healle* **mīn**ne */ (ge)bīdan* (637b–38b)

      'or experience my final day in this mead-hall'

  (e) *þæt hē fram /* **Sige**-*mundes* *secgan / hȳrde*

      ellen- */ dǣdum* (875a–76a)

      'that he heard concerning Sigmund's deeds of valor'

  (f)   **searo**-*nīðas / flēah*

      Eormen- */ rīces* (1200b–1a)

      'he fled the cunning hostilities of Eormenric'

A modified noun is split from a lexical constituent with adjectival function in (12a, b), from an adjectival function word in (12c, d), and from a possessive genitive noun in (12e–f). The split phrase *mē forðgewitenum* is like Modern English *poor me!* except that the heavy adjective follows its modified pronoun. The split modifier can come before the noun, as in (12a, c, e), or after it, as in (12b, d, f). For poetic syntax of this kind I will use the term HYPERBATON, defined as "a figure of speech in which the customary or logical order of words is inverted" (OED, s.v.).

    Hyperbaton is also employed by Old Norse poets. In the 1970s, as Frank (1978: 49) observed, the systematically scrambled syntax of skaldic court poetry was "a murky and still largely mysterious system." Gade (1995) goes a long way toward explaining this system and her findings are also relevant to the syntax of *Beowulf*. As Gade shows (1995: 213–16), constructions like (12a–f), which are very common in skaldic poetry, can also be found in the oldest Germanic poems with traditional meter — not only in Old English and Old Norse but also in Old Saxon and Old High German. These traditional constructions seem to have provided a starting point for the more radical skaldic experiments with split constituents, which are comparable to those in the poetry of E. E. Cummings. Skaldic poems were short enough to be memorized and could be pondered deliberately after presentation. They were crafted to make interpretation difficult, like the sly hints in a crossword puzzle. A minimalist syntactician would situate them between presentation to the faculty of understanding and presentation to the faculty of articulation, as with other syntactic structures that contravene rules of ordinary speech (§1.8). Skaldic poetry also added new rules for sound patterning, with specified positions for rhyme, new constraints on vowel length, and stricter rules for placement of alliterating syllables. Gade (1995: 214) attributes the more radical experiments with syntax in court poetry to the greater difficulty of satisfying metrical requirements with idiomatic word orders.

§1.22. Punctuation

Although there is no apparent syntactic difference between (13a–f) and the instances of hyperbaton in item (12), items (13a–e) are punctuated differently in K4. Item (13f) is a similar instance from Dobbie's ASPR edition.

(13) (a)   *þǣr se / gōda sæt(,)*

     Bēowulf / Gēata   be þǣm ge- / brōðrum twǣm (1190b–91a)

     'there between the two brothers sat the mighty Beowulf of the Geats'

    (b) *him þā / ellen-rōf   and- / swarode(,)*

     wlanc / Wedera lēod (340a–41a)

     'the brave-strong, handsome prince of the people of the Weders answered him'

    (c)   *fela þǣra / wæs(,)*

     wera ond / wīfa (992b–93a)

     'a multitude of those men and women was present'

    (d)   *ond þone / ǣnne heht*

     golde / (for)gyldan(,)   þone ðe / Grendel ǣr

     māne / (ā)cwealde (1053b–55a)

     'and (he) said to compensate with gold the one whom Grendel viciously killed earlier'

    (e) *(ge)spræc þā / (se) gōda   gylp-worda / sum(,)*

Bēowulf / Gēata(,) (675a–76a)

'then the mighty Beowulf of the Geats spoke a certain one of boasting speeches'

(f)   *gūð-bill ge- / swāc(,)*

nacod æt / nīðe (2584b–85a)

'the naked war-sword failed at the fight'

The parenthesized commas in (13a–e) are inherited from K3. Removing them would bring these clauses into conformity with instances like (12a–f), where there is no comma in the K4 text. Since Klaeber's time punctuation has been greatly simplified in English publications, academic ones included. It has become very hard indeed to find a semicolon in a new book and commas occur less frequently than they used to do. One convention that remains unchanged is to punctuate appositions internal to a sentence with a comma on both sides. Now the opening verse in (13a) might be translated as 'there the mighty (one) sat,' where the adjective has become equivalent to a noun by ZERO CONVERSION, without any overt marker to indicate the change from one part of speech to another. Compare *brave* in *none but the brave die young.* But in that case *Bēowulf Gēata* would be a sentence-internal appositive and we would expect a comma after it as well as before it. Using Klaeber's punctuation to waffle about the syntax of the adjective would create nothing but confusion for the vast majority of readers who need to consult K4. Klaeber's punctuation can create semantic confusion as well. For today's reader of English texts the comma in (13d) marks the relative clause as non-restrictive and the preceding clause as an adequate expression of the intended meaning to which the relative clause adds incidental information. In that case (13d) means '(he) said to compensate the one, whom Grendel viciously killed, by the way.' If what comes before the comma expresses the intended meaning, who is this otherwise unspecified 'the one' or 'that one'? The intended meaning is complete only if the relative clause is restrictive, in which case (13d) is mispunctuated. In (13f), as the editors of K4 would have noticed, Dobbie's comma strongly suggests interpretation as 'the war-sword failed, being naked in battle,' where the nakedness of the sword somehow makes it less effective, as a naked warrior might be. But a naked sword is more effective than a sheathed one, not less. *Nacod* modifies *bill,* like *gūð-,* and *æt nīðe* modifies *geswāc,* not *nacod.*

The editors of K4 have accomplished an enormous task in their revised Introduction and Commentary, which incorporates "the vast store of scholarship on *Beowulf* that has appeared since 1936." This is the primary goal of the book, as stated on the opening page. Anyone who consults the entries under 'punctuation' in the topic indexes of OES and Blockley (2001) will soon understand why K4 departs from K3 only where repunctuation is obviously required rather than providing a systematic revision. What the editors have done instead — no small task — is to incorporate relevant findings of Mitchell and Blockley into notes on particular verses while encouraging readers "to experiment continually with repunctuation" (K4: 321). I will respond to the call for experiment by parenthesizing instances that seem unnecessary or misleading to me, as in item (13), and by adding punctuation in square brackets when that seems appropriate. I am no more able than the editors to provide categorical rules for punctuating Old English poetry. Punctuation is to some extent an art and editors of contemporary texts are not entirely in agreement about categorical rules. What can be said now, I think, is that it does no significant harm to punctuate the text in a more contemporary style. Klaeber declares that "our modern stylistic feeling is not necessarily a safe guide for properly judging of Old English sentences, periods, and paragraphs" and leaves appositive variations unpunctuated when in his opinion that would create "awkward cases of overpunctuation" (K3: clxiv). He goes on to declare, again without argument or evidence, that "a rather frequent use of semicolons and of dashes is necessitated by the quality of the old style." It is not at all clear that ease of understanding should be sacrificed to avoid these supposed problems and Klaeber makes no attempt to persuade skeptics otherwise.

Klaeber's punctuation makes it impossible to classify syntactic structures consistently. When there is no secure guide I choose a punctuation that groups verse clauses in a useful way for readers with a variety of interests. Klaeber's punctuation in (13a, b), for example, implies that the adjectives have become noun arguments by zero conversion. If so we would have syntactically independent SV clauses followed by variations. Repunctuated as hyperbatons, (13a-b) have VS structure, with a noun subject after the finite verb. In (13e-f) semantic evidence points toward hyperbaton as the proper analysis, but there is no comparable evidence to guide us in (13a, b). Since SV word order is normative, in prose as well as poetry, the SV analysis may seem preferable in these cases, but variation and zero-conversion are departures from ordinary prose syntax and create significant additive complexity when used in the same clause, while hyperbaton employs a word order that is sometimes obviously required and is well attested in North and West Germanic traditions. Hyperbaton employs no other kinds of complex syntax and associates nouns with adjectives in the usual way. I will classify instances like (13a, b) as hyperbatons.

A similar difficulty of classification is created by the fact that adjectives are sometimes zero-converted to adverbs as well as to nouns in *Beowulf* (K4: cxlix). The two possibilities of interpretation can be difficult to distinguish and further research on this topic would be welcome. I classify compound adjectives as zero-converted arguments in cases like *ēode / ellen-rōf* 'the valor-bold one walked,' since such adjectives typically modify arguments in the poem. The alternative possibility would be to interpret *ellen-rōf* as an adverbial phrase, which seems less consistent with the poet's style. For similar reasons I interpret poetic compounds like *heaðo-torht* 'battle-bright' in *Beowulf* 2553a as adjectives split from their modified nouns by hyperbaton rather than as adjectives zero-converted to adverbs. Adverbial use of a compound adjective seems plausible in a few instances like *grāpode / gearo-folm* '(he) grasped ready-handed' (2085a), where the poetic compound has a meaning closely related to the meaning of the verb.

Mitchell (OES 2: 1003) argues for sparing use of heavy punctuation like colons and semicolons, except in the most plausible instances of subordination identified by Andrew (1940, 1948). This is compatible with current trends in punctuation and would provide a more readable *Beowulf*. If we interpret strictly in accord with formal evidence, the style of *Beowulf* is rather paratactic, with many sentences that are independent or linked by coordinating conjunctions. Obvious cases of subordination in the poem are marked by subordinating conjunctions or have obvious analogues in Modern English, as with omission of *that* in sentences like *Frankie said she would go to Watkins Glen*. Paratactic style contrasts with the HYPOTACTIC style of formal writing that makes intensive use of subordinating conjunctions and employs semicolons to indicate subordination to a main clause of clauses without an overt marker of subordination.

In addition to finding some persuasive instances of subordination without overt marking, Andrew (1940, 1948) proposes categorical rules for employment of heavy punctuation by editors of Old English poetry. Mitchell (OES 1: 675–793) argues that not one of these rules is in fact categorical and his evidence is widely regarded as decisive. As the editors of K4 summarize our present understanding, "it is often impossible to determine with certainty whether a clause is dependent or independent" (K4: 321). The elegant periodic sentences of Classical authors have lent prestige to hypotactic style, especially in academic prose. Mitchell (OES 2: 91) judges that "Andrew's practice reflects his belief that hypotaxis is necessarily superior to parataxis" and that "wherever MnE punctuation can make a sentence periodic rather than paratactic, Andrew finds reason for adopting that punctuation." The most obvious effect of Klaeber's editorial style, which Klaeber nowhere mentions, is to minimize the appearance of parataxis. The punctuation of K3 approximates the long, flowing sentences of Classical rhetoric by bridging across clause boundaries with semicolons and eliding the commas that would normally flank appositions. A particularly unfortunate consequence of Klaeber's style is to elide the boundaries of traditional phrases that provide alliteration and fill out metrical patterns. Obscuring these formulaic elements might give the text a more sophisticated appearance but makes it more difficult to think about what kind of poem *Beowulf* might actually be.

Although he shows that Andrew's proposed rules are tendencies, Mitchell emphasizes that Andrew's findings do sometimes justify interpretation of a formally ambiguous clause as dependent, if not always. Just as valuable and more carefully nuanced than Andrew's are the findings in Blockley (2001), who is familiar with generative theory as well as English historical linguistics. The rules for subordination in her appendix are quite unlike those of Andrew and in some cases are expressed as tendencies, like the violable rules of optimality theory. What editorial responsibility demands is due consideration of alternative possibilities before finalizing punctuation of a text (OES 2: 818). Like Mitchell, Blockley (2001: 1, 40–42) emphasizes the responsibility of editors to punctuate according to the best evidence rather than retreating toward manuscript punctuation in hopes of preserving ambiguities that literary critics should know about. It is hard to understand how that would be helpful, since manuscript punctuation is more difficult to interpret than familiar punctuation and what literary critics require to begin work is a grasp of the most obvious interpretation. A conscientious critic will consult relevant aids to manuscript study, which now include important contributions of digital scholarship, but this is more likely to bear fruit if undertaken after study of a punctuated edition. As Blockley puts it (2001: 40), "an editor who rises to the effort and risk of punctuating a text provides the reader with a more useful and informative document than one who does not." If an editor thinks that a particular ambiguity might be important, of course, that opinion can be provided in a textual note, as with many instances in K4 where the editors discuss alternative interpretations. But avoiding punctuation to valorize remote possibilities of interpretation seems — well — pointless.

§1.23 The main line of argument

The core hypothesis defended in this book is that the order of major constituents in *Beowulf,* as it departs from Old English prose syntax, can be explained by universal principles of language and meter if the normative order in West Germanic poetry was still SOV when *Beowulf* was composed, as seems likely on independent grounds (§1.3). As we shall see, the most common departures from SOV typology are due to rightward displacement of heavy constituents and leftward movement of light constituents. To validate the core hypothesis I must test it against facts determined independently of the theory. Now a researcher who proposes a hypothesis should have as little as possible to do with determining the facts. Ideally a sufficient corpus of facts will have been assessed by eminent researchers before the hypothesis is proposed. K4 obviously qualifies in this regard and I will test my hypothesis against it. I will accept the interpretations of fact in this widely admired edition without demur, except in a few cases where the number of relevant instances is small and pre-theoretical assessments based on frequency of occurrence are less than usually reliable. I seldom find reason to reject Mitchell's claims in OES but cannot agree that Old English had *apo koinou* constructions — a claim that has not been widely accepted (K4: 321).

It seems a very safe bet indeed that anyone interested in this book will already own a copy of K4. I will assume that the reader has K4 ready to hand and will not duplicate all the relevant analytical or bibliographical information in it, providing compact references instead where appropriate. Discussion of intricate metrical and syntactic problems can be decluttered by suppression of diacritics and codicological notations that have no bearing on the topics of interest here, though of course these features of K4 provide valuable information for readers interested in other important topics. A reader who has doubts about my analysis of a difficult construction can consult the relevant note in K4 for previous opinions; and analogous constructions in *Beowulf* will be identified in the same section with the difficult construction. The numbered groups of examples are designed to make it as easy as possible for researchers to test the core hypothesis. It will be most consistent, and of some interest, to test the core hypothesis against the emendations in K4 as well rather than setting them aside. Metrical evidence often provides independent support for these emendations.

A time-honored constraint on theory construction is Occam's Razor, which forbids multiplication of theoretical entities for no good reason. I will exclude from theoretical consideration all of the many interesting and important facts about Old English grammar that have never been shown to affect word order. Grammatical number is irrelevant, for example, when we are concerned with the order of verbs and arguments. Modern English is SVO for plurals as well as singulars. In double-object constructions (§1.8), case inflections can actually be misleading when we want to find out which

object is in closer construction with the verb. Since the main line of argument deals with the order of major constituents, conjunctions and adjuncts
are relevant only when they influence placement of a verb or argument.
Such influences are few in number but not negligible. We will need to consider subordinating conjunctions when they block verb fronting and negative particles when they promote verb fronting (§1.8). As we shall see in
chapter two, modification of a major constituent by a stressed adjunct has
remarkably high frequency in *Beowulf* and the resulting increase in constituent weight has significant consequences. A two-word category II verse
with a modified object is usually displaced beyond the verb to the right periphery, skewing statistical evidence for basic word order. When we factor
out such influences, SOV emerges unmistakably as the norm.

CHAPTER 2

FORMULAIC COMPOSITION

§2.0 Introduction

There are some purely poetic constructions in *Beowulf* (§1.20) but most constructions obey the rules of Old English prose syntax. *Beowulf* differs in this respect from Old Norse skaldic poems that employ conspicuously poetic syntax from beginning to end. From a statistical point of view, however, the syntax of *Beowulf* is anything but prosaic. Consider for example *Cynewulf and Cyneheard,* a well-known prose narrative with heroic content in the *Anglo-Saxon Chronicle,* edited with comments on the style by Cassidy and Ringler (1971: 138–42). This passage is about 450 words long and contains three phrases with an adjective that modifies an immediately adjacent noun: *unryhtum dǣdum* 'unjust deeds' (dat. pl.), *lȳtle werode* 'small troop' (inst. sg.), and *Bryttiscum gīsle* 'British hostage' (dat. sg.). The first 83 lines of *Beowulf* have about the same number of words as the prose passage but theses lines include 21 adjective-noun phrases. Fourteen are like **lange** / **hwīle** 'for a long time' (16a), with an alliterating adjective followed by a stressed noun (cf. 5a, 21a, 29a, 31a, 34b, 54a, 54b, 57a, 58b, 67a, 69a, 75a, 83a). When added to the noun, the adjective creates an ideal two-word realization of a category II verse. In the prose passage, the three adjectives fulfill straightforward descriptive functions in their immediate context. The adjective in **lange** / **hwīle** is equally pertinent to the immediate context in *Beowulf,* a time without a competent leader that was distressing to the Danes because it was long-lasting. In some other two-word verses, however, there is no apparent need for the information provided by the adjective. In verse 31a, for example, Scyld Scefing is called **lēof** / **land**-*fruma* 'beloved leader of the land.' Just three lines later he is called **lēofne** / **þēoden** 'beloved lord' (34b). We learn nothing new from the second instance of *lēof.* In this chapter we will consider how the poet uses modifiers to provide essential information, vivid detail, emphasis on core heroic values, and phraseology that satisfies metrical requirements. Intensive use of these modifiers has very significant effects on word order. We will then revisit *Cynewulf and Cyneheard* for a few more observations about narrative style.

§2.1 The creative ability of poets who use formulaic technique

The foundational work on oral-formulaic theory (Parry 1928) took place at a time when psychology and linguistic theory were influenced by positivistic trends. Lord (1960: 35–36) makes the standard positivist assumptions when he asserts that "the method of language is like that of oral poetry, substitution in the framework of the grammar. Without the metrical restrictions of the verse, language substitutes one subject for another in the nominative case, keeping the same verbs; or keeping the same noun, it substitutes one verb for another." In Skinner (1957), the leading proponent of behaviorism explained language learning as a process of substituting new words for words in previously memorized sentences with reinforcement from parents. This is the context for comparison of the apprentice oral poet to "a child learning words" (Lord 1960: 22).

Behaviorist linguistics received a fatal blow in Chomsky (1959), a review of Skinner (1957). Few now believe that behaviorism can explain "the fundamental fact about the normal use of language, namely the native speaker's ability to produce and understand instantly new sentences that are not similar to those previously heard in any physically defined sense or in terms of any notion of frames or classes of events, nor associated with those previously heard by conditioning, nor obtainable by any sort of 'generalization' known to psychology or philosophy" (Chomsky 1965: 57-58). Roger Brown, a psychologist specializing in child language acquisition, had adopted the new approach by the 1970s. According to Brown (1973: 39), "Chomsky is certainly right in saying that, except for routine greetings and things of that sort, almost every sentence we hear is new to us. New in our lifetime, often new in the whole history of the language." If the human language ability is that powerful, there is no longer any reason to believe, as Milman Parry did, that "the poet who habitually makes his poems without the aid of writing can do so only by putting together old verses and old parts of verses in an old way" (Parry 1933: 181). This is not to say that the formulaic regularities described by Parry are unimportant. Formulaic poets use "routine greetings and things of that sort" far more systematically than participants in an ordinary conversation (Russom 2010). As we shall see, syntactic structures that

68

facilitate composition appear with remarkably high frequency in *Beowulf*. What seems certain now is that inherited phraseology cannot solve every problem of composition. The poet must often work from scratch. The notion that oral-formulaic composition is a sort of cheap trick has nothing to recommend it. Oral poets were the most highly paid professionals of the ancient world because they had skills that took years of hard work to master and because those skills were required for cultural preservation (Watkins 1995: 68–84).

The oral-formulaists who carried on Parry's work came to realize that a behaviorist theory of composition did insufficient justice to Homer and Southslavic oral poets (Foley 1995). A recent survey concludes that no definition of the formula proposed so far has proved adequate to the quite different task of analyzing Old English poetry (Fox 2020: 1–74; cf. Fry 1967). In fact, as we shall see, the *Beowulf* poet employs a variety of formulaic techniques that apply independently of one another and are not restricted to one kind of metrical domain. These techniques can be used to construct a verse, a line, or a clause larger than a line and may apply quite inconspicuously. A verse becomes unmistakably formulaic when several techniques apply simultaneously within it. Although oral-formulaic technique is much harder to explain than Parry supposed, its purpose remains clear: *to solve problems of composition in the general case.* An oral poet knows, for example, what kinds of people, places, and things are required in a heroic narrative and values descriptive phrases for them that are useful in any realization of the genre.

§2.2 Genres as specialized story worlds

In his study of modern urban storytellers with little or no interest in reading, Labov (1972b) observed that their narratives had a hypnotic effect, evoking a deep, attentive silence that a literate orator might envy. Labov's wordsmiths created imaginative worlds that were easy and interesting to enter. The additional challenge confronting oral poets is to construct such worlds with systematically aestheticized metrical language. When we step back from technical detail to consider what the *Beowulf* poet achieves, the demands of formulaic composition seem daunting and we should not be surprised by the difficulty of explaining how it is achieved.

A story cannot represent everything about the natural world that human beings have observed. What can be done — no mean feat! — is to select themes of crucial importance to an audience and create a specialized narrative environment for elaboration of those themes. Many of Labov's most accomplished narrators were barely into their teens and attended schools where bullying was a serious problem. They had developed a "fight" genre describing confrontations with larger antagonists in the narrative environment of the schoolyard. This genre has a well-defined practical goal. As the action unfolds, the narrators let it be known that bullying them would be a costly mistake. They portray themselves as shrewd fighters who are unshakably committed to destruction of the bully. Labov sees nothing particularly childish about them, comparing some scenes in their narratives to memorable scenes in Homer's *Iliad*. Luraghi (1995) employs Labov's methodology for analysis of narrative discourse in several early Indo-European languages, including Homeric Greek.

Beowulf deals with adult problems that confront loved and respected leaders. Though certainly larger than a schoolyard, the poem's imaginative world is selective in a way that facilitates heroic composition. The focal environment is a great wooden hall where the lord's retainers feast with him. Benches occupied by the retainers during the day are converted at night into beds for the younger men. Nearby are the bowers: apartments for young women, married couples, and important guests. What we might call international relations are represented compactly as relations between halls. Outside the hall lie three environments that are well elaborated in ancient Germanic storytelling: the ocean, the wasteland, and the dark forest. The hero must enter these liminal spaces on the way to another hall or to confront evildoers who lurk within.

The alliterative tradition was brought to England by West Germanic peoples who had survived a migration through foreign lands and across an arm of the sea. *Beowulf* is not a nationalistic founding myth like the *Æneid*, however. The poet never mentions England. The idealized political unit in the poem lies to the east and does not result from an invasion. It is a Danish kingdom in the heart of ancient Germania that has expanded by acquiring hegemony over neighboring tribes whose attempts to invade it have failed. The poet mentions an invasion of France by Beowulf's beloved uncle Hygelac, but this Viking-style attack is represented as a rash military adventure and proves fatal to its initiator. Beowulf is praised for avenging his lord and kinsman during the raid, but as for Hygelac, *wēan āhsode* 'he asked for trouble' (1206). Though pronounced with the poet's characteristic understatement, this criticism is severe. The same phrase appears with plural inflection earlier in the poem as *wēan āhsodon* (423b), which evaluates as foolish the attacks of monsters killed by Beowulf. When Beowulf becomes king he follows Hrothgar's example rather than Hygelac's, protecting the Geats from many hostile tribes (2207a–11b). Here as elsewhere the emphasis is firmly on defense, and this emphasis may be very ancient indeed. Some formulaic language in *Beowulf* has survived from an epic tradition more than 5,000 years old, a tradition inherited by speakers of Indo-European languages from India to Ireland that has now been partially reconstructed by historical linguists (Beekes 1995: 41–44).

As described by Watkins (1995: 299–300), Indo-European heroes are gods or mortals strong enough to defend a whole society against nightmarish sociopaths. The archaic hero-tale is structured to repress destructive conflicts by dramatizing the risks to unsavory characters who initiate them. Heroic action is typically situated in a remote past or a mythical otherworld, avoiding mention of conflicts within living memory, which might stir up dangerous resentments. This risk is dramatized in *Beowulf* 2029a–69a, an elaborate digression about a 'peace-weaving' marriage designed to heal the wounds of war. Beowulf fears that war will break out again when an embittered old survivor from the groom's people stirs up a young hot-head whose father was killed by a member of the bride's retinue. Monsters make especially useful villains for the poet because they aren't members of a kinship network that actually exists. *Beowulf* is the binary opposite of imperialistic war propaganda. It is not even a war poem, strictly speaking, since it focuses on fights between a hero and an individual monster. Contempt for initiators of hostilities is expressed systematically throughout. Warfare is represented as an unmitigated disaster. The greatest glory is for heroes whose abilities intimidate potential attackers and for kings who avoid conflict through diplomacy.

§2.3 Narrative syntax

Labov defines pure narrativity as an iconic 'blow-by-blow' technique that presents actions in an amount of recitation time similar to the time required for such actions in the real world. The hypnotic effect of storytelling seems to involve an alignment of the listener's body with the body of a character in the imagined world. To achieve this effect, storytellers adhere to a concrete syntactic design in narrative clauses, encoding each action in a finite main verb with active voice and PUNCTUAL ASPECT. Verbs with punctual aspect represent a single action taking place at a particular point in time and narrative clauses have maximum impact when they follow the order in which actions are imagined to occur. Narrativity is most effective in a sequence of one-clause sentences. The effect is lost in complex sentences with colorless auxiliaries and 'be' verbs, passive constructions, subjunctives representing hypothetical actions, and non-finite verb forms with unspecified temporal boundaries. Hypotaxis can be useful for analysis of complex philosophical problems, in narrative poetry as well as in academic prose, but parataxis is the obvious choice for action sequences.

Heroic epic contrasts sharply with lyric poetry, the predominant English verse form since the end of the nineteenth century. Rather than taking characters forward through imaginary time, the modernist lyric considers topics from various perspectives and moves quickly upward to a higher level of generality. In "The Course of a Particular," for example, the author proceeds from a few autumn leaves to a grim perspective on mortality with cosmic scope (Stevens 1957: 96). Stevens toys rather brutally with sentimental romanticism here, inviting the reader to sympathize with the poor dying leaves at first, then gradually revealing how pathetically silly he thinks that would be. The leaves in the poem are swept passively by wind. They make a crying sound. As the poet reflects on these leaves he observes from time to time that the crying continues. In closing the poet considers one leaf that comes loose from the tree and falls for an unspecified time through the air — a little death that has come to seem disturbingly meaningless rather than moving. The reiterated "cry" is encoded in a finite main verb but does not represent a deliberate act. The crying is continuous and vague rather than punctual and vivid. The leaves perform no other action. Labovian narrativity is excluded here to create an effect of timelessness.

The *Beowulf* poet's narrative skill is conspicuous in a chilling account of Grendel's attack on Heorot (Renoir 1962). Consider item (1), an excerpt in which the giant devours the first warrior he finds in Hrothgar's hall.

(1)   *slāt* / *unwearnum,*

     bāt / *bān-locan,*   *blōd* / *ēdrum dranc,*

     syn-snǣdum / *swealh;*   *sōna* / *hæfde*

     un- / *lyfigendes*   *eal ge-* / *feormod,*

     fēt ond / *folma* (741b-45b)

'(He) slashed the unsuspecting one, bit the bone-container, drank blood from the veins, gobbled in great gulps; soon (he) had entirely devoured the un-living one, feet and hands included'

The passage begins with a blow-by-blow description of the giant's actions in an ordered sequence of monosyllabic finite verbs with punctual aspect: *slāt, bāt, dranc, swealh.* The poet then suspends the action in a passive construction with the colorless finite auxiliary *hæfde* and the non-finite verb *ge-feormed,* a past participle that represents the action sequence as completed rather than taking place. This construction performs an evaluative function, with *sōna* and *eal* underscoring the uncanny speed and thoroughness of actions encoded in the one-verse narrative clauses. Narrative clauses and evaluative clauses work together here to create a shocking reality effect. Verses 741b–45a are followed by a less grisly sequence of narrative clauses in which Grendel seizes Beowulf and is seized by him in return. The poet evaluates Beowulf's counter-move by describing something that had never happened: Grendel had never been gripped so firmly by a human being. Statements about what does not occur suspend the narrative action but the suspension is brief here and the evaluation enhances the reality effect. Unexpected actions are REPORTABLE, creating stronger audience involvement than frequently occurring actions. As any reporter will tell you, *Man Bites Dog* makes a better headline than *Dog Bites Man.*

So far I have assumed that my literary-critical judgments will seem plausible to the reader. I hope that is so, but judgments based solely on a critic's intuition do not explain how a literary effect is achieved or appreciated. What kinds of evidence might be brought to bear on the claim that transitive monosyllables in one-verse narrative clauses enhance the impact of Grendel's violent acts? Precisely *why* might someone be dissatisfied with a prose paraphrase like "after dissecting and eating him, he imbibed his blood and swallowed him quickly"? Consider the evaluative adverb *sōna* in 743b. This has obvious metrical utility, transforming colorless *hæfde,* which is required by the rules of grammar, into a normative two-word verse of type A1 with the finite verb in line-final position. Why imagine that *sōna* serves any other purpose?

Literary effects become conspicuous if the author employs them more than once in close proximity. When we consider the lines preceding item (1) it becomes clear that *sōna* is not an isolated reference to speed. On Grendel's arrival at Heorot, the poet tells us, **duru** *sōna onarn* 'he opened the doors at once' (721b), entering the hall **raþe** *æfter þon* 'right after that' (724b). Something that by no means occurred to the terrifying creature was any thought of delay: *Nē þæt se āglæca* **yl**dan þōhte (739). On the contrary, Grendel seized a sleeping warrior quickly at the first opportunity: *ac hē ge-***fēng** hraðe **forman** sīðe **slæ**pendne rinc (740a–41b). Grendel's reckless advance comes to a sudden halt when Beowulf seizes him with comparable speed and equally hostile intent: *hē onfēng hrāþe* **inwitþancum** (748b–49a). In 724b, *(h)raþe* provides alliteration but does not help the poet create an optimal verse pattern. The adverbs in 721b, 740a, and 748b help fill out the verse but are less conspicuously useful. *Sōna* just happens to do more metrical work than the other adverbs in a systematic rhetorical pattern.

The normative placement for finite verbs in *Beowulf* is at the end of the line on a metrical position where alliteration is unacceptable. Alliteration and verse-initial placement in consecutive lines make *slāt* and *bāt* conspicuous. The poet can front vivid, low-frequency verbs and objects with considerable freedom to highlight reportable features of a narrative event because the Old English inflectional system was more robust than our Modern English system, in which normative word order is more often required to clarify syntactic relations. Linkage by rhyme makes *slāt* and *bāt* even more conspicuous. Rhyme is not governed by the rules of Old English meter, but poets of all kinds employ ORNAMENTAL effects that can be felt even when not foregrounded by metrical rules. Once the pairing of *slāt* and *bāt* is highlighted, syntactically parallel *dranc* and *swealh* in normative line-final position look like a continuation of the verbal patterning with elegant variation. It seems unreasonable to suppose that such an arrangement of formal elements is some sort of accident and that the verbs were chosen solely for their metrical value. There is good evidence here for use of short clauses, short verbs, and emphatic fronting for iconic mimicry of fast, violent actions and for enhancement of this effect by explicit evaluation. As we have seen (§1.5), emphatic fronting is a stylistic option in SOV languages and the fronted verbs in item (1) are ideal candidates, since they convey "information referring to chronologically ordered events that represent the gist of a narrative" (Luraghi 1995: 364).

§2.4 Formulaic modifiers

As we try to understand how alliterative poets learned their craft, we are lucky to have *Skáldskaparmál* (Faulkes 1998), a pedagogical treatise by Snorri Sturluson (1179–1241). During Snorri's lifetime the shift to Christian literacy was well underway. Alliterative poets realized that their poetic culture would not survive unless it was explained in writing. Snorri focuses on two grammatical constructions that are much more common in alliterative poetry than in prose. One is the *KENT HEITI* 'modified noun.' When first introduced in ordinary discourse, people, places, and things are normally denoted by proper nouns like *Beowulf* and *Swede* or common nouns like *boat*. When the identity of the person, place, or thing becomes obvious in subsequent mentions, a pronoun will generally suffice. If the referent of a pronoun would be difficult to identify, the speaker typically reverts to use of an unmodified noun. In alliterative poetry, modified-noun constructions often appear where a pronoun or unmodified noun would usually be expected. Instead of *he* or *Hrōþgār* the *Beowulf* poet often uses expressions like *mǣre þēoden* 'famous king' or *bēaga brytta* 'giver of rings.' Instead of *it* or *boat* we encounter expressions like *sǣ-bāt* 'sea-boat.' As these examples show, the modifier can be realized as an adjective, as a genitive noun, or as the first constituent of a compound. When the *sǣ-bāt* first appears in *Beowulf* 633a there is no obvious need to distinguish it from a lake-boat or a river-boat. Only seagoing boats are mentioned in *Beowulf* and a sea voyage by this one has already been described (207b–24b). The first constituent of *sǣ-bāt* is SEMANTICALLY INESSENTIAL and seems to be used primarily for metrical reasons, transforming a word that does not alliterate into one that does or filling out a verse that would otherwise be too short. Such compound modifiers are common in *Beowulf* and they are often used to modify more than one constituent (K4: cxii; Russom 2010: 72–75). A modified-noun construction with very low frequency in ordinary speech is the metaphorical KENNING, which represents an entity by modifying a noun for a different entity. The ocean is not a road, but in *Beowulf* it can be called the *hron-rād* 'whale-road' or the *swan-rād* 'swan-road.' Snorri provides his young apprentices with long lists of modified-noun constructions designating oft-mentioned people, places, and things in poetic tradition. Although the role of memorization in language learning was overestimated by behaviorists, memorization does play a role in learning constituents that are not generated by the usual internalized rules, such as irregular verbs and phrases with an unpredictable meaning (Pinker 1999). Snorri's phrases for important gods and heroes would have been useful to preliterate poets. As we shall see, however, it was even more useful to master the abstract form of modified-noun constructions and create them as needed for the whole array of characters, scenes, and events that had to be included in a hero-tale.

In item (2) the poet uses modified-noun constructions to versify an imperative clause.

(2) *ond þū / Ūnferð lǣt ealde / lāfe,*
     wrǣtlic / wǣg**-sweord, **wīdcūðne / man
     ***heard**-ecg / **hab**ban* (1488–90)
     'and you let Unferth, the widely-known man, have that old heirloom, the rare patterned sword, hard-edged'

Both the imperative verb and the infinitive take a stressed object in item (2). There is clearly no room for all the major constituents of the sentence in the first verse of the clause. For the opening verse the poet chooses the pronoun subject, the finite verb, and the object of the finite verb, which appear in normative SOV order. The poet uses *ealde,* a semantically inessential adjective, to modify *lāfe,* the object of the infinitive, creating a normative two-word A1 verse for the closing half of the line. In lines two and three the poet uses modified-noun constructions to provide a variation for each argument. Like all variations, these three are semantically inessential. The variations in line two cannot have been used to facilitate composition, however, since this line could be removed with no damage to poetic or narrative form. If a scribe had omitted it, no modern editor would have noticed. The adjective *wrǣtlic* and the compound constituent *wǣg-* are semantically inessential modifiers with primarily generic function. They call attention to the reportably fine way in which a piece of heroic equipment has been manufactured. Semantically inessential *ealde* and *heard-ecg* complete the picture of an effective sword that has withstood the test of time. Modified-noun constructions can perform a variety of artistic functions and the utility of a given modifier can vary from one instance to another. Like a chess master who accomplishes more than one purpose with each move, the *Beowulf* poet knows how to construct phrases with metrical utility that also have relevant semantic content.

§2.5 The meandering style in West Germanic poetry

Another conspicuous feature of Old English poetic style is a tendency to begin a clause in the b-verse and end it in the a-verse. Sievers (1893: 48) identifies this meandering arrangement of verses as a common West Germanic inheritance and illustrates it with a passage from *Beowulf*. The meandering style is obviously not forced by rules of alliterative meter. As Sievers observes, it is not employed by North Germanic alliterative poets, who usually align clause boundaries with line boundaries. It seems reasonable to hypothesize that meandering was an oral-formulaic technique and consider how it might have facilitated composition of long poems. As it turns out, meandering is intimately related to employment of useful variations and modified-noun constructions. Like aspiring poets in the era of *Beowulf,* we can find our way into formulaic technique by attending to conspicuous stylistic traits of this kind. In a corpus of verses with such traits we would expect to find many of the most archaic and most useful phrases, the ones learned first by many generations of apprentice poets.

The opening verse must provide room for every unstressed SP, fixed as well as movable. When insufficient room is left for all the lexical nouns in a clause, one or more of them must be placed elsewhere. A general-case solution for this problem is to create a syntactically coherent verse of two stressed words by adding a modifier to the noun that has to be resituated. As a two-word verse phrase, the modified constituent will conform to the principle of closure and will be suitable for placement toward the end of the clause. The resituated constituent is now heavy and such constituents are routinely displaced rightward in prose and ordinary speech as well as poetry. This technique does nothing to inhibit fast processing of narrative in real time.

Fixed SPs and fronted SPs complicate the syntax of an opening verse (§1.19). The effort required to manage such complexity can be reduced by opening a clause in the second half of the line, where only one constituent needs to alliterate. Metrical constraints make it particularly awkward to construct opening verses of category II, which lack metrical location x1, the normative location for unstressed SPs. In an opening verse of category I, on the other hand, location x1 is available and the number of unstressed constituents before the first stress is not limited by metrical rules.

Unstressed SPs are especially desirable before the first stress in category I when they help distinguish the light foot from an anacrusis (See Appendix E, OE 9.1). The most easily constructed opening verses are of type A7 (xx/Sx). With its Sx foot, this type provides more room in location x1 than verses of type B or C, which have stressed feet with three or four metrical positions. Since the Sx foot corresponds to the most common Old English word pattern, it is easily filled. With only one stress, however, type A7 represents an extreme departure from normative weight and it is restricted to the a-verse by the principle of closure (UM 4). For a verse pattern of such complexity type A7 has a surprisingly high frequency of occurrence, with 294 total instances. This anomaly is clearly attributable to its usefulness. With a single exception (*Beowulf* 1614a), the expected constraint on frequency is suspended only for opening verses that are subject to the SPMR, a clause-level rule that outranks the verse-level constraint on weight (UM 6). Of the 294 A7 verses, 293 are opening verses that contain SPs and the vast majority have two or more unstressed SPs. Typical examples are (3a), with a pronoun and a conjunction; (3b), with a pronoun and an unstressed verb; and (3c), with two pronouns and an unstressed sentential adverb.

(3) (a) *þæt hine on* / **ylde**   *eft* ge- / *wunigen*

      wil-ge- / *sīþas* (22a–3a)

      'so that willing companions will accompany him afterwards in old age'

(b) *habbað wē tō þǣm / **mǣran** **micel** / ǣrende*

   ***Deni**ga / frêan* (270a–71a)

   'we have an important message for the famous lord of the Danes' (hyper-baton)

(c) *hī hyne þā æt- / **bǣron** tō **brimes** <u>faroðe</u>*

   ***swǣ**se / (ge)sīþas* (28a–29a)

   'then they — his own companions — bore him to the shore of the sea'

Since it is available only in the a-verse, type A7 cannot be combined with the strategy of opening a clause in the b-verse. The category I verses available in the second half of the line are of types B and C. The compound foot patterns in these types are somewhat less easy to fill than the Sx foot and take up three or four metrical positions (Sxx, Ssx, Sxs, or Sxxs). When preceded by several unstressed words they make it more difficult to align the metrical pattern with a consistent rhythmical pattern (Russom 2022c: 191–94). From a purely metrical view, on the other hand, types B and C are far less complex than type A7 and are more appropriate for frequent use. When a clause ends with a b-verse, type A7 is available in the following a-verse, but the poet avoids overuse of this complex type by an interesting alternative strategy: use of variation to extend the clause. Two-word verses with modified nouns can paraphrase a variety of clausal constituents and are well suited for employment in the right periphery. When appended to a clause that would otherwise end with a b-verse, a variation can fill the a-verse of the following line and the next clause can open in the b-verse.

   Item (4) is a sentence of five clauses that employs representative strategies for opening verses.

(4) (a) *geþenc nū, se / **mǣra** **maga** / Healfdenes,*

   ***snot**tra / fengel, (b) nū ic eom / **sīð**es fūs,*

   ***gold**-<u>wine</u> / **gum**ena, (c) hwæt wit / **geō** sprǣcon[:]*

   *(d) gif ic æt / **þearfe** **þī**nre / scolde*

   ***ald**re / linnan, (e) þæt ðū mē / ā wǣre*

   ***forð**-ge- / <u>witenum</u> on / **fæder** stǣle* (1474–79)

   'Remember now, famous son of Halfdane, wise king, now that I am desirous of an adventure, gold-friend of men, what we agreed before: that you would always be in the place of a father to me dead (after I died) if I should lose life at your need'

The opening verses in item (4) must accommodate two or three unstressed SPs of a kind that rarely or never appear in anacrusis. It is not surprising to find that all instances are of category I, with the SPs at normative location x1. Clauses (4a, d) begin with type A7, the most convenient type for an opening a-verse with more than one SP. Clauses (4b, c, e) begin in the b-verse, where type A7 is unavailable. The poet chooses type B1 for (4b) and type C3 for (4c, e). The phrase *maga Healfdenes* in (4a) is varied twice by vocative phrases, which can be added quite freely in direct discourse: *snottra fengel,* with an adjectival modifier, and *goldwine gumena,* with a genitive modifier. Both vocative phrases are variations and both make it possible for the next clause to open in a b-verse. In (4e) there is no obvious need for *forðgewitenum,* since the possibility of Beowulf's death has already been introduced in (4d). As with the two variations in item (4), semantically inessential *forðgewitenum* facilitates ideal placement of an opening verse.

What remains to be shown is how regularly the *Beowulf* poet employs the strategies we have identified. To avoid interference from irrelevant factors the corpus employed for frequency counts is restricted to the most directly comparable examples: type A1 verses with two trochaic words, a lexical common noun and a lexical modifier. Phrases with proper nouns are excluded because these phrases have a single referent and are less useful than common nouns. Functional adjectives are excluded because they do not have a fixed metrical value, unlike lexical adjectives, which always have metrical stress in *Beowulf*. For clarity I also exclude verses like *Beowulf* 572a, 1358b, and 2456b, which might be interpreted as Sxx/Sx (A5). Here as generally two-word type A1 provides the most reliable verse pattern for statistical analysis because a change in word order leaves the pattern unchanged, avoiding interference from metrical constraints on foot length, foot weight, and realization of the foot as a word group. Since it is the normative realization of the normative verse pattern, two-word type A1 has a correspondingly high frequency and provides the largest corpus of two-word verses.

We begin with adjectival modifiers. Consider noun phrases like *ealde lāfe* 'old heirloom,' with a lexical noun modified by a lexical adjective. The normative order of lexical nouns and adjectives in Proto-Germanic was probably Adjective-Noun (AdjN). Typologists once thought that AdjN was normative for SOV languages generally but contrary evidence has been found in languages outside Eurasia (Dryer 2007: 101). AdjN does not seem to correlate reliably with OV. However that may be, AdjN is the word order reconstructed for Proto-Indo-European (Beekes 1995: 94-95). NAdj orders in Indo-European languages are later developments or rhetorical options facilitated by robust inflectional systems. It seems simplest to assume that AdjN remained the normative order in Proto-Germanic and this hypothesis is consistent with the ordering of constituents in English compounds, which provide valuable insight into archaic word orders (Lehmann 1969). In compounds corresponding to a verb and its object, for example, the constituents normally conform to the order of a Proto-Germanic OV phrase, with the deverbative noun in final position. OV compounds like *man-eater* still predominate. Innovative VO compounds like *pick-pocket* and *do-nothing* are far less common. In Modern English compounds corresponding to phrases with adjectives and nouns, the predominant order is AdjN. Typical examples are *redhead* and *whitecaps* (wind-blown waves). In Old English, NAdj order is common only in compounds with participial adjectives like *wīn-druncen* 'drunk with wine' and *gold-hroden* 'adorned with gold' (Krahe & Meid 1967: 27). Here the order of constituents imitates the order of phrases like *wīne druncen* (Beo 1467a), with the participle modified by a lexical noun in the dative-instrumental case. Participial adjectives are derived from verbs, so it is not surprising to find them in final position. As the translations show, we now place the participle before the noun at phrase level, but most corresponding compounds are like *gold-plated,* which retains the archaic order of *gold-hroden.*

In the last verse of a clause, adherence to metrical norms is strictly regulated by the principle of closure. Two-word A1 variations with normative word order are ideal for placement in a clause-final a-verse, where they situate the next opening verse in the ideal location. Since they are semantically inessential by definition, variations can be used or not as the poet chooses. Our study corpus contains 57 variations, 52 with AdjN order and 5 with NAdj order. There is no instance in an opening verse, which is hardly surprising, since a variation normally has an antecedent.

(5) (a) **clause-final AdjN instance in a-verse**

    *sē þe / **wæter**-_egesan_ **wuni**an scolde,*

    cealde *strēamas* (1260a–61a)

    'who had to inhabit the water-terrors, the <u>cold currents</u>'

  (b) **non-final AdjN instance in a-verse**

        *þæt hē / **wealdende***

    *ofer / **ealde** riht, ēcean / dryhtne,*

    bitre */ (ge)bulge* (2329–30)

'that he bitterly offended the ruler, <u>the eternal lord</u>, against the Old Law'
(with subjunctive verb)

(c) **non-final AdjN instance in b-verse**

   sweord / *ǣr gebrǣd*

   gōd / *gūð-cyning,*   *gomele* / *lāfe,*

   ecgum / **un**slāw (2562b–64a)

'the good battle-king drew a sword, <u>an old heirloom</u>, keen because of its edges'

(d) **clause-final NAdj instance in b-verse**

   ālegdon ðā tō- / *middes*   *mǣrne* / *þēoden*

   hæleð / *hīofende,*   *hlāford* / *lēofne* (3141–42)

'then sighing men laid down the famous king, <u>the beloved lord</u>, in the midst' (of a pyre)

(e) **non-final NAdj instance in b-verse**

   þæt ðā / *līðende*   *land ge-* / *sāwon,*

   brim-<u>clifu</u> / *blīcan,*   *beorgas* / *stēape,*

   sīde / *sǣ-næssas* (221a–23a; cf. 353a, 2721a)

'that the sailors saw land shining, sea-cliffs, <u>steep headlands</u>, broad-nesses'

Clause-final a-verse variations in other instances like the one in (5a), followed by category I: 83a, 133a, 149a, 201a, 488a, 527a, 572a, 797a, 852a, 1093a, 1209a, 1378a, 1382a, 1398a, 1423a, 1475a, 1547a, 1585a, 1621a, 1688a, 1733a, 1760a, 1779a, 1992a, 2050a, 2078a, 2236a, 2347a, 2384a, 2610a, 2796a, 3029a, 3108a; followed by category II: 166a, 1634a, 1965a, 1912a, 2156a, 2246a, 2610a, 2672a; in non-final variations like (5b): 5a, 345a, 1517a, 1715a; in other b-verse variations like (5c): 416b, 686b, 1358b, 1419b, 2456b.

As the metrical norm, two-word type A1 is usually attracted to the b-verse. Distribution of the 52 AdjN variations is very surprising indeed. There are 46 a-verses and only six b-verses. Among the 46 a-verses, 42 are like the one in (5a), which is immediately followed by an opening b-verse. The opening b-verse is of category I in 34 instances and of category II in eight instances. A clause-final variation in the b-verse would push the opening of the next clause into the following a-verse. There are no such AdjN variations in our study corpus. The remaining eight AdjN instances are non-final, like those in (5b, c). No NAdj instance occurs in a clause-final a-verse.

The instances in item (5) include variations of adjuncts. The adjunct phrases that are not variations are shown in item (6). No NAdj instances occur. The AdjN instances include 44 a-verses and 27 b-verses. The proportion of a-verses is anomalously high but less so than with variations. There are two clause-initial instances (2080a, 2097a).

(6) (a) **clause-final AdjN instance, a-verse**

þæt hīe / **ǣr** drugon   **aldor**- / lēase

lange / hwīle (15a–16a)

'which they had endured without a lord <u>for a long time</u>'

(b) **non-final AdjN instance, a-verse**

mē þone / **wæl**-rǣs   **wine** / Scildunga

fǣttan / golde   **fela** / lēanode (2101–2)

'the friend of the Scyldings paid me a lot <u>with plated gold</u> for that attack'

(c) **clause-final AdjN instance, b-verse**

Heorot / eardode,

sinc-fāge / **sel**   **sweartum** / nihtum (166b–67b)

'(he) inhabited Heorot, the treasure-decked hall, <u>during the dark nights</u>'

(d) **non-final AdjN instance, b-verse**

swylce / **oft** bemearn   **ǣr**ran / mǣlum

swīð-ferhþes / **sīð**   **snotor** ceorl / monig (907–8)

'also, many a wise man lamented <u>in former times</u> the behavior of the head-strong (man)'

Clause-final a-verse adjuncts in other instances like (6a), followed by category I: 114a, 561a, 586a, 1172a, 1357a, 1502a, 1528a, 1542a, 1692a, 1746a, 1761a, 1994a, 2058a, 2237a, 2290a, 2354a, 2467a, 2492a, 2511a, 2692a, 2698a, 2845a, 2898a, 3140a; followed by category II: 849a, 1789a, 1980a, 2140a, 2168a, 2216a, 2392a, 2482a, 2594a, 2780a, 2897a, 3035a; non-final a-verse adjuncts in other instances like (6b): 1413a, 2080a, 2097a, 2211a, 2290a, 2969a; clause-final b-verse adjuncts in other instances like (6c), followed by category I: 877b, 1203b, 1335b, 1729b, 1747b, 1865b, 2159b, 2440b; followed by category II: 1505b, 2178b; non-final b-verse adjuncts in other instances like (6d): 54b, 141b, 275b, 963b, 1011b, 1104b, 1257b, 1324b, 1694b, 2008b, 2030b, 2200b, 2234b, 2571b, 2573b.

There are 37 clause-final AdjN a-verses like (6a). They are followed by an opening verse of category I in 25 instances and of category II in 12 instances. In non-final position there are seven a-verse adjuncts like (6b). Clause-final b-verse instances are not conspicuously limited. There are eleven instances like (6c), eight followed by a category I verse and three followed by a category II verse (including 6c). The sixteen non-final instances like (6d) are not much more common. Adjuncts are inessential by definition but in many instances they are SEMANTICALLY FUNCTIONAL IN CONTEXT, supplying the vivid detail that an absorbing narrative requires. The dark nights in (6c) are important because they characterize Grendel's killings as especially heinous. According to early Germanic law, a killing done openly in daylight is manslaughter; a killing done secretly or at night is murder, a much more serious crime (CV, s.v. *morð, nátt-víg*).

Some constituents otherwise similar to adjuncts seem to be semantically essential or nearly so and are similar in some ways to major sentence constituents. Sentences like *the ball rolled* are rather uncommon. They would be uttered only in special contexts, as for example when someone had asserted that the ball had always remained perfectly still. The verb *roll* is normally accompanied by a modifier like *smoothly* or a prepositional phrase like *to the wall*. In a typical instance like *the ball rolled to the wall*, the prepositional phrase might seem to function like the direct object argument in *the ball approached the wall*. The equivalence breaks down, however, when we compare the corresponding passive sentences. *The wall was approached by the ball* is acceptable but may seem a little odd, since the verb *approach* usually takes an animate agent in the by-phrase of a passive construction. The passive sentence **to the wall was rolled by the ball* is totally unacceptable, not just odd. A somewhat more acceptable passive equivalent would be *the wall was rolled to by the ball*. Such constructions seem to employ a complex transitive verb *roll to* that takes *the wall* as an argument. Though arguably consistent with the rules of an internalized English grammar learned by children without effort, this passive equivalent has the kind of unnecessarily complex syntax that Labov's competent narrators avoid.

For the purposes of this study I do not classify prepositional objects as major constituents in phrases like *to the wall* because even those that resemble arguments have a different distribution. Government by a preposition restricts leftward movement of the noun and prepositional phrases are displaced rightward more often than simplex nouns. The adverb in *the ball rolled smoothly* behaves even less like an ordinary object. The equivalent passive construction, **smoothly was rolled by the ball,* is totally unacceptable and there is no other passive equivalent. For analysis of formulaic technique what matters is how an adverb or prepositional phrase functions semantically on a scale from redundant through generically functional to functional in immediate context and then to quasi-obligatory. Redundant constituents can be added or omitted as required by the meter but quasi-obligatory constituents do not have that kind of formulaic utility.

Items (7a–f) are representative examples of arguments in the corpus. There are 72 instances with AdjN order and six examples with NAdj order. In this group of examples two-word type A1 shows its usual preference for the b-verse, with 51 instances, as compared with 27 instances in the a-verse.

(7) (a) **clause-final AdjN instance, a-verse**

> *þone / **cwealm** gewræc*

ēce / drihten (107b–8a)

'the eternal lord avenged that feud'

(b) **non-final AdjN instance, a-verse**

*nē þǣr nǣnig / **witena** wēnan þorfte*

beorhtre bōte tō / **banan** folmum (157–58)

'none of the wise men needed to expect splendid compensation at the killer's hands'

(c) **clause-final AdjN instance, b-verse**

> *þǣr ge- / **neh**ost brægd*

eorl / Bēowulfes ealde / lāfe (794b–95b)

'very often there an earl of Beowulf's brandished his sword'

(d) **non-final AdjN instance, b-verse**

> *mǣre / þēoden ,*

*æþeling / ǣr-gōd, un**blī**ðe / sæt* (129b–30b)

'the famous king, an excellent chieftain from the old days, sat unhappily'

(e) **clause-final NAdj instance, a-verse**

swā hit oð / dōmes dæg dīope / (be)nemdon.

þēodnas / mǣre (3069–70a; cf. 1291a)

'famous lords solemnly declared that (to be) so until the day of judgment'

(f) **non-final NAdj instance, b-verse**

hēt hine mid þæm / *lācum   lēode* / *swǣse*

sēcean / *(on ge)syn*tum   (1868a–69a; cf. 1341b, 1409b, 1488b)

'told him to seek <u>his own people</u> in health with those treasures'

Clause-final a-verse arguments in other instances like (7a), followed by category I: 116a, 472a, 637a, 889a, 949a, 1598a, 1750a, 2127a, 2572a, 2626a, 2978a; followed by category II: 1303a, 1503a, 2282a, 3131a; non-final a-verse arguments in other instances like (7b): 75a, 334a, 719a, 784a, 1411a, 2199a, 2938a, 2972a; clause-final b-verse arguments in other instances like (7c), followed by category I: 577b, 865b, 978b, 1006b, 1591b, 1943b; followed by category II: 1363b, 1859b; non-final b-verse arguments in other instances like (7d): 34b, 202b, 214b, 231b, 297b, 325b, 466b, 520b, 576b, 896b, 916b, 952b, 1046b, 1245b, 1262b, 1312b, 1400b, 1488b, 1554b, 1677b, 1841b, 1879b, 1915b, 1948b, 2036b, 2044b, 2153b, 2181b, 2207b, 2253b, 2444b, 2615b, 2753b, 2788b, 3079b, 3141b.

There are 16 clause-final AdjN a-verses like the one in (7a), twelve followed by a category I verse and four followed by a category II verse. In non-final position there are nine AdjN instances like the one in (7b). Clause-final AdjN b-verses are not avoided, with nine instances like the one in (7c), seven followed by a category I verse and two followed by a category II verse. Among the 53 AdjN variations in the corpus, only six are non-final b-verses. The 72 AdjN arguments in the corpus afford a striking contrast to the variations, with 40 instances like the one in (7d). The clause-final NAdj instances like (7e) are both a-verses that facilitate placement of the next opening verse. The non-final NAdj instances are both b-verses.

Some relative frequencies remain constant in items (5), (6), and (7) After clause-final a-verses, opening verses of category I always constitute a substantial majority. AdjN instances are always far more common than NAdj instances. Other relative frequencies change systematically as we move from variations in item (5) through adjuncts in item (6) to arguments in item (7). The proportion of instances in clause-final position is far higher for variations than for arguments. The proportion of a-verse instances is anomalously high among variations, less so among adjuncts, and emphatically normative among arguments. These differences in placement are paralleled by differences in semantic function. The variations are semantically inessential by definition and can be used or not as the poet chooses. There is no need to insert them in the b-verse, which would push the opening of the next clause

85

into the more restrictive a-verse. The adjuncts are grammatically inessential by definition but often provide detail that is semantically functional in context. The poet prefers the a-verse for these instances but is less willing to exclude them from the b-verse. The arguments are most difficult to omit. Since they are semantically and grammatically essential, arguments must be expressed unless their reference can be guessed in the immediate context. In examples with modified arguments the usual attraction to the b-verse prevails.

We now turn to constructions with a lexical common noun modified by another common noun in the genitive case. In some languages the word order in such constructions is affected by a semantic feature of the genitive modifier (Dryer 2007: 72). In SVO Modern English, genitive case is normally marked on animate nouns by an inflectional ending and inflected nouns are normally placed before the nouns they modify, as in *John's book*. On inanimate nouns, genitive case is normally marked by *of*, as in *the edge of the razor*. Such genitive constructions normally follow the noun they modify. Exceptions to the animacy constraint tend to be literary archaisms: *The book of John* is a New Testament narrative and *The Razor's Edge* is the title of a novel. In SOV Proto-Germanic, the effect of animacy on word order seems to have been the opposite of its effect in Modern English. GenN order was clearly preferred with inanimate genitives but NGen order seems to have been preferred with animate genitives in the earliest inscriptions (Antonsen 1975: 24). Like Proto-Germanic, OE used inflectional markers for all genitive nouns in the era of *Beowulf*. Marking genitives with *of* developed later.

Our corpus includes 49 variations with genitive modifiers. All have GenN order. There are 41 a-verses and eight b-verses. As with the AdjN variations in item (5), the relative frequency of a-verses is conspicuously elevated.

(8) (a) **clause-final GenN instance in a-verse**

         ðā ge- / **bēah** *cyning,*

   folces / *hyrde* (2980b–81a)

   'then fell the king, <u>guardian of the people</u>'

    (b) **non-final GenN instance in a-verse**

   ne meahton wē ge- / **lǣran** *lēofne* / *þēoden,*

   rīces / *hyrde,* **rǣd** / *ǣnigne* (3079–80)

   'we could not teach the beloved lord, <u>guardian of the kingdom</u>, any advice'

(c) **clause-final GenN instance in b-verse**

> *þēah ðe / **hlā**ford ūs*
>
> *þis / **ellen**-weorc āna / (ā)ðōhte*
>
> *tō ge-**frem**manne, **fol**ces / hyrde* (2642b–44b; cf. 60b, 931b)
>
> 'though the lord, <u>guardian of the people</u>, thought to do this work of valor alone for us'

(d) **non-final GenN instance in b-verse**

> *heht him þā ge- / **wyr**cean **wī**gendra / hlēo*
>
> ***eall** / īrenne, **eor**la / dryhten,*
>
> ***wīg**-bord / **wræt**lic* (2337a–39a)
>
> 'then he — <u>the lord of earls</u> — said to make for him a splendid battle-shield all of iron'

Clause-final a-verse variations in other instances like (8a), followed by category I: 181a, 352a, 454a, 516a, 841a, 887a, 1123a, 1170a, 1555a, 1742a, 1832a, 1835a, 1849a, 2027a, 2146a, 2727a, 2875a, 3088a; followed by category II: 171a, 183a, 259a, 583a, 788a, 984a, 2174a, 2326a; non-final a-verse variations in other instances like (8b): 17a, 35a, 752a, 1752a, 1824a, 2174a; non-final b-verse variations in other instances like (8d): 60b, 697b, 912b, 3154b.

Among the 30 a-verses are 24 clause-final instances like (8a). The next opening verse is of category I in 19 instances and of category II in eight instances. Among the eight b-verses three are clause-final and five are non-final. As with the AdjN variations, most a-verses are clause-final and most b-verses are non-final.

The adjuncts in our corpus that are not variations include 31 with genitive modifiers. The only example with NGen order is 2961b, a non-final verse with an inanimate genitive. There are 20 a-verses and eleven b-verses.

(9) (a) **clause-final GenN instance in a-verse**

> *ne bið þē / **næ**nig(re) gād*
>
> ***worol**de / **wil**na* (949b–50a)
>
> 'for you there will be no lack <u>of the world's pleasures</u>'

(b) **non-final GenN instance in a-verse**

> *hē þǣr for / **feor**me **feorh**-wunde / hlēat(,)*

sweordes / *swengum,* **sunu** / *Hygelāces* (2385–86)

'he — Hygelac's son — got a fatal wound <u>from strokes of swords</u> (in exchange) for hospitality'

(c) **clause-final GenN instance in b-verse**

> *ond his* / ***cwēn*** *mid him*

medo-*stigge* / ***mæt*** ***mægþa*** / *hōse* (923b–24b; cf. 2902b).

'and beside him his queen measured the mead-path with a retinue of maidens'

(d) **non-final GenN instance in b-verse**

> ***myn***te / *(se)* ***mān***-*scaða*   *manna cynnes*

> ***sum***ne *be-* / ***syrwan***   *in* / ***sele*** *þām hēan* (712–13)

'the criminal destroyer intended to ambush one of men's kindred in the high hall'

Clause-final a-verse adjuncts in other instances like (9a), followed by category I: 628a, 1085a, 1152a, 1306a, 1367a, 2219a, 2222a, 2343a, 2614a; followed by category II: 1387a; non-final a-verse adjuncts in other instances like (9b): 281a, 2088a, 2128a, 2224a, 2436a, 2485a, 2945a; non-final b-verse adjuncts in other instances like (8d): 735b, 883b, 982b, 1005b, 1098b, 1716b, 2356b, 2939b.

Eleven of the nineteen a-verses are clause-final instances like (9a), followed by an opening verse of category I in ten instances and of category II in one instance. The eight non-final a-verses like item (9b) are used to fill out a line. The cited clause-final instance in (9c) is followed by a category II verse; the other example is followed by a category I verse. There are eight non-final instances like (9d). As with the AdjN adjuncts in item (6), the frequency of a-verses is less conspicuously elevated in GenN adjuncts, fewer a-verses are clause-final, and most b-verses are non-final.

Arguments in the corpus include 57 with genitive modifiers, 55 with GenN order and two with NGen order (1644b, 2741b). Of the 55 GenN instances, 23 are a-verses and 32 are b-verses. As with the AdjN arguments, there is no elevated frequency of a-verse instances and two-word type A1 shows its usual preference for the b-verse.

(10) (a) **clause-final GenN instance in a-verse**

> *frem*maδ / *gēna*

lēoda / *þearfe* (2800b–01b)

'still meet <u>the people's needs</u>'

  (b) **non-final GenN instance in a-verse**

                 gehȳrde on / ***Bēowulfe***

    *fol*ces hyrde   *fæst-rǣdne* / *(ge)þōht* (609b–10b)

    '<u>the protector of the people</u> heard from Beowulf a firmly considered plan'

  (c) **clause-final GenN instance in b-verse**

    wæs ðā ge- / ***bolgen***   *beor*ges / *hyrde* (2304)

    '<u>the protector of the barrow</u> was enraged'

  (d) **non-final GenN instance in b-verse**

    hwīlum / ***hil**de-dēor*   ***hear**pan* / *wynne,*

    ***gomen**-<u>wudu</u> grētte* (2107a–8a)

    'at times the battle-bold (man) touched <u>the harp's joy</u>, the glee-wood'

Clause-final a-verse arguments in other instances like (10a), followed by category I: 441a, 1058a, 1572a, 1666a, 1797a, 1812a, 1853a, 1887a, 2248a, 2555a, 2567a, 2801a; followed by category II: 724a, 1080a, 1487a; non-final a-verse arguments in other instances like (10b): 150a, 451a, 670a, 810a, 1507a, 2245a; clause-final b-verse arguments in other instances like (10c), all followed by category I: 750b, 1661b, 2345b, 2829b, 3115b, 3133b; non-final b-verse arguments in other instances like (10d): 4b, 96b, 607b, 670b, 810b, 912b, 914b, 1050b, 1270b, 1725b, 1730b, 1732b, 1801b, 1922b, 2107b, 2333b, 2463b, 2505b, 2507b, 2936b, 3121b, 3154b, 3160b, 3170b.

Of the 23 a-verses sixteen are clause-final. Seven of the 32 b-verses are clause-final. The poet must find room for grammatically essential constituents and cannot afford severe constraints on placement of clause-final instances in the b-verse. Both NGen instances are b-verses and neither one is clause-final.

    Constructions with genitive modifiers pattern like those with adjectival modifiers in all important respects. Semantically inessential variations have elevated frequency in the a-verse to facilitate placement of opening verses in the most convenient location. Category I has consistently higher frequency than category II in opening verses because it allows for placement of unstressed SPs in location x1, the ideal location for SPs that must be moved to the opening verse. Another technique for convenient placement of the opening verse is avoidance of b-verses in clause-final position. Semantically inessential constituents are easiest to exclude from the b-verse because they can simply be omitted. The near-total absence of variation in clause-final b-verses shows consistent employment of this strategy by the poet, whether consciously or by intuition. Such a strategy is more difficult to implement with adjuncts, which often perform valuable artistic functions, and most difficult to implement with arguments, which must usually be expressed. This explains the systematic changes in distribution we observe as we proceed from variations to adjuncts and then to arguments. The meandering style invented by ancient West Germanic poets was an oral-formulaic technique. It stands out in high relief when we compare *Beowulf* with Norse Eddic poems like *Völuspá*, which employs fornyrðislag meter, the meter that most closely resembles West Germanic meter. It is clear at a glance that fornyrðislag, which does not employ the meandering style, also makes comparatively little use of variations. The consistently low frequency of NAdj and NGen constructions in our corpus provides good metrical evidence for historical syntacticians. It seems clear that AdjN and GenN orders were strongly preferred at a time when SOV typology still prevailed at clause level.

§2.6 Generic content in modified-noun constructions

Within our corpus of nouns modified by adjectives, most instances refer to giants, heroes, leaders, or Jehovah — major characters in *Beowulf* that need to be mentioned often. The same pairing of noun and adjective occurs in more than half of these instances. The nouns and adjectives are inflected in various ways that have no effect on realization as two-word type A1. Inflectional differences are ignored in the instances listed below, which are grouped according to the meaning of the modified noun. The entry for *ēce drihten* in group Ia below includes *ēcean dryhtne* and *ēcum dryhtne*, for example. Each group of examples is divided into three subgroups. Subgroup 'a' is for sets of two or more verses with the same adjective and the same noun. Subgroup 'b' is for instances with an adjective that is repeated within our test corpus and a noun not otherwise paired with that adjective. Subgroup 'c' is for instances with an adjective that occurs only once within the test corpus.

Group I: Characters in the narrative

Ia. *ēce drihten* 'eternal lord' (108a, 1692a, 1779a, 2330b, 2796a); *geongum cempan* 'young fighter' (1948b, 2044b, 2626a); *lāðan cynnes* 'loathly kindred' (2354a, 2008b); *lēofne mannan* 'beloved man' (297b, 1915b, 1943b, 1994a, 2080a, 2127a, 2897a, 3108a); *lēofne þēoden* 'beloved king' (34b, 3079b); *mǣre þēoden* 'famous king' (129b, 201a, 345a, 797a, 1046b, 1598a, 1715a, 1992a, 2384a, 2572a, 2788b, 3141b); *monegum mǣgþum* 'many tribes' (5a, 75a); *snotere ceorlas* 'wise men' (202b, 416b, 1591b); *snotra fengel* 'wise king' (1475a, 2156a); *wergan gāstes* 'accursed spirit' (133a, 1747b); *wītig drihten* 'wise lord' (1554b, 1841b). With NAdj order: *þēoden mǣrne* 'famous king' (353a, 2721a, 3070a).

Ib. *æþelan cynnes* 'noble kindred' (2234b), *æþele cempa* 'noble figher' (1312b), *āngan brēþer* 'only brother' (1262b), *āngan eaferan* 'only child' (1547a), *earmran mannon* 'unfortunate man' (577b), *earmre teohhe* 'unfortunate band' (2938a), *gomelum ceorle* 'old man' (2444b), *gamelum rince* 'old fighter' (1677b), *wīsa fengel* 'wise king' (1400b), *wīsra monna* 'wise men' (1413a). Additional instances with an adjective also employed in group Ia: *lāðra manna* 'loathly men' (2672a), *mǣran cynnes* 'famous kindred' (1729b), *mǣre cempa* 'famous fighter' (1761a), *mǣrum Gēate* 'famous Geatish man' (1301b). With NAdj order: *hlāford lēofne* 'beloved lord' 3142b, *ðegne monegum* 'many thanes' (1419b).

Ic. *dēorre duguðe* 'dear retainers' (488a), *dyrnra gāsta* 'secretive spirits' (1357a), *ealdum ceorle* 'old man' (2972a), *gyrded cempa* 'belted fighter' (2078a), *hǣðnum horde* 'heathen horde' (2216a), *hālig dryhten* 'holy lord' (686b), *heardran hǣle* 'sturdier men' (719a), *hnāhran rince* 'inferior warrior' (952b), *māran weorode* 'larger troop' (1011b), *rēþe cempa* 'angry fighter' (1585a), *rīce þēoden* 'powerful king' (1209a), *sīdan herge* 'large army' (2347a), *wundum dryhtne* 'injured lord' (2753b), *yldra brōþor* 'older brother' (1324b).

Group II: Relative time

IIa. *ǣrran mǣlum* 'former times' (907b, 2237a, 3035a); *lange hwīle* 'a long while' (16a, 2159b, 2780a); *longe þrāge* 'a long time' (54b, 114a, 1257b); *lȳtle hwīle* 'a little while' (2030b, 2097a, 2571b); *nīowan stefne* 'a new occasion' (1789a, 2594a); *nȳhstan sīðe* 'the last time' (1203b, 2511a); *ufaran dōgrum* 'later days' (2200b, 2392a).

IIb. No instances.

IIc. *forman dōg(o)re* 'the first day' (2573b).

Group III: Fine things

IIIa. *beorhte frætwe* 'bright ornaments' (214b, 896b); *dēore māðmas* 'precious treasures' (2236a, 1528a, 3131a); *ealde lāfe* 'old heirloom' (795b, 1488b, 1688a); *fǣted wǣge* 'plated cup' (2253b, 2282a); *fǣttan goldes* 'plated gold' (1093a, 2102a, 2246a); *gomele lāfe* 'old heirloom' (2563b, 2036b).

IIIb. Instances with adjectives also listed in IIa: *beorhtre bōte* 'bright compensation' (158a), *ealde mādmas* 'old treasures' (472a), *fǣtte bēagas* 'plated rings' (1750a).

IIIc. *fealwe mēaras* 'glossy horses' (865b), *scīran goldes* 'radiant gold' (1694b), *wundnan golde* 'twisted gold' (1382a).

Group IV: The body in combat

IVa. *hāton heolfre* 'hot gore' (849a, 1423a); *heardan clammum* 'strong grips' (963b, 1335b).

IVb. No instances.

IVc. *atolan clommum* 'horrible grips' (1502a), *cūþe folme* 'notorious hand' (1303a), *grimman grāpum* 'grim grips' (1542a), *hālan līce* 'sound body' (1503a), *lāþan fingrum* 'loathly fingers' (1505b).

Group V: Settings and scenic detail

Va. *deorcum nihtum* 'dark nights' (275b, 2211a); *sīde rīce* 'broad kingdom' (1733a, 2199a).

Vb. *cūþe næssas* 'familiar headlands' (1912a), *cūþe strǣte* 'familiar street' (1634a), *wīdan rīces* 'wide kingdom' (1859b), *wīde waroðas* 'wide shores' (1965a).

Vc. *beorgas stēape* 'towering hills' (222b), *blācne lēoman* 'brilliant flame' (1517a), *brāde rīce* 'broad kingdom' (2207b), *cealde strēamas* 'cold currents' (1261a), *ēacne eardas* 'vast lands' (1621a), *fealwe strǣte* 'sparkling street' (916b), *frēcne stōwe* 'fearful place' (1378a), *gearwe stōwe* 'ready place' (1006b), *ginne rīce* 'spacious kingdom' (466b), *hêan hūses* 'lofty residence' (116a), *hrinde bearwas* 'frosted groves' (1363b), *lāðan līges* 'loathsome flame' (83a), *neowle næssas* 'steep headlands' (1411a), *stīge nearwe* 'narrow paths' (1409b), *swǣsne ēðel* 'own dear homeland' (520b), *sweartum nihtum* 'black nights' (167b).

Group VI: Fighting equipment

VIa. *hringed byrne* 'mail made of linked rings' (1245b, 2615b).

VIb. *beorhte randas* 'splendid shields' (231b), **beorhtum byrnum** 'splendid mailcoats' (3140a), *biteran bānum* 'sharp tooth-bones' (2692a), *biteran strǣle* 'sharp arrow' (1746a).

VIc. *brādne mēce* 'broad sword' (2978a), *byrnan sīde* 'broad mailcoat' (1291a), *dēoran sweorde* 'precious sword' (561a), *dȳre īren* 'precious iron sword' (2050a), *ēacnum ecgum* 'large edges' (2140a), *fāgum sweordum* 'decorated swords' (586a), *geolwe linde* 'yellow linden shield' (2610a), *grǣge syrcan* 'grey mailcoats' (334a), *hāre byrnan* 'grey mailcoat' (2153b), *lēohtan sweorde* 'bright sword' (2492a), *sīde scyldas* 'broad shields' (325b).

Group VII: Subjectivity — thought, knowledge, speech, attitude, emotion

VIIa. *dyrnan cræfte* 'secret cunning' (2290a, 2168a).

VIIb. *dyrne langað* 'secret longing' (1879b).

VIIc. *atelic egesa* 'horrible terror' (784a), *eorlic ellen* 'noble bravery' (637a), *frēcnen sprǣce* 'dangerous speech' (1104b), *heardra hȳnða* 'painful humiliations' (166a), *lāðra spella* 'loathsome tidings' (3029a) *mēaglum wordum* 'forceful words' (1980a), *miclan þearfe* 'great need' (2849b); *mildum wordum* 'gracious words' (1172a), *nīwra spella* 'new tidings' (2898a), *sārum wordum* 'painful words' (2058a), *sīdra sorga* 'huge sorrows' (149a).

Group VIII: Miscellaneous abstractions

VIIIa. No examples.

VIIIb. *heardan cēape* 'hard bargain' (2482a), *heardran feohtan*, 'harder struggle' (576b), *heardran hǣle* 'worse luck' (719a), *mǣste cræfte* 'great strength' (2181b), *miclan dōmes* 'great judgment' (978b).

VIIIc. *ealde wīsan* 'the old way' (1865b), *ēce rǣdas* 'great benefits' (1760a), *frēcne dǣde* 'dangerous deed' (889a), *gōdum dǣdum* 'good deeds' (2178b), *grimre gūðe* 'grim warfare' (527a), *lǣnan līfes* 'transitory life' (2845a), *lāðum dǣdum* 'loathsome deeds' (2467a), *nīwe sibbe* 'new kinship' (949a), *sweotolan tācne* 'clear token' (141b), *wīde sīðas* 'wide wanderings' (877b), *wyrsan wrixle* 'a worse exchange' (2969a).

The subgroups within each group differ from one another in characteristic ways, best illustrated by group I, which has many examples in each subgroup. With a single exception, the formulaic verses in subgroup Ia can be used for any instance of a heroic character type: the young fighter who must prove himself, the famous king or hero, the wise king or advisor. There is strong emphasis on the love that attracts followers to a leader and promotes solidarity among close kin or throughout a whole people. The most useful formulas have very high frequency indeed and there is usually no obvious need for the adjective. *Mǣre þēoden*, which has the highest frequency, is inverted three times for use when alliteration on the noun satisfies metrical requirements. A given adjective can be useful for representation of more than one character type. *Snotor* and *lēof* can be used for good kings or for anyone else with admirable qualities such as wisdom, kindness, and generosity. Any monstrous sociopath can be called *werga* 'evil.' The epithet *wergan gāstes* in Ia refers once to Grendel and once to Satan. These expressions differ from Homeric epithets like 'swift-footed Achilles,' which are used more persistently for individual characters and less persistently for multiple characters of the same generic type.

In group Ib the utility of adjectives in Ia is extended by modification of additional nouns. Here *mǣre* describes a kindred and a fighter rather than a king. Rather than inverting *lēofne þēoden* in section Ia to *þēoden lēofne*, the poet employs *hlāford* in *hlāford lēofne,* since in this instance *þēoden* would alliterate incorrectly. We now find synonyms of nouns and adjectives in repeated formulas for a given character type. *Wīsa fengel* (Ib) represents the same type as *snotra fengel* (Ia) and *wīsra monna* represents the same type as *snotere ceorlas*. An example from subgroup Ic is *rīce þēoden*. What changes in Ib and Ic is the frequency of expressions with restricted utility. There are more verses like *earmre teohhe* (Ib), which refers to unfortunate victims of a particular kind of narrative event, or *yldra brōþor* (Ic), which is restricted to a small subset of possible characters. The principle that the most useful expressions have the most stable form is well substantiated in our corpus. This principle applies most often to formulas that express important generic concepts but sometimes to grammatically useful formulas as well. Expressions like *ǣrran mǣlum* and *uferan dōgrum* (IIa) would have been useful during a time when pluperfect idioms like *had done something* and future perfect idioms like *was to do something* had not yet become established. Equivalent constructions with simple tenses are *did something in former times* and *did something in later days*. Within a poem that narrates frequently alternating phases of of joy and sorrow, *lange hwīle* and *longe þrāge* can represent a reportably long phase, *lȳtel hwīle* can represent a reportably short phase, and *nīowan stefne* can represent resumption of a previous state, whether happy or calamitous. With a single exception, all expressions of relative time occur in section IIa. The exception is *forman dōg(o)re* (IIc), which can only be used for the first day in a cycle. The only repeated phrase with this kind of re-stricted usefulness is *nīehstan sīðe,* which has the minimal frequency for inclusion in subsection IIa.

Below are the instances in our corpus with genitive modifiers. To high-light important similarities and differences, I retain the categories employed for instances with adjectival modifiers and order these categories in the same way.

Group I: Characters in the narrative

Ia. *bēaga bryttan* 'distributor of rings' (35a, 352a, 1487a); *eorla drihten* 'lord of earls' (1050b, 2338b); *folces hyrde* 'shepherd of the people' (610a, 1832a, 1849a, 2644b, 2981a); *manna cynnes* 'the kindred of men' (712b, 735b, 810b, 914b, 1725b); *rīces hyrde* 'guardian of the kingdom' (2027a, 3080a); *sinces brytta* 'distributor of treasure' (607b, 1170a, 1922b, 2071a), *wuldres wealdend* 'ruler of heaven' (17a, 183a, 1752a).

Ib. *gumena bearna* 'the children of men' (1367a), *gumena cynnes* 'the kindred of men' (1058a), *gumena dryhten* 'lord of men' (1824a), *hringa fengel* 'lord of rings' (2345b), *hringa hyrde* 'guardian of rings' (2245a), *hringa þengel* 'lord of rings' (1507a), *weoroda ræswan* 'leader of hosts' (60b), *werodes wīsa* 'leader of hosts' (259a), *ylda bearnum* 'children of men' (150a), *ylda waldend* 'ruler of men' (1661b), *ðēodnes dohtor* 'king's daughter' (2174a), *þēodnes ðegne* 'king's thane' (1085a).

Ic. *beorges hyrde* 'guardian of the barrow' (2304b), *bronda lāfe* 'residue of the fire' (3160b), *cumbles hyrde* 'guardian of the banner' (2505b), *cyniges þegnas* 'king's thanes' (3121b), *dǣda dēmend* 'judger of deeds' (181a), *eotena cynnes* 'kindred of the giants' (883b), *frætwa hyrde* 'guardian of treasures' (3133b), *fyrena hyrde* 'guardian of sins' (750b), *hæleða bearna* 'children of men' (2224a), *helle hæfton* 'slave of hell' (788a), *hordes hyrde* 'guardian of the hoard' (887a), *hūses hyrdas* 'guardians of the house' (1666a), *lēoda dugoðe* 'army of the people' (2945a), *mægþa hōse* 'troop of maidens' (924b), *nipða bearna* 'children of men' (1005b), *rodera rǣdend* 'ruler of the heavens' (1555a), *sāwele hyrde* 'guardian of the soul' (1742a), *sceaþena þrēatum* 'troops of foes' (4b), *sigora waldend* 'controller of victory' (2875a), *sweorda lāfe* 'remnant of the swords' (2936b), *wigena strengel* 'chief of warriors' (3115b), *winia bealdor* 'emboldener of warriors' (2567a), *wuldres hyrde* 'guardian of heaven' (931b). With NGen order: *ealdor ðegna* 'the thanes' chieftain' (1644b), *waldend fīra* 'the men's ruler' (2741b).

95

Group II: Relative time

No examples

Group III: Fine things

IIIa, b. No examples.

IIIc. *eorla ǣhte* 'the possessions of earls' (2248a), *mægnes mēde* 'the reward of strength' (2146a), *recedes geatwa* 'furnishings of the hall' (3088a)

Group IV: The body in combat

IVa, b. No examples.

IVc. *fēondes fingras* 'the demon's fingers' (984a)

Group V: Settings and scenic detail

Va, b. No examples.

Vc. *eorþan scēata* 'the corners of the earth' (752a), *foldan scēatas* 'the corners of the earth' (96b), *hæleþa rīce* 'kingdom of heroes' (912b), *lāþes lāstas* 'the loathsome one's footprints' (841a), *lēoda fæsten* 'fortress of the people' (2333b), *māga rīce* 'the kindred's kingdom' (1853a), *recedes mūþan* 'the building's mouth' (724a), *rodores candel* 'candle of the sky' (1572a), *wintrys wylmum* 'winter's turbulence' (516a), *worolde dǣlas* 'parts of the world' (1732b),

Group VI. Fighting equipment

VIa. *mēces ecge* 'sword's edge' (1812a, 2614a, 2939b)

VIb. *ecgum sweorda* 'swords' edges' (2961b).

VIc. *billes ecgum* 'sword's edge' (2485a), *hāres hyrste* 'the old man's armor' (2988a), *homera lāfe* 'remnant of hammers, sword' (2829b).

Group VII: Subjectivity — thought, knowledge, speech, attitude, emotion

VIIa. *eorþan wynne* 'joys of the world' (1730b, 2727a), *mægenes wynnum* 'joys of strength' (1716b, 1887a).

VIIb. *worolde wilna* 'joys of the world' (950a), *worolde wynne* 'joys of the world' (1080a), *mōdes brecða* 'grief of mind' (171a), *mōdes myrðe* 'distress of mind' (810a).

VIIc. *bealuwa bisigu* 'the distress of attacks' (281a), *billa brōgan* 'terror of swords' (583a), *dēofles cræftum* 'devil's skills' (2088a), *eorles cræfte* 'earl's skill' (982b), *hearpan wynne* 'joy of the harp' (2107b), *heofones wynne* 'joy of heaven' (1801b), *heortan sorge* 'sorrow of the heart' (2463b), *heortan wylmas* 'surgings of the heart' (2507b), *lēoda þearfe* 'the need of the people' (2801a), *mannes reorde* 'the man's voice' (2555a), *metodes hyldo* 'the favor of God' (670b), *werudes egesan* 'terror of the army' (3154b), *þegnes þearfe* 'thane's needs' (1797a), *þēofes cræfte* 'thief's cunning' (2219a).

Group VIII: Miscellaneous abstractions

VIIIa. *worolde līfes* 'the life of this world' (1387a, 2343a).

VIIIb. *fēonda fēorum* 'the lives of foes' (1152a), *fēondes fæðmum* 'the clutches of foes' (2128a), *mægenes fultum* 'support of might' (1835a), *mægenes strenge* 'strength of might' (1270b).

VIIIc. *dryhtnes dōme* 'God's judgment' (441a), *frēonda fēorum* 'the lives of friends' (1306a), *fyrena frōfre* 'relief of pain' (628a), *mæges dǣdum* 'kinsman's acts' (2436a), *mōdgan mægnes* 'power of physical strength' (670a), *sweordes swengum* 'strokes of the sword' (2386a), *weotena dōme* 'judgment of wise men' (1098b), *wyrmes dǣdum* 'dragon's deeds' (2902b).

Once again the largest number of instances is for important characters in group I. In fact this is the only group with a large number of formulaic repetitions. Fortunately, group I supplies many informative examples and the same general principles can be seen to apply. As a glance at subsection Ic will show, there are many examples with restricted reference, whereas all examples in subsection Ia permit unrestricted reference to a character type. With the exception of *manna cynne,* these useful constructions identify characters by reference to a role that is appropriate for any instance of their type. Once again we find unique expressions with the same referents as a repeated phrase, for example *gumena cynnes* (Ib) and *niþða bearna* (Ic), which have the same types of referents as *manna cynne* (Ia). In addition to a strikingly lower frequency of instances in subgroup 'a,' groups II–VIII also show consistently fewer instances of subgroup 'b' than of subgroup 'c'. Unlike adjectives, which often encode simple properties of diverse entities, genitives encode complex relations between entities. Not surprisingly, oral poets found it difficult to find genitive nouns that could be used appropriately with all instances of a core generic category. Among these categories character types stand out as exceptional. They can be defined in terms of essential generic actions expressed by agent nouns that are modified by a noun in the genitive case. As a king, for example, Hrothgar is the type of character who ought to protect his people. His inability to perform that function creates dramatic conflict and narrative momentum for Beowulf's adventure in Denmark. The conflict is heightened by use of phrases like *folces hyrde* 'protector of the folk' (610a) at a point in the narrative when the threat to Hrothgar's people is the topic of discussion. Use of agent nouns in phrases with normative metrical and syntactic form would have been especially valuable and the tradition seems to have conserved some of them from an era before the split of West Germanic from North Germanic. Eddic poetry in fornyrðislag, the Norse meter most closely related to the meter of *Beowulf,* employs two-word A1 verses like *gumna dróttin* and *seggja dróttin,* both of which mean 'lord of men.' Compare *gumena dryhten* (Ib), the Old English cognate of *gumna dróttin.*

When we consider the distribution of all examples within a well-defined corpus, it becomes obvious that semantically inessential modifiers were heavily used for their metrical value. The kinds of formulas studied by Snorri's pupils provided important general-case solutions to problems of verse construction. It seems equally clear that formulaic technique was not the preliterate equivalent of cutting and pasting. Even in a corpus like the one explored here, which is designed to isolate the most useful and most archaic constructions, we find many unique instances. Some of them resemble repeated phrases and may have been derived from them by a kind of analogy. Since analogy is notoriously difficult to define, however, it is hard to explain how it makes a poet's job easier. If we feel certain that analogy would be helpful, which would not be unreasonable, why we feel certain would be equally hard to explain.

Many clauses would be less effective if their semantically inessential variations were removed. Consider for example item (12).

(12) *hī hyne þā æt-* / **bæron** *tō* / **brimes** *faroðe,*

  swæse / *(ge-)***sīþas** (28a-29a)

  'then they bore him to the shore of the sea, his dear companions'

Here the variation performs important literary functions in the immediate context, clarifying the reference of the pronoun *hī*, adding the kind of detail that maintains a reality effect, and underscoring the cultural significance of the companions' loyal behavior. A brief return to the Chronicle entry for 755 will show what can happen when references are less clearly specified.

Our passage for comparison is situated within the climactic phase of the dispute between King Cynewulf and his political rival Cyneheard. The action begins when Cyneheard learns that the king is accompanied by a small retinue and attacks him in a fortified compound with a larger force, offering life and wealth to the king's men if they will abandon him. They refuse and are killed along with the king. Then an even larger force of the king's men surrounds the attackers. They offer life and wealth to Cyneheard's men if they will abandon him. What happens next is narrated in the following passage.

Ond þā cuǣdon hīe þæt him nǣnig mǣg lēofra nǣre þonne hiera hlāford, ond hīe nǣfre his banan folgian noldon, ond þā budon hīe hiera mǣgum þæt hīe gesunde fram eodon. Ond hīe cuǣdon þæt tæt ilce hiera gefērum geboden wǣre þe ǣr mid þām cyninge wǣrun; þā cuǣdon hīe þæt hīe hīe þæs ne onmunden "þon mā þe ēowre gefēran þe mid þām cyninge ofslǣgene wǣrun." [And then they said that to them no kinsman was more beloved than their lord, and they would never follow his killers, and then they offered to their kinsmen that they might go from there unharmed. And they said that the same thing was offered to their companions who were previously with the king; then they said that they would have none of that "any more than your companions who were slain with the king."].

As the editors observe (Cassidy & Ringler 1971: 138), familiarity with heroic concepts of loyalty can help us figure out how the pronouns refer: that the offer to depart unharmed is made by certain men in the king's retinue to their relatives in Cyneheard's retinue, that the companions mentioned are members of the king's retinue killed in the original attack, and that the comparison is between the determination of those loyal retainers to die with the king and the determination of Cyneheard's retainers to die with Cyneheard. Old English listeners might have understood all this without too much headscratching if the passage were recited to them but it is hard to imagine anyone paying rapt attention to such language. Far better to spin the passage out in a leisurely series of verse clauses with concrete variations identifying the referents and semantically inessential adjectives providing compact evaluations of cultural significance. The literate scribe was an incompetent narrator.

§2.7 Return to the main line of argument

Use of a stressed modifier for its metrical utility creates the kind of heavy constituent that is often displaced rightward in prose and ordinary speech. When realized as a verse of two stressed words, the modified constituent has the metrical simplicity required by the principle of closure for placement at the end of a verse clause, where it can situate the next opening verse in the most convenient location. When the modified constituent is an argument, this formulaic technique disrupts SOV typology. As we saw in chapter one, SOV typology is also disrupted by fronting of unstressed arguments to the opening verse, which reduces syntactic complexity toward the end of the clause, another important effect of the principle of closure. Additional disruptions of normative word order result from constraints on pairing of feet to create verse patterns and from constraints on mismatch to patterns that are acceptable. These linguistic and metrical disruptions must be factored out for proper assessment of word order.

A theory has value to the extent that it explains a variety of phenomena with general principles that are simple or elegant in the relevant scientific senses of these terms. Here I apply the universalist theory to every complete verse clause available in the K4 text, whether as a manuscript reading or as an editorial emendation, except for the few clauses that contain hypermetrical verses. Hypermetrical patterns have low frequency in the poetic corpus and require special methods of analysis (Hartman 2020). Chapters three through nine are devoted to syntactic constructions that provide adequate data for analysis. Low-frequency remainders that are harder to analyze are discussed in chapter ten. The possible arrangements of major constituents with specified metrical values are quite numerous even within clauses of the most familiar types, for example those in chapter three, which have a subject, a transitive verb, and a direct object. The same syntactic, metrical, and formulaic principles apply over and over again, but the discussions are not repetitious in the usual sense because each set of metrically defined constituents has unique characteristics. I have not been able to devise a more compact presentation of the evidence.

In addition to providing a comprehensive test for the core hypothesis, sorting all the verse clauses used by the poet into groups with similar syntax and meter has independent value for projects in several fields of study. Formulaic theorists will find rich concentrations of traditional phrases in many of these groups. Literary critics will find evidence to distinguish tradition from individual talent. Syntacticians interested in a particular kind of construction will find comprehensive data sets for deeper analysis. Textual critics faced with a peculiar verse will find it easy to determine how frequently such a verse occurs in *Beowulf* and how it departs from traditional norms. Comparison with other narratives in alliterative meter should yield new insights into linguistic and metrical evolution. I have tried to find language that would make the book accessible to all these groups of potential users.

CHAPTER 3

SOV CLAUSES AND THEIR DERIVATIVES

§3.0 Introduction

This chapter is devoted to verse clauses with a subject, one or more objects, a finite main verb, and no other major constituents. These clauses include instances in which a major constituent is expressed as a relative pronoun or understood rather than expressed. Verse clauses are organized into groups according to the metrical values of the major constituents. One-verse clauses provide a special kind of evidence because all metrical rules apply to the same verse. These clauses will be discussed separately from multi-verse clauses. In notations for grammatical patterns, 'S,' 'V,' 'O,' and 'Io' will represent stressed subjects, main verbs, direct objects, and indirect objects. Unstressed major constituents will be represented as 's,' 'v,' 'o',' and 'io.'

In section after section the instances with the highest frequency are those with the fewest departures from SOV typology. This is particularly obvious in sections with a large number of instances. Adherence to SOV typology restricts use of alternative word orders for metrical convenience. The poet rarely employs unusual word orders for the sole purpose of providing alliteration, for example. Departure from normative syntax usually avoids a pairing of foot patterns that is widely regarded as unacceptable (K4: 330–35). In many other instances the unusual word order greatly reduces metrical complexity, as measured by the universalist theory of Old English meter. For discussion of word orders that would cause metrical problems I will use the numbered designations for rules and principles in the Appendix.

When two major constituents share the same verse in a multi-verse clause the preference for SOV typology is remarkably strong. To assess the

strength of this preference we will need to distinguish major sentence constituents sharing a verse from those occupying different verses. I will use a
forward slash to represent a boundary between verses. Thus for example
S/OV will be used for SOV clauses with the subject in one verse and major
constituents of the verb phrase in a following verse. For concision and readability in lists of examples, multi-verse clauses will be identified by the number of the opening verse. The closing verses are easy to identify in verse
clauses as redefined here (§1.19).

§3.1 Instances with all major constituents stressed

Here and in §§3.2–4 we consider clauses in which there are no unstressed
verbs or personal pronouns and the SPMR has no influence on the order of
major constituents.

§3.1a One-verse instances

Two important causes of departure from normative word order in *Beowulf*
are the restricted size of the verse and the use of stressed modifiers. When a
major constituent of a phrase is modified by a semantically inessential adjunct, as often happens, it may not fit within the same verse as the other
major constituents. Expressing a clause within a single verse normally requires an unusual word order or a technique of compression such as leaving
a major constituent unexpressed or expressing it as a pronoun. Only five
verses in *Beowulf* have stressed subjects, stressed accusative objects, and
stressed main verbs in SOV order. All are heavy verses of type D3 or D4
with the compound foot occupied by a word group. Their low frequency in
the poem is due to their metrical complexity.

(1) (a) ***sceft*** / *nytte hēold* (3118b)   SOV
      'the shaft did (its) duty'   S/Sxs (D3)
  (b) ***þegn*** / *nytte behēold* (494b; cf. 1520b)   SOV
      'the thane did (his) duty'   S/Sxxs (D4)

As the cited examples in (1a, b) make clear, grouping verses with similar
syntax together can provide useful data for identification of formulaic similarities even when the number of instances is small. The arrow–shaft in (1a)
behaves like the dutiful thane in (1b). Implicit personifications of this kind

occur throughout the poem and allow for employment of the same formulaic structures for animate and inanimate objects.

Three verses otherwise similar to (1a, b) are followed by an additional verse within the same clause.

(2) (a)   **wint(e)r** / *ȳþe belēac*   SOV

     īs-ge-/binde (1132b–33a)

     'winter locked the waves in ice-bonds'   S/Sxxs (D4)

   (b)   **līg** / *ealle forswealg,*   SOV

     gǣsta gīfrost (1122b–23a; cf. 2609b–10a)

     'fire, greediest of demons, devoured all things'   S/Sxxs (D4)

Items (2a, b) contain heavy adjunct verses displaced to the right periphery. In (2a) the verb is modified by *īsgebinde*, an adjunct noun compound in the dative-instrumental case. In the verses like (2b) the phrase *gǣsta gīfrost* is a variation of the subject *līg*. As with adjuncts generally, these heavy constituents are irrelevant to the SOV structure of the opening verses in (2a, b), which are syntactically complete. Here and subsequently I classify syntactically complete verses as one-verse clauses and exclude adjuncts from the notation. As we saw in chapter two, clause-final variations like *gǣsta gīfrost* often provide an alliterative link to the next clause and situate its opening verse in the second half of the line, the most convenient location for beginning a clause.

In (3a, b) the object is dative rather than accusative. In (3b) the dative object is elaborated as a PARTITIVE GENITIVE construction in which the adjective *eallum* is zero-converted to a noun meaning 'all instances' and the partitive genitive phrase *gumena cynnes* designates the set of things to which *eallum* refers.

(3) (a) **secg** / *weorce gefeh* (1569b; cf. 1214b, 3155b).   SOV

     'the man rejoiced in (enjoyed) his work'   S/Sxxs (D4)

   (b)   **metod** / *eallum wēold*   SOV

     gumena / *cynnes* (1057b–58a)

     'the creator ruled all (every one) of the kindred of mankind'   S/Sxs (D4)

Although the objects are dative in (3a, b), the verbs are not genuinely intransitive (OES 1: 125). The inanimate dative object *weorce* is not the usual kind of indirect object that occurs in sentences with an accusative direct object. Item (3a) bears a closer logical resemblance to sentences like 'the man enjoyed his work,' where 'work' is an inanimate direct object. In the K4 glossary verbs like *gefeh* are said to be used 'with the dative' and I will interpret dative arguments like *weorce* as direct objects. As we shall see, the *Beowulf* poet also employed genitive direct objects and a few unambiguously instrumental direct objects. I will refer to these dative, genitive, and instrumental direct objects as OBLIQUE OBJECTS.

Blake (2001) distinguishes between two kinds of case. ABSTRACT CASE represents purely syntactic relations among constituents, such as the relation between a verb and its subject, direct object, or indirect object. In Old English the direct-object relation of a noun to a verb is normally marked with an accusative ending on the noun and the indirect-object relation is normally marked with a dative ending. Abstract case must always be present on an argument noun for checking against the corresponding case feature of a verb but need not be represented by a difference in the form of the noun. In Modern English only pronouns have different case forms for subjects and objects. Lexical subjects and direct objects are distinguished by word order alone. The inflections on oblique objects represent INHERENT CASE, which is assigned to an argument by a particular verb. In his work on Kalkatungu, an Australian language, Blake (2001: 47–59) identifies several constructions in which an inherent case normally used for objects is used for subjects. As Blake observes (2001: 59), the same kind of mismatch between abstract subject case and inherent case occurs in Modern German passive constructions. The subject of the passive construction ordinarily has nominative case, as in *Er wird gesehen* 'he is seen,' with nominative *Er*. This corresponds to active constructions like *Sie sieht ihn* 'she sees him,' with accusative *ihn*. When a German verb assigns inherent dative case to an oblique object, however, the subject of the corresponding passive construction remains in the dative case. Thus we have *Ihm wird geholfen* 'he is helped,' with dative *ihm*, corresponding to active sentences like *Sie hilft ihm*, 'she helps him,' with an oblique object in the dative case. Verbs that assign inherent case to an object assign the same case to a subject in the corresponding passive construction. The resistance of inherent case to change can be attributed to the fact that it provides semantic information not reducible to a purely syntactic function. In the German example, dative case marks the subject as a beneficiary. An Old English example with a subject in the genitive case is *bēne / (ge)tīðad fēasceaftum / men* 'some favor (was) granted to the unfortunate man' (*Beowulf* 2284b–85a). Here the inherent genitive case expresses the meaning 'some,' as with genitive case in French constructions like *du pain* 'some of the bread, some bread.' Dative direct objects are less common than accusative ones and genitive direct objects are less common still. For concision in lists of examples I indicate only the most likely interpretations for ambiguous case forms. When the inflected form of an object could be accusative or dative, I classify it as accusative; when an object could be dative or genitive, I classify it as dative; when an object could be dative or instrumental, I classify it as dative. The other possibilities of interpretation are specified in the K4 glossary.

The SOV verses in items (1–3) have two things in common that determine their placement. First, all examples are heavy and morphologically complex type D variants and their placement late in the clause is progressively more inhibited as the number of verses in the clause increases (§1.19). It is not surprising to find that all these examples occur in the first verse of the clause, the one most tolerant of complexity. Secondly, all examples end in finite verbs. If we considered the complexity of types D3 and D4 in isolation, we would expect placement to be inhibited in the b-verse and the fact that all examples appear in the b-verse would be very surprising. This constraint on verse complexity is overcome, however, by a higher-ranking preference for line-final placement of finite verbs (OE 1.3). The strength of this tendency becomes conspicuous when we consider all instances of types D3 and D4. *Beowulf* contains 155 D3 verses. Of the 78 instances ending in finite verbs, 75 are b-verses. Of the 80 remaining instances, only 16 are b-verses. Type D4, the most complex type, is attested only 19 times in the poem. All twelve instances ending in a finite verb are b-verses. Only two of the remaining seven instances are b-verses. When the influence of finite verbs is removed, the complexity of the verse pattern exerts an obvious influence; but that influence is insufficient to overcome the preference for placement of a stressed finite verb in line-final position at normative metrical location s4. The predominance of the constraint on verb placement is attributable to UM 6, the universal tendency for norms at higher levels of metrical structure to exert more influence than norms at lower levels. Since it specifies a location within a line abstracted from an SOV clause, the verb-placement norm is at a higher level of structure than norms for verses abstracted from phrases below clause level. UM 6 comes into play only when the norms at both levels of structure are sufficiently low-ranking to be violated, as in this instance. The preference for line-final placement of finite verbs cannot overrule the constraints on pairing of foot patterns to create verse patterns, which are rules of such high rank that they are never violated.

There are four one-verse instances with OSV structure. The verses like (4a) are one-sentence clauses; in those like (4b) the major constituents are followed by semantically inessential variations.

(4) (a) **wyrm** / *hāt gemealt* (897b; cf. 2706b)   O S V

  'heat dissolved the dragon'   S/Sxs (D3)

 (b)   **sunu** / *dēað fornam,*   O S V

  wīg-*hete* / **Wedra** (2119b-20a; cf. 1377b)   S/Sxs (D3)

  'death, the battle-hatred of the Weders, snatched away (her) son'

OSV is rare as a basic word order. Most OSV orders are created by fronting an object from its normative position in an SOV or SVO language. OSV order in (4a) is most plausibly explained as fronting of the prominent object to highlight a contrast between the vanquished dragon and his triumphal slayer Sigurd, the topic of discussion in the previous clause. As we have observed (§1.5), this kind of fronting is often encountered in Indo-European SOV languages and follows from the universal 'iconicity of distance' principle that brings constituents closely related in meaning closer together in the discourse. In late Proto-Germanic, when alliterative meter was born, subjects were distinguished from objects by a robust inflectional system and a fronted accusative noun was readily identifiable as a direct object. Although some case distinctions had been lost by the Old English period, fronting to highlight relations between clauses was still available to poets as a workable option. In Modern English, with its paucity of case forms and correspondingly stricter constraints on word order, this kind of fronting usually employs wordier constructions like 'As for the dragon, he was dissolved by his own fire.' In (4b) *sunu* is fronted to highlight the relation of kinship between Grendel and his mother, represented in the previous clause as seeking vengeance for her son's death in accord with Germanic custom. SOV and OSV are the only attested orders in *Beowulf* for one-verse clauses with stressed subjects, objects, and main verbs. There are no instances with SVO order. In clauses like (4a, b) the objects were clearly not fronted from underlying final position in a sentence with SVO typology. The number of examples in items (1–4) is rather small but their evidence points decisively toward SOV as the normative order in the poem. Verb-second order is avoided rather than favored.

§3.1b Multi-verse instances

The most common clause pattern is S/OV, as in (5a, b), where the stressed
subject is in the opening verse and the constituents of the verb phrase share
a later verse. Items (5c–e) have an indirect object added to the S/OV structure. As the terms 'direct' and 'indirect' imply, a direct object is in closer
syntactic composition with the verb and its referent is more directly affected
by the action of the verb (§1.2). When there are two stressed objects, the
verb normally shares a verse with the direct object, as in (5c–e), seldom with
the indirect object. In (5d) a simplex indirect object is fronted to a stressed
position before the subject. In (5e) a heavy indirect object is displaced to the
right periphery. The unstressed adverbs *oft* 'often' (5c) and *þā* 'then' (5d, e)
are movable SPs placed at location x1, the normative metrical location for
unstressed SPs of all kinds. Instances with oblique objects are identified in
the lists of examples with S/OV structure.

(5) (a) **hæle / hilde-dēor   Hrōðgār** / *grētte* (1816)   S/OV

      'the battle-bold man greeted Hrothgar'

  (b)   **cyning**-*balde* / *men*   S/OV

      from þǣm / **holm**-*clife* **hafelan** / *bǣron*

      earfoð- / *līce heora* / **ǣ**ghwæþrum,

      fela- / *mōdigra* (1634b–37a)

      'men bold as kings bore the head from the sea-cliff, with difficulty for each
      pair of them, of (those) very brave ones'

  (c) *oft* / **Scyld Scēfing   sceaþena** / *þrēatum,*   S/Io/OV

     monegum / **mǣgþum,   meodo**-*setla* / *(of)tēah*

     (4–5, gen. obj.; cf. 1725a–27a)

     'Scyld Scefing often denied mead-benches to troops of attackers, to many
     tribes'

  (d) *ond ðā* / **Bēowulfe   bēga** / *(ge)hwæþres*   Io/S/OV

     eodor / **Ing**-*wina onweald ge*- / *tēah,*

     wicga / *(ond)* **wǣpna** (1043a–45a; cf. 1050a–53a)

     'and then to Beowulf the protector of Ing's friends (the Danes) gave posses-
     sion of each of two (things), horses and weapons'

  (e) *ond þā* / **frēolic wīf   ful ge**- / *sealde*   S/OV/Io

     ǣrest / **Ēast**-*Dena **ēþel**- / **wearde** (615–16; cf. 2020–21)

     'and then the excellent woman first gave a cup to the land-guardian of the
     East-Danes'

(f)   *lange / þrāge*   S/OV

æfter / gūð-ceare **Gren**des / mōdor,

ides[,] / āglæc-wīf, *yrmþe / (ge)munde* (1257b–59b)

'for a long time after the distress of battle Grendel's mother, a lady, a formidable woman, brooded about the injury'

Opening verses in other S/OV examples like (5a): 3a, 689b, 834a, 972b
(hyperbaton), 1212a, 1364a, 1395a, 1448a, 1816a, 1945a, 2098a (dat. obj.),
2481a, 2486a (gen. obj.), 2559a, 2579a, 2647a (gen. obj.), 2846a, 2948a,
3020a, 3062b; Like (5b): 86a, 207b, 314b, 316b, 433b (gen. obj.), 457a,
583b, 685b, 850b, 867b, 923b, 982a, 1030a, 1046a, 1076a, 1089a, 1099b,
1148a, 1213b, 1240b, 1368a, 1510b, 1634b, 1642b, 1737b, 1978b, 2016b,
2120b, 2223a, 2264b, 2413b, 2677b, 2791b, 2928a, 3148b, 3160b.

Arrangement of the major constituents in (5a) conforms to OE 1.1, OE 1.2,
and OE 1.3. The constituents are realized as a single line, the caesura falls
in the ideal location between the subject and the constituents of the verb
phrase, and the verb occupies normative metrical location s4. Within the b-
verse the constituents of the verb phrase observe normative OV order. In
the instances like (5b) the major constituents are not expressed in a single
line. As in (5a), however, the subject occupies the opening verse and the
verb stands in normative syntactic position at the end of the clause, observing normative OV order with its object. In the cited example for (5b) normative placement of *bǣron* is achieved by filling the a-verse of this line with
from þǣm holmclife, a prepositional phrase that is semantically inessential.
The phrase is aesthetically functional, however, insofar as it clarifies spatio-
temporal relations, making the narrative action easier to visualize. The third
line in (5b) is inessential but semantically functional in the immediate narrative context, highlighting the reportably huge weight of the giant's head.
The final verse, *felamōdigra,* provides no relevant information, since the
bravery of Beowulf's companions has been emphasized many times before.
The same can be said for *hildedēor* and *cyningbalde,* the alliterating subject
modifiers in (5a, b). These generic adjectives are used primarily for metrical
reasons.

  Item (5f) has the same syntax as (5a). I represent it separately because
Klaeber assumed that *lange þrāge* modified the previous verse and inter-
preted line 1257 to mean that Grendel's mother lived for a long time after
Grendel was killed by Beowulf. As the K4 editors observe in their note to
the line, this makes no sense because she dies only a day later than her son.
Since no problems with Kuhn's Laws or the SPMR would arise, I see no

problem with including 1257b–58a in the following clause. Punctuated as in (5f), the clause makes sense and expresses important generic content. The obligation to take swift vengeance is strongly emphasized in ancient Germanic narratives. When he hears that Grendel's mother has killed Hrothgar's close companion, for example, Beowulf tells the king that it would be best to defer mourning and pursue the killer at once (1384–85). From this perspective a single day would be a long time to brood before seeking vengeance. Like the dragon in 2302b–6a, Grendel's mother is impatient for the next opportunity to attack at night.

The remaining SOV clauses are represented in item (6). When subject and object share a verse they appear in normative SO order. In (6e) a heavy indirect object has been displaced to the right periphery.

(6) (a) *oþ þæt / **hrefn** blaca   **heofones** / wynne*   S/O/V
     ***blīð**-heort / **bodode** (1801a–02b)*

     'until the black raven, happy-hearted, announced heaven's joy (the sun)'

  (b) *þonne him / **Hūnlāfing**   **hilde-** / lēoman,*   S/O/V
     ***billa** / sēlest,   on / **bearm** dyde (1143a–44a)*

     'when Hunlafing placed the battle-flame, best of swords, in the lap to him (his lap)'

  (c)   ***Al-walda** / þec*   SO/V
     *gōde / (for)**gylde** (955b–56a; cf. 2131a–32a)*

     'the Almighty should reward you with good things' (subjunctive verb)

  (d) *þæt næfre / **Grendel** swā <u>fela</u>   gryra / (ge)<u>fremede</u>,*   SO/V/Io
     atol / æg-læca,   ealdre / þīnum,
     *hȳnðo / on **Heorote** (591a–93a)*

     'that Grendel, the horrid awe-inspirer, would never have done so many terrible things, injuries in Heorot, to your lord' (subjunctive verb)

Opening verses in other S/O/V examples like (5a, b): 331b, 503b, 701a (gen. obj.), 1285a, 1499b, 2318a, 2462b, 2507a, 2718a, 2958b.

Most of these instances have S/O/V distribution of the major constituents, with each one in a separate verse, as in (6a, b). In (6b) *him* is split by hyperbaton from other constituents of the phrase *him on bearme,* a possessive dative construction that corresponds to Modern English 'in his lap.' Since it is an adjunct STP rather than an SP indirect object, *him* is not represented in the syntactic notation for (6b). The verses like (6c, d) have a subject and an extraneous object in one verse and the verb in a following verse. If the verb had been moved leftward out of the a-verse it would leave a trace after the object and the a-verse would be a psychologically complete SOV constituent (§1.8). The verb remains in core position to the right of the object, however, and there is no trace of it in the a-verse. The subject and object are in normative order but do not form a natural syntactic constituent. This departure from the verse norm (OE 2) restricts the frequency of clauses like (6c, d). The rarest kind of enjambment in *Beowulf* splits closely bound constituents that are immediately adjacent, as in the first line of (6d), where the constituents of a partitive genitive construction are split by the midline caesura. In (6c) this particularly jarring kind of enjambment is avoided by interposition of an adjunct between the object and the verb. Here as in many other cases metrical complexity is reduced by situating the enjambment as early as possible, in accord with the principle of closure (UM 4).

Although there are no one-verse SVO clauses, multi-verse SVO clauses have significant frequency. These clauses are subject to an interesting constraint. If the basic pattern were SVO, we would expect most instances to have an S/VO pattern, with the caesura at the natural point of syntactic division between subject and verb phrase. In fact most instances have the pattern SV/O. Relative to an SVO norm, SV/O creates a major syntactic mismatch, splitting the constituents of the verb phrase and placing an extraneous verb in the same verse with the subject. Relative to an SOV norm, however, SV/O is created by displacing the object to the right periphery of the clause, which creates a major syntactic break between verb and object. The intervening metrical boundary is matched by this derived syntactic boundary. The vast majority of displaced objects occur in a two-word verse shared by a stressed object with a stressed modifier, employing the formulaic technique discussed in chapter two.

Item (7a) is a representative SV/O clause.

(7) (a)   ***frēa* / *scēawode***   SV/O

   fīra / ***fyrn****-geweorc* ***for****man* / *sīðe* (2285b–86b)

   'the chieftain inspected the ancient work of men for the first time'

 (b)   ***scyld* / *wēl gebearg***   SV/O/Io

   līfe ond / *līce* ***læs****san* / *hwīle*

   mǣ*rum* / *þēodne* (2570b–72a, dat. obj.)

   'the shield protected life and body for the famous chieftain for less time'

 (c)   *þā se* / ***ellor****-gāst*   S/VO *(of)lēt / līf-dagas   ond þās / lǣnan gesceaft* (1621b–22b)

'when the alien spirit relinquished (his) life-days and this transitory world'

(e)   *ond s[ē] / ān ðā gēn*   S/VO

lēoda / <u>duguð</u>e,   sē ðǣr / lengest hwearf,

weard / wine-geōmor,   wēnde / (þæs) ylcan (2237b–39b, gen. obj.)

'and the one of the retainers of that people who longest moved about there, a lord sad for friends, still expected the same (thing)'

Opening verses in other SV/O examples like (7a): 208b, 213b, 215b (dat. obj.), 320b (dat. obj.), 557b, 572b, 688b, 890b, 1024b, 1080b, 1161b, 1198b, 1223b, 1374b, 1423b, 1440b, 1494b (dative object), 1521a, 1524b (dat. obj.), 1567b, 1689b, 1751b, 1846b, 1882b (gen. obj.), 1890b, 2216b (as emended), 2249b, 2288b, 2488b, 2536b, 2554b, 2814b, 3060b; in other S/VO examples like (7c): 771b (dat. obj), 2702b (dat. obj.).

Although the object is displaced to the right periphery in (7a), subject and verb observe normative order in their shared verse and the verb occupies normative metrical location s4. In item (7b) both objects are heavy and both are displaced rightward. In (7c) the verb alliterates at metrical location s1a, the least favorable location for stressed verbs, and the following noun alliterates in accord with the RULE OF PRECEDENCE, a strong preference for alliteration on the most prominent constituent in a verse (OE 6.1, OE 7.2). Departure from normative verse placement in (7c) avoids *līf-dagas / (of)lēt,* with a short vowel on the s position in type E (Ssx/S), which would contravene OE 8.3. Even with a change in alliteration, the verb-final alternative to (7d), **(þæs) ylcan / wēnde,* would have easily avoidable anacrusis, which is ruled out by OE 9.6.

In (8a, b) each major constituent of an SVO clause occupies a different verse.

(8) (a) *hūru / Gēata lēod,   georne / <u>truwo</u>de*

mōdgan / mægnes,   metodes / hyldo (699–70, gen. obj.)

'indeed the man of the Geats earnestly trusted (his) valiant strength (and) the grace of the creator'

(b)   *Heaðo- / Scilfingas(,)*

nīða / (ge)nǣgdan   nefan / Hererīces (2205b–6b)

'the Battle-Scyldings approached Hereric's nephew with hostile intents'

(c) *þæt mid / Scyldingum   sceaðona / nāthwylc,*   S/V/O *dēogol* / *dǣd*-*hata[,]* **deorc**um / *nihtum*

*ēawe*ð / *(þurh)* **eg**san **un**cūðne / nīð,

*hȳn*ðu / *(ond)* **hrā**fyl (274a–77a)

'that among the Scyldings some unknown (one) of enemies, a raging aggres-
sor, shows uncanny malice in the dark nights through terror, oppression, and
destruction of human bodies'

Opening verses in other examples like (8a): 30b (hyperbaton), 1154a, 2278a,
2785a, 2888b, 2924a (dat. obj.), 3120a.

The cited instance in (8a) provides a good example of conjuncts simply juxtaposed rather than linked by a conjunction as in Modern English. Note also
the absence of a possessive pronoun for something inalienably possessed, in
this case a person's strength (*mægen*). The finite verb occupies normative
location s4 in the examples like (8a). In (8b) the verb occupies metrical
location s2 at the end of the a-verse. In (8c) placement of the verb at metrical
location s1a avoids **(þurh)* **eg**san / *ēawe*ð, an unacceptable type A1 variant
with easily avoidable anacrusis, contravening OE 9.6. Placement of the verb
at location s1a often avoids contravention of this QUASI-OBLIGATORY rule,
which is violable but rarely violated.

Verse clauses with VSO order are created by leftward movement of the
finite verb to a stressed position. All three possible clause patterns are represented: V/S/O, V/SO, and VS/O.

(9) (a) *ge-* / **worh**ton ðā **Wedra** / *lēode*   V/S/O

  hlǣw on / **hōe** (3156a–57a)

  'then the people of the Weders constructed a tumulus on the hill'

  (b) *þenden* / **rēa**fode **rinc** / ōðerne (2985; cf. 652a–3a)   V/S

  'meanwhile (one) warrior plundered the other (one)'

  (c) *(for)***wrāt** / **Wedra** helm **wyrm** on / *middan*   VS/O

  (2705; cf. 1539a–40a, 1713)

  'the protector of the Weders pierced the serpent in the middle'

  (d) **set**ton / **sǣ**-*mēþe* **sīde** / *scyldas*   VS/O

  rondas / **regn**-*hearde*, wið þæs / **rec**edes weal

  (325–26; cf. 94–95, 723a–24a)

  'the sea-weary (ones) set the broad bucklers, wonderfully strong shields,
  against the wall of the building'

  (e) **grēt**te / **gold**-*hroden* **guman** on / *healle* (614)   VS/O 'the gold-adorned (one) greeted the men in the hall'

(f) *(on)geat þā / (se) gōda   grund-* / *wyrgenne,*   VS/O

*mere-wīf / mih*tig   (1518a–19a; cf. 1506–7, 2247a–48a, imperative)

'then the outcast of the deep, the mighty sea-woman, perceived the powerful (man)'

(g) *hwanon / ferigeað gē   fǣtte / scyldas,*   VS/O

grǣge / syrcan   ond / grīm-helmas,

here-sceafta / hēap?   (333a–35a)

'whence did you bring decorated shields, grey mail-coats and grim helmets, (and) a heap of battle-shafts (spears)?'

Opening verses in other examples like (5a): 620a, 758a, 794b, 1408a, 1537a, 1870a, 2244a, 2756a, 2926a, 3178a.

Although S/V/O and V/S/O clauses depart from normative order, their frequencies are not much lower than those for S/O/V clauses. Departure from normative order becomes more tolerable when major constituents occupy separate verses (OE 2.3). This is attributable to the obvious fact that clauses with each major constituent in a separate verse cannot violate the severe constraints on stressed major constituents sharing a verse, which seldom depart from normative order and are seldom paired in such a way as to split a constituent from its natural partner by enjambment. These severe constraints follow from the definition of the normative verse as a natural syntactic constituent with two words in normative order (OE 2). Stressed constituents sharing a verse in (9b) observe normative SO order, but stressed constituents sharing a verse in (9c–g) are out of normative SV order. In these instances, constraints on words sharing a verse are violated because normative order would violate a higher-ranking constraint. In the other examples like (9c, d, f) the same violation would occur as in the cited examples. With normative SV order (9c) would be **Wedra helm / (for)wrāt* (Sxs/S: M1), and (9d) would be **sǣ-mēþe / set*ton (Ssx/Sx: H5). If *–hroden* in (9e) could be resolved, the SV alternative **gold-hroden / grētte* would have the acceptable pattern Ss/Sx; but since the second syllable in *–hroden* is closed by a consonant, resolution is blocked by KALUZA'S LAW (OE 8.6), and the verse has the unacceptable H5 pattern. The SV alternative to (9f), **þā se / gōda (on)geat,* is not acceptable to the poet as a variant of type B2 (x/Sxxs). Because alliteration is universally associated with prominence, alliteration on a weakly stressed finite verb occupying a subordinate s position causes substantial complexity (OE 7.5). Whenever possible in such cases the poet arranges the major constituents as a type A1 verse like (9f). There are four B2 verses in *Beowulf* like *ac in compe gecrong* (2505a), but all four begin with a fixed SP conjunction (cf. 760a, 2353a, 2767a). Departure from normative SV order in these instances would do more harm than good, creating otherwise unattested A1 variants like *(ac ge)crong in / compe,* with a fixed SP conjunction in a disyllabic anacrusis. The poet almost always departs from normative word order to avoid anacrusis and especially to avoid placing SPs in anacrusis (OE 9.2). In item (9f) as we have it the anacrusis is of the ordinary prefixal kind. VS order in (9g) is not a departure from SOV typology because SOV languages front interrogative verbs routinely, as with imperative and hortative subjunctive verbs (§1.5). In (9g), moreover, the finite main verb, being more prominent than the pronoun object, is the appropriate occupant of the more prominent lift (OE 6.1).

When we move beyond the most widespread orders in the world's languages, the most common pattern in verse-clauses is OV/S. Relative to an SOV norm, OV/S is created by displacing a heavy subject phrase to the right periphery of the clause, leaving the constituents of the verb phrase to share a verse in normative OV order. There are no clauses in *Beowulf* with O/VS structure, which would require placement of the stressed object before the stressed subject and departure from normative order in the verse shared by subject and verb. A one-line verse clause with O/VS structure would also have enjambment between the closely bound constituents of the verb phrase.

(10) (a)   *þone / **cwealm** gewræc*   OV/S

         ēce / drihten (107b–8a)

         'the eternal Lord avenged that killing'

    (b) *þone / **hring hæfde   Hige**lāc / Gēata,*   OV/S

         ***nefa** / Swertinges **nȳh**stan / sīðe* (1202–03)

         'Hygelac of the Geats, nephew of Swerting, had that ring on (his) last expedition'

    (c)   *hwīlum / **syl**lic spell*   O/V/S

         *reh**te** / (æfter) **rih**te   rūm-heort / cyning* (2109b–10b)

         'at times the great-hearted king recited a wondrous tale with skill'

    (d)   *nalles / **frætwe** geaf*   OV/SIo

         ealdor / <u>dugo</u>ðe (2919b–20a; cf. 305b–6a)

         'the chieftain by no means gave treasure to his retinue'

    (e) *þenden / **hæ**lo ābēad   **heorð**-ge- / nēatum(,)*   OV/Io/S

116

gold-<u>wine</u> / ***Gēata*** (2418a–19a)

'while the gold-friend of the Geats said farewell to (his) hearth-companions'
Opening verses in other examples like (10a): 147a, 608b, 625a (dat. obj.),
815b, 886a (hyperbaton), 1146a, 1237b, 1573b, 1600b, 1681b, 1931b,
2267a, 2460b, 2562b, 2575b, 2583b (genitive object), 3094b.

The most common instances are those like (10a), with the verb in normative
location s4. In (10b) placement of the verb at metrical location s3 makes it
possible to arrange the major constituents as a single line. In (10c) placement
of the verb at location s1a avoids *(*æfter*) ***rihte*** / ***rehte****, an unacceptable type
A1 variant with easily avoidable anacrusis. In (10d, e) the inanimate direct
object shares a verse with the verb in normative order, with the indirect
animate object more distant. In (10d) the subject shares a displaced type II
verse with an indirect object, observing normative SIo order. In (10e) subject and indirect object are out of normative order but do not share a verse.

Emphatic fronting of a stressed object to the left periphery creates the
O/SV order of items (11a–f). Unlike displaced objects, which usually fill a
whole verse, fronted objects rarely do so. Stressed constituents like *beot,
word, gold-sele, and sīð-fæt* are fronted less often than unstressed constituents
but much more often than whole-verse constituents. *Sīðfæt* can scan as Sx
in (11f) because it is an ordinary-language compound with a secondary constituent likely to undergo reduction rather than a poetic neologism with a
more prominent secondary constituent (Russom 1987: 92–97). Modern
English makes some use of emphatic fronting (*spaghetti I like, mushrooms I
don't*). Instances of this kind generally have pronouns marked for subject
case, making the fronted constituent easy to identify as an object. Most often, however, modern speakers conform to normative SVO order and use
stress for emphasis instead.

(11) (a)   ***Bēot*** *eal wið* / *þē*   O/S/V

     sunu / *Bēanstānes* ***sōðe*** / *(ge)læste* (523b–24b)

     'the son of Beanstan truly fulfilled his boast against you'

   (b) *swā ðā* / ***mæl****-ceare* ***maga*** / *Healfdenes*   O/S/V

     singāla / ***sēað*** (189a–90a)

     'thus the son of Halfdane continually brooded over the trouble of that
     time'

   (c) *swylce* / ***giōmor-gyd*** ***Gēa****tisc* / *mēowle*   O/S/V

     æfter / ***Bīowulfe*** *bunden-* / *heorde*

117

sang / *sorg*-cearig,   *sæide* / *(ge)neahhe* (3150–52)

'also, a Geatish woman with hair bound up, lamenting (her) grief, sang a sad song in memory of Beowulf, said earnestly' (anticipating a that-clause)

(d) *siþðan* / *gold*-sele   **Grendel** / <u>*warode*</u> (1253; cf. 1609, 2651b–52b)   O/SV

'after Grendel occupied the gold-hall'

(e) *ðām* / *wīfe þā* **word**   **wēl** / *līcodon,*   OS/V

gilp-<u>*cwide*</u> / **Gēa***tes* (639a–40a, dat. obj.)

'those words, the boasting speech of the Geat, well pleased the woman'

(f) *ðone* / *sīð*-*fæt him*   **snotere** / *ceorlas*   OIo/S/V

lȳthwōn / *lōgon* (202a–3a)

'wise men little criticized that journey to him' (did not dissuade him from going)

Opening verses in other examples like (11a): 104b, 164a, 1018b.

In (11a, d, e) the finite verb occupies normative location s4. In (11b, f) the object is fronted to provide alliteration for the opening verse and the verb occupies location s2 in the second line. In (11b) the fronted object comes closer to the topic of discussion in the previous passage by way of introducing a new passage marked as *fit III* in the manuscript. The iconically fronted object in (11f) refers to the topic of the preceding clause. In (11c) a verb suitable for emphasis is fronted to a stressed position at metrical location s1a, avoiding **sorh*-cearig / *song,* a dispreferred variant of type E with a short syllable on the s position (OE 8.3). As in item (9), the common realizations (11a–c) have each major constituent in a separate verse. Such realizations have the kind of clause structure that is most tolerant of departure from word order norms. In the verses like (9d) stressed constituents sharing a verse observe normative SV order. Stressed constituents sharing a verse are out of normative order in (11e, f). In (11e) OS order avoids **(þā)* **word** *ðām* / **wīfe***,* type A1 with avoidable anacrusis. In (11f) departure from normative IoO order matches the more prominent compound object to the more prominent lift in accord with OE 6.1.

Items (12a, b) have VOS order — SOV order turned around backwards.

(12) (a)   *oþ ðæt* / **eft** *byreð*   V/O/S

ofer / **lagu**-strēamas   *lēofne* / *mannan*

wudu / **wunden**-hals   *tō* / **Weder**-mearce (296b–98b; cf. 1014b–17a) 'until the wood (ship) with curved neck (prow) bears the beloved man over the sea-currents to the land of the Weder-Geats'

(b) *swylce / **oft** bemearn* **ǣrran** */ mǣlum*   V/O/S

    swīð-*ferhþes /* **sīð** **snotor** *ceorl / monig* (907–8)

    'likewise, in former times many a wise man often lamented the behavior of the strong-minded (one)'

(c) **bær** */ (on)* **bearm** *scipes* **beorht**e */ frætwa*   V/O/S

    Wælses */ eafe*ra (896a–97a)

    'Waels's heir bore bright treasure into the interior of the boat'

(d) *ðonne /* **sægdon** *þæt* **sǣ**- */ līþende* (377)   VO/S

    'also, seafarers said that' (anticipating a that-clause)

(e) **wearp** */ (ðā)* **wunden**-mǣl **wrǣ**ttum */ (ge)bunden*   VO/S

    yrre / ōretta (1531a–32a; cf. 2367–68)

    'the angry warrior threw away the decorated sword, wrapped with ornaments'

(f) *(ge)***wēold** */* **wīg**-*sigor* **wītig** */ drihten,*   VO/S

    rodera */* **rǣ**dend (1554a–55a)

    'the wise lord, ruler of the heavens, determined victory in the fight'

(g) **geald** *þone /* **gūð**-*rǣs* **Gēa**ta */ dryhten,*   VO/S/Io

    Hrēðles */ eafo*ra, *þā hē tō /* **hām** becōm,

    Iofore */ (ond) Wulfe* mid */* **ofer**-māðmum (2991–93)

    'when he came home the lord of the Geats remunerated the battle-attack to Iofor and Wulf with exceeding treasure'

In (12a–c) the modified subject and modified object are displaced to the right periphery but do not maintain normative OV order. The complexity of VOS order is mitigated in these clauses by placement of each major constituent in a separate verse. Even in this small sample important trends hold true. The most common pattern, (12a), has the verb in normative location s4; and there is a metrical explanation for placement of the verb on metrical location s1a in (12c). With normative verb-final order the opening verse would be **(on) **bearm** scipes / **bær**, with unacceptable anacrusis in type E (OE 9.7). In (12d–g) constituents sharing a verse are out of normative OV order, again for metrical reasons. In the opening verse of (12d) the verb is more prominent than its object and VO order aligns linguistic prominence with metrical prominence (OE 6.1). In (12e) normative OV order would create the unacceptable pattern *Sxs/S (M1). In (12f) the result would be a type E verse with a short syllable on the s position, contravening OE 8.3. The verse as we have it is an unremarkable D variant with ordinary prefixal anacrusis. In (12g) the result would be a type B verse with the prominent secondary stress of a poetic compound on the x position of the Sxs foot, violating OE 4.3, a constraint of the highest rank.

The normative double-object construction has an indirect object in the dative case and a direct object in the accusative case. There are no Old English equivalents to Modern English prepositional dative constructions like *Frankie gave a Maserati to Brett,* with the indirect object expressed as a prepositional phrase (§1.8). In *Beowulf* all objects are expressed as nouns that are governed directly by the finite verb rather than by an intermediary preposition. The double-object constructions in (13a–c) have objects with inherent oblique case.

(13) (a) *þætte / **freoðu**-webbe **fēores** / (on)sǣce* $S/O^1V/O^2$

        *æfter / **lige**-torne **lēofne** / mannan* (1942–43)

        'that a peace-weaver should deny life to a beloved man after a pretended injury'

    (b) *nō þǣr **wǣg**-flotan **wind** ofer / ȳðum* $O^2/S/O^1V$

        sīðes / (ge)twǣfde (1907a–08a)

        'there the wind over the waves by no means denied a journey to the wave-floater (ship)'

    (c) *þone / **yldestan** ōret- / mecgas* $O^2/S/O^1V$

        ***Bēowulf** / nemnað* (363a–64a)

        'fighting men call the leader Beowulf'

I notate the inanimate object in such constructions as a primary direct object (O^1) and use O^2 to notate an animate secondary object or a personified secondary object like the ship in (13b). Items (13a, b) have genitive primary objects and accusative secondary objects. Both objects are accusative in (13c). The inanimate object is direct no matter what case it bears, in the sense of being in closer construction with the verb. The syntactic proximity of verb and inanimate object provides an iconic representation of the fact that an agent generally applies the action of a transitive verb more directly to an inanimate mediating object than to an animate object, as in ordinary double-object constructions with dative indirect objects. Sentences like *they gave him to the sea* are perfectly appropriate in relation to a sea burial but in that context the gift is no longer animate, the agents control the body directly, and the personified sea is out of their control. The translations for

(13a, b) are meant to bring out the similarity between their animate objects and dative indirect objects. Naming constructions like (13c) have somewhat different semantics but the same iconic principle applies: the speaker controls the name directly but not the named individual and the name mediates between the speaker and the individual who is addressed or mentioned. *Beowulf* is consistent with the representation of double-object constructions by Bárány (2024), in which all inanimate themes share a closely-bound head-complement construction with the finite verb and all animate recipients occupy a specifier position more distant from the finite verb (§1.8).

The examples with all major constituents stressed in §3.1 provide strong evidence for the claim that the basic order was SOV when the oral-formulaic tradition was founded and that the *Beowulf* poet strongly prefers SOV order at clause level. We will return to verse clauses with all major constituents stressed in §3.11 after exploring the influence of metrical constraints in the remaining transitive clauses.

§3.2   Clauses with an unexpressed or relativized subject, a stressed transitive verb, and a stressed direct object

A pronoun argument refers to a readily identified entity in the discourse — something recently mentioned, for example. When an argument is very easy to identify, it may be unexpressed rather than pronominalized. Since a signed postcard identifies the writer to a friend, constructions like *arrived safe and sound, wish you were here* can leave the subject unexpressed, making best use of limited writing space. In less intimate discourse, Modern English would require an expressed pronoun subject in these sentences, unlike NULL-SUBJECT languages with a robust inflectional system that provides adequate information about the subject (Radford 1997: 227, 518). When a subject pronoun would be required in Modern English prose, the subject may be unexpressed in *Beowulf*. Since unexpressed arguments have no overt locations, I represent them in an artificial way for consistency, notating them in lower case and placing them between parentheses before the notations for stressed constituents. In some instances the poet leaves more than one argument unexpressed. I notate such arguments in normative order as (so), (sio), and (s.io.o), using parentheses to indicate non-expression and adding a stop when necessary to distinguish 'io' from other uses of 'i' and 'o' in notations. Most verse clauses with unexpressed subjects are easy to interpret because they are immediately preceded by one or more clauses in which a subject referring to the same entity is expressed in the first such clause. I use the term COREFERENTIAL to designate the semantic relation between a pronoun — expressed or unexpressed — and its antecedent. Unexpressed subjects are also easy to interpret if they are defined in a following relative clause. Relativized pronoun arguments are fixed SPs and their placement cannot be disrupted by the SPMR. I notate them as 'ws', 'wo,' and 'wio.' These notations are not parenthesized because relative pronouns are expressed in specified syntactic positions.

§3.2a One-verse instances

With the subject unexpressed or relativized it is possible to construct one-verse transitive clauses with normative weight. Constraints on frequency are far weaker than for the clauses in §3.1a and many verse types are represented. The examples in item (14) have unexpressed subjects. As printed in K4, 1889b qualifies for inclusion in the list of examples like (14a), but Pascual (2021) makes a strong case for emendation of the finite verb form to an infinitive governed by a verb of motion.

(14) (a) *bēagas / dǣlde* (80b)   (s)OV

        '(he) distributed rings'

    (b) *sinc-fato / sealde* (622a)   (s)OV

        '(she) handed out treasure-cups'

    (c) *symb(e)l-wynne / drēoh* (1782b; cf. 659b, 1760b, gen. obj.)   (s)OV

        '(you) enjoy the pleasures of feasting' (imperative)

Other examples like (14a): 14b, 119b, 131b, 152b, 154b, 166b, 169b, 172b, 179b, 204b, 226a, 241b, 259b, 315b, 341b, 390b, 401a, 422b, 423b, 564a, 633a, 654b, 667b, 668b, 682a, 711b, 742b, 874b, 895b, 943b, 1200b, 1205a, 1233b, 1239a, 1254a, 1265a, 1290b, 1421b, 1501b, 1519b, 1526b, 1545b, 1549a, 1564b, 1567a, 1619b, 1633b, 1656b, 1669b, 1687b, 1701b, 1723a, 1889b, 1904b, 1982b, 2027b, 2046b, 2055b, 2080b, 2097b, 2108b, 2121b, 2134a, 2141a, 2154b, 2231a (as emended), 2246b, 2296b, 2300a, 2319b, 2360b, 2431b, 2439b, 2469b, 2489b, 2535a, 2539b, 2576b, 2594b, 2610b, 2661b, 2662b, 2691b, 2706a, 2723b, 2776b, 2780b, 2793b, 2834a, 2930b, 3006a, 3007a, 3014a, 3014a, 3043b, 3131b; with dative object: 30a, 227b, 598b, 743a, 827b, 1014a, 1397b, 1533b, 1626b, 1993b, 2133b, 2370b, 2379a, 2540b, 2599a, 3119b; with unambiguously instrumental object: 2703b; with genitive object: 82b, 600b, 1217b, 1624b, 1627b, 1757b, 2055a, 2097b, 2298b, 2322b, 2953b.

Here as generally the most common clause pattern shows the fewest departures from SOV typology. Most instances have (s)OV order, like (14a–c). In
the clauses like (14c) the verb is an imperative left in its underlying final
position rather than fronted for emphasis. As a glance at the lists of other
examples will show, the vast majority of (s)OV clauses are b-verses, with the
finite verb in normative metrical location s4. A conspicuous formulaic technique in this group is substitution of a poetic compound for an ordinary
word. In (14b), for example, the reference is to a scene in which Queen
Wealhtheow hands out cups of mead to everyone in the hall. The cup presented to Beowulf is represented by the ordinary word *full* (verse 628b). The
compound *sinc-fæt* in (14b) refers to the same kind of cup but is unattested
in prose. A plural object like *fato* 'cups' is required here but *sinc-* is used
primarily to supply the required alliteration and fill out the line. Similar
clauses among the other examples include *sund-nytte drēah* 'engaged in
swimming skill' (2360b) and *nearo-þearfe drēah* 'encountered trouble-dis-
tress' (422b). In *sund-nytt* the essential constituent is the first one; in *nearo-
þearf* either constituent could serve as the essential one.

In item (15) the subject is relativized rather than unexpressed. The
stressed constituents observe normative OV order. In all instances the finite
verb occupies normative metrical location s4.

(15) *þæt mīne / **brēost** wereð* (453b)   wsOV

    'which protects my breast'

Other examples with accusative object: 103b, 1367b, 1610b, 1977b, 2041b,
2251b, 2898b, 2982b, 3073b, 3126b; with dative object: 52b, 143b, 1887b,
2595b, 2861b.

Relative pronouns are unacceptable in anacrusis and are restricted to clause-
initial syntactic position by rules of ordinary grammar. They are accordingly
restricted to metrical location x1 in a verse of category I.

In one-verse clauses the other possible arrangement with unexpressed
subjects is (s)VO, with verb and object out of normative order.

(16) (a) ***mǣton / mere*-*strǣta*** (514a)   (s)VO

        '(you two) measured the sea-street (ocean)'   Sx/Ssx (D6)

    (b) ***eah*todan / eorl-<u>scipe</u>** (3173a)   (s)VO

        '(they) praised heroic behavior'   Sxx/Ss (A6)

    (c) ***mearcað / mōr*-*hopu*** (450a)   (s)VO 'marks (traverses) the moor retreats'   Sx/Ssx (D6)

(d) *(on)fōh þissum / **fulle**, frēo-drihten mīn,*   (s)VO

    *sinces / **brytta*** (1169a–70a; cf. 1216a–17a)

    'receive this cup, my dear lord, distributor of treasure'   Sxx/Sx (A5)

(e) ***lēofa** / Bīowulf, **lǣst** eall / tela* (2663; cf. 2162b)   (s)VO

    'dear Beowulf, (you) endure everything well'   Ss/Sx (A3)

(f)   ***ðolod**(e) ǣr / fela*   (s)VO

    ***hond**-ge- / mōta* (1525b–26a)

    '(it) previously survived many (a one) of hand-to-hand combats'

                  ?Ss/Sx (A3)

Other examples with a non-reversible Sx/Ssx pattern: 204a, 496a, 1512a, 1610a, 2018a, 2051a, 2252a, 2439a, 2738a.

The (s)OV alternative to (16a), **mere-strǣta / mǣton,* would have the unacceptable pattern *Ssx/Sx (H5). The unacceptable result of OV order in (16b) would be ****eorl**-*scipe* / **eah**todan* (*Ss/Sxx: H1). On the other hand, the OV alternative to (16c) would have an acceptable type A3 pattern, Ss/Sx, with resolution of the secondary constituent *-hopu.* As a vivid, low-frequency main verb, *mearcað* is suitable for emphasis, the only apparent reason for fronting in this case. In the verses like (16d, e) an imperative verb is routinely fronted. The verb is the most prominent constituent in the opening verse of (16f), so VO order provides the best alignment of linguistic and metrical prominence here (OE 6.1). The K4 text underdots the final *-e* of *ðolode* for elision and the verse then scans as type A3. This is a somewhat problematic scansion, however. Elision does occur in Germanic alliterative verse but it is not very common and in the securely attested cases both adjacent vowels are unstressed.

    In addition to creating long heavy verses, OV order in (17a, b) would place an Sxs foot in first position.

(17) (a) ***wræc** / **Wedera** nīð* (423a; cf. 448a, 1150a)   (s)VO

    '(I) avenged the persecution of the Weders'   S/Sxs (D3)

(b) ***ȳðde** / **eotena** cyn* (421a; cf. 625a, 1274a)   (s)VO

    '(he) destroyed the kindred of the giants'   Sx/Sxs (D6)

The unacceptable alternatives for these verses would be *Sxs/S (M1) and *Sxs/Sx (MH1).

OV order would also have metrically unacceptable consequences in (18a–d).

(18) (a) **lufode** / *(ðā)* **lēode** (1982a)   (s)VO

'(he) cherished the people'   Sx/Sx (A1)

(b) *(of)***sæt** *þā* / *(þone)* **sele**-*gyst* (1545a)   (s)VO

'(she) then attacked the hall-guest'   Sx/Ss (A2)

(c) *for-* / **grand gramum** (424a, with dative object)   (s)VO

'(I) crushed the foes'   x/Ssx (C2)

(d) *ge-* / **myne mǣrþo** (659a)

'(you) remember fame' (be mindful of your reputation)

In (18a) the (s)OV alternative would have unnecessary anacrusis. In (18a) anacrusis is avoided altogether. In (18b) the anacrusis is of the ordinary prefixal kind. The unacceptable (s)OV alternative for (18c) is *Sx/S (O4), with *gramum* resolved obligatorily on the first lift (OE 8.1). Routine fronting of an imperative verb in (18d) avoids a rare variant of type A1 with an extrametrical prefix and an unresolved syllable on the second lift (K4: 330).

The remaining examples with a single object are in item (19).

(19) (a) **eg**sode / **eorlas** (6a)   (s)VO

'(he) awed the earls'   Sxx/Sx (A5)

(b) **wearp** / **wæl**-*fȳre* (2582a)   (s)VO

'(it) spewed deadly fire'   S/Ssx (D2)

(c) *(ā)***brēot** / **brim**-*wīsan* (2930a; cf. 501a)   (s)VO

'(he) destroyed the sea-kings'   (x)S/Ssx (D2 with anacrusis)

(d) **wunað** / **wæl**-*reste* (2902a; cf. 598a)   (s)VO

'(he) lives on (lies dead on) the slaughter-couch'   S/Ssx (D2)

(e) **bāt** / **bān**-*locan* (742a; cf. 1954a–57a)   (s)VO

'(he) bit the bone-locker (body)'   S/Ssx (D2)

When the most complex foot of normal weight, Sxx, shares the verse with a normative Sx foot, placement of the complex foot after the normative one contravenes the principle of closure in a particularly conspicuous way (UM

4, OE 3.6). When the second foot is realized as a finite verb, the alternative with OV order, Sx/Sxx (type D5), is almost entirely restricted to a pan-Germanic formula for introducing speeches (§1.14). In (19c), the alternative **brim**-*wīsan* / *(ā)***brēot** would eliminate the anacrusis but the usual reduction in complexity would be offset by placement of the weakly stressed alliterating verb on the subordinate S position in type E, which is more complex than type D due to departure from normative placement of the heavier foot in verse-final position (see OE 7.5). The complex type E alternative for (19d) would have resolution as well as alliteration on a finite verb occupying the subordinate S position. The only such example in *Beowulf* is **gold**ǣht *on-* / **gite** (2748a). In the alternative for (19e), **bān**-*locan* / **bāt,** there would be significant additive complexity due to placement of a short syllable on the s position, which is strongly dispreferred in type E (OE 8.3). The fronted verbs in item (19) are suitable for emphasis. They perform a significant rhetorical function that might be the most important reason for fronting in some cases. High-frequency *wunað* 'lives, inhabits, dwells' is normally inconspicuous but in (19d) it is used in a grimly ironic metaphor with a meaning contrary to expectation and its prominence is enhanced.

Item (20) is a double-object construction with a dative primary object and an accusative secondary object.

(20) (a) **cyning** / *ealdre binēat* (2396b)   (s)O^{2}O^{1}V

'(he) deprived the king of life / denied life to the king'

In the K4 glossary the verb is defined as 'deprive of' in reference to something in the dative-instrumental case. Translating as 'deprived the king of life' renders the animate argument as direct. As in items (13a, b), however, the oblique inanimate object in (20) shares a verse with the verb in normative OV order and the accusative animate object is more distant from the verb. In such constructions the inanimate object is apprehended as direct even though it has oblique case and the animate object is apprehended as indirect even though it has accusative case.

§3.2b Multi-verse instances

When they occupy separate verses in (s)OV clauses like (21a–c), verbs and objects can be modified with semantically inessential constituents that provide alliteration and perform other important metrical functions.

(21) (a) *oððe /* **hring**-*sele* **hon**dum / <u>styrede</u> (2840)   (s)O/V

       'or (someone) disturbed the ring-hall with hands'

  (b)   *ond his /* **ellen**-*weorc*   (s)O/V

    duguð*um /* **dēm**don (3173b–74a; cf. 283a–84a, 916a–17a)

       'and (they) honored his courageous work with praises'

  (c) *þēah ðe /* **hord**-*welan* **hēol**de / *lange* (2344)   (s)O/V

       'though (he) had long guarded the accumulated wealth'

Opening verses in other (s)O/V examples like (21a): 300a, 470a, 830a, 1091a, 1583a, 2477b.

The instances like (21a) are one-line clauses with the verb in normative metrical location s4. In the clauses like (21b) the verb alliterates optionally at metrical location s2 in a following line. In (21c) placement of the verb at metrical location s1a in the b-verse makes it possible to construct a one-line clause. The preceding verb subordinates the adverb so there is no violation of the rule of precedence (OE 6.1, OE 7.2).

Verses with modified objects are usually displaced to the right periphery, increasing the frequency of (s)V/O clauses relative to (s)O/V clauses.

(22) (a)   **þrym**mum / cwehte   (s)V/O

    mægen-<u>wudu</u> / **mun**dum (235b–36a)

       'mightily (he) shook the power-wood (spear) with hands'

  (b) *ond on /* **geogo**ðe *hēold* **gin**ne *rīce,*

    hord-*burh /* **hæle**þa (466; cf. 2253a–54a, as emended)   (s)V/O

       'and in youth (I) ruled a spacious kingdom (and) a treasure-fortress of heroes'

  (c) *ond æt /* **gū**ðe *forgrāp* **Gren**deles / mǣgum

    lāðan / cynnes (2353a–54a, dat. obj.)   (s)V/O

       'and in combat (I) crushed Grendel's family of a loathsome kindred'

Opening verses in other examples like (22a): 122b, 135a, 161b, 421b, 959b, 1405b, 1502b (dat. obj.), 1581b, 1663b (dat.obj.), 1749b, 1811b, 1959b, 2179b, 2393b, 2614b, 2748b, 2897b (gen. obj.).

In (22a) the verb stands at normative metrical location s4. In (22b) placement of the verb at location s2 allows for realization of the clause as a line. In (22c) placement of the alliterating verb on the s position of a type B2 verse contravenes OE 7.5. Movement of the verb to the S position would do more harm than good in this case because the verse contains a fixed SP, *ond*. If the verb were fronted the result would be *(ond for)grāp æt / gūðe*, with disyllabic anacrusis that includes a conjunction.

In (23a–e) the verb alliterates on the first S position of the verse.

(23) (a) *ā-* / *lēdon þā* *lēofne* / *þēoden*,   (s)V/O

     bēaga / *bryttan*,   *on* / *bearm* scipes,

      mærne / *(be) mæste* (34a–36a)

     'then they laid down the beloved lord, giver of rings, famous, in the interior of the ship'

   (b) *ond be-* / *timbredon* *on* / *tȳndagum*   (s)V/O

     beadu-rōfes / *bēcn* (3159a–60a; cf. 96a–97a, 2933)

     'and in a ten-day period (they) built the monument of the battle-bold (man)'

   (c) *(of)slōh ðā* / *(æt þǣre) sæcce*,   *þā mē* / *sǣl āgeald*,   (s)V/O

     hūses / *hyrdas* (1665a–66a; cf. 1557a–59a)

     'then in the fighting — when opportunity offered for me — (I) slew the guardians of the house'

   (d) *sǣlde* / *(tō) sande* *sīd-fæþme* / *scip*   (s)V/O

     onc(e)r-bendum / *fæst* (1917a–18a; cf. 2936)

     '(he) secured the broad-beamed ship to the sand firmly with anchor lines'

   (e) *healdeð* / *hige-mǣðum* *hēafod-* / *wearde*   (s)V/O

     lēofes / *(ond) lāðes* (2909a–10a)

     'he maintains the death-watch of a beloved (one) and a loathed (one) for the sake of a weary-hearted one (for Beowulf's sake)'

Opening verses in other examples like (23a): 2516a, 2800b (imperative), 2968b.

Verb placement causes minimal complexity in the type I examples. In (23a) the verb is followed by a less prominent adverb and verb-initial order aligns linguistic and metrical prominence in compliance with OE 6.1. In (23b) the verb alliterates as the only stressed syllable in the verse. Placement of the verb at metrical location s1a in type II verses avoids violation of higher-ranking constraints in (23c–e). In (23c) verb-initial order avoids placement of an alliterating verb on an s position in type B, contravening OE 7.5. In the examples like (23d) verb-final order would create unacceptable anacrusis in the opening verse. In (23e) the unacceptable result of verb-final order would be *__hige-mǣðum__ / __healdeð__ (*Ssx/Sx: H5). In many of these instances placement of the verb at location s1a also makes it possible to arrange the major constituents as a single line, reducing complexity in another way (OE 1.1).

In (24a–d) an indirect object is added.

(24) (a)   *nallas* / __bēa__*gas geaf*   (s)OV/Io

       __Denum__ *æfter* / __dōme__ (1719b–20a)

           '(he) by no means gave rings to the Danes after fame' (in pursuit of fame)

     (b)   *hāres* / __hyrste__   __Hige__*-lāce* / __bær__ (2988)   (s)O/IoV

          '(he) bore the armor of the old (man) to Hygelac'

     (c)   __man__*-dryhtne* / __bær__   (s)IoV/O

       __fǣ__*ted* / *wǣge* (2281b–82a)

          'he bore the ornamented cup to (his) earthly lord'

     (d)   __word__*-rihta* / <u>*fela*</u>   (s)O/VIo

       __sægde__ / *(ge)sīðum* (2631b–32a)

          '(he) gave a lot of spoken instructions to his companions'

     (e)   *ond on-* / __sǣl__ *meoto,*   (s)VO/Io

       sige-hrēð[,] / __secgum__ (489b–90a)

          'and unfold (your) story, glory of victory, for men' (imperative)

Opening verses in other examples like (24a): 97b, 2937b; like (24c): 1178b (imperative), 2470a, 2810b, 2997a.

In the clauses like (24a) a heavy indirect object is displaced to the right periphery and the verb shares the verse with the direct object in normative order, as usual. In (24b–e) the modified direct object is too large to share the verse with the verb and is displaced to the right periphery. The indirect object and the verb share a verse in normative order in (24b, c). Departure from normative IoV order in (24d) avoids *__(ge)sīðum__ / __sægde,__ with unacceptable anacrusis (OE 9.6). Verb fronting is routine in (24e), an imperative construction.

Items (25a, b) are double-object constructions with an unexpressed subject.

(25) (a)   *þæt* / __syð__*þan nā*   (s)O^2/O^{1}V

> *ymb* / **brontne** *ford* **brim-** / *līðende*
>
> *lāde* / *(ne)* **let**ton (567b–69a)
>
> 'so that they did not deny the seafarers a journey'

  (b)   **frioðo**-*wǣre* / **bǣd**   (s)O^{1}V/O^2

> *hlā*ford / *sīnne* (2282b–83a)
>
> 'he asked his lord forgiveness'

Both primary inanimate objects have oblique genitive case and both second-ary animate objects are accusative. The inanimate objects share a verse with the verb in normative order as usual, with the animate objects more remote.

When a relative pronoun is the only major constituent in the opening verse, as in (26a–d), I follow 'ws' by a slash and interpret the clause as a multi-verse instance. As expected, word order is OV when the direct object shares a verse with the verb. There are no exceptions with ws/VO order.

(26) (a)   *nō his* / **līf**-*gedāl*   ws/OV

> *sārlīc* / *þūhte* **secga** / *ǣnegum*
>
> *þāra þe* / **tīr**-*lēases* **trode** / *scēawode* (841b–43b)
>
> 'by no means did his separation from life seem painful to any of the men who inspected the track of the (one) bereft of triumph'

  (b) *sē þe un-* / **murn**līce **mād**mas / *dǣleþ,*   ws/OV

> *eor*les / **ǣr**-*gestrēon* (1756a–57a)
>
> 'who unregretfully deals out treasures, ancient wealth of earls'

  (c)   *sē þe* / *longe hēr*   ws/OV

> *on ðyssum* / **win**-*dagum* **worolde** / *brūceð* (1061b–62b, gen. obj.)
>
> 'who experiences the world here for a long time in these days of strife'

  (d)   *sē ðe* / **waldendes**

> *hyl*do *ge-* / **healdeþ** (2292b–93a; cf. 2364b–65a)   ws/OV
>
> 'who retains the ruler's favor'

Opening verses in other examples like (26a): 909a (dat. obj.), 1051a, 1407a, 1686a, 2272a, 2383a; like (26b): 1135a, 2212a, 2407a.

The preceding clause is included in item (26a) to illustrate relations between pronouns and their antecedents. The relative pronoun *þe* in this example is preceded by the pronoun *ðāra*, a genitive personal pronoun that has **secga** as its antecedent in the main clause. The fixed position of relative pronouns is clause-initial because that places them closer to the antecedent in the main clause, in accord with iconicity of distance (§1.4). The tendency toward initial placement of subjects in human languages can be explained in the same way, since subjects are typically familiar from previous discourse and pronoun subjects often have antecedents in the preceding clause. An alternative to (26a) with a personal pronoun subject would translate as 'by no means did his separation from life seem painful to the men. They inspected the track,' etc. Iconicity of distance can also be achieved by fronting an object pronoun closer to its antecedent. Case-matching pronouns like *þāra* are optional before a relative pronoun and add the same kind of clarification provided by optional fronting of a pronoun object. Since the evident purpose of pronouns like *þāra* is to clarify the relation of the relative pronoun to its antecedent, I interpret two-word constructions like *þāra þe* as compound relative pronouns and translate them with a single Modern English word, as in (26a–d).

Clauses with relative pronouns are adjuncts to a sub-constituent of a larger clause. They tend to be shorter in *Beowulf* than clauses with unexpressed subjects and to employ fewer modified constituents. Most instances of ws/OV are one-line sentences like (26a) or syntactically complete one-line clauses like (26b) with a semantically inessential adjunct in the following line. Item (26c) begins in the b-verse and the finite verb occupies normative location s4 in the following line. The clauses in (26d) begin in the b-verse and the verb occupies metrical location s2 in the following a-verse. Enjambment in the cited example appears immediately after the opening verse as usual.

The remaining instances with relative pronouns have the object and the verb in separate verses. Most are like (27a–d), with wsO/V order. As we have seen in §3.1b, S/OV has far higher frequency than SO/V, which splits the constituents of the verb phrase and groups an extraneous object with the stressed subject. The poet is less reluctant to group a stressed object with a relativized subject. This is not unexpected. Relative pronouns have been fronted to higher-level positions and lie outside the core of the clause (Radford 1997: 305–7), which is the usual domain of application for typological constraints on the ordering of movable words (§1.8). In the opening verse of a wsO/V clause the object is the *only* constituent of the core — not extraneous to another major constituent of the core — and the extraneous relative pronoun cannot be relocated. Clauses like (27a), with wsO/V structure, are not much less frequent than clauses like (26a), with ws/OV structure. There is a similar elevation of relative frequency for s/VO, where the unstressed SP subject is largely restricted to metrical location x1 by Kuhn's

first law and the SPMR (§3.5). In both kinds of clause, constraints on placement of the subject thwart employment of the OV/S and O/SV orders that
are preferred for alliteration on the object when all constituents are stressed
and movable.

(27) (a) *þāra þe / **lēod**-fruman   **lan**ge / (be)gēate* (2130)   wsO/V

   'which befell the leader of the people for a long time'

   (b)   *sē ðe / **worna** fela[,]*   wsO/V

   ***gum**-cystum / **gōd**[,] **gūð**a / (ge)dīgde,*

   ***hil**de- / **hlem**ma* (2542b–44a; cf. 2807b–08b)

   'who, strong in manly virtues, survived a great number of wars, of battle-
   clashes'

   (c)   *sē þe / **sōð** ond riht*   wsO/V

   ***fremeð** on / **fol**ce* (1700b–01a)

   'who supports truth and justice among the people'

   (d)   *sē ðe / **flō**da begong*   wsO/V

   ***heoro**-gīfre / (be)**hēold   hund** / missera,*

   ***grim** ond / **grǣ**dig* (1497b–99a)

   'who, very ravenous, ruled that domain of waters for a hundred seasons,
   grim and greedy'

   (e) *sē þe ǣr / **lange** tīd   **lēof**ra / **man**na [,]*   ws/O/V

   ***fūs** æt / **faro**ðe[,]   **feor** / **wlā**tode* (1915–16, gen. obj.)

   'who for a long time previously sought (looked for) the beloved man, eager
   at the shore'

   (f)   *sē þe / **fela** ǣror*   wsO/Io/V

   ***mō**des / **myrð**e   **man**na / cynne,*

   fyren**e[,] / (ge)**fremede (809b–11a)

   'who previously caused much grief of mind (and) injustices for the kindred
   of men'

Opening verses in other examples like (27a): 79a, 370a, 378a, 3086a; like
(27d): 869a, 993b, 2685a.

The verse with the verb has room for semantically inessential constituents
like *lange* in (27a), *on folce* in (27c), and *heorogīfre* in (27d). Instances like
(27a) are syntactically complete one-line clauses with the verb in normative
location s4. In (27b) the clause begins in the b-verse and the verb appears

at normative location s4 in the following line. In (27c) the verb occupies metrical location s1a and the following noun alliterates in accord with the rule of precedence (OE 6.1, OE 7.2). Here verb-initial order avoids *on / **folce fremeð**, with a resolved and alliterating verb on an s position in type B, which would contravene OE 7.5 and OE 8.5 as well. In the verses like (27d) the verb appears at location s2, where alliteration is optional. In (27e) there are no movable major constituents in the opening verse so a slash is placed after 'ws' in the notation. In (27f) direct and indirect objects occupy separate verses so departure from normative IoO order is unremarkable. Though closer to the verb than **mōdes / myrðe, manna** / cynne is not in close syntactic composition with the verb, which shares a verse with *fyrene,* a variation of the inanimate direct object. Phrases like *fyrene (ge)fremede* can be used whether the noun is an object argument or a variation.

In (28a–c) a type II verse containing the object is displaced to the right periphery. In (28c) the relative pronoun is the only major constituent of the opening verse.

(28) (a) *þone ðe* / **oft** *gebād*   *īsern-* / *scūre* (3116; cf. 495)   wsV/O

   'who often lived through iron showers (attacks with spears or arrows)'

   (b)   *sē þe ǣr æt* / **sæcce** *gebād*   wsV/O

   wīg-*hryre* / **wrāðra** (1618b–19a; cf. 2042b–43a, 2258b–59b, 3003b–5b)

   'who at a battle often experienced the downfall in combat of enemies'

   (c) *þām ðe* / **unrihte**   **in**ne / *(ge)hȳdde*   ws/V/O

   wrǣtte / *(under)* **wealle** (3059a–60a; cf. 1428a–30a, 1796a–97a)

   'who wrongly hid ornaments under the wall inside'

In the opening verses of (28a–c) the poet uses adverbial modifiers to displace the verb from metrical location s1a, the least appropriate location for finite verbs and the only position in which they are normally required to alliterate. Each modifier is semantically inessential and provides the only alliteration for the verse it occupies. In (28a) placement of the verb at metrical location s3 makes it possible to express the major constituents as a single line. In (28b) opening the clause in a b-verse places the verb at normative metrical location s4. In (28c) the relative pronoun shares the opening verse with a semantically inessential constituent that supplies the alliteration.

§3.3 Instances with an unexpressed or relativized object, including instances with unexpressed or relativized subjects

Objects are expressed more often than subjects because they refer less often to something previously mentioned. Unexpressed objects, as defined here, occur with verbs that are normally transitive. When such verbs appear without an expressed object, information in the immediate context usually makes it clear what object is intended (OES 1: 232–34). Consider for example verse 48b, *lēton holm beran* '(they) let the sea bear (him).' The note to this verse in K4 posits an understood object because *beran* normally takes a direct object and the understood object is the topic of discussion in preceding clauses.

Verbs with understood objects differ from intransitive verbs that are etymologically related to a transitive verb with the same linguistic root. These genuinely intransitive verbs occur without objects independently of the context, as in *oak firewood burns well,* where intransitive *burns* has the same form as transitive *burns* in *she burns firewood to heat her cabin.* An Old English intransitive verb of this kind is *beornan* 'burn,' which is identical in form to the etymologically related transitive form. The subject of such intransitive verbs corresponds to the object of the corresponding transitive verb. Constructions with a single major constituent are relatively uninformative with respect to the major line of argument in this book. When the single constituent is a verb, however, placement within the metrical line provides some useful information about basic sentence structure. I treat constructions without expressed arguments as verse clauses if a verb is expressed. Some examples are discussed in this section.

§3.3a One-verse instances

In (291a–f) the object is easy to identify because one or more immediately preceding clauses have a coreferential object and that object is expressed in the first such clause. The close relation to the preceding clause is often marked by a conjunction, as in (29a–c).

(29) (a) *swā his / **fæder** āhte* (2608b)   (o)SV
      'since his father owned (it)'

    (b) *ond ge- / **læste** swā* (2990b)   (so)V
       'and (he) performed (it) thus'

    (c) *ond be / **heal**se genam* (1872a, 1101b)   (so)V
       'and (he) took (him) by the neck'

(d) *gēafon / (on) gārsecg* (49a; cf. 1159a)   (so)V

   '(they) relinquished (him) to the ocean'

(e) *slāt / unwearnum* (741b)   (so)V

   '(he) rent (him) irresistibly'

Other (o)SV examples like (29a): 24a, 93b, 490b, 666b, 706b, 1503b 1786b, 1975b; other (so)V examples like (29b): 532a, 1452b, 1453a, 1718a, 2917a, 2983a, 3176a.

Fronting is required in the cited example for (29b) because type A7 verses like *ond swā ge- / lǣste* are unacceptable in the b-verse. Placement of the verb at metrical location s1a avoids unnecessary anacrusis in the clauses like (29d). In (29e) fronting provides rhetorical emphasis on a vivid verb in the blow-by-blow description of Grendel eating a warrior (§2.3). Fronting is required for alliteration here but not for any other evident metrical reason. With the appropriate change in alliteration the verse would be a two-word variant of type E (Ssx/S).

In Modern English, 'it' can be used as the object of a main clause in constructions like *I resent it that you have failed to pay me*, where *it* anticipates a following that-clause. Similar constructions in *Beowulf* usually employ the neuter pronoun *þæt* in both clauses, as for example in *ic þæt gehȳre, þæt þis is hold weorod* 'I hear it that this is a loyal troop' (line 290). In (30a–e) *þæt* is unexpressed in the main clause. In such instances the unexpressed object in the main clause is understood from an immediately following clause rather than from a close antecedent. In the examples like (30d) the unexpressed object is understood from a following indirect question. Item (30e) is a similar instance followed by a direct question.

(30) (a) *ðā se / eorl ongeat* (1512b)   (o)SV

      'then the earl understood (that)'

   (b) *secgað / sǣ-līðend* (411a; cf. 2329a)   (o)VS

      'seafarers say (that)'

   (c) *wordum / bǣdon* (176b)   (so)V

      '(they) asked (that) with words'

   (d) *men ne / cunnon* (162b; cf. 1313b, 3067b)   (o)SV

      'men do not know (that)

   (e) *meþel-wordum / frægn* (236b)   (so)V

'(he) asked (that which follows) with formal words'

Other (o)SV examples like (30a): 857b, 967b, 987b, 1522b, 2650b, 2874b, 3129b; other (so)V examples like (30c): 67b, 536a, 821b, 2156b, 2187a.

The two (o)VS examples in item (32b) front the finite verb to its least appropriate location and contravene the strong preference for normative ordering of stressed major constituents that share a verse. In the cited example fronting the verb to location s1a avoids *Ssx/Sx (H5). Fronting in *Beowulf* 2329a eliminates easily avoidable anacrusis.

Items (31a–c) have relativized arguments. In (31d) a following relative clause specifies the referent of an unexpressed object.

(31) (a) *ðāra þe ne / wēndon* (937a)   ws(o)V

       'who did not expect (that)' (anticipating a that-clause)

    (b)   *þone / god sende*

      folce / (tō) frōfre (13b; cf. 1123b–4a)   woSV

       'whom God sent as a consolation to the people'

    (c) *þæs se / man gespræc* (1398b)   woSV

       'what the man said'

    (d)   *bill / ǣr gescōd*   (o)SV

     — *ecg wæs / īren* — *eald- / hlāfordes* (2777b–78b)

     'the old lord's sword — its edge was iron — injured (someone)'

Item (31a) has an unexpressed object and a relativized subject. Verse-initial *ðāra* matches a genitive noun antecedent in the main clause. The object is relativized in (31b, c). In (31c) genitive *þæs* does double duty: it is the oblique genitive object of *þancian* 'thank' in the preceding main clause as well as the relativized object of the subordinate clause.

§3.3b. Multi-verse instances

In (32a–f) a direct object is unexpressed. In (32d) as generally I interpret adjectives like *grim* as zero-converted subjects when no other subject is expressed in the verse clause.

(32) (a)   *gomela / Scilding,*   (o)/S/V

*fela- / fric*gende[,] *feorran / rehte* (2105b–6b)

'the old Scylding, knowing many things, recited (something) from long ago'

(b)   *nymþe / līges fæþm*   (o)S/V

swulge / (on) swaþule (781b–82a)

'unless the embrace of fire swallowed (it) in flame'

(c) *ofer- / hogode* ðā   *hringa / fengel* (2345; cf. 480–81, 1465a–66a)   (o)V/S

'the lord of rings scorned (that)' (anticipating a that-clause)

(d)   *fæste / hæfde*   (o)V/S

grim on / grāpe (554b–55a)

'the fierce (one) had (me) firmly in (her) grip'

(e)   *þrȳð-swȳð be- / hēold*   (o)V/S

mæg / Higelāces (736b–37a)

'the mighty strong kinsman of Hygelac beheld (that)'

(f)   *hider / ūt ætbær*   (so)V/Io

cyninge / mīnum (3092b–93a)

'(I) brought (it) outside to my king'

In (32a) the stressed constituents are in normative order and the stressed verb occupies normative metrical location s4. In (32b) the verb is fronted to avoid *(on) swaþule / swulge,* with the easily avoidable anacrusis that is ruled out by OE 9.6. In (32c) a rearrangement of the constituents in normative order would end the line with ðā *ofer- / hogode,* violating the constraint against placement of type A7 in the b-verse. Rearrangement to achieve normative order in the other instances like (32c) would violate the same constraint. The two verses in (32d) must satisfy contrasting alliterative requirements and no rearrangement of their constituents would be acceptable with the stressed verb in its normative syntactic position at the end of the clause. What the poet *could* do here was to situate the stressed verb at normative metrical location s4 by placing an alliterating adverb on the first lift of the b-verse. The poet also situates the verb at normative location s4 in (32e, f). In (32e) a compound adjective is split by hyperbaton from the heavy noun phrase it modifies, which is too large to share a verse with the adjective. In (32f) a heavy indirect object is displaced to the right periphery.

In (33a, b) an object is relativized.

(33) (a)   *þone* ðe / *Grendel* ær   woS/V

> *mā*ne / *(ā)cwealde* (1054b–55a)
>
> 'whom Grendel wickedly killed earlier'

(b) *þē ūs / sēceað tō Swēona / lēoda* (3001)   woV/S

   'which the people of the Swedes seek from us'

(c) *ðǣm tō / hām forgeaf Hrēþel / Gēata*   wioV/S/O

   *ān*gan / *dohtor* (374a–75a)

   'to whom at home (in exogamic marriage) Hrethel of the Geats gave his
   own daughter'

Opening verses in other examples like (33a): 70a, 878a, 2048a.

The instances like (33a) have normative syntactic placement of the major
constituents. The other examples like (33a) are one-line clauses with the
verb at normative metrical location s4. In (33b) a heavy subject phrase has
been moved to the right periphery. Constituents of the postpositional phrase
ūs tō 'at us, from us' are split by hyperbaton. In (33c) the relativized object
is indirect. Placing the modified subject in the opening verse would create
unacceptable anacrusis here. The heavy arguments are accordingly displaced
to the right periphery, where they observe normative SO order. Alliteration
in the opening verse is supplied by the adjunct prepositional phrase *tō ham*
'at home,' which is semantically inessential but provides a concrete detail
relevant to the immediate context.

§3.4 Clauses with an unexpressed verb

Analysis of poetic word order depends crucially on the position of the verb
in relation to other constituents. I do not discuss constructions as verse
clauses if no verbal constituent is expressed. Constructions with an unexpressed finite verb are discussed only if an infinitive or participle is expressed
(chapters 8–10). In constructions with unexpressed verbs, nouns that resemble arguments can often be interpreted as appositions rather than as reduced
clauses. Consider item (34) for example.

(34) *ge- / grētte þā guma / ōþerne,*   V/SO

   *Hrōð*gār / *Bēowulf* (652a–53a)

   'one man, Hrothgar, greeted the other, Beowulf'

Here instead of interpreting *Hrōðgār Bēowulf* as a clause with the verb *gegrētte* unexpressed I interpret each name as a variation of a noun in the preceding line and include 653a in the number span for the verse clause.

§3.5 Clauses with an unstressed SP subject and all other major constituents stressed

Clauses with unstressed arguments provide an opportunity to assess constraints on SPs that occupy unstressed positions in the opening verse. In many instances Kuhn's Laws do not make the required distinctions among unstressed metrical locations and placement of SPs is determined by rules of the universalist theory.

§3.5a One-verse instances

Like unexpressed arguments, pronoun arguments leave good room for other major constituents in a clause. There are many one-verse sOV constructions with SP pronoun subjects. All instances are of type B or C, with the unstressed SP in normative metrical location x1. Kuhn's laws do not explain why these unstressed SPs rarely occupy an unstressed location after the first stress. In the universalist theory this is explained by verse-level constraints that restrict placement of SPs at metrical locations normally occupied by unstressed prefixes and negative particles with the lowest prominence (OE 9.2).

(35) (a) *hēo þā / **fǣhðe** wræc* (1333b)   sOV

        'she avenged the feud'

    (b) *þæt hē his / **frēond** wrece* (1385a)   sOV

        'that he should avenge his friend'

Other examples like (35a): 7b (gen. obj.), 108b, 114b, 247b, 366b, 383b, 392b, 417b, 420b, 522b, 563b, 599b, 628b, 798b, 950b, 1207b, 1273b, 1355b, 1370b, 1470b (dat. obj.), 1613b, 1664b (dat. obj.), 1739b, 1849b, 1966b, 2127b, 2150b, 2355b, 2446b, 2633b, 2653b, 2698b (gen. obj.), 2732b, 2818b, 2834b, 3000b (as emended); like (35b): 80a, 437a, 2620a 2633a, 2989a (dat. obj).

Most instances are b-verse clauses like item (35a), with the stressed finite verb on a subordinate lift at normative metrical location s4. The clauses like (35b) have the verb on a subordinate lift at metrical location s2.

There are predictably fewer sVO instances like (36a–c), where constituents sharing a verse are out of normative order and the verb occupies metrical location s1a.

(36) (a) *þæt ge- / **bearh** fēore* (1548b)   sVO

      'that protected life'

  (b)   *ic ge- / **nēðde** <u>fela</u>*   sVO

      *gūða / (on) **geogoðe*** (2511b-12a)

      'I survived a multitude of battles in youth'

  (c) *(hē ge)**fēng** þā / **fetel**-hilt(,)   freca / Scyldinga[,]*

      *hrēoh ond / **heoro**-grim* (1563a)   sVO or VO/S

      'he (or 'the warrior of the Scyldings') grasped the linked sword, rough and

      battle-grim'

In (36a) is a rare example with a finite verb that alliterates before a more prominent noun that does not alliterate, contravening OE 7.2. The verb is suitable for emphatic fronting, with low frequency and high information content. The poet expends much artistic effort to provide the alliteration required by OE 7.2 but will occasionally disregard this rule to provide emphasis. Clauses like (36a) show that emphatic fronting has a semantic motivation and is not a purely metrical device. In most cases it increases effort rather than reducing effort; in occasional instances like (36a) it creates unusual complexity rather than reducing complexity. In (36b) *fela* 'much, many, a great number' is a high-frequency quantifier that functions as the object. The low prominence of *fela* makes it appropriate for the less prominent lift, so linguistic and metrical prominence are properly aligned in accord with OE 6.1 and there is no violation of OE 7.2. Item (36c) has alliteration on the following noun, in conformity with OE 7.2, but is remarkable for another reason. It is the only clause with an unstressed pronoun in anacrusis at location x5, the least suitable location for SPs of major category like pronouns. This may be an example of syntactic modernization. When the *Beowulf* manuscript was produced in the late tenth or early eleventh century, unexpressed pronoun subjects were already less common than when the poem was composed. A scribe in the later era might well add such pronouns reflexively (K4: cxlix–cl). With removal of *hē*, removal of the editorial

140

comma, and insertion of a comma before the semantically inessential adjectives, we have an unremarkable alternative with ordinary prefixal anacrusis and *freca Scyldinga* as a heavy displaced subject rather than a variation.

In (37a, b) a low-frequency verb suitable for emphasis is fronted to a stressed position before the unstressed subject in a verse of normative type A1, the type most tolerant of metrical complexity. This stressed metrical position coincides with the syntactic 'C(OMP) position,' the site occupied by a complementizer like 'that' if one is present. When not filled by a complementizer the C position can be occupied by a fronted verb, which can be stressed or unstressed. In these particular instances fronting of the prominent verb to the unfilled C position in the main clause is promoted by negation of the verb (§§1.5, 1.8).

(37) (b) *(ne) hēdde / (hē þæs) heafolan* (2697a, gen. obj.)   VsO

    'he did not heed (pay attention to) the head'

  (d) *(ne ge)feah hē /(þǣre) fǣhðe* (109a, gen. obj.)   VsO

    'he did not enjoy that feud'

In addition to conforming with Old English syntactic norms, placement of the unstressed pronouns after the verb in (37a, b) is preferable to placing them before the verb at normative location x1. With VsO order we have a common kind of monosyllabic anacrusis in (37a) and the usual kind of disyllabic anacrusis in (37b). With sVO order the anacruses would be unlike anything attested in *Beowulf,* with location x5 occupied by *hē þæs* in (37a) and by *hē þǣre* in (37b).

In (38a, b) placement of an unstressed subject pronoun in anacrusis is avoided by fronting stressed objects.

(38) (a)   *metod hīe / (ne) cūþon*   O s V

    dǣda / dēmend (180b)

    'they did not know the Creator, judge of deeds'

  (b) *Gode / (ic) þanc secge* (1997b)   Io.sOV

    'to God I say thanks'

The fronted objects are lexical nouns suitable for emphasis. The K4 text indicates elision between *gode* and *ic* in (38b). Both adjacent vowels are unstressed here, as in clear cases of elision between the lifts in type B variants

141

(Russom 1998: 139–44). In (38b), as usual, the inanimate direct object is in close construction with the verb and the indirect object is more distant.

§3.5b Multi-verse instances

The clauses in item (39) have the subject in one verse and constituents of the verb phrase in a following verse where they observe normative order. The examples like (39a, b) have the verb at normative metrical location s4.

(39) (a) *þæt hē / **Hrōþgāres hām** ge- / sōhte* (717)   s/OV

   'that he sought out Hrothgar's home'

   (b) *hū hē / **wērig-mōd** on / **weg** þanon,*   s/OV

   ***nīða** / (ofer)cumen,   on / **nicera** <u>mere</u>*

   ***fǣge** / (ond ge)**flȳmed   feorh**-lāstas / bær* (844a–46b)

   'how he, weary-hearted, overcome in respect of the hostile encounters, doomed and put to flight, bore the remains of his life away from there into the bay of water monsters'

   (c) ***hwīlum** / **hilde-dēor   hearpan** / wynne,*   s/OV

   gomen**-<u>wudu</u> / **grētte (2107a–8a)

   'at times the battle-bold (man) coaxed joy from the harp, glee from the wooden instrument'

   (d)   *þæt wit on / **gār**secg ūt*   s/OV

   ***al**drum / nēðdon* (537b–38a; cf. 1326b–27a)

   'that we risked our lives out on the sea'

Opening verses in other one-line examples like (39a): 88a, 132a, 279a, 508a, 562a, 1102a, 1129a, 1204a, 1206a, 1334a, 1589a, 1721a, 1946a, 2075a, 2084a, 2114a, 2385a, 2391a, 2528a, 2534a, 2839a, 2850a, 2973a, 3027a; in examples like (39b): 1a, 623a, 1182b, 1351b, 2093b, 2099b, 2135a, 2351b; like (39c): 634a, 958a, 1892a, 2028a, 2115a, 2132b, 2468a, 2943a.

The examples like (39a) are single lines or one-line clauses followed by adjunct verses. In the examples like (39b) the space between subject and object is filled by adjunct phrases and the verb appears at the end of a later line. Many of these adjunct phrases add detail relevant to the immediate context. In (39b), for example, the second, third, and fifth verses contribute to a representation of abject defeat. When a stressed verb occupies metrical location s2, alliteration on the verb is optional but the poet usually supplies it, as in (39c). The only exceptions are those in (39d). In (39a–d) the poet goes well beyond minimum requirements of the verse form.

In (40a–d) a stressed indirect object is placed in the usual way, either before or after a verse shared by the direct object and the finite verb.

(40) (a) *hē þǣm* / ***bāt**-wearde* ***bun**den* / *golde*   sIo/OV

            ***swurd** ge-* / ***seal**de* (1900a–01a; cf. 2157)

            'he gave a sword bound with gold to the boat-guardian'

    (b)   *þǣr hē* / ***worna**<u>*fela*</u>*   s/Io/OV

            Sige**-* / *Scyldingum*   ***sorge / *(ge)<u>fremede</u>,*

            ***yrm**ðe* / *(tō) aldre* (2003b–5a)

            'where he caused a lot of sorrows for the Victory-Scyldings, misery forever'

    (c)   *þā hē þæs* / ***wǣp**nes onlāh*   sOV/Io

            ***sēl**ran* / ***sweord**-frecan* (1467b–68a, with genitive object)

            'when he loaned the weapon to a better swordsman'

    (d) *ful oft ic for* / ***lǣs**san* ***lēan*** / *teohhode,*   s/OV/Io

            ***hord**-* / *weorþunge* ***hnā**hran* / *rince,*

            ***sǣm**ran* / *(æt) **sæc**ce* (951a–53a)

            'very often I provided a reward, a treasure-honor, to a poorer warrior, worse in combat'

In (40a, b) all constituents observe normative order. In (40c, d) a modified indirect object is displaced to the right periphery. The textbook examples of Old English indirect objects are beneficiaries. As Mitchell observes, however (OES 1: 567–68), a bare dative noun can also be used for victims. The indirect object (40b) is a DATIVE OF DISADVANTAGE that represents something unpleasant given to an unfortunate recipient, as in constructions like *the judge gave a three-year sentence to Light-fingered Lou.*

In (41a–d) the poet obtains the required alliteration and reduces total verse complexity by placement of an indirect object in the same verse with the verb, leaving the direct object more distant in these unusual instances. OE *feondum* in the cited example for (41a) is a dative of disadvantage of the kind sometimes called a DATIVE OF SEPARATION (OES 1: 568), representing someone deprived of something rather than given something.

(41) (a)   *ic þæt* / ***hilt** þanan*   sO/IoV

fēondum / (æt)ferede (1668b–69a)

'I took that hilt away from the foes'

(b)   oft hīo / **bēah**-wriðan   sO/IoV

secge / **seal**de (2018b–19a)

'often she gave a ring-band to a warrior'   sO/IoV

(c)   þǣr hīo / **nægled** sinc

hæleðum / sealde (2023b–24a)

'where she gave studded treasure to warriors'

(d) swylce þū ðā / **mādm**as   þē þū / **mē** sealdest,   sO/IoV

Hrōðgār / lēofa,   **Higel**āce / (on)send (1482–43)

'likewise, dear Hrothgar, you send to Higelac the treasures you gave to me'

Placement of the object in the same verse with the verb here would create problems even with the required changes in alliteration. In (41a) the result would be *(þæt) **hilt** æt- / ferede, with unnecessary anacrusis. In (41b) the OV alternative **bēah**-wriðan / sealde scans as *Ssx/Sx (H5). Kaluza's law (OE 8.6) rules out resolution of -wriðan, so this alternative could not be scanned as Ss/Sx (type A3). In (41c) the OV alternative would be ***nægled** sinc / sealde, a b-verse with the unacceptable pattern *Sxs/Sx (MH1). The OV alternative in (41d) would be ðā / **mādm**as onsend, a type B2 variant (x/Sxxs). This variant is acceptable under certain conditions but it is light relative to the A1 norm and employs the most complex foot pattern, Sxxs. As we have seen (§1.19), the additive complexity of such verses is governed by the principle of closure and severely restricts their placement late in the clause. B2 variants ending in a finite verb appear 95 of 96 times as the first verse of a clause. The only instance placed later is tō / Heorute ātēah 'took to Heorot' (766b). Type E variants like **Higel**āce / (on)send, though rendered somewhat complex by employment of an extrametrical prefix, appear after the opening verse in seven of eighteen instances and were clearly considered more suitable for late placement. Satisfying alliterative requirements was one reason for departure from normative object placement in (41a–d) but not the only reason.

The most common realization of sO/V fits the major constituents into a single line with the verb in normative location s4, as in (42a).

(42) (a) þæt ðū þone / **wæl**-gǣst **wih**te / (ne) grētte (1995)   sO/V

'that you should by no means confront the slaughterous demon'

(b)   *tō þæs þe hē / **wīn**-reced,*   sO/V

     *gold-<u>sele</u> / **gumen**a,   **gearw**ost / wisse,*

     *f**ǣt**um / **fāh**ne* (714b–16a)

     'to the point where he most clearly perceived the wine-building, gold-hall of men, decorated with ornaments'

(c)   *þæt hē þā / **wēa**-lāfe **weot**ena / dōme*   sO/V

     ārum / hēolde (1949b–51a)

     'that he would maintain the survivors of calamity with honors by wise men's advice'

(d)   *hīe / **dȳgel** lond*   sO/V

     ***war**igeað, / **wulf**-hleoþu, **wind**ige / næssas,*

     *frēcne / **fen**-gelād* (1357b–39a)

     'they inhabit a mysterious land — wolf-slopes, windy headlands, dangerous fen-waters'

(e)   *swā ic / **Hring**-Dena **hund** / missera*   sO/V

     ***wēold** under / **wol**cnum* (1769a–70a, gen. obj.)

     'thus I ruled the Ring-Danes for a hundred half-years beneath the clouds'

(f)   *þ**ǣ**r hē / **h**ǣ**ð**en gold*   sO/V

     ***war**að / **win**trum frōd* (2276b–77a; cf. 1723b–24a)

     'where he guards heathen gold, wise in winters'

(g)   *þā hē / **bior**ges weard*   sO/V

     *sōhte, / **searo**-nīðas* (3066b–67a)

     'when he sought out the guardian of the barrow (and) cunning attacks'

Opening verses in other examples like (42a): 418a, 513a, 533a, 556a, 578a, 661a, 862a, 1086a, 1141a, 2012a, 2346a, 2410a, 2522a (gen. obj.), 2619a, 2645a, 2699a, 3008a; like (42b): 245b, 530a, 698b, 2349b, 3175a; like (42c): 1098a, 1604b, 1992b, 2329b (dat. obj.), 2747b, 3112b.

With the subject realized as a pronoun, as (42a) shows, there is room for alliterating modifiers like *wæl-* before the object in the a-verse and *wihte* before the verb in the b-verse. In (42b) the subject and verb phrase are separated by semantically inessential material that situates the finite verb at normative location s4. In (42c) the verb occupies location s2. Items (42d–f) have the verb at dispreferred location s1a. The verb-final alternative to (42d) would scan as type A3 (Ss/Sx) but would be stylistically anomalous. In the verse as it stands *wulf-hleoþu* is grouped with other quite different geographical features that together make up the mysterious land. If it stood before the verb, *wulf-hleoþu* would be interpreted as a variation synonymous with *dȳgel lond* and it would be unclear why other geographical features were mentioned after the verb. The verb-final alternative in (42e) would have the alliterating finite verb on an s position in type B3 (xx/Sxs), contravening OE 7.5. With verb-final order the verse containing the verb in (42f) would have the pattern*Sxs/S (M1). In (42g) the pattern would be *Ssx/Sx (H5).

As we have seen (§3.1b), the poet is very reluctant to split constituents of the verb phrase in SOV clauses where all major constituents are stressed. There are only four SO/V clauses to set beside more than ten times as many with S/OV structure. Among instances with unstressed subjects, however, the frequency of sO/V instances is not much lower than the frequency of s/OV instances. The difference is attributable to metrical constraints on unstressed SP arguments, which are restricted to the first verse of the clause by the SPMR and strongly prefer normative location x1. As alternatives to SO/V, the orders O/SV and OV/S allow for alliteration on the object while maintaining normative order between stressed major constituents sharing a verse. With unstressed subjects, on the other hand, the orders O/sV and OV/s would place an unstressed SP in the second verse of the clause, violating the SPMR. The only viable orders allowing for alliteration on the object are s/OV and sO/V. That being the case, an elevated frequency of sO/V would be expected. Independent support for this explanation is provided by clauses with relative pronoun subjects that are confined to initial position by grammatical constraints of ordinary language. The frequency of wsO/V clauses is also elevated relative to the frequency of ws/OV clauses (§3.2b).

In (43a–f) subject, verb, and direct object occupy separate verses. Item (43b) follows a direct question with the verb fronted after *hū* 'how.' Despite the absence of verb fronting, item (43b) appears to be a second question and is punctuated with a question mark in K4. In (43c) the stressed objects share a verse in normative IoO order. In the b-verse of the first line *ealles* is split by hyperbaton from *ðāra frætwa*.

(43) (a)   *ðǣr hīo* / **syððan** *well*   s/O/V

        in / **gum**-*stōle,   gōde[,]* / *mǣre,*

        līf-*ge-* / *sceafta* **lifigende** / *brēac* (1951b–53b, gen. obj.)

        'where on a throne she well enjoyed her allotted time (while) alive, famous (and) powerful'

        (b)   *ac ðū* / **Hrōðgāre**   sIo/O/V *wīd-cūðne / **wēan** **wih**te / (ge)bēttest,*

mǣrum / ðēodne? (1990b–92a)

'and you allieviated that widely-known affliction somewhat for Hrothgar, the famous king?'

(c) *ic ðāra / **frætwa** **frēan** / ealles ðanc,*   s/IoO/V

    wuld(u)r- / cyninge, **wordum** / secge,*

    ēcum / dryhtne (2794a–96a)

'for all of those treasures I say thanks with words to the Lord, the glory-king, the eternal leader'

(d) *þæt hē / **gēnunga** **gūð**-ge- / wǣdu*   s/O/V

    ***wrā**ðe / (for)wurpe* (2871a–72a; cf. 379b–81a, 2922a–23a, gen. obj.)

'that he rashly threw those war-garments entirely away'

(e) *forþan hē tō / **lange** **lēode** / mīne*   s/O/V

    wanode / (ond) **wyrde*** (1336a–37a)

'because he diminished and destroyed my people too long'

(f) *þǣr ic, / **þēoden** mīn, **þīne** / lēode*   s/O/V

    weorðode / **weorcum*** (2095a–96a; cf. 1580a–81a, 2181a–83a)

'there, my lord, I honored your people with achievements'

(g) *þæt se / **mon**-dryhten sē ēow ðā / **māð**mas geaf* (2865) (subject fragment)

'that the earthly lord who gave you those gifts...'

Opening verses in other examples like (43a): 718a, 937b (dat. obj.), 1157b, 2788a.

In (43a–c) the verb occupies normative metrical location s4. The verb occupies location s2 in (43d). In (43e) both lifts are occupied by finite verbs and there is no violation of OE 6. In the verses like (43f) placement of the verb at metrical location s1a avoids adverse metrical consequences. In the cited example the result would be an a-verse with the rare pattern Sx/Sxx (D5), otherwise attested only in an archaic formula for introducing direct discourse (§1.14). As it stands the verse has the more complex foot first, in accord with the principle of closure (UM 4). The other undesirable results would be *hilde-dēor / hēold* (*Sxs/S: M1) and *on / sweofote / slōh*, where the alliterating verb contravenes OE 7.5. The a-verse in (43g) anticipates the cited example in (43d). The relative clause in the b-verse of (43g) continues for five more lines that describe occasions on which Beowulf gave retainers the splendid armor that they should have used, but did not, to defend their lord at need. This clause is so long and so intricate that its verb would be difficult to associate with the remote subject *mondryhten*. The poet accordingly starts again with the resumptive pronoun *that* to provide a more readily interpretable subject for (43d).

If Old English had SVO typology, multi-verse sVO clauses would be expected to favor s/VO structure, with the subject in one verse and the verb-phrase constituents in a later verse. In fact there are no examples of s/VO. The most common structure is sV/O. The cited example in (44a) has *mǣste* split from its modified constituents by hyperbaton.

(44) (a)   *þǣr hēo ǣr / **mǣste** hēold*   sV/O

*worolde / **wyn**ne* (1079b–80a)

'where she had most joy of the world'

(b) *þanon hē ge- / **sōh**te **Sūð**-Dena / folc*   sV/O

ofer / ȳða gewealc (463a–64a, dat. obj.)

'thence he sought the people of the South-Danes over the rolling of the waves'

(c) *ðā hīe ge- / **truwedon** on / twā healfa*   sV/O

*fǣste / **frioðu**-wǣre* (1095a–96a)

'then on the two (opposing) sides they ratified a firm compact of peace'

(d) *ac hē ge- / **fēng** hraðe **forman** / sīðe*   sV/O

*sl**ǣ**pendne / rinc* (740a–41a, gen. obj.; cf. 3029b–30a, gen. obj.)

'but he swiftly seized a sleeping warrior at the first opportunity'

Opening verses in other examples like (44a): 574b, 575b, 618b, 1079b, 1180b (hyperbaton), 1251b (gen. obj.), 1302b, 1460b (dat. obj.), 2138b, 2523b, 2686b, 2736b (gen. obj.), 2880b, 3090b, 3124b; like (44b): 47a, 465a, 520a, 671a, 1142a, 1270a, 3081a, 3163a; like (44c): 175a (gen. obj.), 751a, 2039a.

Relative to an SVO norm, sV/O would split the verb from its natural partner in the verb phrase and place it in the same clause with an extraneous subject. Relative to the poet's SOV norm, sV/O involves displacement of an object to the right periphery, which is routine if the object is heavy, in prose as well as poetry. The clauses like (44a) have the verb in normative location s4. The clauses like (44b) have the verb on the last lift of the a-verse at location s2 or at location s1b in a verse with a single stressed constituent. Placement of the verb in the a-verse achieves normative realization of the major constituents as a single line (OE 1.1). In the instances like (44c) the verb is the

most prominent constituent in the opening verse and occupies metrical location s1b. In the instances like (44d) the verb stands in metrical location
s1a before a less prominent adverb, the b-verse is filled by an adjunct phrase,
and the object occupies the a-verse in the next line.

In (45a–d) subjects, verbs, and direct objects occupy separate verses and
the heavy direct objects are displaced to the right periphery. Constituents
sharing a verse in (45d) observe normative SIo order.

(45) (a) *ic þǣre / **sōcne** singāles / wæg*   s/V/O

        *mōd-ceare / **micle*** (1777a–78a)

        'I continually suffered great mental anguish from that persecution'

   (b) *ac hē / **wæccende** wrāþum / (on) andan*

        bād / bolgen-mōd beadwa / (ge)þinges* (708–9, gen. obj.)   s/V/O

        'but he, waking against the foe, awaited with wrathful heart the result of
battle'

   (c) *þonne hē on / **ealu**-bence **oft** ge- / sealde*   s/V/Io/O

        heal- / sittendum **helm** ond / byrnan,*

        þēoden / (his) þegnum* (2867a–69a)

        'when he, the lord, often gave a helmet and mailcoat to those sitting in the
hall, his thanes'

   (d) *nǣfre ic / **ǣnigum** men ǣr ā- / lȳfde,*   sIo/V/O

        *siþðan ic / **hond** ond rond **hebban**/ mihte,*

        *ðrȳþ-ærn / Dena būton / **þē** nūða*

        (655a–57b, excluding verse-internal parenthesis)

        'since I could lift hand and shield, I never entrusted the great hall of the
Danes to any man except you now'

Opening verses in other examples like (45a): 254b (hyperbaton), 627a, 887b,
1197a (hyperbaton), 1318a (hyperbaton), 1486a, 1655a, 2799a (hyperbaton),
3104a, 3130a.

Most instances are like (45a, c, d), with the verb at normative metrical location s4. In (44b) placement of the verb at metrical location s1a avoids **bolgen-
mōd** / **bād** (*Sxs/S: M1). The following noun alliterates in accord with the
rule of precedence. The modified objects in (44c) are both displaced to the
right periphery, where they observe normative IoO order. In (44d) the
whole-verse direct object is displaced and modifiers of the subject and the
indirect object provide alliteration for the first line.

There is one example with an unstressed pronoun after the first stress. Here as generally I interpret Old English phrases like *tō þē,* with expressed prepositions, as adjunct prepositional phrases rather than as indirect objects of advantage or disadvantage. Indirect objects are still bare datives in *Beowulf*. They acquired *to* as the inflectional system declined and case endings were replaced by prepositions.

(46) *ðonne / wēn(e) ic tō þē   wyrsan / (ge)þingea* (525, gen. obj.).   VsO
          'then I expect a worse result from you'

In *Beowulf* 338a and 442a the manuscript has *wen ic* rather than *wene ic,* with elision or contraction of the verbal inflection with the unstressed pronoun (K4: 333). If the same kind of elision occurred in item (46), as seems likely, the a-verse scans normally as type B4 (xx/Sxxs). Item (46) is unusual in having an unstressed SP pronoun on an x position in an Sxxs foot. If *wene ic* became one phonological word by elision or contraction, however, *ic* would lose meaningful prominence and become a less inappropriate occupant of this x position — something comparable to an inflectional ending. Since the verb is followed by a less prominent stressed pronoun, linguistic and metrical prominence are correctly aligned and there is no violation of the rule of precedence. Departure from normative placement of the verb makes it possible to realize the major constituents as a single line.

§3.6 Instances with unstressed objects

§3.6a One-verse instances

In (47a, b) unstressed objects are fronted to normative metrical location x1, the stressed constituents observe normative SV order, and the verb occupies normative location s4.

(47) (a) *hīe / wyrd forswēop* (477)   oSV
              'fate swept them off'
       (b) *þæt him / Onela forgeaf,*   oioSV
              his / gædelinges gūð-ge- / wædu
              fyrd-searo / fūslīc (2616b–18a)
              'Onela gave that to him — his kinsman's combat equipment, army-gear in readiness'

150

Other examples like (47a): 232b, 441b, 452b, 488b, 545b, 579b, 852b, 915b, 1048b, 1068b, 1205b, 1291b, 1436b, 1481b, 1491b, 1658b, 1985b, 2050b, 2219b (as emended), 2230b (as emended), 2236b, 2629b, 2772b, 2784b, 2872b, 2883b; with dative object: 250b, 852b, 2323b, 2976b.

In (47b) an unstressed direct object has been fronted beyond the unstressed indirect object within location x1. As a result the object is closer to its antecedent in the previous clause, which describes Onela's gift in detail.

In (48a, b) both subject and object are unstressed. In (48a) þē is a late form of accusative þec. Item (48b) is a syntactically complete clause followed by adjunct material.

(48) (a) *hē þē æt / **sun**de oferflāt* (517b)   soV

        'he overmatched you in swimming'

   (b)   *fela ic / **lā**þes gebād,*   osV

    *gryn**na / (æt) **Gren**dle* (929b–30a)

        'I have endured a lot of loathly afflictions from Grendel'

Other examples like (48a): 28a, 109b, 290a, 372a, 435a, 535a, 632a, 798a, 929b, 1185b, 1392a, 1671a, 1722b, 1826a, 1833b, 2005b, 2217b, 2300b, 2427b, 2638b, 2713b, 2787b, 2875b, 2976a; with dative object: 292b, 560b, 722b, 968b, 1821b, 2668b, 3103b; with genitive object: 586b.

In (48a) the unstressed arguments occupy location x1 in normative 'so' order. The 'os' order in (48b) gives appropriate positional emphasis to the intensifier *fela,* which functions as the object here.

In (49a–c) the only unstressed object is indirect. Reflexive dative pronouns like *him* in (49b) indicate that the action encoded by the verb — fearing for oneself, in this case — is initiated by the subject, presumably for the benefit of the subject. I take 'feared for himself' as analogous to 'cared for himself, observed caution' and interpret *him* in (49b) as an indirect object beneficiary.

(49) (a) *hē mē / **mē**de gehēt* (2134b)   sioOV

        'he promised me a reward'

  (b) *nō hē him þā / **sæc**ce ondrēd* (2347b; cf. 2492b–93a)   sioOV

        'he by no means feared combat for himself'

   (c)   *ic þē / **an** tela*   sioVO *sinc-ge-* / *strēona* (1225b)

        'I will give you a great number of precious treasures'

Other examples like (49a): 472b, 1085b, 1220b, 1584b, 2146b, 2165b.

In (49a, b) all constituents are in normative syntactic order, the verb occupies its normative metrical location at line end, and the stressed constituents observe normative OV order. VO order in (49c) avoids **ic þē / tela an,* an unacceptable variant of xx/Ss (type A8) with the Ss foot realized as a word group (OE 3.4).

    In (50a, b) verb fronting to a stressed position avoids placement of an unstressed pronoun object in anacrusis. As we have observed, the only instance of such anacrusis in the poem, item (36c), may be due to scribal modernization.

(50) (a) *reste* / *(hine þā) rūm-heort* (1799a; cf. 688a, 2593a–94a)   VoS

       'the great-hearted (man) rested himself then'

   (b)   *gyrede hine* / *Bēowulf*   VoS

     eorl-ge- / *wǣdum* (1441b–42a)

     'Beowulf dressed himself in a hero's garments'

Absence of alliteration on *Bēowulf* in (50b) seems to violate the rule of precedence but might have been more tolerable because the protagonist's name has high frequency in the discourse and would have undergone SEMANTIC BLEACHING, a reduction in phrasal prominence that was destined to play a more conspicuous role in Middle English alliterative meter (Russom 2009: 44).

§3.6b Instances in multi-verse clauses

As with the corresponding one-verse clauses, the most common multi-verse clauses with unstressed objects have oSV structure, with subject and verb in normative order.

(51) (a) *þæt þec* / *ymb-sittend egesan* / *þȳwað* (1827)   oS/V

       'that your neighbors threaten you with terror'

   (b)   *þæt him his* / *wine-māgas*   oS/V

     georne / *hȳrdon* (65b–66a)

'that his kindred friends eagerly obeyed him'

(c)   *hine* / **sorh**-*wylmas*

    lemedon / *(tō)* **lange** (904b–05a; cf. 1509b–10a)   oS/V

    'the surges of sorrow oppressed him too long'

(d) *þæt* / **mǣg**-*wine*   **mīne** / *(ge)wrǣcan,*   oS/V

    fǣhðe / *(ond) fyrene* (2479a–80a)

    'my kindred friends avenged that — the feud and the violence'

(e)   *hine* / **hā**lig *God*   oS/IoV

    for / **ār**-*stafum*   **ūs** *on*- / *sende,*

    tō / **West**-*Denum* (381b–83a)

    'holy God has sent him as tokens of favor to us, the West-Danes'

Opening verses in other examples like (51a), with the verb at the end of a b-verse: 1106a (as emended), 1514a, 1794a (dat. obj.), 2428b, 2437a, 2514b, 2916a; like (51b), with the verb at the end of an a-verse: 1716a, 2274b, 2379b.

The stressed verb occupies normative location s4 in (51a, e). In (51b) the verb stands in normative syntactic position at metrical location s2, its preferred location when it occupies the a-verse. In (51c) the verb occupies location s1a. The alternative with verb-final order, *(tō)* **lange** / **lemede,** would have avoidable anacrusis. In (51d) the verb shares a verse with an extraneous modifier of the subject, creating enjambment. Normative realization of the line as a clause compensates for the complexity caused by the enjambment, which occurs between the first two verses as usual. In (51e) the unstressed object *hine* is fronted to normative metrical location x1. The stressed indirect object pronoun shares a verse with the stressed finite verb, observing normative order. In this unusual instance emphatic stress would be appropriate on the pronoun and the verb occupies a position that matches its subordinate phrasal stress. The prominence of stressed pronouns relative to finite verbs deserves consideration in a larger corpus of examples.

In the remaining oSV clauses a fronted pronoun object is the only major constituent in the opening verse and the subject observes normative order with the verb. Since the fronted object leaves a trace between subject and verb (§1.8), the SV constructions are psychologically complete and the subject is not extraneous to the verb in the verse that they share.

(52) (a) *þæt ðec,* / **dryht**-*guma,*   **dēað** *ofer*- / *swȳðeð* (1768)   o/SV

'that death will overpower you, troop-man'

(b)   *þæt ðē / **feor** ond nēah*   o/SV

     *ealne / **wīde**-ferhþ   **weras** / ehtigað* (1221b–23a)

     'that far and near, entirely throughout time, men will praise you'

(c)   *hwæt, hyt / **ǣr** on ðē*   o/SV

     *gōde / (be)**gēaton*** (2248b–49a)

     'indeed, powerful men found it in you' (found gold in the earth)

(d)   *hyne þā mid / **han**da **heoro**- / drēorigne,*   o/S/V

     ***þēo**den / mǣrne, **þegn** / un(ge)met(e) till*

     ***wine**-dryhten / his **wǣ**tere / (ge)l<u>afe</u>de,*

     ***hil**de / sǣdne* (2720a–23a)

     'with hands then the extremely good thane laved him with water — the

     famous king, his friend and lord, blood-stained, exhausted by battle'

Opening verses in other examples like (52a): 2828a, 2836a; like (52b): 518b, 694b; like (52d): 559a, 813a, 2233a, 2964b.

The examples like (52a) are one-line clauses with the verb in normative syntactic and metrical position. In those like (52b) subject and verb share a verse at the end of a later line. In the cited example semantically inessential **feor** *ond nēah* and *ealne* **wīde**-*ferhþ* have generic significance in the immediate context, highlighting the poet's role in the ancient world: creating widespread, deathless glory for anyone who provides crucial protection to a social group. Item (52c) is the only instance with the verb at the end of an a-verse. Each major constituent occupies a separate verse in (52d), leaving much room available for semantically inessential constituents. The bare clause is *hyne þā þegn gel<u>afe</u>de*. The semantically inessential constituents add concrete detail and evaluative generic material to a passage in which a thane who has come to his lord's aid in combat continues the attempt to save the lord's life with pathetically ineffective stubbornness.

     In two instances an unstressed object precedes an unstressed subject.

(53) (a) *þæt hē on / **Bīo**wulfes **bearm** ā- / legde* (2194)   os/V

       'he laid that on Beowulf's lap'

   (b) *fela ic on / **giogo**ðe **gūð**-rǣsa / (ge)næs,*   os/V

       ***orleg**- / hwīla* (2426a–27a)

       'in my youth I survived a lot of attacks in combat, of battle-times'

In (53a) fronting of the object shortens the iconic grammatical distance from its antecedent in the previous clause, the sword given to Beowulf. In (53b) it seems necessary to interpret *fela* as the direct object rather than as an adverb because *genēsan* does not take genitive objects like *gūðrǣsa*. As an intensifier, *fela* is appropriate for positional emphasis.

In (54a–d) a heavy subject phrase is displaced to the right periphery. Unstressed accusative *mē* in the cited examples for (54a, d) is a late scribal variant of accusative *mec*.

(54) (a)   *mē tō / **grun**de tēah*

     fāh / **fēond**-*scaða* (553b–54a)   oV/S

     'the hostile attacker dragged me to the bottom'

   (b) **hūru** *þæt / (on)hōhsnode* **Hemminges** / *mǣg* (1944)   oV/S

     'indeed Hemming's kinsman moderated that'

   (c) *ðā hyne ge- / **sōh**tan   on / **sige**-þēode*   oV/S

     hearde / **hild**(e)-*frecan[.]* (2204a–05a)

     'when doughty battle-warriors, the War-Scylfings, sought him among

     the victory-people'

   (d) *þā mē þæt ge- / **lǣr**don   lēode / mīne*   o^{2}o^{1}V/S

     *þā / **sē**lestan,   **snot**ere / ceorlas,*

     þēoden / *Hrōðgār* (415a–17a)

     'then my most capable people, wise men, taught me that, Lord Hrothgar'

     (suggested that to me)

Opening verses in other examples like (54a): 265b, 1587b (dat. obj.), 1735b, 2280b; like (54b): 194a, 750a, 778a (gen. obj.), 1591a.

In (54a) the clause begins in the b-verse with the verb in normative location s4. In (54b) normative realization of the clause as a line compensates for verb placement at the end of the a-verse. The first line (54c) is completed by a semantically inessential verse and the very heavy subject is displaced to the following a-verse, leaving the b-verse available for the opening of the next clause. Item (54d) is a double-object construction with two unstressed accusative objects. The animate secondary object precedes the inanimate primary object, which stands closer to the verb as usual.

In the remaining oVS clauses the unstressed object shares the opening verse with an adjunct that provides the alliteration and the stressed constituents occupy following verses.

(55) (a)   *swā hine / **fyrn**-dagum*   o/VS

        ***worhte** / **wǣpna** smið* (1451b–52a)

        'as the smith of weapons crafted it in days of old'

     (b) *þæt hine on / **ylde** **eft** ge- / wunigen*   o/V/S

        ***wil**-ge- / **sīþ**as* (22a–23a; cf. 3069a–70a)

        '(so) that willing companions might accompany him in old age'

Departure from normative SV order in (55a) avoids **wǣpna smið / **worhte*** (*Sxs/Sx: MH1). In the instances like (55b) a semantically inessential adverb provides alliteration for the b-verse and situates the verb at normative metrical location s4. The stressed constituents occupy separate verses and the heavy modified subjects are displaced to the right periphery.

Items (56a–e) have an unstressed indirect object. Both subject and object are unstressed in (56d–f). Enjambment in the cited example for (56b) occurs as usual in the earliest possible location. Stressed constituents observe normative OV order. Unstressed constituents sharing a verse observe normative 'sio' order.

(56) (a)   *him ðæs / **gūð**-kyning,*   ioS/OV

        ***Wede**ra / þīoden, **wrǣce** / leornode* (2335b–36b)

        'for him the fighting king, lord of the Weders, devised vengeance for that'

     (b) *sōna mē se / **mǣra** **mago** / Healfdenes,*   io/S/OV

        *wið his / **sylf**es **sunu** **setl** ge- / tǣhte* (2011–13; cf. 550–1)

        'promptly the famous son of Halfdane assigned me a seat with his own sons'

     (c) *him þā / **hil**de-dēor **hof** / mōdigra*   ioS/O/V

        ***torht** ge- / **tǣh**te* (312a–13a)

        'Then the battle-brave (one) pointed out to them the residence of the bold (ones)'

     (d) *ic ðē / **þū**senda **þegna** / bringe,*   sioO/V

        ***hæle**þa / (tō) **hel**pe* (1829a–30a)

        'I (will) bring you thousands of thanes, of warriors, for support'

     (e)   *ic **mē** mid / **Hrun**tinge*   sio/OV

        ***dōm** ge- / wyrce* (1490b–91a)

        'I will create fame for myself with Hrunting (a sword)'

     (f) *ic him þā / **māð**mas þe hē / **mē** sealde,*   sioO/V

        ***geald** æt / **gūð**e* (2490a–91a)

'at the fight I remunerated him the treasures that he gave me'
Opening verses in other examples like (56a): 16b, 177a, 1056a, 1552a, 1880b; like (56d): 1541a, 1653a, 3153a.

The most common instances are ioS/OV constructions like (56a), with the indirect object and stressed subject in the opening verse and the direct object sharing a b-verse with the verb in normative order. Item (56e) is a similar example with an unstressed subject. The indirect object occupies a separate verse in the clauses like (56b), which have the same arrangement of stressed constituents as (56a). Items (56c, e) have the verb at metrical location s2. In (52c, d, f) the stressed constituents occupy separate verses. In (56f) placement of the verb at metrical location s1a avoids *æt / gūðe geald*, a dispreferred type B variant with an alliterating verb on the s position (OE 7.5).

Items (57a–f) are the remaining examples with unstressed indirect objects. Constituents sharing a verse in (57a–c) observe normative OV and SV orders.

(57) (a)   *swā unc / **wyrd** getēoð*   ioOV/S

        ***metod** / **manna** gehwæs* (2526b–27a)

        'as the creator of all men determines fate for us'

  (b) *þǣr him / **Hygd** gebēad   **hord** ond / rīce,*   ioSV/O

        *bēagas / (ond) **brego**-stōl* (2369a–70a; cf. 696b–98a)

        'there Hygd gave him a treasure-hoard and a kingdom, rings and a kingly seat'

  (c)   *him þæs / **en**de-lēan*   ioO/SV

        *þurh / **wæteres wylm**   **waldend** / sealde* (1692b–93b; cf. 2155a–56a)

        'the Lord gave them a final retribution for that through a flood of water'

  (d) *ac mē / **eorla** hlēo   **eft** ge- / sealde*   ioS/V/O

        *mā**ð**ma / **meni**geo,   **maga** / Healfdenes* (2142–43; cf. 1866–67)

        'but the protector of earls, Halfdane's son, afterwards gave me a lot of treasures'

  (e) *him ðā ge- / **giredan**   **Gēa**ta / lēode*   ioV/S/O

        *ā**d** on / eorðan   **un** / -wāclicne,*

        ***hel**mum / (be)hongen,   **hil**de- / bordum,*

        beorh**tum / **byrnum (3137a–40a)

        'for him then the people of the Geats prepared a pyre on the earth, not sparingly, hung about with helmets, with battle-shields, with bright mail-coats'

(f) *mē þone / **wæl-ræs** **wine** / Scildunga* ioO/S/V

*fǣttan / golde **fela** / lēanode,*

manegum** / **māðmum (2101a–3a; cf. 1841a–42a)

'to me the Scyldings' friend amply remunerated that deadly attack with ornamented gold, with many treasures'

In (57a) a very heavy subject verse is displaced to the right periphery. Verses with modified heavy objects are displaced to the right periphery in (57b, d). In (57e) the heavy subject and object have both been displaced and maintain normative SV order. In (57c, f) a compound object smaller than a verse is fronted to complete the opening verse. A general-case strategy for managing clauses with one or more unstressed SPs is to situate all the unstressed constituents at metrical location x1 and follow them with any poetic compound smaller than a verse. The result will be an opening verse of type I with the normative number of stresses and normative realization of the compound foot as a compound word.

Items (58a–f) are double-object constructions with secondary unstressed objects. All instances have the verb at normative metrical location s4. The verb in (58f), which looks like an infinitive, is a spelling variant of a finite subjunctive form.

(58) (a) *sumne / **Gēata** lēod* o^2S/O^1V

*of / **flān**-bogan **fēores** / (ge)twǣfde,*

***ȳð**-ge- / winnes* (1432b–34a.; cf. 1763a–66a)

'the man of the Geats denied one life (deprived one of life), of power on the waves'

(b) *nalæs hī hine / **lǣssan** **lācum** / tēodan* so^2/O^1V

***þēod**-ge- / strēonum,* (43a–44a; cf. 2377a–78a)

'they did not provide him lesser gifts (or) great treasures'

(c) *oþ þæt hine / **yldo** benam* o^2SV/O^1

***mægenes** / wynnum* (1886b–87a)

'until age denied him the joys of strength'

(d) *swā him / **wyrd** ne gescrāf* o^2SV/O^1

hrēð** æt / **hilde (2574b–75a)

'since fate did not grant him victory in battle'

(e) *þone on / **gēar**-dagum   **Gren**del / nemdon*   o²O¹V/S

   ***fold**- / būende* (1354a–55a)

   'in days of yore earth-dwellers called him Grendel'

(f) *þæt hit / **sǣ**-līðend   **syð**ðan / hātan*   o²S/V/O¹

   Bī**owulfes / **Biorh (2806a–07a)

   'so that seafarers might call it "Beowulf's Barrow" afterwards'

(g) *Ic þē þā / **fǣh**ðe   **fēo** / lēanige,*   so²O¹/V

   ***eald-**ge- / strēonum,   swā ic / **ǣr** dyde,*

   ***wund**nan / golde* (1380a–82a)

   'I will remunerate you the feud with old treasures, with woven gold, as I
   did before'

The primary object is genitive in (58a), dative in (58b, c), and accusative in
(58d–g). The secondary object is dative in (58d, g) and accusative in the
other instances. When the verb shares a verse with an object in these clauses,
it is always the inanimate object, and the animate object is more remote,
irrespective of case. In (58e) a personal name is the abstract inanimate object.
Item (58f) is a similar example with a place name.

§3.7 Instances with unstressed finite main verbs

In main clauses verbs fronted to unstressed positions typically occupy a C
position in the left periphery, with the subject following. Verb movement to
C is restricted to auxiliaries in Modern English but in *Beowulf* main verbs
also move before the subject, not only in imperative and hortative subjunctive clauses but also in indicative clauses. When the C position is filled by a
subordinating conjunction, movement of a verb before the subject is
blocked, with rare apparent exceptions (§1.8).

§3.7a One-verse instances

As the most prominent SPs, unstressed main verbs are never used for anacrusis (at location x5) and are never placed after the first alliteration of the
verse (at location x2, x3, or x4). They are confined to normative location
x1, which means that they occur only in verses of category I.

(59) (a) *ne wiston hīe / **drih**ten God* (181b; cf. 681a, gen. obj.)   vsO

'they knew not the lord God'

    (b) *cūþe hē / **duguðe** þeaw* (359b; cf. 487b–88a)   vsO

    'he understood the custom of the court'

    (c) *hē āh / **ealra** geweald* (1727b)   svO

    'he has control of everything'

    (d) *druncon / **wīn weras*** (1233a)   vOS

    'the men drank *wine*'

Items (59a, b) have vsO order, with a high-frequency main verb fronted to an unstressed C position before the unstressed subject. This is the usual location for unstressed verbs in main clauses and is strongly preferred when such a verb is negated, as in (59a). Item (59c) has the less usual sv order, with the verb fronted to a position between the subject and other constituents of the verb phrase. Here putting the subject pronoun first shortens the iconic distance to its antecedent, a rather remote noun subject in a long previous clause. A position before other constituents of the verb phrase is available for verb fronting when the C position is filled. In (59d) the object *wīn* is fronted to a stressed position before the subject, emphasizing the reportable character of a drink less widely available in the Germanic north than beer or ale. The verb that predictably accompanies a beverage is fronted to an unstressed position.

§3.7b Multi-verse instances

In (60a–f) an unstressed main verb is fronted to an unoccupied C position at location x1. Stressed constituents occupy separate verses.

(60) (a)   *ne seah ic / **wīdan** feorh*   vs/O

        *under / **heofones hwealf heal-** / sittendra*

        medu**-drēam / **māran (2014b–16a; cf. 336b–37b, 1612a–15a)

        'I did not see throughout life under the vault of heaven more mead-joy of those sitting in a hall'

    (b)   *gehȳrde on / **Bēowulfe***   v/S/O

    ***fol**ces / hyrde **fæst**-rǣdne / (ge)þōht* (609b–10b)

    'the guardian of the people heard in Beowulf a firmly resolved intention'

    (c) *geslōh þīn / **fæder fǣh**ðe / mǣste* (459)   vS/O

    'your father struck up the greatest feud'

(d) *sende ic /* **Wylfingum** *ofer /* **wæteres** *hrycg*　　　　　　vsIo/O

　　*eal*de */ mādmas* (471a–72a; cf. 270a–71a)

　　'I sent ancient treasures to the Wylfings over the ridge of water (ocean)'

(e) *ālegdon ðā tō- /* **middes** **mǣrne** */ þēoden*　　　　　　v/O/S

　　hæleð */* **hīofende,** **hlāford** */* **lēofne** (3141–42)

　　'the lamenting warriors laid down the famous king, the beloved lord, in the
　　middle (of a funeral pyre)'

Opening verses in examples like (60e): 675a, 746a, 1020a, 2809a.

In these clauses with a fronted verb the unmoved direct object is the last
expressed constituent in the core. In the verses like (60e) a heavy modified
subject has been displaced beyond an object. In the cited example the subject is followed by a variation of the object, imitating normative SO order.

§3.8. Clauses with an unstressed argument and an unexpressed or relativized subject

Omission of the subject and compact expression of an argument make it
easier to realize a clause as a single verse. The number of one-verse instances
is larger than the number of multi-verse instances.

§3.8a One-verse instances

In (61a–e) an unstressed object SP occupies normative location x1. In (61d)
the objects are juxtaposed paratactically rather than linked by an overt conjunction as in Modern English.

(61) (a)　　　　　*hit on /* **ryht** *gescēd*　　　　　　(s)oV

　　　　ȳðe- / līce (1555b–56a; cf. 3087b–88a)

　　　　'(he) decided it justly (and) easily'

　　(b) *ðā þæt on- /* **funde** (809a, 1497a, 3009a)　　　　(s)oV

　　　　'then (he) discovered that' (anticipating a that-clause)

　　(c) *ond him /* **fæste** *wiðfēng* (760a, dat. obj.)　　　　(s)oV

　　　　'and (he) seized him firmly'

　　(d)　　　　　*ond him /* **hǣl** *ābēad,*　　　　　　(s)ioOV

　　　　wīn-*ærnes / (ge)***weald** (653b; cf. 1759b–60b, 2640b)

　　　　'and (he) offered him luck (and) possession of the wine-hall'

(e) *ond hine þā /* **hēafde becearf** (1590b)   (s)o²O¹V

    'and then (he) severed him (his) head' (cut off his head)

(f) *ond þæt ge- /* **æfn**don swā (538b)   (s)oV

    'and accomplished that accordingly'

(g)   *nē mē /* **swōr** *fela*   (s)ioVO

    āða / *(on)* **un**riht   (2738b–39a)

    '(I) did not swear a lot of oaths wrongfully for myself'

The verb occupies normative location s4 in (61a, d, f). In the examples like (61b) the verb occupies location s1b and alliterates as the only stressed constituent in the verse. Placement of the alliterating verb on an s position in (61c) violates OE 7.5. This is a violable constraint but a strong one and there are many instances of compliance for each violation. The ease with which OE 7.5 could be violated more often is shown by the many otherwise similar instances in which the alliterating verb has been moved out of an s position that is normative by purely syntactic criteria. The poet took obvious pains to comply with OE 7.5. In the examples like (61d) the only unstressed object is indirect and the stressed constituents observe normative OV order. Item (61e) has an accusative animate object and a dative inanimate object, the reverse of the situation in ordinary constructions with indirect objects. As usual the inanimate object stands closer to the verb and the animate object is more distant despite its accusative case. In (61f) the verb is more prominent than the following high-frequency adverb and alliterates appropriately on the most prominent lift. The VO order in (61g) is required for metrical reasons. Since *fela* would have to be resolved if it stood before the verb on the first S position, **nē mē / **fela** swōr* would have an Ss word group in type A8 (xx/Ss), contravening OE 3.4.

    Placement of the unstressed object SP in location x2 or x4 occurs under special conditions in (62a–d).

(62) (a) **weh**te / *(hyne)* **wæ**tre (2854a; cf. 2640a)   (s)Vo

    '(he) would awaken him with water'

    (wanted to awaken him, past subjunctive)

(b) **cen** *þec / (mid)* **cræf**te (1219a)   (s)Vo

    '(you) declare yourself with strength' (imperative)

(c) *(be)***beorh** *þē / (ðone)* **bealo**-nīð, **Bēo**wulf / *lēofa,*   (s)Vo²O¹

    secg / *betesta* (1758a–59a)

'(you) guard yourself (against) serious offense, dear Beowulf,

best of men' (imperative)

(d) **hēold** *hine / fæste* (788b; cf. 142b–43a)   (s)Vo

'(he) held him firmly'

Verb-final order in (62a) would place a disyllabic pronoun at metrical location x5, creating anacruses that would be dubious as well as avoidable. An imperative verb is routinely fronted before a pronoun subject in (62b, c). Item (62b) is another example of the many instances in which the poet moves an alliterating verb away from a verse-final s position to comply with OE 7.5. Item (62c) is a double-object construction in which the primary and secondary objects are both accusative. Placement of the verb at metrical location s1a avoids two violations in the verb-final alternative, *þē ðone / **bealo**-nīð (be)**beorh**: violation of OE 7.5 and placement of a prominent secondary root on the first x position of the Sxxs foot, which violates OE 4.2, a rule of highest rank. Placement of *þē* at metrical location x2 avoids dubious and unnecessary anacrusis. Alliteration on the direct object in (62c) complies with the rule of precedence. The cited example in (62d) occurs within the blow-by-blow description of Beowulf's fight with Grendel, a scene in which several vivid action verbs are fronted for emphasis (§2.3). The verb in the other example is also appropriate for emphatic fronting. With the required change in alliteration, the verb-final alternatives would be acceptable variants of type B3 (xx/Sxs). Emphasis seems to be the main reason for fronting here.

In (63a, b) the subject is relativized.

(63) (a) *þā ðæt / **þǣr** dydon*   wsoV

(3070b; cf. 1461b, 2222b, dat. obj., 2468b, dat. obj.)

'who put that there'

(b) *þē ūs / **bēa**gas geaf*   wsioOV

(3009b; cf. 2635b, 2865b–66a, 3034b–35a)

'who gave rings to us'

All instances have normative placement of stressed and unstressed constituents. The closely related examples like (63b) all describe the core heroic concept of treasure-giving. All end in *geaf*. The pronouns vary in number to satisfy grammatical requirements. Varying alliterative requirements are met by employment of *māðmas* and *hringas*, which have the same metrical pattern as *bēagas*.

§3.8b Multi-verse instances

The clauses in (64a–e) have two objects, one stressed and one unstressed. The present-tense verb is used for future tense in (64a), as often in Old English. Compare the Modern English future tense in *I'm leaving for London tomorrow*. The general principle in play here is that present tense is more vivid than future tense, as shown by the frequency with which reporters, novelists, and everyday conversationalists use present tense in their narratives.

(64) (a) *ond þē tō / **gēoce gār**-holt / bere,*   (s)io/OV

        ***mægenes** / fultum* (1834a–35a; cf. 1272a–73a, with dative object)

        'and as help (I) bring a forest of spears for you, the support of strength'

  (b) *nē him þæs / **wyrmes wīg**   for / **wiht** dyde,*   (s)ioO/V

        eafoð** ond / **ellen (2348a–49a)

        'and for himself (he) by no means heeded the serpent's fighting ability, its strength and courage'

  (c) *ond him ge- / **sealde seofan** / þūsendo,*   (s)ioV/O

        ***bold** ond / **brego**-stōl* (2195a–96a; cf. 2989b–90a)

        'and (he) gave him seven thousand (units of land), a hall and a kingly throne'

  (d) ***geaf** him / (ðā mid) **Gēa**tum **gūð**-ge- / wǣda*   (s)Vio/O

        ǣghwæs** / **unrīm (2623a–24a)

        '(he) gave him battle-garments, absolutely countless, in the presence of the Geats'

  (e)   *ond hig / **wigge** belēac*   (s)oV/Io

        manigum** / **mǣg**þa geond þysne / **middangeard,

        æscum** / (ond) **ecgum (1770b–72a)

        'and (I) closed them to (protected them from) many a one of tribes throughout this middle-earth by combat with spears and swords'

The major constituents are realized as syntactically complete one-line clauses in (64a–d). In the examples like (64a) a stressed verb and its direct object share a verse in normative syntactic order and the verb occupies normative metrical location s4. In (64b), which has the same order of major constituents, interjection of the adjunct phrase *for wiht* mitigates the enjambment between object and verb. In (64c) a heavy direct object is displaced to the right periphery. Placement of the verb at location s1b makes it possible to realize the major constituents as a single line. In (64d) placement of the verb at metrical location s1a avoids *him ðā mid / Gēatum geaf*, a violation of OE 7.5. In (64e) **manigum / mǣgþa,** a modified oblique object in the dative case, is displaced to the right periphery and followed by two displaced adjunct verses.

Relativized subjects are followed in normative order by an unstressed direct object in (65a, b) and by an unstressed indirect object in (65c, d). Stressed constituents sharing a verse observe normative OV order. The verbs occupy normative metrical location s4.

(65) (a) *þæt mec / **ǣr** ond sīð **oft** ge- / lǣste* (2500; cf. 1344)   wso/V

       'which often served me before and afterwards'

   (b) *þē hine æt / **frum**sceafte **forð** on- / sendon*   wso/V

      *ǣnne / (ofer) ȳðe **umb**(o)r- / wesende* (45–6)

      'who sent him forth alone over the waves at the beginning, (he) being a child'

   (c) *þone þe him on / **sweo**fote **sā**re / (ge)tēode* (2295)   wsio/OV

      'who did an injury to him in sleep' (while he was sleeping)

   (d)   *þē him / **elles** hwǣr*   wsio/OV

      *ge- / **rūm**licor **ræste** / sōhte* (138a–40a)

      'who sought a roomier resting place elsewhere for himself'

The major constituents are realized as one-line clauses in (65a–c). The adverbs that perform required metrical functions in (65a) are semantically inessential but functional in context, emphasizing the well-tested excellence of a sword nevertheless destined to fail Beowulf in his fight with the dragon. In (65b) the semantically inessential constituents add important detail to a description of Scyld's mysterious arrival in Denmark. In (65c) the prepositional phrase that provides alliteration for the opening verse adds a detail relevant to the immediate context. In (65d) the clause begins in the b-verse. The adjuncts *elles hwǣr* and *gerūmlicor* add functional detail to an ironic turn of speech.

§3.9 Clauses with an unstressed argument and an unexpressed or relativized object

As in §3.8, the number of one-verse instances is large relative to the number of multi-verse instances.

§§3.9a One-verse instances

Items (66a–c) have the most common clause pattern.

(66) (a) *swā ic /* ***ǣr** dyde* (1381b)   (o)sV

       'as I did (that) before'

   (b) *nǣnig heora /* ***þōhte*** (691a; cf. 503a)   (o)sV

       'none of them thought (that)'

   (c)   *hē on-/* ***fēng** hraþe*   (o)sV

     *in**wit-þancum* (748b–49a)

       'he seized (him) quickly with hostile intentions'

Opening verses in other examples like (66a): 29b, 444b, 956b, 1058b, 1238b, 1676b, 1779b, 1830b, 1891b, 2070b, 2521b, 2859b; like (66c): 1396b, 2208b, 2395b, 2519b, 2656b, 2855b.

In nine of the twelve instances like (66a) a non-alliterating form of *dōn* 'do' is preceded by an adverb or adverbial phrase. Alliterative requirements for these nine verses are satisfied by *ǣr* 'before' (4X), *nū gȳt* 'still' (2X), *oft* 'often,' *nū gēn* 'still,' and *wið Grendle* 'against Grendel.' The verbs all occupy normative metrical location s4. In (66b) the verb alliterates at metrical location s1b as the only stressed constituent and the following b-verse initiates a that-clause specifying the referent of the unexpressed object. The instances like (66c) have the verb at metrical location s1a in the b-verse. The following constituent is a weakly stressed adverb or postposition, so metrical and linguistic prominence are properly aligned in conformity with OE 6.

Items (67a, b) anticipate that-clauses specifying the reference of the unexpressed object.

(67) (a) ***wisse** / (hē) gearwe* (2339b, 2725b; cf. 960b)   (o)Vs

       'he readily perceived (that)'

   (b) ***secge** / (ic þē tō)* ***sōðe**, **sunu** / Ecgláfes,* (590)   (o)Vsio

       'I say (that) to you in truth, son of Ecglaf'

In the verses like (67a) the alliterating verb at location s1a is more prominent than the stressed adverb. Linguistic prominence is properly aligned with metrical prominence and single alliteration is acceptable. In (67b) the prominent lexical noun *sōðe* alliterates after the alliterating verb as required by the rule of precedence. The (o)sV alternatives to (67a, b) would be unacceptable A1 variants with easily avoidable anacrusis.

Items (68a–e) are double-object constructions used to anticipate that-clauses. The stressed verb occupies normative location s4 in (68a, c, e) and location s1b in (68b, d).

(68) (a) *þā mē / **sǣl** āgeald* (1665b; cf. 401b, 2690b)   (o)ioSV

'when an opportunity made (that) possible for me'

   (b) *mē man / **sægde*** (1175a)   (o)iosV

'someone said (that) to me'

   (c) *ic ðē / **lange** bæd* (1994b)   (o^1)so^{2}V

'for a long time I asked you (that)'

   (d) *þæt ðū mē ne for- / **wyrne**, **wīgendra** hlēo,*   (o^1)so^{2}V

   frēo-wine / folca (429a)

'that you not deny me (that), protector of warriors, distinguished friend of the people' (with subjunctive verb)

   (e) *þæt hig þæs / **æðelinges** **eft** ne / wēndon* (1596)   (o^1)sO^{2}V

'that they did not expect (that) of the atheling' (expect the atheling to do that)

Items (68a, b) have dative indirect objects of the ordinary kind. In (68b) queen Wealhtheow fronts her indirect object pronoun before the subject pronoun *man* 'someone,' a reference to the kind of unnamed retainer that is generally out of focus in the poem. In (68c, d) the unexpressed primary object refers to an abstract inanimate request in the following that-clause. The K4 glossary identifies *ðē* in (68c) as a late variant of accusative *þec* because the verb requires an accusative animate object. On the analogy of other double-object constructions I classify this animate object as secondary even though it has accusative case. In (68d) *mē* represents the dative form, since the verb requires dative case on the animate object. In (68e) *forwyrnan* takes an animate secondary object in the genitive case. The Modern English translation for (68e) expresses the secondary object with a prepositional phrase but *þæs æðelinges* is an argument governed directly by the verb, not by an intervening preposition. The unexpressed primary object is the inanimate state of affairs expressed in the that-clause.

In (69a–d) the direct object is relativized and the stressed verb stands at the end of the clause at normative metrical location s4.

(69) (a) *þā þū / **nū** hafast* (1174b)   wosV

      'which you now have'

   (b) *þe hē him / **ǣr** forgeaf* (2606b)   wosioV

      'which he gave him previously'

   (c) *ðe him / **God** sealde* (1271b, 2182b; cf. 72b, 2173b)   woioSV

      'which God gave him'

   (d) *þe þū / **mē** sealdest* (1482b; cf. 2490b)   wosIoV

      'which you gave *me*'

Opening verses in other examples like (69a): 15a, 831b, 1298b, 1476b, 1625b, 1748b, 1858b, 2704b, 2751b.

All instances have the major constituents in a single verse, with adjunct verses following in some cases. In (69a, b, d) the relativized object is followed by the other major constituents in normative syntactic order at their normative metrical locations. In (69c) the unstressed indirect object is fronted to normative metrical location x1. In (69d) contrastive stress on the pronoun *mē*, which provides the alliteration, distinguishes the speaker from his uncle, a possible future recipient of the gift. The other example differs only in having third-person singular *sealde*. Contrastive stress distinguishes *mē* from other possible gift recipients here as well.

§3.9b Multi-verse instances

In (70a–d) the major constituents are arranged in a single line.

(70) (a) *swylce hē on / **eald(e)r**-dagum   **ǣr** ge- / mētte*   (o)s/V

      (757; cf. 1828, 2664)

      'such (ones) as he encountered before in the days of (his) life'

   (b) *þonne wē ge- / **hēton**   ūssum / **hlā**forde*   (o)sV/Io

      *in / **bīor**-sele* (2634a–35a)

      'when we promised (that) to our lord in the beer-hall'

   (c) *ac mē ge- / **ūðe**   ylda / waldend* (1661)   (o)ioV/S 'but the ruler of men granted (that) to me'

(d) *ac hē / sōðlīce   sægde / (ofer) ealle* (2899)   (o)s/V

'but he said (that) truly over all' (so that all could hear)

The instances like (70a) have the verb at normative metrical location s4. In (70b, c) realization of the major constituents as a line requires placement of the verb at metrical location s1b. In (70b) the subject is unstressed and a heavy indirect object is displaced to the right periphery. In (70c) the indirect object is unstressed and the heavy subject is displaced. Placement of the verb at location s1a in (70d) is required for metrical reasons. Even with the required change of alliteration, the verb-final alternative *(ofer) ealle / sægde* would have unusual and easily avoidable anacrusis.

In (71a–e) the direct object is relativized.

(71) (a) *hwæt wit tō / willan   ond tō / worð-myndum*   wos/Io/V

       umb(o)r-wesendum / ǣr   ārna / (ge)fremedon (1186–87)

       'what (kinds) of benefits we provided as delights and honors for him as a child'

   (b) *þē him se / eorð-draca   ǣr ge- / worhte* (2712)   woioS/V

       'which the earth-dragon did to him previously'

   (c) *ðāra þe hē ge- / worhte   tō / West-denum*   wosV/Io

       oftor / micle   ðonne on / ǣnne sīð (1578–79)

       'which he did to the West-Danes much more often than on one occasion'

   (d) *þæt him on / ðearfe lāh   ðyle / Hrōðgāres* (1456)   wo.ioV/S

       'that Hrothgar's spokesman lent to him in need'

In (71a, b) the stressed constituents occupy separate verses in normative syntactic order and the verb occupies its normative metrical position at line end. In (71c, d) stressed arguments are displaced to the right periphery. Placement of the verb at metrical location s2 makes it possible to express the major constituents of these clauses as a single line.

§3.10 Clauses with an unexpressed argument and an unstressed main verb

In all instances the main verb occupies metrical location x1, the only permissible location for unstressed main verbs. The only relevant difference between a-verse and b-verse examples is the possibility of double alliteration in the a-verse.

§3.10a One-verse instances

(72) (a) *sōhte / **holdne** wine* (376b)   (s)vO

'(he) sought a loyal friend'

(b) *geaf mē / **sinc** ond **symb**(e)l* (2431a; cf. 78b, 1809b)   (s)vioO

'(he) gave me treasure and feasting'

(c) *con him / **land** geare* (2062b)   (s)vioO

'(he) knows the land readily for himself'

(d) *swā dēð / **ēa**dig mon*   (2470b)   (o)vS

'as a fortunate man does (that)'

(e) *gesaga him ēac / **wordum*** (388a)   (so)vio

'(you) say (that) to him with words' (imperative)

(f) *geþenc nū, se **mæra   maga** / Healfdenes,*   (so)v

*snot**tra** / fengel* (1474a–76a)

'(you) remember (that), famous kinsman of Halfdane, wise king'

(imperative)

Like (72a): 264a, 518a, 539a, 926b, 1201b, 2606a, 2737b.

The main verb in (72a) must be unstressed for metrical reasons. Since the s position of the Sxs foot is occupied by a prominent noun, OE 5.1 requires alliteration on *holdne*; but if *sōhte* bore metrical stress it would have to alliterate, and alliteration on *holdne* would then be unacceptable. With verb-final order the unacceptable result would be **holdne wine / sōhte* (*Sxs/Sx: MH1). The poet's arrangement of constituents is the only acceptable one. In the examples like (72b) the verb is fronted to an available C position and the unstressed indirect object follows. Item (72c) is a similar example with a reflexive indirect object beneficiary. A conjunction occupies the C position in (72d) but does not block fronting of the verb before the subject. This is a putative example of 'doubly filled COMP' (§1.8). In (72e, f) a high-frequency imperative verb of cognition is fronted to an unstressed position rather than to a stressed position. In the first line of (72f), as the note in K4 points out, the definite article *se* is retained in *se mæra maga Healfdenes,* an adjunct vocative construction. The enjambment comes immediately after the opening verse as usual and makes it possible to arrange the major constituents in a single line.

§3.10b Multi-verse instances

Items (73a–d) have an unexpressed subject, an unstressed verb, and all other constituents stressed.

(73) (a) *nam on / **Ongenðīo** īren- / byrnan,* (s)v/O

      heard *swyrd / **hilted** ond his / **helm** somod* (2986–87)

      '(he) took from Ongentheow an iron corslet, a sharp hilted sword, and his helmet as well'

  (b) *forgeaf þā / **Bēowulfe** **brand** / Healfdenes* (s)vIo/O

      segen / *gyldenne* **sigores** / *(tō) lēane,*

      hroden / ***hilde**-cumb(o)r,* **helm** *ond / byrnan* (1020–22; cf. 2994a–95a)

      'then as a reward of victory the child of Halfdane gave to Beowulf a golden standard, an ornamented war-banner, a helmet, and a mailcoat'

  (c) *onsend / **Higelāce,** gif mec / **hild** nime,* (s)vIo/O

      beadu**-scrūda / **betst, *þæt mīne / **brēost** wereð,*

      hrægla / *sēlest* (452a–43a)

      '(you) send to Hygelac, if combat takes me, the best of battle-shrouds, worthiest of combat garments, which protects my breast' (imperative)

  (d)   *sealde his / **hyrsted** sweord,* (s)vO/Io

      *īrena / cyst, **ombiht**- / þegne* (672b–73b)

      '(he) gave his ornamented sword, choicest of iron, to the attendant thane'

Opening verses in other examples like (73a): 948b (imperative), 1242a, 2221a, 2361a.

The instances like (73a) are syntactically complete opening verses. Conjuncts like those in the second line of (73a) can be added freely, like adjuncts, but are included in the complex object of the verb. In this particular case the whole second line could be omitted without adverse metrical consequences and its only apparent function is to add details relevant to immediate context. In (73b, c) the stressed constituents occupy separate verses in normative IoO order. In (73d) the heavy indirect object is displaced beyond the heavy direct object.

§3.11 Retrospect

The unique feature of this chapter is §3.1, which contains all the clauses in the poem that are most directly relevant to determination of typological word order, with a stressed subject, a stressed direct object, a stressed verb, and no other major constituents. Let us review the attested arrangements of major constituents in §3.1, drawing on principles shown to operate in §§3.2–10 as well. Below are the total frequencies for clauses with SOV, SVO, and VSO orders, the most common basic orders in human languages.

Common typologies:	SOV	SVO	VSO
One-verse clauses:	SOV: 10	SVO: 0	VSO: 0
1/2 division:	S/OV: 55	S/VO: 4	V/SO: 2
2/1 division:	SO/V: 3	SV/O: 34	VS/O: 10
1/1/1 division:	S/O/V: 12	S/V/O: 10	V/S/O: 11
Totals:	80	48	23

On the basis of total frequency SOV stands out as the leading contender for basic word order. The evidence of total frequency is confirmed by the frequencies for the possible arrangements, which are consistent with UM 1, the fundamental hypothesis that metrical constituents are abstracted from linguistic constituents, and with UM 2, a corollary to UM 1 that derives norms for metrical constituents from norms for the corresponding linguistic constituents. These principles predict that the favored realizations of verses, lines, and clauses will be consistent with the syntactic norms of Proto-Germanic, assuming that its basic order was SOV, as seems most likely on independent grounds (§§1.5, 1.6). Among the most common word orders the only one attested in §3.1a is SOV. In the multi-verse clauses of §3.1b, as predicted, the most common arrangement is S/OV, with the subject specifier in one verse and a following verse shared by constituents of the verb phrase in OV order. As predicted, the least common arrangement with SOV order in multi-verse clauses is SO/V, where the subject in a higher-level specifier position shares a verse with an extraneous lower-level object that is split from the verb in the verb phrase. SVO is next-highest in total frequency but the frequencies for arrangements in multi-verse clauses are inconsistent with SVO typology. The 2/1 division, which would have an extraneous lower-level constituent of the verb phrase sharing a verse with the higher-level subject, should be the least common in SVO typology, but in fact it is the most common. The 1/2 division, with verb and object sharing a verse in normative order, should be the most common, but has far lower frequency. VSO order is ruled out as a contender by its low total frequency and also by its favored distribution, V/S/O. As we have seen, arrangements with each major constituent in a separate verse are the ones most tolerant of departure from normative word order.

Now consider the attested frequencies for arrangement of constituents in OSV, OVS, and VOS clauses, which correspond to the least common basic orders in human languages.

Rare typologies:	OSV	OVS	VOS
One-verse clauses:	OSV: 4	OVS: 0	VOS: 0
1/2 division:	O/SV: 3	O/VS: 0	V/OS: 0
2/1 division:	OS/V: 1	OV/S: 16	VO/S: 5
1/1/1 division:	O/S/V: 6	O/V/S: 1	V/O/S: 4
Totals:	14	17	9

The only attested one-verse order, OSV, is derived from SOV order by emphatic fronting of an object suitable for emphasis. Like VSO order, OSV and VOS orders are ruled out as basic not only by their low total frequencies but also by their favored distribution, which has each major constituent in a separate verse. Although OVS is a rare typology, OVS clauses have higher frequency than VSO clauses, and this is due almost entirely to the frequency of OV/S, the only arrangement that puts constituents of the verb phrase in a verse with OV order. The least common OSV arrangement, OS/V, is the one with a verse shared by the subject and object in OS order, which departs from normative order in an SOV language. In the more common O/SV arrangement the SV verse conforms to SOV typology. This arrangement is most plausibly interpreted as an example of object fronting that leaves a trace between subject and verb. On that interpretation the SV clause is psychologically complete.

If the differences among word orders were subtler we might require a larger sample of data or advanced techniques of statistical analysis. In fact we are dealing with gross statistical discrepancies that are obviously not due to chance and therefore need to be explained. The explanation is provided by two independent hypotheses that are quite simple in the relevant scientific sense: (1) that the meter arose in a language with SOV word order and (2) that metrical constituents are abstracted from linguistic constituents. As we have seen (§1.3), other researchers have argued that Proto-Germanic had SOV typology and the traditional term *enjambment* presupposes that boundaries between verses and lines normally fall at natural points of syntactic division. The innovation employed here is a generative rule system that applies to syntax as well as morphology and phonology. This universalist system provides metrical evidence that is especially useful for testing linguistic theories, since it predicts what arrangements of linguistic constituents should be favored in a given meter. In chapters four through ten we will see that the SOV hypothesis and the universalist system predict the observed relative frequencies for arrangements of major constituents in all the attested syntactic constructions. Verse clauses with infinitive constructions, discussed in chapter 9, will provide further evidence for the role of animacy in determining which of two objects is in closer construction with the verb.

CHAPTER 4

SV CLAUSES AND THEIR DERIVATIVES

§4.0 Introduction

This chapter is devoted to clauses with a subject and an intransitive verb. Interpreted literally, the term 'intransitive' implies that intransitive verbs cannot have objects. This may seem true in Modern English, where animate recipients in intransitive clauses must be assigned case by a preposition rather than by a verb. We cannot say *that worked him* to mean *that worked for him*. However, Old English intransitive clauses can include datives of advantage or disadvantage that function in many ways like animate dative arguments governed by transitive verbs. The equivalent of *that worked him* is perfectly idiomatic in Old English and nothing but the verb is available to assign dative case to the pronoun. Compare *that helped him,* where a verb with an inanimate subject assigns uncontroversial object case to the pronoun. I interpret datives of advantage or disadvantage in intransitive clauses as arguments and refer to them as indirect objects.

Since intransitive clauses have fewer major constituents than the clauses in chapter three, the possible combinations are fewer. There are fewer sections and they provide larger samples of instances with the same set of metrically specified constituents. As a result there is strikingly clear evidence for constraints on the word order of major constituents sharing a verse and on placement of finite verbs within the line. The larger the sample, the easier it is to assess the relation between metrical complexity and relative frequency. It becomes particularly obvious here that the poet departs from SV order primarily to avoid adverse metrical consequences and that most other departures are of a kind often employed in SOV languages for emphasis, to clarify syntactic relations between adjacent clauses, or to mark a transition

175

to a new topic. The smaller number of major constituents leaves more room for adjuncts that provide alliteration and fill out a line. There are especially large samples of adjunct prepositional phrases, many of which provide detail relevant to immediate context as well as doing important metrical work.

§4.1. Instances with stressed subjects and verbs

§4.1a One-verse instances

Since one-verse SV clauses have only two major constituents, two-word realizations of verse types are common and many types can be constructed. The SV examples in item (1) fill each foot of a category II verse with a stressed word. The only extrametrical constituents that appear in these clauses are unstressed prefixes, the strongly preferred constituents for placement on extrametrical positions. The prefixes are required in a few cases here to express the relevant meaning of the verb.

(1) (a) *roderas / rēotað* (1376a)   S V

      'the skies weep'   Sx/Sx (A1)

  (b) *dryht-<u>sele</u> / dynede* (767a)   S V

      'the troop-hall resounded'   Ss/Sx (A3)

  (c) *brimu* / *swaþredon* (570b)   S V

      'the seas subsided'   S/Sxx (D1)

  (d) *Wīglāf* / <u>*maðelode,*</u> *Wēohstānes* / *sunu* (2862)   S V

      'Wiglaf spoke, Weohstan's son'   Sx/Sxx (D5)

  (e) *sǣ-genga / fōr* (1908b)   S V

      'the sea-goer (a boat) advanced'   Ssx/S (E)

  (f) *scaþan* / *ōnetton* (1803b; cf. 306b)   S V

      'the warriors hastened'   S/Ssx (D2)

Other examples like (1a): 212b, 226b, 327b, 328b, 419a (with prefixed verb), 703b, 760b, 817b (with prefixed verb), 1120b, 1328a, 1376a, 1602b, 2558b, 3048a; like (1b): 303b, 1121a, 1317b, 1906b, 2031a, 2256b, 2293b, 2457b, 2552a, 2906b; like (1c): 81b, 286a, 402b, 570b, 611b, 725b, 770b, 1117b, 1566b, 1630b, 1799b, 1898b, 2085b; like (1d): 348a, 360a, 371a, 405a, 456a, 499a, 529a, 631a, 925a, 957a, 1215a, 1321a, 1383a, 1473a, 1651a, 1687a, 1817a, 1840a, 1999a, 2425a, 2510a, 2631a, 2724a, 3076a; like (1e): 321b, 850a, 1401b, 1908b, 1965b, 2313b.

The verse lists provide good samples for many common verse patterns. Instances of types B, C, and D with a compound in the second foot have low frequency because verbs derived from compounds have low frequency in Old English. The rare examples in (1f) are type D2 verses with an Ssx verb in the second foot. In both cases the verb is *ōnettan* 'hasten,' an archaic verbal compound that has reduced secondary stress, as with other compounds in which the secondary root was no longer easily identifiable as a wordlike constituent (OEG: 32).

VS clauses comparable to the SV clauses in item (1) have predictably lower frequency. Item (2) contains the only instances in type II. There is no violation of the rule of precedence in (2a) because the following constituent has high frequency and correspondingly low prominence. In the other examples the second constituent is more prominent than the verb and alliterates in accord with the rule of precedence. In (2c, f, g), as in most cases, I interpret compound adjectives as zero-converted subjects when there is no expressed noun or pronoun subject (§1.22). The alternative interpretation of (2f) would be '(he) walked in a valor-bold way,' with an adverb zero-converted from an adjective. The reader should bear in mind that I have selected the interpretation with a zero-converted noun for consistent grouping of examples, not with any dogmatic intention. My choice has been guided in part by the high frequency of unambiguous instances in which a poetic compound adjective modifies an expressed argument and the lower frequency of unambiguous instances in which a verb is modified by such a compound.

(2) (a) *swīgedon / ealle* (1699b; cf. 1137b)   V S

   'all fell silent'   Sxx/Sx (A5)

  (b) *beorhtode / benc-swēg* (1161a)   V S

   'the bench-noise resounded'   Sxx/Ss (A6)

  (c) *þolode / ðrȳð-swȳð* (131a; cf. 726a)   V S

   'the mighty powerful (one) suffered'   Sx/Ss (A2)

  (d) *eteð / ān-genga*   *un-* / *murnlīce* (449a; cf. 2455a–57a)   V S

   'the lone-walker eats without regret'   S/Ssx (D2)

  (e) *burston / bān-locan* (818a)   VS

   'the bone joints burst'   Sx/Ssx (D6)

  (f) *ēode / ellen-rōf* (358a; cf. 1616a, 1909a)   VS

   'the valor-bold (one) walked'   Sx/Sxs (D7)

  (g) *gȳtsað / grom-hȳdig* (1749a)   VS

    'the unfriendly (one) grasps' (hoards ungenerously)   Sx/Ssx   (D6)

In all these examples verb fronting avoids placement of an alliterating finite verb on an s position, which violates OE 7.5. Items (2a, b) effect transitions to new phases of the narrative, a recognized function of verse-initial order in early Indo-European languages (§1.5). In (2a) VS order coincides with the hush that falls over hall-dwellers when an important character is about to deliver a speech; in (2b) excited talk at the end of a speech moves the narrative toward the next phase. VS order in (2a) avoids the rare D5 pattern of *ealle / swigedon* (Sx/Sxx), a violation of OE 3.6 with the complex Sxx foot in the wrong position. As we have observed (§1.14), this pattern appears only once in the b-verse. VS order in (2b) avoids **benc-swēg / beorht*ode, with the unacceptable pattern *Ss/Sxx (H1). Items (2e, g) avoid ***bān**-*locan / **bur**ston* and ***grom**-*hȳdig / **gȳt**saδ*, both with the unacceptable pattern *Ssx/Sx (H5). Item (2e) would qualify as Ssx/S (type E) if *locan* could be resolved, but that is blocked by Kaluza's law (OE 8.6). All the verbs are appropriate for emphatic fronting except *ēode* in (2f). This high-frequency verb of motion must be fronted to avoid the pattern *Sxs/Sx (MH1). Normative verb placement would create the same unacceptable pattern in the other examples like (2f), which have more vivid verbs.

    Items (3a, b) are type E verses with a stressed word in each foot. They differ from (1e) in having a word boundary internal to the first foot.

(3) (a) **gūd**-*rēc ā*- / *stāh* (1118b)   SV

       'the war-smoke (from a warriors' funeral pyre) rose up'   Ssx/S (E)

  (b) **drēa**m-*lēas ge*- / *bād* (1720b)   SV

       'the joyless (one) remained'   Ssx/S (E)

Other examples like (3a): 1789b, 2302b, 2487a, 2584b, 2680b, 3144b, 3146b.

All the other examples like (3a) are of type E, all are free of extrametrical syllables, and in every instance the unstressed constituent in the first foot is a prefix. Most of these are b-verses with the finite verb in normative metrical position s4.

    In the remaining SV verses of type II the metrical pattern is completed with the help of a stressed adjunct. In most instances the adjunct is the adverbial constituent of a quasi-compound. These instances might also be interpreted as two-word realizations (§1.14). The instances like (4b) have a noun in the dative-instrumental case used adverbially. Most instances in item (4) are of subtype D3, the type most commonly used for one-verse clauses with three stressed constituents (§3.1).

(4) (a) *fyrst / forð gewāt* (210a)	SV
'time went onward'	S/Sxs (D3)
(b) *draca / morðre swealt* (892b)	SV
'the dragon died from the assault'	S/Sxs (D3)
(c) *weras / on sāwon* (1650b; cf. 1422b)	SV
'the men looked on'	S/Ssx (D2)
(d) *fēþa / eal gesæt* (1424b)	SV
'the troop sat down entirely (as one)'	Sx/Sxs (D7)
(e) *werod / eall ārās* (651b)	SV
'the troop arose as one' or 'the whole troop arose'	D7 or S/Sxs (D3)

Other examples like (4a): 18b, 55b, 301b, 569b, 721b, 761b, 782b, 1160b, 1416b, 1570b, 1588b, 1615b, 1800b, 1912b, 2113b, 2213b, 2254b, 2331b, 2693b; like (4b): 496b, 515b, 1131b, 1422a, 2138a, 2593b, 2672b, 2966b; like (43e): 999b, 1790b, 2824b, 3030b.

In verses like (4a, c, d) the defining adverbs bear stress, in contrast to intensifying adverbs like *micle* 'much,' which are unstressed in pre-verbal position. If the adverbs were unstressed in (4a, d), these verses would have the unmetrical pattern *Sxx/S (O6). The stressed adverb alliterates in preference to the following constituent, as with the first constituent of a noun or adjective compound. There is little or no departure here from normative realization of a compound foot as a compound word. Evidence for quasi-compound status is weaker in verses like (4b), where the verb is modified by a dative-instrumental noun, since a lexical noun normally alliterates in preference to a finite verb no matter what function the noun performs. Item (4d) shows the 'semi-adverbial' use mentioned under the head word for *eal(l)* in the K4 glossary. If *eall* were in close constituency with the subject, mandatory placement of the foot boundary at the major syntactic break would yield the unacceptable pattern *Sxs/S (M1). I accordingly translate *eal* as a modifier of the verb meaning 'entirely' or 'as one.' Item (4e) could be scanned like (4d), but in this instance grouping *eal* with the verb would yield an acceptable Ssx/S verse of type E and *werod eal* would translate as 'the whole troop.' For this interpretation of *weorod eal* the less common noun-adjective order would be required.

The remaining VS clauses of type II are in item (5). The pronoun *him* in (5b, f) is excluded from the clause notation because it is a possessive dative, an STP rather than an SP.

(5) (a) *līxte / (se) lēoma* (1570a; cf. 311)   VS

      'the light gleamed'   Sx/Sx (A1)

  (b) *(Ne ge)mealt / (him se) mōd-sefa* (2628a)   VS

      'the courageous heart to him (his heart) did not weaken'   Sx/Ssx (A1)

  (c)   **samod** / *ǣrdæge*

    ēode / eorla sum, *æþele / cempa*   VS

    self mid / *(ge)sīðum* (1311b–13a)

    'at dawn one of the earls, a glorious champion, went with his companions'

                               Sx/Sxs (D7)

  (d) *fēhð ōþer / tō* (1755b; cf. 2673a)   VS

      'another (person) succeeds thereto (to an inheritance)'   Ssx/S (E)

  (e) *(ā)rās þā / (se) rīca, ymb hine / rinc manig,*   VS

    þrȳðlīc / þegna hēap (399a)

    'the mighty (one) arose then, (with) many a man — a magnificent band of thanes — around him'   Sx/Sx (A1)

  (f)   **hruron** him / *tēaras,*   VS

    blonden- / *feaxum* (1872b–73a)   SxSx (A1)

    'the tears to him — to the grey-haired (man) — fell' (his tears fell)

In (5a) verb-final order would create unacceptable anacrusis (OE 9.6). The simplest imaginable scansion for a verb-final alternative to (5b) would be **(him se) mōd-sefa ne / (ge)mealt*, with unacceptable anacrusis in type E (OE 9.7). The verb-final alternative to the second verse in (5c) would scan as **Sxs/Sx* (MH1). The verb-final alternative to (5d), **ōþer / tō fēhð*, would be an unacceptable type A8 variant (OE 3.4). The verb-final alternative to (5e), *þā se / rīca ārās*, would have an alliterating finite verb on an s position, contravening OE 7.5. The poet prefers to place the alliterating verb on the initial S position of type A1 verses like (5a). The normative type A1 has no inherent metrical complexity. Rearranging more complex types as A1 variants can reduce complexity if the resulting mismatches are tolerable.

As expected, most SV clauses of type I are b-verses like (6a–e), with normative order, a word group in the second foot, and the verb at normative metrical location s4. Item (6f) is the only instance in the a-verse. There are no instances with a compound verb like *ōnettan* in the second foot.

(6) (a) *þā his / mōd āhlōg* (730b)		SV
	'then his heart laughed'	x/Sxs (B1)
(b) *syððan / mergen cōm* (2103b, 2124b)		SV
	'after morning came'	xx/Sxs (B3)
(c)	*oþ þæt / ende becwōm,*	S V
	swylt æfter / synnum (1254b–55a)	
	'until the end came, death after sins'	xx/Sxxs (B4)
(d) *þon / þā dydon* (44b)		SV
	'than *they* did' (with contrastive stress)	x/Ssx (C2)
(e) *þonne / dæg līxte* (485b)		SV
	'when day dawned'	xx/Ssx (C4)
(f) *þā se / wyrm onwōc* (2287a)		S V
	'then the serpent awoke'	x/Sxs (B1)

Other B1 examples of like (6a): 66b, 310b, 356b, 369b, 405b, 573b, 1235b, 1528b, 1667b, 2403b, 2567b, 2577b, 2697b, 2700b, 2715b, 2769b, 2851b, 2978b, 3058b; of type B3 like (6b): 115b, 151b, 622b, 1077b, 1121b, 1960b, 2051b, 2103b, 2201b, 2303b, 2359b, 2388b, 2474b; of type C2 like (6d): 589b, 777b, 954b, 966b, 1343b, 1362b, 1648b, 1660b, 1741b, 2031b, 2445b, 2447b, 2499b, 2572b, 2745b; of type C4 like (6e): 23b, 731b, 1042b, 1375b 2058b.

Item (6a) represents a suspenseful moment when Grendel snickers to himself as he slouches toward the Scylding warriors he expects to eat. More often the intransitive verb encodes a quiet period between action scenes, for example to mark the passage of time, as in (6b, e).

There are just a handful of type I instances with VS order.

(7) (a)	*þanon / wōc fela*	VS
	geōsceaft- / gāsta (1265b–66a)	
	'then awoke (were born) a multitude of demons from the depths of time'	
		xx/Ssx (C4)
(b)	*ðā ge- / bēah cyning,*	VS

folces / *hyrde* (2980b–81a)

'then fell the king, guardian of the people'   x/Ssx (C2)

(c) *þonne* / **hniton** *fēþan* (1327b, 2544b)   VS

'when troops clashed'   xx/Ssx (C4)

In all of these instances the major constituents are realized as a b-verse, so alliteration is permitted only on the first lift. Item (7a) conforms to the rule of precedence: alliteration is not required on high-frequency constituents like *fela* when they follow an alliterating verb. Departure from normative order in (7a) is required for proper placement of the alliteration but not for that reason alone. With obligatory resolution of *fela*, the SV alternative **þanon* / **fela** *wōc* would be an unacceptable A8 variant with two stressed words (OE 3.4). The instances with prominent verse-final nouns in (7b, c) must violate the rule of precedence to avoid violation of the higher-ranking constraint against alliteration on the subordinate lift of the b-verse, which has highest rank and applies categorically. The only acceptable place for the alliterating verb in the opening verse of (7b) is at metrical location s1a. Even with the required changes in alliteration, the verb-final alternative to (7c) would contravene OE 8.5, since *hniton* would have to be resolved in order to create an acceptable verse pattern. The verbs in (7b, c) are quite vivid and suitable for emphatic fronting. Here as generally the poet uses plausible departures from SOV order — not just any departures — to avoid adverse metrical consequences.

§4.1b Multi-verse instances

Departure from normative order becomes more tolerable when major constituents occupy separate verses (OE 2.3). V/S instances are not much less common than S/V instances. The S/V instances in item (8) have the verb at normative metrical location s4. Those like (8a) arrange the metrical constituents as a single line; those like (8b) have the major constituents in separate lines.

(8) (a) *syððan* / **ðēod**-*cyning* **þyder** *on-* / *cirde* (2970)   S/V

'after the people's king went there'

   (b) *syððan* / **Gēa**ta <u>cyning</u> **gūð**e / *ræsum*,   S/V

      frēa-<u>wine</u> / *folca* **Frēs**-*londum* / *on*,

      Hrēðles / <u>eafo</u>ra **hioro**-*dryncum* / *swealt*,

bille / (ge)bēaten (2356a–59a)

'after the king of the Geats, the people's lord and friend, Hrethel's heir,

perished in Frisian lands from sword-drinks (bloodthirsty swords), beaten

down by blades'

Opening verses in other instances like (8a): 99a, 111a, 163a, 224b, 258a, 552a, 766a, 901a, 1373a, 1754a, 2144a, 2273a, 2951a, 2960a, 2970a; like (8b): 129b, 604b, 1000b, 1096b, 1359b, 1594b, 2053a, 2059a, 2325b, 2356a, 2592a (as emended), 2596a, 2893b, 3036b.

With just one major constituent per verse, S/V clauses provide ample room for semantically inessential modifiers. Alliteration for the first verse in (8a) is supplied by a semantically inessential compound constituent. Semantically inessential verses can be arranged rather freely around the two verses with major constituents. The second and third a-verses in (8b) are epithets of a kind often used to fill out a line. The fourth a-verse states somewhat redundantly that the king's death was by the sword; but such verses often explain a complex preceding metaphor like *hioro-drync*, which might be difficult to process in real time.

In (9a, b) the clause-final verb stands at the end of an a-verse at metrical location s2 or s3.

(9) (a)   *beornas / gearwe*   S/V

    on / stefn stigon (211b–12a)

    'the men eagerly climbed onto the prow'

 (b) *ðisse / ansȳne al-wealdan / þanc*   S/V

   lungre / (ge)limpe (928a–29a) (subjunctive verb)

   'for this sight thanks to the all-wielder should promptly take place'

Opening verses in other examples like (9a): 547b, 1279b, 1400b, 1736b, 2263b, 2675a.

Since the verb occupies a non-initial lift in the a-verse it is not required to alliterate by the rule of precedence but the poet alliterates on the verb in all these instances. The instance in (9b) violates Kuhn's second law, since *ðisse* is a clause-initial STP not accompanied by an SP. The universalist theory does not impose this constraint on SPs and is consistent with (9b). The weight of whole-verse constituents like *ðisse / ansȳne* explains why they are not often moved to the beginning of a clause and no other explanation is required.

Metrical constraints require placement of the verb at metrical location s1a in (10a–c). In (10d) *brogdenmǣl* is split from its modified subject by hyperbaton.

(10) (a)   ***hring***-*īren* / *scīr*   S/V

         song *in* / ***searwum*** (322b–23a)

         'the shining iron ring-mail sang in the war-gear'

      (b)   ***wæl***-*fȳra* / *mǣst*

         hlynode / *(for)* ***hlāwe*** (1119b–20a)

         'the greatest of corpse-fires (funeral pyres) roared in front of the barrow'

      (c)   ***Hen****gest* *ðā* / *gȳt*   S/V

         wæl-*fāgne* / ***wint(e)r***   ***wunode*** / *(mid)* *Finne* (1127b–28b; cf. 2863)

         'Hengest still dwelt with Finn then during the slaughter-stained winter'

      (d)   *þā þæt* / ***hilde***-*bil*   S/V

         *(for)****barn*** / ***brogden***-*mǣl* (1666b–67a; cf. 2487b–88a, as emended)

         'then the pattern-welded war-sword burned up'

       (e)   *swylce* / ***self*** *cyning*   S/V

         of / ***brȳd***-*būre*,   ***bēah***-*horda* / *weard*,

         tryd*dode* / ***tīr***-*fæst*. *ge-* / ***trume*** *micle*,

         cys*tum* / *(ge)****cȳþed*** (920b–23a)

         'also, the king himself, guardian of the ring-hoard, secure in glory, known for good qualities, walked with a large retinue'

Opening verses in other examples like (10a): 1007a, 1878a, 2072b, 2269b, 2628b, 2830a, 2881b, 3117a; like (10b): 1256b, 1492a, 1738b, 2241b, 2258a.

Departure from placement norms in (10a) avoids alliteration on a finite verb with subordinate stress occupying a subordinate s position (OE 7.5). In (10b) the verb in the a-verse is followed by a more prominent constituent that alliterates in accord with the rule of precedence. In (10c) the verb alliterates in the b-verse before a more prominent constituent that does not alliterate, contrary to the rule of precedence. In both instances verse-final placement of the verb would create unacceptable anacrusis (OE 9.6). Verb fronting is required in (10d, e) to avoid the unacceptable patterns *Sxs/S (M1) and Ss/Sxx (H1).

In the V/S clauses of item (11) the verb occupies normative metrical position s4 and the subject is displaced to the right periphery. In several instances like (11b) the displaced subject is split from a modifier by the verb in a common type of hyperbaton.

(11) (a)   *him on* / ***bearme** læg*   V/S

     mādma / ***mænigo,*** (40b–41a)

     'on his breast lay a multitude of treasures'

(b)   *ðā se* / ***wīsa** spræc*   V/S

     sunu / *Healfdenes* (1698b–99a)

     'then the wise son of Halfdane spoke'

(c)   ***wīde*** / *sprungon*   V/S

     hilde- / *lēoman* (2582b–83a)

     'the battle-flames spread widely'

(d)   *þenden* / ***þǣr** wunað*   V/S

     on / ***hēah**-stede **hū**sa* / *sēlest* (284b–85b)

     'while the best of houses stands there on the high place'

Opening verses in other examples like (11a): 40b, 726b, 775b, 1037b, 1041b, 1281b, 1434a, 1547b, 1571a (single alliteration), 1923b, 1980b, 2214b, 2225b, 2404b, 2556b, 2599b, 2714a, 2956b; with hyperbaton, as in (11b): 171b, 994b, 1133b, 1190b, 1338b, 2566b, 2742b.

All subjects are heavy modified constituents suitable for displacement. In most of these phrases the poet supplies optional alliteration, as in (11a). In (11b) the genitive modifier is a relative's name that does not happen to alliterate with the subject noun. In (11c) the subject is a compound in which the secondary constituent is less prominent than an independent noun and less appropriate for alliteration. In (11d) the modifier is a high-frequency comparative form that provides an appropriate occupant for the non-alliterating lift in the b-verse.

Items (12a–f) are V/S clauses with the verb out of normative metrical location s4.

(12) (a)   *þæt tō* / ***healle** gang **Healf**-_denes_ / _sunu_* (1009)   V/S

     'that Halfdane's son went to the hall'

(b)   *ac in* / ***campe** gecrong **cumb**les* / *hyrde,*   V/S

     æþeling / *(on)* ***elne*** (2505a–06a)

'but the standard-bearer, the atheling, fell in battle, in bravery'

(c) *nō þȳ / leng leofað   lāð-ge- / tēona,*   V/S

   *syn*num / *(ge)swen*ced (974a–75a)

   'none the longer lives the loathly spoiler, afflicted with sins' (simple present
   for future)

(d) *(ge)swāc æt / sæcce   sweord / Bīowulfes,*   V/S

   gomol ond / græg-mæl (2681a–82a; cf. 1013, 1977a–98a)

   'Beowulf's sword, ancient and gray-colored, failed at the fight'

(e) *seomode / (on) sāle   sīd-fæþmed scip*   V/S

   on / ancre fæst (302a–3a)

   'the broad-beamed ship stayed on the hawser, fast at anchor'

(f) *ofer þǣm / hongiað   hrin*de / bearwas   V/S

   'over it hang frost-covered groves' (1363; cf. 2036a–37b, 2177–78)

Opening verses in other examples like (12c): 32a, 2903a, 3047a, 3169a; like
(12e): 217a (avoids anacrusis in type E), 1543a (removes Sxs foot from initial
position).

These clauses provide insight into the relative strength of important rules.
As we have frequently seen, the poet avoids violating OE 7.5 if possible by
placement of alliterating finite verbs on the initial S position of type A1, as
in (12d), rather than on the subordinate s position of type B or C. In (12a)
rearrangement as type A1 is thwarted by the complementizer *þæt*, which
would create an unnecessary and otherwise unattested kind of anacrusis. The
anacrusis in (12d) is of the ordinary prefixal kind that adds the least complexity to type A1, the pattern most tolerant of additive complexity. In
(12b), the type A1 verse created by verb fronting would be *(ac ge)crong on
/ com*pe, with an an otherwise unattested form of disyllabic anacrusis that
includes a fixed SP conjunction. The poet will not tolerate an anacrusis this
complex to obtain conformity with OE 7.5. In (12c) the usual rearrangement
would not yield the tolerant type A1, rather type B with a resolved finite
verb at location s1a, a variant attested only twice in the poem (333a, 2345a).
Here too the cost of rearrangement outweighs the benefit. In (12e) verb-
final order would create unnecessary anacrusis and place the Sx and Sxx feet
in the wrong positions, contrary to OE 3.6. Verb placement at metrical location s1b is unproblematic in the examples like (12f), where there is no
other candidate for the required alliteration and no mismatch of linguistic
prominence to metrical prominence.

186

The verses in item (13) have a stressed indirect object added to the stressed subject and verb.

(13) (a)   *ed*wenden / *cwōm*   V/Io

        tīr-ēad(i)gum / menn   **tor**na / *(ge)hwylces* (2188b–89b)

        'a reversal of every misfortune occurred for the victory-blessed man'

(b)   *swylce hira /* **man**-*dryhtne*   Io/SV

        þearf ge- / sǣlde (1249b–50a; cf. 2227)

        'as need arose for their human lord'

(c)   *syððan* **Bēowulfe**   **brā**de *rīce*   Io/S/V

    on / **hand** *gehwearf* (2207a–08a)

    'afterwards a broad kingdom came to hand for Beowulf'

(d)   *syððan /* **Ingelde**   Io/VS

    weallað / **wæl**-*nīðas* (2064b–65a)

    'after deadly hostilities raged for Ingeld' (dative of disadvantage)

(e)   **Sige**-*munde / (ge)sprong*   IoV/S

    æfter / **dēað-dæge**   **dōm** */ unlȳtel* (884b–85b; cf. 783b–84b)

    'no little fame arose for Sigmund after (his) death-day'

Opening verses in other instances like (13a): 2116b (hyperbaton), 2941b.

In (13a, e) the verb occupies normative metrical location s4. The verb occupies location s2 in (13b, c) and location s1a in (13d). It might also be possible to interpret (13c) as an instance of hyperbaton in which the direct object splits possessive dative *Bēowulfe* from its modified noun *hand*. In that case *Bēowulfe on hand* would be excluded from the notation as an adjunct modifier of the verb and the clause pattern would be S/V. In (13d, e) a modified subject has been displaced to the right periphery. Metrical requirements explain why the verb and subject in (13d) are out of normative order in the verse they share. The SV alternative **wæl-nīðas / weallað* scans as *Ssx/Sx (H5).

§4.2 Instances with unexpressed or relativized subjects

The instances with an unexpressed subject are all one-verse clauses. The only multi-verse instances have a relativized subject in one verse and the verb in a later verse.

§4.2a One-verse instances

In (14a–f) the clause-final verb occupies normative metrical location s4 at the end of a b-verse. The most common realizations are like (14a).

(14) (a)   *ðǣr on / **wicge** sæt* (286b)   (s)V

      'where (he) sat on a horse'

  (b)   *ac him tō- / **gēanes** rād* (1893b; cf. 1542b)   (s)V

      'and (he) rode towards them'

  (c)   ***mægen**-strengo / slōh* (2678b)   (s)V

      '(he) struck with great strength'

  (d)   ***yrringa** / slōh* (1565b)   (s)V

      '(he) struck angrily'

  (e)   *nō þæs / **frōd** leofað*

      ***gume**na / bearna* (1366b–67a)   (s)V

      'no (one) so wise lives of the children of men'

  (f)   *nalles æfter / **lyfte**   **lā**cende / hwearf*   (s)V

      ***mid**del- / nihtum* (2832a–33a)

      '(he) by no means wheeled flying through the air in the midnight hours'

Like (14a): 144b, 507b, 635b, 749b, 1171b, 1442b, 1536b, 1537b, 1603b, 1893b, 1913b, 2299b, 2308b, 2618b; like (14c): 8b, 514b, 849b, 2268b, 2510b; like (14d): 745b, 759b, 1404b.

In all these instances the verb is preceded by an adverbial modifier that supplies the obligatory alliteration. The preposed adverbials are more prominent than the finite verbs, so there are no violations of the rule of precedence. The instances like (14a) have prepositional phrases in adverbial function. The two instances like (14b), with postpositional phrases, differ only in the choice of motion verb. The instances like (14c) have a dative-instrumental noun in adverbial function. Alliteration is supplied by an adverb in (14d), by an adverbial phrase in (14e), and by a present participle in (14f). In most cases a linguistically acceptable construction would remain if the adjuncts were removed from their clauses and the adjuncts are semantically inessential in that sense. In some cases, however, the result of omission would be a grammatically acceptable construction that did not make good sense in context. Reduced to *ac rād,* for example, (14b) would seem bizarrely pointless. Such adjuncts, though semantically inessential at verse level, are required at discourse level. In a traditional phrase repeated verbatim or with minimal change a metrically useful adjunct can be semantically redundant in one instance and indispensable in another.

Less often the verb occupies the last lift of the a-verse, at location s2, s3, or s1b.

(15) (a)   *on ge- / **weald** gehwearf **worold**- / cyninga*   (s)V
           *ðǣm / **sē**lestan   be / **sǣm** twēonum* (1684a–85a)
           'it passed into the ownership of the best of worldly kings between the two seas'

     (b)   *ond for / **dol**-gilpe   on / **dēop** wæter*   (s)V
           aldrum / nēþdon (509a–10a)
           'and for foolish boasting (you) gambled with (your) lives in deep water'

     (c)   *elne / (ge)**ē**odon* (1967a; cf. 1691a)   (s)V
           'they walked boldly'

     (d)   *swā / **rī**xode* (144a; cf. 630)   (s)V
           'in this way he prevailed'

In (15a) the only alliteration for the opening verse is provided by a prepositional phrase in adverbial function. I interpret *woroldcyninga* as an adjunct modifier of *geweald* and *ðǣm sēlestan* as an adjunct modifier of *woroldcyninga*. In (15b) the first line contains prepositional phrases that modify the verb and the (s)V clause follows them. In the clauses like (15c) the verb alliterates optionally at location s2 after an alliterating adverb. In the clauses like (15d) the verb alliterates at metrical location s1b as the only stressed constituent.

In (16a–h) the finite verb occupies metrical location s1a, the least appropriate location. In (16a) *sum* refers to the subject but **eahta** *sum* seems most appropriate as a modifier of the verb describing the manner in which the subject went. I interpret **eah**ta *sum* as an adverbial modifier rather than as a zero-converted subject. I also interpret **gearo**-*folm* as an adverbial modifier in (16d), where the meaning of the poetic compound is closely related to the meaning of the verb. Departure from normative verse placement in (16a–g) avoids verse patterns that are rare or unacceptable. The imperative verb is routinely fronted in (16h).

(16) (a)   *ēode / **eah**ta sum* (3123a)   (s)V

'he went one of eight' (he went in a group of eight)

(b) *rǣsde / (on ðone) rōfan* (2690a; cf. 356a, 402a)   (s)V

'(he) rushed into the bold (one)'

(c) *wōd þā / (þurh þone) wæl-rēc* (2661a; cf. 515a, 2852a)   (s)V

'(he) advanced then through the deadly fumes'

(d) *grāpode / gearo-folm* (2085a; cf. 2119a)   (s)V

'(he) grasped ready-handed'

(e) *ond nō / mearn fore* (136b)   (s)V

'and (he) did not feel remorse for that'

(f) *fērdon / forð þonon   fēþe-lāstum[,]*   (s)V

ferhþum / fægne (1632a–33a)

'(they) fared forth from there in foot-troops, happy in heart'

(g) *geōmrode / giddum* (1118a)   (s)V

'(she) sorrowed in songs'

(h) *(ne) sorga, / snotor guma* (1384a)

'do not sorrow, wise man'

Other instances like (16a): 1390a, 2717b, 2746a, 3084a.

The SV alternative to (16a), *eahta sum / ēode* (*Sxs/Sx: MH1), violates the
*MORPHOLOGY rule against placement of a complex Sxs or Sxxs foot in
first position. The same kind of problem would arise in the other examples.
In the verses like (16b) verb-final order would create unnecessary anacruses.
The alternative to (16c),*þā þurh þone / **wæl-rēc wōd**, would have the prominently stressed constituent of a poetic compound on the x position of the
Sxs foot, violating OE 4.2; and occupation of the s position by alliterating
wōd would contravene OE 7.5 as well. The same problems would arise in
the other examples. Verb-final order in (16d) would create *__gearo-folm /
grāpode,__* with the unacceptable pattern *Ss/Sxx (H1). In (16e) the verb
could not occupy final position because that would put *fore* at metrical location s1a, where resolution is obligatory. The resulting pattern would be
xx/Ss (type A8), which is unacceptable in the b-verse. In the opening verse
of (16f) verb-final order would create *__forð þonon / fērdon__*, with the unacceptable pattern *Ssx/Sx (H5). Here *þonon* would bear weak but metrically
significant stress in phrase-final position after *forð*. Scansion of such a verse
as Ss/Sx (A3) would require resolution on the s position, but since the last
syllable of *þonon* is closed by a final consonant, resolution is blocked by

Kaluza's Law. Verb-final order in (16g) would place the complex Sxx foot after the normative Sx foot, contravening OE 3.6.

We have seen many examples in which violation of OE 7.5 is avoided by rearranging the constituents as a type A verse with the verb in metrical location s1a. The instances like (17a, c) are additional examples of this kind.

(17) (a) *wēox* under / *wolcnum* (8a)   (s)V

       '(he) flourished beneath the skies'

    (b) *sē ðe* / *lengest leofað   lāðan* / *cynnes,*   wsV

       fǣre bifongen (2008a–9a)

       'whoever lives longest of that loathly kindred, surrounded by perils'

    (c) *site* nū / *(tō) symle* (489a)   (s)V

       '(you) sit down to the feast now' (imperative)

Like (17a): 307a, 327a, 714a, 926a, 1119a, 1132a, 1251a, 1501a, 2179a, 2288a, 2919a, 2975a; like (17c): 660a, 1218b.

The number of type A verses like (17a, c) is significant and the absence of type B alternatives like *under / *wolcnum* *wēox* is a SYSTEMATIC GAP requiring explanation. In (17b) placement of the alliterating verb on the more prominent lift would create a type C variant with resolution of a finite verb on the S position, a variant attested only three times in the poem (659a, 1326b, 2544b). Here as in (12b, c) the cost of fronting the verb to location s1a outweighs the benefit. Far from probing the rule and finding it wanting, SYSTEMATIC EXCEPTIONS like (17b) testify to the validity of OE 7.5. This rule cannot be formulated within the system of Sievers (1893) because Sievers assigns the final stress in types B and C to a primary lift rather than to a subordinate lift. It seems simplest to assume that OE 7.5 would also inhibit reversal of instances like (17c), though the systematic gap is not conspicuous here because imperative verbs are routinely fronted for emphasis.

The verses in item (18) have relativized subjects. Those like (18a) are of type B; those like (18b) are of type C.

(18) (a) *sē þe in* / *þȳstrum bād* (87b)   wsV

       'who dwelt in the shadows'

    (b) *sē þe* / *wēl þenceð* (289b)   wsV

       'who thinks properly'

Other examples like (18a): 192b, 500a, 825b, 1617b, 1883b, 2238b, 3125b; like (18b): 98b, 113b, 506b, 996b, 2601b.

The instances like (18a, b) have single alliteration and do not contravene OE 7.5. Since the verbs do not alliterate in these type I verses, there are no impediments to normative verb placement and all instances have clause-final order. The clause-final verb stands in normative metrical location s4 in all instances except 500a. The constraints on alliteration in type B apply in type C as well but a little more dramatically. There is no verb-final a-verse with alliteration on the verb in type C, not even a systematic exception comparable to (17b).

　　We are left with item (19).

(19) (a) *bāt* / *unswīðor* (2578b)　　　　　　　　　　　　　　　(s)V

　　　　'(it) cut no more strongly' (anticipating a than–clause)

With the required change in alliteration, **unswīðor** / *bāt* would scan as Ssx/S (type E). The vivid monosyllabic verb **bāt** seems to be fronted to an alliterating position for emphasis in (19a) and not simply because it provides the alliteration (compare *Beowulf* 742a).

§4.2b Multi-verse instances

In (20a–c) the subject is relativized and the verb stands at normative metrical position s4.

(20) (a) *þā ðe mid* / **Hrōðgāre** *on* / **holm** *wliton* (1592; cf. 1342)　　ws/V

　　　　'who gazed on the sea with Hrothgar'

　(b) *sē þe of* / **flān**-*bogan* **fyrenum** / *scēoteð* (1744; cf. 1935)　　ws/V

　　　　'who wickedly shoots from an arrow-bow'

　(c)　　　　　　*sē ðe* / **nēh** *geþrong*　　　　　　　　　　　　　wsV

　　hǣðnum / **horde** (2215b–16a)

　　　　'who pressed near the heathen hoard'

Alliteration for the verse containing the verb is supplied by a prepositional phrase in (20a) and by an adverbial noun in (20b). In (20c) the verb splits the alliterating preposition *nēh* from its governed object in a typical instance of hyperbaton. *Nēh* bears stress here as an adverb would do in pre-verbal position. As the entry for *nē(a)h* in the K4 glossary points out, the word sometimes functions as an adverb.

§4.3 Instances with an unstressed subject pronoun and a stressed verb

§4.3a One-verse instances

Items (21a–e) are b-verse clauses with normative word order, the unstressed subject in normative metrical position x1, and the stressed verb in normative metrical position s4. As expected, these instances have the highest frequency.

(21) (a) *gyf hēo / **gȳt** lyfað* (944b)   sV

      'if she still lives'

   (b) *hē tō / **healle** gēong* (925b)   sV

      'he went to the hall'

   (c) *oð þæt hē / **morðre** swealt* (2782b)   sV

      'until he died from the attack'

   (d)   *hē ge- / **wērgad** sæt,*   sV

    *fēðe- / cempa, **frēan** eaxlum / nēah* (2852b–53b)

      'he sat wearied — that foot-soldier — near to the shoulders of his lord'

   (e)   *oþ þæt hē / **āna** hwearf,*   sV

    *mǣre / þēoden[,] **mon**-drēamum / from* (1714b–15b)

      'until he — that famous lord — passed alone from the joys of mankind'

   (f) *þē þū hēr / **tō** lōcast* (1654b; cf. 681b, 2866b)   sV

      'which you gaze at here'

Like (20a): 400b, 430b, 680b, 900b, 1385b, 1466b, 1556b, 1824b, 2077b, 2289b, 3106b, 3167b; like (20b): 264b, 358b, 404b, 419b, 512b, 539b, 632b, 676b, 772b, 891b, 1074b, 1113b, 1209b, 1215b, 1295b, 1337b, 1382b, 1392b, 1430b, 1485b, 1506b, 1532b, 1540b, 1568b, 1572b, 1679b, 2019b, 2096b, 2362b, 2409b, 2471b, 2568b, 2598b, 2624b, 2679b, 2724b, 2756b, 2796b, 2992b.

In most instances the required alliteration is supplied by an adverb, as in (21a), or by a prepositional phrase with adverbial function, as in (21b). Observe that the prepositional phrases have significantly higher frequency than the adverbs, probably because prepositional phrases can encode many more kinds of appropriate detail. Alliteration is supplied by an adverbial noun in (21c) and by a participial adjective in (21d). I interpret simplex *āna* in (21e) as an adjective zero-converted to an adverb rather than as an adjectival modifier of the subject in a phrase with the meaning 'he alone.' Interpretation of *āna* as an adjective here would assert for no particular reason that the famous lord was the only one who died. In this cautionary digression the emphasis is on the lonely death of a leader who abused his followers. The third verse of (21e) is realized as a postpositional phrase. A prepositional phrase would be metrically acceptable here but the poet did not modernize the word order. In (21f) the postposition in the cited example subordinates the finite verb as adverbial *tō* would do in an Old English quasi-compound. In the other instances postpositional *on* and *ongean* have the same subordinating effect as the corresponding adverbs.

In (22a–c) the verb stands at the end of the a-verse.

(22) (a) *þæt hit / **eal** gemealt[,] **īse** / (ge)līcost* (1608) sV

'that it melted entirely, most like unto ice'

  (b) *oð ðæt hī oð- / **ēodon** earfoð- / līce* sV

    *in / **Hrefnes Holt** hlāford- / lēase* (2934–35; cf. 2200a–1a)

    'until with great difficulty they escaped lordless into Raven's Wood'

  (c) *gif þæt ge- / **gangeð*** (1846a)

    'if that happens' (anticipating a that-clause)

In (22a, b) the line with the major constituents is completed by a semantically inessential adjunct. Placement of (22c) in the a-verse makes the b-verse available for opening the that-clause in the ideal location, with the finite verb of this clause at normative location s4. The verb in (22a) occupies the subordinate lift in an a-verse of type I and alliteration on the more prominent adverb suffices. In the clauses like (22b, c) the verb alliterates at metrical location s1b as the only stressed constituent.

In (23a–d) the verb occupies metrical location s1a, its least appropriate location.

(23) (a) *(ne ge)**wēox** hē / (him tō) **willan**[,] ac tō / **wæl**-fealle* Vs

    *ond tō / **dēað**-cwalum **Deniga** / lēodum* (1711–12)

    'he did not mature according to their desire, rather as slaughter and deadly injury for the people of the Danes' (with possessive dative *him*)

(b) *(ge)bīde / (gē on) beorge*   *byr*num / <u>wered</u>e,   Vs

    secgas / (on) searwum (2529a–30a)

    '(you) abide on the hill protected by mailcoats, oh men in war-gear'

                                                                             (imperative)

(c) *wunað hē / (on) wiste* (1735a)   Vs

    'he lives amid feasting'

(d)   *hē him / rǣhte ongēan* ,   sV

    fēond [,] mid / folme (747b–48a)

    'he — that enemy — reached out toward him with (his) hand'

In the opening verse of (23a), normative syntactic order would create **hē him tō / willan ne gewēox,* with the pattern *x(xx)/Sxxxs. Besides contravening OE 7.5 with alliteration on *gewēox,* the compound foot in this pattern is unacceptable because it does not correspond to an Old English word pattern. In (23b) leaving the imperative verb in core-final position would create an otherwise unattested kind of disyllabic anacrusis with a SP pronoun and a preposition. As it stands (23b) has ordinary prefixal anacrusis in a pattern of normative type A1, the pattern most tolerant of anacrusis. The verb-final alternative to (23c), **hē on / wiste wunað,* would be a very unusual type B verse with a resolved and alliterating verb on the s position, contravening both OE 7.5 and OE 8.5. The poet avoids these problems in the usual way, by rearranging the constituents as a type A1 verse. In (23d) fronting highlights a verb suitable for emphasis as well as providing the alliteration.

§4.3b Multi-verse instances

In these relatively few s/V examples the clause is extended beyond the opening verse by adjunct modifiers of the verb.

(24) (a) *syððan ic on / yrre*   *uprihte / (ā)stōd* (2092)   s/V

    'after I stood upright in anger'

  (b)   *git on / wæteres ǣht*

    seofon-niht / swuncon (516b–17a; cf. 252b–54a, 1138b–39b)   s/V

    'you toiled a sennight (a week counted as seven nights) in the domain of the water'

(c) *þæt hē bī / **wealle**[,]   **wīs**- / hycgende[,]*   s/V

   (ge)sæt on / sesse (2716a–17a)

   'that he sat, wise-thinking, on a seat'

Opening verses in other examples like (24a): 526a, 1753a, 1780a, 2034a, 3049b.

Most instances are like (24a), with the verb in normative metrical and syntactic position. In (24b) the verb occupies location s2 in the a-verse. In (24c) the stressed verb occupies metrical location s1a, its least appropriate location. As verb placement departs from the norm in (24b) and farther from the norm in (24c), the frequency of instances in this small sample falls as expected, just as in larger samples we have considered. Verb fronting in (24c) avoids contravention of OE 7.5 by rearranging the constituents as a type A1 verse with ordinary prefixal anacrusis.

§4.4 Instances with an unstressed object and a stressed verb

Since we are concerned with intransitive verbs in this chapter, the only relevant objects to consider are indirect.

§4.4a One-verse instances

Stressed constituents sharing a verse in (25a–c) observe normative SV and IoV orders. In (25b) as generally in such constructions I interpret the reflexive dative pronoun as an indirect object beneficiary that happens to have the same referent as the subject.

(25) (a) *þæs ðe hire se / **willa** gelamp* (626b)   ioSV

   'because the wish had come to pass for her'

   (b) *ond him / **Hrōþgār** gewāt   tō / **hofe** sīnum,*   ioSV

   *rīce[,] / (tō) **ræste*** (1236a–37a; cf. 662–63)

   'then Hrothgar, the powerful (man), walked for himself to his apartment, to his bed'

   (c) *(hū) **lomp** ēow / (on) **lāde**,   **lēofa** / Bīowulf* (1987)   Io.sV

   'how went (it) for you on the journey, dear Beowulf?'

The verb occupies normative metrical location s4 in (25a), location s2 in (25b), and s1a in (25c). In (25c) a main verb has been fronted to C after an

operator (*hū*) in a higher-level specifier position (§1.9). This kind of fronting
no longer occurs with main verbs in English. *How did it go for you?* would
be idiomatic usage today but *how went it for you?* probably sounds like an
archaism in a historical novel. Arranging the constituents of (25c) as a type
A1 verse avoids contravention of OE 7.5. The adverbial anacrusis in (25c)
is unusual but there is a similar example in 2093a.

§4.4b Multi-verse instances

Items (26a–d) have an unstressed indirect object in location x1 of the opening verse and a major constituent in a following verse. The indirect object
beneficiary is identical to the subject in (26d, e).

(26) (a) *gif him / **þyslīcu** **þearf** ge- / lumpe*   io/SV
         (2637; cf. 340a–41a, 1774a–75a)
         'if such a need should arise for him'

   (b)   *oþ þæt him / **eft** onwōc*   iøV/S
         hēah / **Healf**dene (56b–57a)
         'until eminent Halfdane awoke for him' (was born to him)

   (c) *ðǣm / **fēower bearn**   **forð**-ge- / rīmed*   ioS/V
       *in / **worold** wōcun,   **weoroda** / rǣswan,*
       ***Heorogār** / (ond) **Hrōðgār**   ond / **Hālga** til* (59–61)
       'four children, leaders of hosts, were born to him in succession: Heorogar
       and Hrothgar and worthy Halga, leaders of hosts' (fourth child mentioned
       in a separate clause)

   (d) *gif him þonne / **Hrēþrīc**   tō / **hofum** Gēata*   ioS/V
       *(ge)þingeð[,] / **þēod**nes bearn* (1836a–37a; cf. 1853b–54b)
       'then if Hrethric, the king's son, intends (to go) to the courts of the Geats
       for himself'

   (e)   *him se / **ōðer** þonan*   ioS/V
       ***losað** / **lif**gende* (2061b–62a)
       'the other (one) escapes for himself alive'

In the clauses like (26a) the major constituents are arranged in a single line
with the unstressed object in normative location x1 and the stressed constituents in normative order. The example in *Beowulf* 340a–41a employs hyperbaton to achieve this arrangement. In (26b) a heavy modified subject is

displaced to the right periphery. In (26c) the opening line is filled out by a semantically inessential compound and the finite verb alliterates on the s position in type B, contravening OE 7.5. The alternative with the verb on the S position would be a rare form of type A1 with an unresolved short syllable on the second lift. Placing the verb at metrical location s1a in the instances like (26d) avoids the unacceptable pattern *Sxs/Sx (MH1). In (26e) an alliterating finite verb is resolved on the first S at metrical location s1a. The alternative with verb-final order would contravene OE 7.5 and OE 8.5 in *lifigende / losað*, an easily reversible two-word variant of type E. The closest parallel to this alternative in *Beowulf* is *gold-æht on- / gite* 'see the golden treasures' (2748a), but in this instance reversal would create the unacceptable type C variant **on- / gite gold-æht*, with a prominent compound constituent on the x position of the Ssx foot (OE 4.3).

§4.5 Instances with an unexpressed or relativized subject and an unstressed indirect object

§4.5a One-verse instances

In (27a–e) an unstressed indirect object stands at location x1, its normative metrical location. The subject is unexpressed in (27a–d) and relativized in (27e).

(27) (a) *him / **wiht** ne spēow* (2854b; cf. 3026b)   (s)ioV
        '(that) did not work for him at all'

    (b) *swā him ful / **oft** gelamp* (1252b; cf. 76b–77a)   (s)ioV
        'as (that) had very often happened to him'

    (c) *swā him ge- / **met** þince* (687b)   (s)ioV
        'as (it) seems proper to him'

    (d) *hwæþere mē ge- / **sælde** * (574a; cf. 890a)   (s)ioV
        'however, (it) it turned out well for me'

    (e) *þǣm þe him / **selfa** dēah* (1839b)   wsioV
        'who fends for himself himself (without aid)'

In (27a–c) the unexpressed subject has an antecedent in the immediately preceding clause. The other examples like (27a, b) have prepositional phrases rather than adverbs as the adjuncts that supply the alliteration. Item (27d) is an impersonal construction of the kind in which an unexpressed subject occurs routinely without an antecedent. The other example like

(27d) differs only in having *him* rather than *me*. In (27a–c, e) the stressed verb stands in normative metrical location s4. The instances like (27d) have the verb at metrical location s1b in a type A7 pattern restricted to the a-verse.

§4.5b Multi-verse examples

Since they are quite compact, (s)ioV and wsioV constructions usually fit within a single verse. No multi-verse examples happen to occur in *Beowulf.* Item (28) is a wsio/V example from an early Old English poem that is metrically similar to *Beowulf.*

(28) *þæt him on his / **in**ne swā / **earm**e gelamp* (*Genesis* 1567)   wsio/V

   'what so shamefully happened to him in his dwelling'

Here two adjuncts, a prepositional phrase and a root adverb, supply the required alliteration and make it possible to express the clause as a line. The verses are common realizations of types A7 and B1.

§4.6 Instances with unstressed main verbs

§4.6a One-verse instances

In (29a–c) a main verb has been fronted to metrical location x1 in the opening verse, the only location permissible for such verbs when they are unstressed.

(29) (a)   *ēode / **Wealh**þēo forð,*   vS

   ***cwēn** / Hrōðgāres **cyn**na / (ge)myndig* (612b–13b; cf. 404b–4a as emended, 1600a)

   'Wealhtheow came forth, Hrothgar's queen, mindful of courtesies'

   (b) *āhlēop ðā se / **gom**ela* (1397a)   vS

   'the old (man) leapt up then'

   (c) *ne frīn þū æfter / **sæ**lum* (1322a)   vS

   'don't you ask about happiness' (imperative)

The instances like (29a) have colorless verbs of motion and perception suitable for unstressed usage. In (29b) a more vivid verb of motion marks a transition to the next action sequence. It (29c) a high-frequency imperative verb of speaking is fronted to an unstressed position before the unstressed subject. Here as in other cases the early Indo-European technique of fronting for emphasis can be distinguished from the emphasis provided by Germanic expiratory stress.

A fronted verb marks a point of narrative transition in (30a, b). The referent of the unexpressed subject in (30b) is specified in a following relative clause.

(30) (a) *cōm þā tō* / **Heorote** (1279a)   (s)v

    '(she) came then to Heorot'

  (b) *þonne cwið æt* / **bēore** (2041a)   (s)v

    'then (he) speaks at the beer-drinking'

Other examples like (30a): 1188a, 1232a, 1573a, 1782a, 2460a.

The other examples like (30a) also have a high-frequency verb of motion in location x1 followed by a prepositional phrase that supplies the alliteration. The main verb of speaking in (30b) has such high frequency in the narrative that it usually appears on an unstressed position.

§4.6b Multi-verse instances

In (31a–d) an unstressed verb of motion is fronted to clause-initial position at a transitional point in the narrative.

(31) (a) *gesæt ðā on* / **næsse** *nīð-heard* / *cyning* (2417)   v/S

    'then the battle-brave king sat down on the headland'

  (b) *ēodon him þā tō-* / **gēanes, Gode** / *þancodon,*   v/S

    ðrȳðlic / **þeg**na *hēap* (1626a–27a)

    'then went toward him — (and) thanked God — that mighty troop of thanes'

  (c)   *gewāt him* / **hām** *þonon*   vio/S

    gold-*wine* / **gum**ena (1601b–2a)

    'the gold-friend of men went home for himself'

  (d)   *ēode* / **weorð** *Denum*   v/S

    æþeling / *(tō)* **yp**pan (1814b–15a)

    'the atheling, dear to the Danes, went to the throne'

Opening verses in other examples like (31a): 1210a, 1316a, 1888a, 2538a.

Most instances are like (31a), with a prepositional phrase providing alliteration for the a-verse and a heavy subject displaced to the right periphery. The alliterating constituent in (31b) is the stressed postposition of a postpositional phrase. In (31c) the alliterating adverbial is *hām* 'home, homeward,' a noun with accusative case encoding motion toward a goal. In (31d) alliteration is supplied by a complex adjectival modifier of the subject.

§4.7. Retrospect

The unique feature of this chapter is §4.1a, with its very large number of one-verse clauses that have stress on all major constituents. These clauses provide especially convenient evidence for syntactic constraints on verse structure because their word orders cannot be disrupted by Kuhn's laws or the SPMR. They provide equally convenient evidence for metrical constraints on verse structure, since all metrical rules apply to the same verse. As we observed in §3.1a, one-verse SOV clauses have low frequency because they have such complex metrical patterns. SV clauses allow for construction of less complex verse patterns and the large sample of one-verse instances has made it possible to discuss them type by type in §4.1a. We now abstract away from these detailed discussions to highlight constraints that apply in all instances with a stressed subject, a stressed verb, and no other major constituent.

One-verse clauses:	SV: 178	VS: 30
in a-verse	42	21
in b-verse	136	9
Multi-verse clauses:	S/V: 56	V/S: 44
verb on last lift of a-verse:	6	11
verb before last lift of a-verse:	19	7
verb on last lift of b-verse:	29	25
verb before last lift of b-verse:	2	1

Among the SOV clauses surveyed in §3.11, one-verse instances with complex syntax are outnumbered by multi-verse instances that place major constituents in less complex verses. Among the less complex SV clauses one-verse instances outnumber multi-verse instances by 178 to 56. The poet obviously prefers to realize an SV clause as a verse and it is easy to see why. The more prominent major constituent is the noun subject and it occupies the more prominent lift in accord with OE 6.1. Since linguistic and metrical prominence are properly aligned, the rule of precedence does not apply, and alliteration is required only on the subject. If its word patterns create an acceptable verse pattern, an SV clause provides a ready-made verse with optimal two-word form that can be used in either half of the line. VS order in one-verse clauses occurs for metrical reasons. Most instances in items (2) and (5) avoid verse patterns ruled out by Sievers (1893) and Bliss (1967), patterns that are widely regarded as unacceptable (K4: 330–35). In the remaining instances, VS order avoids violation of OE 3.4 (item 5d), OE 3.6 (item 2a), and OE 7.5 (item 5e). Departure from normative SV order is also subject to stylistic constraints. Most verbs in VS clauses are vivid, low-frequency constituents suitable for emphatic fronting.

The larger sample of one-verse instances makes it easier to assess their normative placement within the line. An SV clause in the b-verse has its verb in normative location s4 and b-verse instances have much higher frequency as expected (OE 1.3). Departure from normative word order creates significant metrical complexity in one-verse clauses with VS order and they cannot be placed so as to put the verb at normative location s4. As a result, the principle of closure inhibits placement of these clauses toward the end of the line and a-verses outnumber b-verses (UM 4, OE 5.3). The verb can be placed at normative location s4 in multi-verse V/S clauses, however. This explains why V/S clauses outnumber VS clauses, in contrast to clauses with SV order. When the finite verb appears on the first of two lifts, the word on the second lift is usually more prominent and in these cases double alliteration is strongly preferred (OE 7.2). Since double alliteration is ruled out in the b-verse, most one-verse instances with the verb before the last lift are a-verses.

CHAPTER 5

EXISTENTIAL AND PREDICATE ADVERBIAL
CLAUSES

§5.0 Introduction

The *Beowulf* poet typically uses 'be' verbs to provide the required grammatical functions for a verb phrase that has most of its semantic content in a constituent such as a predicate noun, a predicate adjective, or a participle. In this chapter we will discuss predicative use of adverbials with 'be' verbs as well as use of 'be' verbs to assert an existential status. Predicate adverbials (Pd, pd) are major sentence constituents similar to predicate adjectives. To distinguish the ordinary use of adverbs as adjuncts from their use as major sentence constituents we will need to distinguish existential constructions with adjunct adverbials from constructions in which the semantic content of the verb phrase is concentrated in an adverb.

Existential 'be' verbs in Indo-European languages are often similar in meaning to the verbs from which they evolved — verbs with senses like *exist, stay, persist, dwell, appear, be present, happen, occur, become, arise,* and *remain* (OED, s.v. *be*). English *be* often means 'have or occupy a place' or 'remain or go on in its existing condition.' It means 'be the case' in constructions like *It's not (the case) that I dislike you, it's just that I disapprove of you.* Existential clauses are used to introduce a new entity into a discourse or, when negated, to assert the absence of an entity. After an entity is introduced or declared absent its existential status is presupposed and does not need to be reasserted. Narratives that prioritize audience involvement restrict use of existential 'be' verbs to required functions and use verbs at the other extreme of vividness for compelling action sequences whenever possible.

Old English existential constructions employ three 'be' verbs, all no-tated as (B, b). These verbs have extremely high frequency, extremely sparse information content, and extremely low prominence. OE *wesan* 'be' has the highest frequency and the lowest prominence. Nearly synonymous *bēon,* in existential usage, typically represents continuous existence (DURATIVE as-pect) or repeated occurrence (ITERATIVE aspect). The existential meaning of OE *weorðan* 'become' is 'to arise,' in the sense of coming into existence or beginning to occur (INGRESSIVE aspect). Since they have the lowest promi-nence, Old English 'be' verbs are the most likely to occupy verse-final po-sition when stressed, the most likely to be fronted to unstressed positions, and the least likely to alliterate. Verb fronting to stressed positions, a major consideration in chapter four, is extremely rare with 'be' verbs. The only example in this chapter is item (2c) below.

§5.1 Instances with all major constituents stressed

§5.1a One-verse instances

Items (1a–d) have a stressed subject and a stressed verb. There are no in-stances with BS order, which would require alliteration on B.

(1) (a)   **fela** *þǣra* / *wæs(,)*   SB

      wera *ond* / **wīfa** (992b–3a)

      'a multitude of men and women was present'

    (b) *þǣr se* / *ōþer wæs* (1815b; cf. 1188b–90a)   SB

      'where the other (one) was situated'

    (c) *siþðan* / **morgen** *bið* (1784b)   SB

      'when morning comes into being'

    (d)   *þenden* / **hyt** *sŷ,*   SB

      glēd-*eg(e)sa* / **grim** (2649b–50a)

      'while heat should continue, grim flame-terror'

In (1a, b) forms of *wesan* express presence at a location in space and time, a sense of the verb emphasized in (1b) by *þǣr* 'where.' In (1c) *bēon* expresses the ingressive aspect of dawning. In (1d) a subjunctive form of *wesan* has durative aspect, emphasized by *þenden* 'while.'

§5.1b Multi-verse instances

Items (2a–c) are multi-verse existential constructions with all major constituents stressed. The disyllabic variant *hæþnes* is required in (2a) to avoid the
unacceptable pattern with two long feet (*Sxx/Ssx: L2). In (2b), as the note
in K4 explains, *uncer Grendles,* literally 'ours Grendel's,' is an archaic ellip-
tical dual construction meaning 'of us two, me and Grendel.' Resolution of
-sporu to avoid this problem would contravene the rule of the coda (OE
8.2).

(2) (a)   *foran / **ǣghwylc** wæs,*   B / S

      ***steda** nægla ge- / hwylc,*   ***stȳle** ge- / līcost,*

      ***hǣþ(e)nes / hand**-sporu **hilde**- / rinces,*

      ***egl'** un- / hēoru* (984b–87a)

      'before each (one), every (one) of the places of the nails, was hand-spurs
of the heathen fighting man, most like unto steel, hideous, vicious'

   (b)   *ǣghwæðrum / wæs*   IoB / S

      ***bealo**- / hycgendra **brōga** / (fram) ōðrum* (2564b–65b)

      'for each (one) of the grim-thinking (antagonists) there was terror from the
other'

   (c) *hwylc / **orleg-hwīl** **un**cer / Grendles*   S / B

      wearð** on / (ðām) **wange (2002a–3a)

      'what time of strife — mine (and) Grendel's — occurred in that place'

   (d)   *þā ðǣr / **sōna** wearð*   B / IoS

      ***ed**hwyrft / **eor**lum* (1280b–81a)

      'then a reversal immediately occurred for the earls there'

   (e)   ***Denum** eallum / wearð,*   IoB / S or B / S

      ***cea**ster- / būendum, **cēn**ra / (ge)hwylcum,*

      ***eor**lum / **ealu**-scerwen* (767b–69a)

      'for (or 'by') all the Danes, dwellers in the fortress, each of those bold (men),
a dispensing of ale began to occur'

There is no metrical impediment to BS order in existential clauses like (2a,
b), where *wesan* bears stress at normative metrical location s4. The heavy
subjects are displaced beyond the verb as usual to the right periphery of the
clause. In (2b) *ǣghwæðrum* is split from its modified noun by the verb in a
typical instance of hyperbaton. Item (2c) contains a rare instance of finite

wearð alliterating at metrical location s1a, with alliteration on the following noun as required by the rule of precedence. This instance occurs at the beginning of Beowulf's response to Hygelac, who has asked with polite vagueness whether Beowulf confronted Grendel as promised. Here *wearð* might have the force of 'did in fact occur' and if so it would be more suitable for emphatic fronting and alliteration. In (2d, e) *wearð* occupies normative metrical position s4 with no special force. In (2e) the problem is to explain how *ealuscerwen,* literally 'dispensing of ale,' could indicate distress, as it seems to do. The note in K4 finds linguistic problems with all the proposed explanations, most of which interpret nouns referring to the Danes as indirect objects. The Danish retainers in distress here receive ironically euphemistic but pretty rough criticism for hiding in outbuildings rather than confronting Grendel in the hall (590a–601a; cf. 138–43). The alternative translation represents *Denum* and *eorlum* as dative-instrumental adjuncts and interprets the ale dispensed by the Danes as that which they had earlier imbibed.

Items (3a, b) are predicate adverbial constructions that employ the idiom *tō banan weorðan,* literally 'to turn (transition) into a slayer.' This is usually accompanied by a dative of disadvantage referring to the victim. OE *bana,* Modern English *bane,* is related to a verb for 'slay' employed in an Indo-European heroic formula (§1.0).

(3) (a)   *siþðan / **Cā**in wearð*   SB/Pd/Io

         *tō / **ecg**-banan   **ā**ngan / brēþer*

         ***fæde**ren- / mǣge* (1261b–63a)

         'after Cain became a sword-slayer to (his) only brother, a paternal relative'

     (b) *ond / **Heardr**ēde   **hilde**- / mēceas*   Io/S/PdB

         *under / **bord**-hrēoðan   tō / **bonan** wurdon* (2202–3)

         'and battle-swords became slayers to Heardred under (his) protecting shield'

Denying (3a, b) would not assert that their subjects didn't exist; the existence of these subjects is presupposed in the usual way. Here the verb serves primarily as a bearer of tense and of the person and number features required for checking with the subject. The semantic content of the predicate is concentrated in a prepositional phrase that has adverbial function. Clauses like (3a, b) are much like predicate adjective constructions, in which the verb serves primarily as a LINKER and the semantic content of the predicate is concentrated in an adjective.

The need for a term like 'predicate adjective' is obvious because adjectives typically function as adjunct modifiers of nouns. Since nouns in the nominative case typically function as subjects, the need for a term like 'predicate nominative' is equally obvious. As the name implies, adverbs typically modify verbs, so the need for a term like 'predicate adverbial' is less obvious. Adverbs can also be used predicatively, however, as can noun phrases and prepositional phrases in adverbial function (OES 1: 452). I represent instances like (3a, b) as predicate adverbial constructions and classify predicate adverbials as major sentence constituents.

§5.2 Instances with unexpressed or relativized subjects

Items (4a, b) are existential constructions. Those in (4a) use the simple present to assert the existence of a future state of affairs. Item (4b) asserts the existence of entities in past time.

(4) (a)   *semninga / bið*   (1767b; cf. 1762b)   (s)B

         'suddenly (it) will happen' (anticipating a that-clause)

   (b) *swylce ðǣr / iū wǣron*   (2459b)   wsB

         'such as / which existed there before'

The other instance like (4a) is very similar. I analyze the adverbs in these instances as adjuncts that add incidental information to a verb with existential meaning. In (4b) *swylce* functions as a relativized subject. I interpret *ðǣr* as an adjunct adverbial modifier of this clause, following Mitchell (OES 1: 623–26), who finds few if any clear cases in *Beowulf* of *þǣr* as a semantically empty constituent that 'anticipates and takes the place of a subject that is yet to be expressed.' A clear case of such anticipatory usage in Modern English would be *there are inexpensive homes here, much less expensive than there in California,* where the first instance of *there* would create a contradiction if interpreted in the same way as the second.

§5.3 Instances with unstressed subjects

§5.3a One-verse instances

In (5a–c) the unstressed subject occupies normative location x1 and the stressed verb stands in normative metrical and syntactic position.

(5) (a) *þǣr hē / longe wæs*   (3082b)   sB

'where he was for a long time'

(b)   *þū on / **sǣ**lum wes*   sPdB

       ***gold**-wine / **gum**ena* (1170b–71a)

       'you be in happiness (rejoice), gold-friend of men' (imperative)

(c) *þæt hē on / **fylle** wearð* (1544b)   sPdB

       'that he transitioned into a fall' (started to fall)

In (5a) the adverb *þǣr* functions as a conjunction and a finite form of *wesan* expresses the existential meaning 'occupy a place.' Item (5b) has an expressed subject and an imperative verb that remains in clause-final position rather than being fronted for emphasis. With the usual word order we would have *wes þū on / **sǣ**lum,* with a type A7 pattern that is unacceptable in the b-verse. The existence of the subject is presupposed in the usual way and meaning is concentrated in the prepositional phrase, which functions as a predicate adverbial. Item (5c) employs a finite form of *weorðan* in a predicate adverbial construction with the same clause pattern as (5b). In (5c) *weorðan* serves primarily as a marker of ingressive aspect, focusing on the point at which the subject starts to fall.

§5.3b Multi-verse instances

(6) (a) *þæt hē in **nīð**-sele **nāth**wylcum / wæs* (1513)   sPd/B

       'that he was in an unwelcoming hall who knows what kind'

(b) *þēah ðū þīnum / **brōð**rum tō / **banan** wurde,*   sIo/PdB

       ***hēa**fod- / **mǣ**gum* (587a—88a)

       'although you became a slayer to your brother, a close relative'

(c) *syððan ic for / **duge**ðum **Dæg**hrefne wearð*   s/IoB/Pd

       *tō / **hand**-bonan, **Hū**ga / **cempan*** (2501–2)

       'after I became a hand-slayer to Day-Raven, champion of the Franks, in front of the war-bands'

(d)   *hē his / **lēo**dum wearð,*   sIoB/Pd

       ***eal**lum / **æþel**lingum tō / **ald**(o)r-ceare* (905b–6b)

       'to his people, to all the athelings, he became a great sorrow'

In (6a) the existence of the subject is presupposed and the prepositional phrase has predicate adverbial function. Items (6b, c) employ the same archaic idiom as in item (3a, b). Item (6d) is a similar construction with a different prepositional phrase. The compound *hēafod-mǣgum* in (6a) parallels *fæd(e)ren-mǣge* in (3a). Both (6a) and (3a) end with a semantically inessential variation of the indirect object, underscoring the horror of killing within the family, which is regulated by taboo rather than by law in early Germanic culture. Item (6b) represents a killing done in defense of one's lord. This clause ends with a semantically inessential verse underscoring the worthiness of Beowulf's opponent, a champion of the major military power in Western Europe. The compound *hand-bana* in (6b) parallels *ecg-bana* in item (3a). In both instances the semantically inessential compound constituent provides alliteration with the following verse. The constituent *hand-* is semantically functional in (6b), since Beowulf overtaxes swords and prefers to fight by hand.

§5.4 Instances with unstressed objects

Since 'be' verbs are intransitive, the only objects to consider are indirect. Item (7) is a one-verse instance in which both the indirect object and the subject are unstressed.

(7) *him þæt tō / **mear**ce wearð* (2384b)

    'that became the limit for them' (caused their deaths)

In this predicate adverbial construction the verb functions primarily as a marker of ingressive aspect. Fronting the indirect object brings it closer to the coreferential subject of the preceding clause in accord with iconicity of distance.

    Items (8a, b) are the multi-verse-instances with the verb in line-final position.

(8) (a)   *þæt ðū mē / ā wǣre*   sioB/Pd

     forð-*ge-* / <u>*witenum*</u>   *on* / **fæder** *stæle* (1478b–79b)

     'that you would always be in the place of a father to me having passed away (after I died)'

    (b)   *him* / **Grendel** *wearð,*   ioSB/Pd

     mǣrum / **magu**-*þegne[,]*   *tō* / **mūð**-*bonan* (2078b–79b)

     'Grendel became a mouth-killer to him, to that splendid thane'

In (8a) the subject is unstressed and appears in normative location x1. Item (8b) is an additional instance of the archaic formula in items (3) and (6). The relation between (6b) and (8b) is particularly close. In both a semantically inessential compound constituent provides alliteration with a variation of the indirect object. In both the compound constituent is semantically functional in context: Beowulf kills with his bare hands and the cannibalistic Grendel kills with his mouth. The *Beowulf* poet employed *hand-* and its obscene equivalent *mūð-* to mark the antagonists in an archaic plot that pitted a sociopathic attacker against a defender who would go on to rule well for fifty winters of peace and prosperity (2207a–9a). What we have here is a formula of the kind posited in Watkins (1995): a memorable expression of a core generic concept which is maintained even when language change makes its original linguistic form unusable. In this particular formula, as we have observed, the core concept was maintained by replacing a lost verb with a surviving noun from the same linguistic root. The rebuilt Germanic formula was largely restricted to contexts where the Indo-European formula had been used (Watkins 1995: chapter 43).

§5.5 Instances with relativized predicate adverbials

Item (9) is a one-verse clause in which the predicate adverbial *hwanan* refers to the point at which transition to a new place began.

(9) *hwanan ēowre / **cyme** syndon* (257b)   wpdSB
     'whence your arrivals are' (where you come from)

This clause differs significantly from item (1b), where *þǣr* refers to the place occupied by the subject, emphasizing a sense already present in the verb and serving primarily as a conjunction. In item (9) the conjunction *hwanon* creates a substantive change in meaning. Without *hwanon,* (9) would assert the occurrence of the arrival rather than the location of the departure.

In item (10) a relativized predicate adverbial shares the verse with the verb and the modified subject is displaced to the right periphery. The stressed adverb *syððan* is a semantically inessential adjunct that provides alliteration for the opening verse.

(10)   *tō hwan / **syðð**an wearð*   pdB/S
     hond*-*rǣs* / *hæleða (2071b–72a)

'to what (conclusion) the hand-attack of warriors continued afterwards'

Here *tō hwan* refers to the end point of an action specified by the modified subject and *wearð* marks this action as durative in addition to providing mandatory grammatical information. The existence of the battle is presupposed in the usual way.

§5.6 Instances with unstressed verbs

Since they have the highest frequency and the lowest prominence, 'be' verbs are the ones most likely to be fronted to an unstressed position.

§5.6a One-verse instances

Items (11a–e) are existential constructions with the unstressed verb at normative location x1. Many instances represent the presence or absence of joyful activities in a hall, with particular emphasis on poetic entertainment. Old English *þǣr* is used in several examples — but not all of them — to bring out the sense of occupying a place, foreshadowing its more systematic employment in Modern English existential constructions. Item (11d) is the main clause of a complex sentence stating that no king existed who dared to attack the speaker. In Modern English (11d) translates as 'no folk-king existed' or 'there was no folk-king.' We no longer use constructions like 'the folk-king wasn't.'

(11) (a)   *þǣr wæs* / ***hearpan*** *swēg*   bS

       swutol sang / *scopes* (89b–90a)

       'the sound of the harp, clear song of the poet, was present there'

     (b)   *ac þǣr is* / ***māðma*** *hord*   bS

       gold / *unrīme* ***grim***me / *(ge)cēapod* (3011b–12b)

       'but a hoard of treasures is present there, uncountable gold grimly purchased'

     (c)   *nis þǣr* / ***hearp***an *swēg*   bS

       gomen *in* / ***gear***dum (2458b–59a; cf. 2555b–56a)

       'the sound of the harp is not present there'

     (d)   *næs sē* / ***folc***-*cyning,*   bS

       ymb(*e*)- / *sittendra* / *ǣnig* / *ðāra* (2733b–34b; cf. 2262b–63a)

'No folk-king existed, (not) any (one) of those settled nearby,' anticipating
a relative clause

(e) *næs / **Bēowulf** ðǣr* (1299b; cf. 889b)   bS

'Beowulf was not present there'

Opening verses in other examples like (11a): 497b, 611a, 1063a, 1232b,
1761b, 1778b, 2105a, 2231b, 2472a, 2762b, 2910b, 2982a.

In the instances like (11a–c) the semantically inessential adverb *þǣr* occupies
an unstressed position before the unstressed verb. In (11a) and many similar
examples the unstressed constituents occur in normative order, with the
verb last. Normative order can also occur after a conjunction, as (11b) shows.
The negated verb in (11c) is fronted before the adverb to initial position, its
usual position in prose (OES: 661). In (11e) the adverb has stress in phrase-
final position. The similar instance, *Beowulf* 889b, has stress on the clause-
final postposition of an adjunct postpositional phrase.

Items (12a–d) are predicate adverbial constructions in which both verb
and subject are unstressed.

(12) (a) *hēo wæs on / **ofste*** (1292a; cf. 932a, 3087a)   sbPd

'she was in haste'

(b) *ne wæs hit / **lenge** þā gēn* (83b; cf. 1361b)   bsPd

'it was not still long' (there was not still a long waiting time)

(c) *bēo ðū on / **ofeste*** (386a)   bsPd

'be thou in haste'

The unstressed constituents observe normative order in (12a). In (12b) the
negated verb is fronted as usual to the C position. Contraction of *ne wæs* to
næs, as in (11e), is very common in this position but does not seem to be
obligatory. Contraction of negated verbs is much rarer when the verb has
clause-final stress and does not occur with *næs* in *Beowulf,* though there is
one clause-final instance with subjunctive singular *nǣre* 'might not be'
(860b). In (12c) the imperative verb is routinely fronted. With its extremely
low prominence, the imperative 'be' verb is fronted to an unstressed position
rather than to a stressed position. With high-frequency constituents of this
kind fronting to an unstressed position is the most appropriate way to provide emphasis.

In (13a–c) are existential constructions with an unstressed indirect object adjacent to the unstressed verb.

(13) (a)   *him wæs / **bēga wēn**,*   iobS

         *eal**dum** / **infrōdum**,   ōþres / swīðor* (1873b–74b)

         'a likelihood of two things occurred to him, one of the two more strongly'

     (b) *þā him wæs / **elnes þearf*** (2876b; cf. 201b, 1835b)   iobS

         'when need of courage arose for him'

     (c) *ne **bið** þē / **wilna** gād* (660b; cf. 949b–50a)   bio/S

         'a lack of pleasures will not arise for you'

     (d) *næs him / **ænig þearf*** (2493b)   bio/S

         'no need arose for him,' anticipating a that-clause

Normative 'iob' order is observed in (13a) and after a conjunction in (13b). The negated 'be' verbs in (13c, d) are fronted to initial position as usual, disrupting the normative order of unstressed constituents.

A prepositional phrase functions an adverbial adjunct in (14a) and as a predicate adverbial in (14b, c).

(14) (a) ***hrēam** wearð / (on) **Heorote*** (1302a)   S b

         'an outcry arose in Heorot'   Sx/Sx (A1)

     (b) ***ār** wæs / (on) **ofo**ste* (2783a; cf. 210b–11a, 2014a)   SbPd

         'the messenger was in haste'   Sx/Sx (A1)

     (c) ***hēan** wæs / lange* (2183b)   SbPd

         'the shame was lengthy'   Sx/Sx (A1)

Here the unstressed 'be' verb stands at location x2 rather than at normative location x1, a mismatch that is permissible only for the very lightest verbs. It occurs once with the auxiliary *sceal* (1060b) but is otherwise restricted to the 'be' verbs *wesan, bēon,* and *weordan.* In (14a, b) clause-initial placement of the 'be' verb would create the type A1 variants **(wearð) *hrēam (in) / Heorote* and **(wæs) ār on / ofoste),* with totally unacceptable placement of the verb in anacrusis. With normative word order these verses would become *hrēam / (in) Heorote wearð* and *ār / (on) ofoste wæs,* variants of the complex type D3 (S/Sxs) made still more complex by addition of an extrametrical syllable. There are only four instances of such a variant in *Beowulf* (1114a, 1531a, 1539a, 3084a). Placing the unstressed verbal SP in an unusual location creates the simplest verse pattern, type A1, the pattern most tolerant of metrical complexity. Item (14c) would scan as type C if the verb occupied normative location x1. Emphatic fronting of a suitably vivid argument noun is the only apparent reason for placement of the unstressed 'be' verb after the stressed subject.

§5.6b Multi-verse examples

Items (15a, b) are existential constructions with the unstressed verb in the opening verse and the modified subject displaced to the right periphery.

(15) (a) *ðā wæs on* / ***morgen   mīne*** / *(ge)frǣge*   b/S

      ymb þā / ***gif**-healle   **gūð**-rinc* / *monig* (837–38)

      'then in the morning, according to my information, many a fighting man appeared around the gift-hall'

  (b)   *næs ðæs* / ***wyr**mes þǣr*   b/S

      *on*sȳn / *ǣnig* (2771b–72a; cf. 2192b–93b, 1905a–6a)

      'any trace of the dragon wasn't there'

The people who appear in (15a) are visitors from far and near. They are introduced into the discourse for the first time here and their existence is not presupposed. The prepositional phrase in (15a) is an adjunct adding detail relevant to the immediate context. The verb follows the adverb in normative order. In (15b) the bare verb is used in its existential sense and *þǣr* is an adverbial adjunct. An idiomatic Modern English translation would be 'there wasn't any trace of the dragon there,' with the DUMMY subject *there* occupying subject position, or 'no trace of the dragon was there,' with the negative particle attracted to an indefinite constituent in clause-initial position (Labov 1972a).

Items (16a–d) are predicate adverbial constructions. An indirect object has been added in (16b, d), two further instances of the archaic *bana* construction.

(16) (a)   *þā wæs* / ***frōd*** *cyning,*   bS/Pd

      hār / ***hilde**-rinc[,]* *on* / ***hrēon*** *mōde*

      (1306b–7b; cf. 536b–37a, 2580b–81b)

      'then the old king, that hoary battle-warrior, was in a rough mood'

  (b) *wearþ hē* / ***Heaþolāfe***   *tō* / ***hand**-bonan*   bsIo/Pd

      mid / ***Wilfingum*** (460a–61a)

      'he became a hand-killer to Heatholaf among the Wylfings'

(c) *þā wæs on / **sālum** **sin**ces / brytta,*   bPd/S

   ***gamol**-feax / (ond) **gūð**-rōf* (607a–8a; cf. 835b–36a)

   'then the distributor of treasure, grey-haired and battle-bold, was
   in a happy mood'

(d) *wearð him on / **Heorote** tō / **hand**-banan*   bio/Pd/S

   ***wæl**-gǣst / **wǣ**fre* (1330a–31a)

   'the wandering slaughter-demon became a hand-killer to him in Heorot'

In (16a) the verb follows the adverb as usual. In (16b, d) the verb is fronted
to an available C position, marking a transition to a new action sequence. In
(16c, d) a heavy modified subject is displaced to the right periphery of the
clause. *Hand-bana*, the poetic compound that refers to *Beowulf* in (6c), refers
to Beowulf's father in (16b) and to Grendel's mother in (16d).

   Items (17a, b) are predicate adverbial constructions with negated verbs.

(17) (a)   *ne wearð / **Heremōd** swā*   bSPd/Io

   ***eaforum Ecg**-welan, **Ār**- / Scyldingum* (1709b–10b)

   'Heremod was not thus to the heirs of Ecgwela, the honorable Scyldings'

   (b)   *ne wæs his **droht**oð þǣr*   bS/Pd

   *swylce hē on / **eald**(e)r-dagum **ǣr** ge- / mētte* (756b–57b)

   'his experience there was not as he encountered in former days'

In (17a) the negated 'be' verb is fronted as usual to a syntactic C position at
metrical location x1. The high-frequency predicate adverb is placed appropriately at location s4, with the more prominent noun supplying the alliteration for the b-verse. In (17b) *swylce* does double duty as predicate adverbial in the main clause and relativized object of the following clause.

§5.7 Instances with an unstressed verb and an unexpressed or relativized subject

Items (18a, b) are existential constructions that would require expression of
the subject in Modern English. In (18c) the existence of the unexpressed
subject is presupposed and meaning is concentrated in a prepositional phrase
that functions as a predicate adverbial.

(18) (a) *swā wæs / **Bīowulfe*** (3066a)   (s)bIo

'(it) happened thus to Beowulf'

(b) *ne wæs þǣm / ōðrum swā* (1471b)   (s)bIo

'(it) did not happen thus to the other (one)'

(c) *bīo nū on / ofoste* (2747a)   (s)bPd

'(you) be now in haste' (imperative)

In (18a) the verb follows the adverb as usual. In (18c) the subject of an imperative clause is routinely unexpressed and the imperative verb is routinely fronted to initial position.

The opening verses in (19a, b) are predicate adverbial clauses in which the referent of an unexpressed subject is specified in a following relative clause.

(19) (a) **sōna** / *(wæs on)* **sun**de   *sē þe ǣr æt* / **sæcce** *gebād*

wīg-*hryre* / **wrāð**ra (1618a–19a)   (s)bPd

'at once he who lived to see the death of foes in combat was in the sound (fjord)'

(b) *næs ðā on* / **hlyt**me   *hwā þæt* / **hord** *strude* (3126)   (s)bPd

'who plundered that hoard was not determined by lot'

In (19a) *sē* refers to the subject of the preceding clause and *þe* is the relativized subject of the following clause. In (19b) *hwā* functions as subject of both clauses. The unstressed verb in (19a) occupies metrical location x4 for metrical reasons. In normative location x1 the verb would create an unnecessary verbal anacrusis that would be unacceptable under any conditions (OE 9.5, OE 9.6).

§5.8 Retrospect

A special feature of the previous chapter is the abundance of examples with all major constituents stressed (§4.7). Finite main verbs are moved to unstressed positions in only 18 verses, as compared with more than five hundred stressed instances. The 'be' verbs in this chapter are moved to unstressed positions 56 times, as compared with only 21 stressed instances. The stark contrast in distribution is due to the equally stark contrast in prominence between main verbs and 'be' verbs, which have much higher frequency and much lower information content (§1.4). A stressed subject shares a verse with a stressed 'be' verb in six existential clauses, all with

216

normative SB order and all with the verb in normative line-final position (992b, 1188b, 1784b, 1815b, 2649b).

In §4.3a we observed that the poet employs stressed root adverbs less often than prepositional phrases in adverbial function, which can provide more kinds of vivid narrative detail. Of the stressed predicate adverbials in this chapter, 27 are prepositional phrases, one is a postpositional phrase (899b), and nine are stressed root adverbs. In the following chapters we will observe a consistent pattern of word placement in verses with a stressed 'be' verb and a stressed predicate adjective, noun, or participle. The number of predicate adverbial constructions is small but a similar pattern emerges. If the verb is stressed and the prepositional phrase is small enough they always share a verse in normative PdB order and the stressed verb always occupies normative line-final position, as in *þū on / sǣlum wes* 'be thou in happiness' (1170b; cf. 587b, 1544b, 2203b, 2384b). If the prepositional phrase fills a whole verse it is displaced beyond a stressed verb to the right periphery, as with *tō / ecg-banan* 'as a sword-slayer' (1262a; cf. 906b, 1479b, 2079b, 2502a).

CHAPTER 6

PREDICATE ADJECTIVE CLAUSES

§6.0 Introduction

In this chapter, as in chapter five, we are concerned with verbs of the lowest prominence that are fronted to unstressed positions with the highest frequency. When stressed these 'be' verbs are strongly attracted to the least prominent lift of the line at metrical location s4. Instances like (9g) below, where the stressed verb alliterates at metrical location s1a, are extremely rare. Predicate adjectives are notated as 'Pj' for stressed usage and as 'pj' for unstressed usage.

§6.1 Instances with all major constituents stressed

There are no one-verse instances with all constituents stressed. Verses like item (1) could easily have been constructed, however.

(1) *eorl* / *yrre* wæs (constructed)	SPjB
'the earl was angry'	S/Sxs (D3)

As we observed in section 3.1, type D3 verses with three stressed constituents are metrically complex, exceeding normative weight and realizing a compound foot as two words. Given three stressed words like those in item (1), the poet always moves the 'be' verb to an unstressed metrical position, creating a verse with normative weight. Departure from normative syntactic order would be particularly easy for hearers to process in such cases because 'be' verbs are so often fronted to unstressed positions in ordinary language. Since the SOV instances in §3.1 have such low frequency, it is not surprising to find that there are no comparable instances in a less common construction with a 'be' verb. No special rule is required to explain the absence of verses like item (1).

Items (2a–e) are multi-verse instances. Stressed constituents that share a verse observe normative syntactic orders (PjB, SPj, SB).

(2) (a) ond þā / **cear**-wylmas **cōl**ran / wurðaþ   S/PjB

      (282; cf. 120b–22a, 858–61)

      'and the seething sorrows will become cooler'

  (b)   him on / **eax**le wearð   B/SPj

      syn-dolh / **sweo**tol (816b–17a)

      'a huge wound became evident on his shoulder' (with possessive dative STP pronoun)

  (c) ond þā / **sīð**-frome, **sear**wum / **gear**we[,]   Pj/SB

      wīgend / **wǣ**ron (1813a–14a)

      'and then the warriors were ready in armor, eager for the journey'

  (d)   **lā**stas / **wǣ**ron   SB / Pj

      æfter / **wald**-swaþum **wī**de / (ge)**sȳ**ne,

      gang ofer / **grun**das (1402b–4a; cf. 593b–94a, 3071a–73a)

      'the footprints — the track over the lands — were widely visible along the forest paths'

  (e) **ǣt** þǣm / **ā**de wæs **ēþ**-ge- / **sȳ**ne   B/Pj/S

      swāt-fāh / **syr**ce, **swȳn** / eal **gyl**den,

      eofer / **ī**ren-heard, **æþe**ling / **man**ig

      wundum / (ā)**wyr**ded (1110a–13a; cf. 1243b–46a)

      'easily visible at the pyre was a bloodstained corselet, a pig all golden — iron-hard boar — (and) many an atheling doomed by wounds'

Alliteration for verses with major constituents is provided by compound modifiers like *cear*- in (2a) and *ēþ*- in (2e), and by adjunct adverbials like *him on eaxle* in (2b) and *wīde* in (2d). The verses like (2a) have the subject in one verse and constituents of the verb phrase sharing a later verse. In (2b) the stressed verb is fronted to normative metrical position s4 in the opening verse. In (2c) a predicate adjective suitable for emphasis is fronted before the subject to the left periphery and the line is completed with a variation of this adjective that fills a type II b-verse. Such heavy variations are usually displaced rightward rather than fronted, as in (2d), where the clause-final variation allows for placement of the next opening verse in the most convenient location. In (2e) the verb is followed by a displaced predicate adjective phrase followed out of normative order by a displaced subject phrase. Here as generally expression of each major constituent in a separate verse makes multiple departures from word-order norms more acceptable. The other instance like (2e) is similar, with *ēþgesȳne* followed by a list of combat equipment.

In (3a, b) an indirect object has been added. Stressed constituents sharing a verse observe normative IoB and SPj orders.

(3) (a)	***Hæðcynne*** / *wearð,*		IoB/SPj
	Gēata / *dryhtne,* ***gūð*** / *onsæge* (2482b–83b; cf. 2169b–70b)		
	'warfare became oppressive for Haethcyn, lord of the Geats,'		
(b)	*syððan* / ***un***derne		Pj/Io/S/B
	Fron*cum* / *(ond)* ***Frȳ****sum* ***fyll*** / *cyninges*		
	wīde / ***weor****ðeð* (2911b–13b)		
	'after the king's death becomes widely apparent to the Franks and Frisians'		

In (3a) an indirect object smaller than a verse has been fronted, signaling that it identifies the previously unnamed subject of the previous clause, in accord with iconicity of distance. The verb in (3a) has been fronted before the subject to complete the opening verse and occupies normative metrical position s4. Item (3b) is another example of metrical complexity mitigated by placement of the major constituents in separate verses. Here a one-word predicate adjective is fronted to complete the opening verse and a heavy modified subject is displaced rightward beyond the heavy indirect object. The order of verses cannot be switched in the second line because the indirect object verse has double alliteration.

§6.2 Instances with an unexpressed or relativized subject

Item (4), the only one-verse instance, has a relativized subject and all constituents in normative order.

(4) *þām ðǣr* / ***sēl****ra wæs* (2199b)	wsPjB
'who was superior there'	

The relative pronoun subject is in the dative case because its antecedent in the previous clause is a dative beneficiary.

Items (5a–c) are the multi-verse instances. Stressed constituents sharing a verse observe normative IoB and PjB orders.

(5) (a)   *ond þyssum /* **cnyh***tum wes*   (s)IoB/Pj

     lāra */* **līð***e* (1219b–20a)

       'and (you) be gracious in counsel to these boys' (imperative)

     (b)   *forðām ge- /* **sȳ***ne wearð*   (s)PjB/Io

     yl*da / bearnum,* **un***dyrne /* **cū***ð*

     gyd*dum /* **geō***more* (149b–51a)

       'therefore (it) became evident to the children of men, openly known through sad songs'

     (c) *sē þe /* **man***na wæs* **mæge***ne / strengest*   wsB/Pj

     on / **þæ***m dæge* **þys***ses / līfes* (789–90)

       'who was strongest in might in that era of this (earthly) life'

In (5a, c) a modified predicate adjective is displaced to the right periphery. The imperative verb is not fronted for emphasis in (5a) and remains in core position after the indirect object. In (5b) a modified indirect object is displaced, followed by a heavy variation of *gesȳne*. The verb occupies normative metrical location s4 in (5a, b). In (5c) placement of the verb at metrical location s2 makes it possible to realize the major constituents as a syntactically complete line.

§6.3 Instances with unstressed subjects

Expression of a major constituent as a pronoun makes a clause easier to fit within a single verse. In this section one-verse clauses begin to outnumber multi-verse clauses.

§6.3a One-verse instances

The clauses in item (6) have a subject as the only unstressed major constituent.

(6) *swā hit ge- /* **dē***fe wæs* (561b, 1670b)   sPjB

     'since it was fitting'

Other examples: 682b, 1255b, 1508b, 1831b, 1941b, 2187b, 2378b, 2480b, 3174b.

In all of these instances the unstressed subject occupies normative metrical location x1 and the stressed constituents stand in normative PjB order, with the verb at normative metrical position s4. The adjective *gedēfe* in the identical cited instances also appears in 3174b, which has *bið* rather than *wæs*.

§6.3b Multi-verse instances

In (7a–d) semantically inessential modifiers provide alliteration, expanding the clause beyond the opening verse.

(7) (a)   *þæt hē / **syð**þan wæs*   sB/Pj

         *on / **meodu**-bence **mā**þme / (þȳ) weorþra,*

         yrfe- / lāfe (1901b–3a)

         'that he was afterwards the more honored on the mead-bench because of the treasure, an heirloom'

    (b) *þēah ðe hē / **dǣda** gehwæs **dyr**stig / wǣre* (2838)   s/PjB

         'although he was daring in respect of every deed'

    (c) *ðā wit æt- / **som**ne on / **sǣ** wǣron*   sPj/B

         *fīf-nihta / **fyrst*** (544a–45a)

         'then we were together on the sea (during) five nights' time'

    (d) *þæt hīe / **oft** wǣron anwīg- / gearwe,*   sB/Pj

         *(gē æt) **hām** gē / (on) herge, gē ge- / **hwæþer** þāra,*

         *efne swylce / **mǣ**la* (1247a–49a)

         'that they were often combat-ready, both at home and in the army, and in both of those (simultaneously), even at such times' (anticipating an 'as' clause).

Opening verses in other examples like (5a): 753b, 913b, 1435b.

In several instances constituents are arranged as in (7a, d), where the compact subject and verb fit into the same verse with a more prominent modifier that supplies the alliteration. In these clauses a heavy adjectival phrase is displaced to the right periphery. Stressed constituents share a verse only in (5b), where they observe normative PjB order. In (7a–c) the verb occupies its normative metrical position at line end. In (7d) placement of the verb at metrical location s2 allows for realization of the major constituents as a line.

§6.4 Instances with unstressed objects

§6.4a One-verse clauses

Here as generally clauses with unstressed objects have lower frequency than those with unstressed subjects. Items (8a, b) are the one-verse examples. In (8b) *gifeðe* translates most idiomatically as a Modern English past participle but is adjectival in form.

(8) (a) *þēah hē him / **hold** wǣre* (2161b; cf. 203b) sioPjB

'although he was loyal to him'

(b) *him þæt / **gifeðe** ne wæs* (2682b) iosPjB

'it was not (something) granted to him'

The two verses like (8a) have the unstressed constituents in normative order. These verses are identical except for the adjective, which is *lēof* 'dear' in 203b. In (8b) the unstressed indirect object is fronted before the unstressed subject, linking this explanatory statement to the relevant antecedent in the preceding clause.

§6.4b Multi-verse clauses

Items (9a–e) have the unstressed constituents in normative location x1. Stressed constituents sharing a verse observe normative PjB, SB, and SPj orders.

(9) (a) *þæs þe him / **ȳþ**-lāde **ēaðe** / wurdon* (228; cf. 945a–46a, 1269) ioS/PjB

'in respect of the fact that the sea-paths became pleasant for them'

(b) *ond him / **wīf**-lufan* ioS/PjB

*æfter / **cear**-wælmum **cōlran** / weorðað* (2065b–66b)

'and after overwhelming sorrow, love of the woman will become cooler for him'

(c) *þǣr mē / **gifeðe** swā* ioPj/S/B

*ǣnig / **yrfe**-weard **æfter** / wurde*

*līce / (ge)**lenge*** (2730b–32a)

'if any inheritance-guardian related to my body had been granted to me'

(d)   *swā mē* / ***Higelāc*** *sīe,*   ioSB/Pj

mīn / ***mon***-*drihten,*   ***mōdes blīðe*** (435b–36b)

'so may Hygelac, my mortal lord, be generous of heart to me' (an oath)

(e) *oð ðe him* / ***Ong(e)nðēowes*** ***eaferan*** / *wǣran*   io/SB/Pj

frome, / ***fyrd***-*hwate* (2475a–76a)

'until Ongentheow's heirs were aggressive and warlike to him'

(f) *þǣr unc* / ***hwīle*** *wæs*   ***hand*** *ge-* / *mǣne* (2137)   ioB/SPj

'there for a time hand was shared for us two' (we fought hand-to-hand awhile)

(g) *ond gē him* / ***syndon***   *ofer* / ***sǣ***-*wylmas*   sioB/Pj

heard- / ***hic***gende   ***hider*** / *wilcuman* (393–94)

'and to them you bold-thinking men are welcome here beyond the sea-swells'

In the verses like (9a) the major sentence constituents are realized ideally as a single line with the stressed constituents in normative syntactic order. The caesura falls between the stressed subject and the stressed constituents of the verb phrase. In (9b) the clause begins in a b-verse and a semantically inessential a-verse situates the verb at normative location s4 in the following line. The a-verse is semantically functional in the immediate context. In (9c) the verb is in normative metrical position s4 and an unmodified predicate adjective has been fronted to the opening verse, where it provides the only alliteration. In (9d, e) the heavy type II verse containing the adjective is displaced to the right periphery. In (9f) the poet creates a one-line clause by fronting the 'be' verb to metrical location s2 in the opening verse, where semantically inessential *hwīle* provides the alliteration. In (9g) the unstressed arguments share location x1 in normative order and the stressed constituents occupy separate verses. In addition to filling out lines and situating the verb in normative position, the semantically inessential second and third verses of (9g) highlight the core generic concept of travel on the sea as a test of heroism. In this unusual example the 'be' verb is the most prominent constituent in the opening verse and alliterates at metrical location s1b.

§6.5 Instances with unstressed verbs

§6.5a   One-verse instances

Most examples have the stressed constituents in normative SPj order, as in (10a, e, f).

(10) (a) *wæs sēo /* **hwīl** *micel* (146b)   bSPj

'that time was long'

(b) *ðā wæs /* **swīgra secg,   sunu** */ Ecglāfes,*   bPjS

on / **gylp**-*spræce* **gūð**-*ge-* / *weorca* (980–8; cf. 467b, 1376b, 3007b)

'then the man — Ecglaf's son — was quieter in boasting talk of fighting
accomplishments'

(c) *næs him /* **hrēoh** *sefa* (2180b)   bPjS

'the heart to him (his heart) was not savage'

(d) *him bið /* **grim** *sefa* (2043b; cf. 49b, 2419b–20a)   bPjS

'his heart is grim'

(e) *him wæs /* **sefa** *geōmor* (2632b)   bSPj

'his heart was sad'

(f) *ðā wæs /* **Hygelāc** *dēad* (2372b)   bSPj

'when Hygelac was dead'

Other examples like (10a): 133b, 191b, 467b, 1250b, 1282b, 1376b, 1616b,
1742b, 2684b, 3085b, 3105b (hortative subjunctive).

In the examples like (10a) the C position is empty and the verb moves to it.
In (10b) the verb follows a clause-initial adverb. In (10c) a verb contracted
with a negative particle is routinely fronted. Alliteration in (10b–d) is provided by vivid unmodified adjectives suitable for emphatic fronting before
the stressed subject. Normative SPj order in (10c, d) would have required
resolution of *sefa* on the first lift, creating an unacceptable A8 variant with a
word group in the Ss foot (OE 3.4). The verses like (10c, d) are closely
related, with adjectives of similar meaning and minor inflectional variations.
In (10e) the verse-final adjective is trochaic and resolution of *sefa* creates an
ordinary type C verse. Item (10f) contains an apparent example of a subordinating conjunction that fails to block verb fronting (§1.8). The death of
Hygelac has been described not long before in 2354b–59a, so an independent sentence translating as 'Hygelac was dead then' would have an awkward
appearance. When used as adverbs, constituents like *þā* do not inhibit fronting in the same way, as shown for example by the three instances in (10b).

The unstressed verb occupies location x2 or x4 under special conditions
in (11a–e).

(11) (a) **stræt** *wæs /* **stān**-*fāh* (320a)   SbPj

'the street was stone-paved'

(b) **sweord** wæs / **swātig** (1569a; cf. 1459a)   SbPj

'the sword was bloody'

(c) **Bēow** wæs / **brēme** — **blǣd** / wīde sprang —   SbPj

Scyldes / eafera **Scede**landum / in (18–19, as emended)

'Beow, Scyld's heir, was famous in south Sweden — his glory spread widely'

(d) **word** wǣron / **wyn**sume (612a; cf. 1230a)   SbPj

'the conversations were enjoyable'

(e) **hrēo** wǣron / **ȳþa** (548b; cf. 769b, 1323b–26a)   PjbS

'rough were the waves'

Other examples like (11a): 755a, 761a, 1785a, 1925a.

In the examples like (11a) verb-final order would create verses like **strǣt / stān-fāh wæs*, with the prominently stressed constituent -fāh on an x position in a heavy D3 pattern (S/Sxs), violating OE 4.3. This problem does not arise in the verse-final alternative to (11b), **sweord / swātig wæs*, type D3 with an unstressed suffix on the x position. As we have observed, however (§6.1), the poet always avoids the complex type D3 when movement of the 'be' verb to an unstressed position yields a type A1 variant like (11b). Unemended and with normative syntactic order (11c) would be **Bēowulf / brēme wæs* (Sx/Sxs, type D7). Type D7 is even more complex than type D3 because it is long as well as heavy. If type D3 is avoided, type D7 is sure to be avoided as well. The verb-final alternative to (11d), **word / wyn*sume / *wǣron*, scans as *S/Ss/Sx or *S/Ssx/Sx. Both patterns are unacceptable because they have three feet. The verb-final alternative to (11e), **ȳþa / hrēo wǣron*, would be type D6, a long heavy pattern comparable in complexity to type D3. The predicate adjective is suitable for emphatic fronting here. In many cases a normative syntactic pattern rejected by the poet would create more than one metrical problem. In the verb-final alternative to (11d), for example, the verb would bear stress in clause-final position. Since the matching [w] in wǣron can be disregarded only when the word is metrically unstressed, **word / wyn*sume / *wǣron* would have triple alliteration, which is permissible only under extremely restricted conditions (Russom 1987: 77). For reasons of space I must generally be content to identify only one metrical problem that requires a departure from normative syntax. Readers familiar with alliterative meter will notice other problems as well.

§6.5b Multi-verse instances

In (12a–c) the unstressed 'be' verb occupies normative metrical location x1 and the stressed constituents occupy separate verses. In (12b) the superlative form *sēlest* functions as an intensifier equivalent to 'very.'

(12) (a)   *wæs þǣre / **burnan** wælm*   bS/Pj
    heaðo**-fȳrum / **hāt (2546b–47a)
    'the surging of that stream was hot with hostile fire'

  (b) *þā wæs / **þēod**-sceaða **þrid**dan / sīðe,*   bS/Pj
    *frēcne / **fȳr**-draca, **fǣh**ða / (ge)myndig* (2688–89)
    'then the enemy of the people — the dangerous fire-dragon — was mind-ful of hostilities for the third time'

  (c) *forþan bið / **and**git ǣghwǣr / sēlest,*   bS/Pj
    *ferhðes / **fore**-þanc* (1059a–60a; cf. 2316–17)
    'therefore discernment — forethought of mind — is most useful in all situations'

  (d) *ðā wæs on / **bur**gum **Bēow** / Scyldinga,*   b/S/Pj
    *lēof / **lēod**-cyning[,] **lon**ge / þrāge*
    *fol**cum** / (ge)frǣge* (53a–55a)
    'then in the strongholds Beowulf of the Scyldings, beloved king of (his) people, was well-known to (various) tribes for a long time'

Opening verses in other examples like (12a): 2316a, 2946a; like (12b): 484a, 2149b, 2860a, 2900a.

The predicate adjective stands at the end of a syntactically complete clause in (12a–d), its normal location when the verb is fronted. The syntactically complete clauses in (12c) are followed by adjuncts. The verb moves to an empty C position in the verses like (12a). In the remaining instances the verb follows an unstressed adverb.

A few instances have less usual word orders.

(13) (a)   *þā wæs / **eft** hraðe*   b/Pj/S
    ***gearo** / **gyrn**-wræce **Grend**eles / mōdor* (2117b–18b)
    'then quickly again Grendel's mother was intent on avenging injury'

  (b)   *wæs tō / **fore**-mihtig*   bPj/S
    ***fēond** on / fēþe* (969b–70a)

'the enemy was too pre-eminently mighty in departure' (too good at run-
ning away)

(c)   *Here-* / *Scyldinga*   S/bPj

   betst / ***beado****-rinca   wæs on* / ***bæl*** *gearu* (1108b–09b)

   'the best fighting man of the Battle-Scyldings was ready on the pyre'

In (13a, b) predicate adjectives suitable for emphasis precede the subject. In
(13c) an unstressed verb appears well after the opening verse. This is a very
unusual violation of Kuhn's Laws and the SPMR.

   In (14a–e) indirect objects have been added to clauses with the unstressed verb at location x1. When an adverb is present in these instances it
precedes the verb.

(14) (a)   *wæs se* / ***fruma*** <u>*ege*</u>*slīc*   bSPj/Io

   lēodum / *(on)* ***lan****de* (2309b–10a; cf. 1575b–76a)

   'the onset (of the flying dragon) was terrifying for people on land'

(b) *þær wæs* / ***Hond****sciō   **hild** on-* / *sæge,*   bIo/SPj

   feorh-<u>*bealu*</u> / ***fæ****gum* (2076a–77a; cf. 2122b–23b)

   'there combat was threatening to Hondscio — a life-bale for the doomed
   (man)'

(c) *wæs ge-* / ***hwæþer*** *ōðrum   **lifigende*** / ***lāð*** (814b–15a)   bSIo/Pj

   'each one was loathsome to the other living (while alive)'

(d) *hēr is* / ***æghwylc eorl*** *ōþrum* / *(ge)trȳwe,*   bS/IoPj

   mōdes / ***milde,   man****-drihtne* / *hold* (1228–29)

   'here each earl is true to the other, friendly of heart, loyal to the earthly
   lord'

(e) *ðā wæs on* / ***ūh****tan   mid* / ***ær****dæge*   b/S/IoPj

   Grend*les* / ***gūð****-cræft   **gumum*** / *undyrne* (126–27)

   'then in the morning with the coming of day Grendel's power in combat
   was evident to men'

What remains constant in these various word orders is that stressed constituents sharing a verse observe normative orders: SPj in (14a, b), SIo in (14c),
and IoPj in (14d, e).

   In (15a–c) the unstressed verbal SP occupies location x2 under special
conditions.

(15) (a) **hreþe** *wæs æt /* **holme** **hȳð**-*weard / geara* (1914)   b/SPj

      'at the sea the harbormaster was ready at once'

  (b)   **dēað** *bið /* **sēlla**   SbPj/Io

    eorla */ (ge)hwylcum þonne /* **edwīt**-*līf* (2890b–91b)

    'death is better for each (one) of earls than a life of shame'

  (c) **eft** *wæs /* **ānrǣd,** *nalas /* **elnes** *læt,*   bPj/S

    mǣrða */ (ge)***myndig**[,] **mǣg** */ Hȳlāces* (1529–30)

    'the kinsman of Hygelac was resolute again, by no means slow of courage, mindful of glorious deeds'

Placement of the verb at normative location x1 would create unnecessary anacrusis in (15a). With verb-final order the opening verse of (15b) would be **dēað** */ sēlla bið,* type D3. Here as usual the poet prefers to rearrange the constituents as a type A1 verse with the verb at metrical location x2. In (15c) the heavy modified subject is displaced to the right periphery and the two lines are completed by semantically inessential verses. The verb-final alternative for the opening verse would be **anrǣd** */* **eft** *wæs* (Ss/Ss), a type A4 variant with two words in the second foot, attested only once in the poem (*Beowulf* 330a). As it stands (15c) is a variant of type A2 (Sx/Ss), attested 47 times.

§6.6 Instances with an unstressed verb and an unexpressed or relativized argument

These compact clauses fit easily into a single verse and there are no multi-verse examples. All instances have unexpressed subjects. Indirect objects are generally optional. They are often added to clauses like (16a) but it would be hard to justify positing an unexpressed indirect object in such cases.

§6.6a One-verse instances

The subject is unexpressed in (16a–c) and relativized in (16d). In all instances the unstressed verb occupies normative location x1. The verb stands first in (16a, b); in the remaining examples it stands second.

(16) (a) *wæs ðā /* **dēaðe** *fæst* (3045b)   (s)bPj

    '(he) was then fixed in death'

  (b) *næs ðā /* **long** *tō ðon* (2591b, 2845b)   (s)bPj

'(it) was not long until that (time)'

(c) *þā wæs* / *ēað-fynde* (138a)   (s)bPj

'then (he) was easily locatable'

(d) *ac wæs* / *wīde cūð* (2923b)   (s)bPj

'for (it) was widely known'

(e) *þē is* / *wīde cūð* (2135b)   wsbPj

'which is widely known'

Other examples like (16a): 137b, 1173a (imperative); like (16c): 2880a, 3058a.

The cited examples in (16a, b) have the verb preceding adverbial *ðā*. Item (16a) makes it clear that this order is acceptable, since there is no apparent metrical reason for the less usual order. Fronting is strongly promoted in (16b) by negation of the verb, and by the imperative verb in another verb-initial example like (16a). The instances in (16c) have the more usual adverb-verb order. The verb follows a coordinating conjunction in (16d) and a relative pronoun in (16e). Ironic understatements like the identical instances in (16b) emphasize the suddenness of a narrative event. By falling so obviously short of appropriate emphasis such phrases hint that a great deal of emphasis would be justified. Sometimes the understatement is followed by a corresponding assertion with appropriate emphasis, as for example in 739a–41a.

The unstressed verb occupies verse-medial locations x2 and x4 under special conditions in (17a, b).

(17) (a)   *cwico wæs* / *(þā) gēna,*   (s)Pjb

wīs ond / *(ge)wittig* (3093b–94a)

'(he) was still alive then, aware and conscious'

(b) *sēlre* / *(bið) æghwǣm* (1384b)   (s)Pjb

'(it) is better for everyone'

Normative syntax in (17a) would create **þā gēna* / *cwico wæs*, an unacceptable variant of type A8 with obligatory resolution of the predicate adjective (OE 3.4). The result in (17b) would be *sēlre* / *æghwǣm bið*, a rare violation of OE 4.3 with a secondary constituent of reduced stress on the second x position in type D7 (Sx/Sxs). In both instances the problem is avoided by situating the 'be' verb on an unstressed position, which cannot be clause-initial, since that would place the verb in anacrusis. The adjectives are suitable for emphatic fronting to the clause-initial lift, which positions the verbs acceptably.

§6.7 Instances with an unstressed verb and an unstressed subject

§6.7a One-verse instances

(18) (a) *Ic wæs / **syfan**-wintre* (2428a)   sbPj

     'I was seven years old'

  (b) *þæt wæs / **yl**dum cūþ* (705b)   sbIoPj

     'that was known to people' (anticipating a that-clause)

  (c) *næs hīo / **hnāh** swā þēah* (1929b)   bsPj

     'she was not stingy, however'

  (d) *wæs þū, / **Hrōðgār**, hāl* (407a)   bsPj

     'be thou healthy, Hrothgar'

  (e) *wes þū ūs / **lārena** gōd* (269b)   bsioPj

     'be thou good to us in respect of counsels'

  (f)   *þæt hit wearð / **eal**-gearo,*   sbPj

  ***heal**-ærna / mǣst* (77b–78a; cf. 1353)

     'that it became entirely ready, greatest of hall-buildings'

Other examples like (18a): 309a, 469b, 811b, 1475b, 1560a, 1825b, 1844a, 2000a, 2412b, 2527b, 3157b; like (14c): 2141b, 2967b, 2975b, 3074a.

Most instances have the unstressed constituents in normative 'sb' order, as in (18a, b, f). In (18b) a stressed indirect object is added in normative position before the predicate adjective. As usual in verses like (18c), the negated and contracted 'be' verb occupies the C position before the unstressed subject. In (18d, e) the imperative 'be' verbs are routinely fronted to an unstressed position in accord with their low prominence. In (18e) an unstressed indirect object follows the unstressed subject in normative order. The verses like (18f) have subordinating conjunctions, which block fronting of the verb before the subject as usual. The other example has *næfne* 'except that.'

§6.7b Multi-verse instances

In (19a) *lang,* a predicate adjective of extent, governs genitive case in *fīftiges fōtgemearces* (OES 1: 88, 559).

(19) (a) *sē wæs / **fīftiges** **fōt-ge-** / mearces*   sb/Pj

        lang *on / **lege**re* (3042a–43a; cf. 196a–98a, 898a–902a)

        'it was long to the extent of fifty foot-marks in its resting-place' (fifty feet long as it lay)

    (b)   *þæt bið / **driht**-guman*   sbIo/Pj

        un- */ lifgendum **æfter** / sēlest* (1388b–89b)

        'that is best for the dead fighting man afterwards' (simple present for future)

    (c)   *þæt hīe sint / **wil**cuman*   sbPj/Io

        Deniga */ lēodum* (388b–89a)

        'that they are welcome to the people of the Danes'

    (d)   *bēo þū / **suna** mīnum*   bsIo/Pj

        dædum */ (ge)dēfe,* **drēam-** */ healdende* (1226b–27b)

        'having happiness, be thou just in deeds to my sons'

Items (19a, b) are like (18a, b) except that the predicate adjective occupies a separate verse. In (19c) a modified indirect object fills a separate verse displaced to the right periphery. Verb fronting before the subject is blocked as usual by *þæt*. Item (19d) has fronting of an imperative 'be' verb to an unstressed position, as in (18d, e). Wealhtheow's use of *bēo*, with durative aspect, instead of the more usual *wes* signifies that Hrothulf should continue to be loyal to her sons.

§6.8 Instances with an unstressed verb and an unstressed object

§6.8a One-verse instances

Since unstressed objects have generally lower frequency than unstressed subjects, there are fewer instances than in §6.7. Items (20a, b) are the one-verse instances.

(20) (a) *þæt mē is micle / **lēofre*** (2651)   siobPj

        'that is greatly preferable to me'

    (b) *wæs him se / **man** tō þon lēof* (1876b)   bioSPj

        'to him the man was dear to that extent' (that dear to him)

Item (20a) has the normative order of unstressed constituents. In (20b) the unstressed verb has been fronted before the indirect object, marking the transition to an explanatory digression.

§6.8b Multi-verse instances

The third line in (21a) is a list of names in apposition to *bearna hwylc*. In (21b) the last two verses vary the preceding statement and anticipate a relative clause adding information about the senior inheritor.

(21) (a) *næs ic him tō / **līfe** **lāðra** / ōwihte,*   bsio/Pj

         ***beorn** in / **burgum**, þonne his / **bearna** hwylc,*

         ***Herebeald** / (ond) **Hæðcyn** oððe / **Hygel**āc mīn* (2432–34)

         'to him I wasn't ever a more loathly man in the dwellings than any of his children, Herebeald and Haethcyn or my (lord) Higelac'

     (b)   *him wæs / **bām** samod*   iobSPj

         *on ðām / **lēod**scipe **lond** ge- / cynde,*

         ***eard**, / ēðel-riht ōðrum / swīðor*

         sīde / rīce (2196b–98a)

         'the property in that land — home (and) ancestral domain — was due to them both, a spacious realm more abundantly to one of the two' (anticipating a relative clause)

Item (19a) has routine fronting of the negated and contracted 'be' verb to an available C position at location x1. In (19b) the unstressed constituents are in normative order.

§6.9 Instances with an unexpressed subject and an unstressed SP

There are no multi-verse instances. Items (22a–c) are one-verse instances with an unstressed indirect object.

(22) (a) *swā mē / **gifeð**e wæs* (2491b; cf. 299b, 2696b)   ioPjB

         'as (it) was granted to me'

     (b) *hwæþre mē / **gyfeþe** wearð* (555b)   ioPjB

         'however, (it) was granted to me'

     (c) *næs him / **wih**te ðē sēl* (2687b; cf. 2277b)   bioPj

         '(it) was none the better for him'

     (d) *þēah him / **lēof** ne wæs* (2467b; cf. 2332b)   ioPjB

         'though (he) was not dear to him'

In (22a, b) the choice of 'be' verb varies for no apparent reason (OES 1: 314). If *weorðan* was already becoming less distinct from *wesan* in the era of *Beowulf*, it is not surprising that the verb of lower frequency was obsolete by the Early Modern English period, surviving in a few archaic expressions like *woe worth the day*. Verse 299b, a similar instance with *gifeðe*, has *bið*. In (20c) the unstressed negated and contracted verb is routinely fronted before the unstressed indirect object. The other instance like (20c) is the same except for having *ne bið* rather than *næs*. In the verses like (20d) a subordinating conjunction blocks verb fronting as usual and the negated verb remains in archaic line-final position. The other instance has a different predicate adjective but is otherwise the same as the cited example.

§6.10 Instances with unexpressed predicate adjectives

The only examples in *Beowulf* are one-verse instances in clauses of comparison. In (23a–c) *swā* and *þonne* serve as the markers of comparison. The unexpressed predicate adjectives are understood from the immediately preceding clauses.

(23) (a) *swā hyt / ǣror wæs* (3168b)   (pj)sB

'as it was (useless) before'

   (b)   *ðonne is / ēower sum,*   (pj)bS

secg on / *searwum* (248b–49a)

'than one of you is (large), a warrior in armor'

   (c)   *swā bið / mægþa cræft,*   (pj)bS

wīg-gryre / wīfes,   be / wǣpned-men (1283b–84b)

'as the prowess of female humans — a woman's fearsomeness in combat — is (less) in comparison with male humans'

Item (23a) completes an assertion that the dragon's gold became as useless as it had been before being unearthed. Here the verb follows the subject, as it would normally do after a subordinating conjunction. In (23b, c), however, the verb precedes the subject and is situated immediately after the marker of comparison, which does not have the usual inhibiting effect of a subordinating conjunction. This suggests that the second clause in comparative constructions is coordinated with the first clause rather than subordinated, in which case the variation between verb-fronting constructions and

verb-final constructions would be expected. Item (23b) completes an assertion by Hrothgar's harbormaster that Beowulf is the largest human he has
ever seen. Item (23c) completes an assertion that Grendel's mother was less
terrifyingly strong than Grendel in proportion as the average female warrior
is less terrifyingly strong than her average male counterpart. This assertion
is in the poet's own voice. It presupposes the existence of formidable woman
warriors. It is relevant to add that Grendel's mother would have killed Beowulf if God had not intervened, according to the poet (1550–56) and to
Beowulf himself (1655–58). The poet cannot be saying that no woman is fit
for combat. Plural *mægþa* in the opening verse of (23b), which parallels plural *men* in the third verse, makes it clear that *wīfes* in the second verse is a
generic singular variation of *mægþa*. The poet is comparing two large groups,
both of which contain individuals with varying fitness for combat, rather
than assessing the fitness of any individual within a group.

§6.11 Instances with unexpressed 'be' verbs

Instances are not discussed as clauses if the predicate adjective is the only
major constituent expressed. The instances considered in this section also
have expressed arguments and provide evidence for normative word orders.

§6.11a One-verse instances

In (24a–d) the verb is understood from an immediately preceding clause.
Note the similarity between (24a) and the Modern English construction with
and before the final constituent and no expressed conjunction between the
earlier constituents.

(24) (a)   ***Hygd*** / *swīðe geong,*   (b)SPj

  wīs[,] / ***wēl-þungen*** (1926b–27a)

  'Hygd (was) very young, wise, (and) accomplished'

 (b) ***fæger*** / ***fol***dan bearm (1137a; cf. 770a, 1925b)   (b)PjS

  'fair (was) earth's breast'

 (c) ***lēodum*** / ***līðost   ond*** / ***lof***-geornost (3182)   (sb)IoPj

  '(he was) most gracious to the people and most eager for fame'

 (d) ***wīd-cūþ*** / ***werum*** (1256a)   (sb)IoPj

  '(that became) widely known to men'

Like (24a): 1230b, 1594a, 1743b, 2420b, 2728b.

Item (24a) has the stressed constituents in normative SPj order. In the clauses like (24b) stressed adjectives suitable for emphasis are fronted to the left periphery and the stressed constituents are out of normative order. With adjectives in final position these verses would have the unacceptable patterns *Sxs/S (M1), *Ssx/Sx (H5), and *Sxx/S (O6). Stressed constituents observe normative IoPj order in (24c). In the alternative to (24d) with the predicate adjective in final position, *werum* would be resolved obligatorily on the first S position and the verse would have only three metrical positions. In the verse as it stands *werum* can stand unresolved in a common realization of type A3 (Ss/Sx).

§6.11b Multi-verse instances

The stressed constituents occupy separate verses in item (25).

(25) *mīn* / **yldra** *mǣg* un- / **lifigende,**   (b)S/Pj

    bearn / *Healfdenes* (468a–69a; cf. 2171)

    'my elder kinsman, the son of Halfdane, (was) not living'

Here a modified predicate adjective that would overburden the opening verse occupies the following b-verse. The verb is unexpressed so there is no evidence for movement or displacement.

§6.12 Other constructions with predicate adjectives

It is difficult to distinguish predicate adjective constructions with 'be' verbs from constructions with certain other verbs. In (26a–c), for example, the semantic content of the verb phrase is concentrated in the adjective and OE *standan* 'stand' could be replaced by a 'be' verb with no change in truth value. In (26d), similarly, *grēow* could be replaced by *wearð* 'became.' In ordinary usage the 'stand' verb is used for human beings rising to an upright position and the 'grow' verb is used for plants or animals rising toward their mature height. Observe that the subjects of *standan* in (26a–c) are neither plants nor animals. The subject in (26d) is a body part rather than a plant or an animate creature.

(26) (a)   *þonne* / **blōde** *fāh*   S/PjB

    hūsa / *sēlest* **heoro**-*drēorig* / *stōd*

    wēa / **wīd**-*scofen* **witena** / *(ge)hwylcum* (934b–36b)

'when the best of dwellings remained polluted with blood, sword-gory —
a far-reaching woe for each (one) of the wise men'

(b)   *oð þæt / īdel stōd*   PjB/S

hū̆sa / sēlest (145b–46a)

'until the best of dwellings became empty'

(c)   *þæt þæs /* **sele** *stande,*   SB/Io/Pj

reced */ sēlesta,* **rinca** */ (ge)hwylcum*

īdel / (ond) **un**nyt (411b–13a)

'that this hall, best of buildings, remains empty and useless to each (one)
of men'

(d)   *hwæþere him on /* **ferhþe** *grēow*   B/SPj

brēost-*hord /* **blōd**-*rēow* (1718b–19a)

'but within his heart his soul became bloodthirsty'

It would be awkward to represent the adjectives in these instances as zero-
converted adverbial modifiers of a main verb. To do so would imply that
words like 'empty' and 'sword-gory' could represent ways of standing like
'aside,' or that 'bloodthirsty' could describe a way of growing like 'vigor-
ously.' Compare **stōd** *on /* **stapole** 'stood on the platform' (*Beowulf* 926a), a
straightforward description of where a human being was taking an upright
posture. In this instance the verb retains sufficiently vivid meaning to be
fronted to the most prominent S position of the verse, with the noun alliterating in accord with the rule of precedence. In (26a–d), on the other hand,
the verb occupies a subordinate S position where alliteration is unnecessary,
as a stressed 'be' verb would normally do. Item (26a) has normative word
order, with the caesura in the ideal position between the subject and the
constituents of the verb phrase. In (26b) a heavy modified subject is displaced to the right periphery. In (26c) a heavy variation is displaced, remaining adjacent to the adjunct it varies. In (26d) the light verb is fronted to
normative metrical location s4 and completes the opening b-verse.

Speakers of Modern English know that *I consider Burgess reliable* means
the same thing as *I consider Burgess to be reliable*. In early generative grammar
the more compact construction was sometimes explained as deletion of underlying *be* from the wordier construction. In the minimalist theory *Burgess
reliable* can be represented as an adjective phrase that serves as the complement of *consider* and some other verbs of mental activity (e.g. *find* and
think.). Within such a complement both *Burgess* and *reliable* would receive
accusative case. No underlying 'be' verb would be posited. *Burgess is reliable*

238

would be derived by movement of *Burgess* out of the adjective phrase to subject position in a higher clause headed by a 'be' verb (Chomsky 1993: 8–9). *I consider Burgess to be reliable* would incorporate *Burgess to be reliable* into the finite-verb domain of *consider* as an infinitive complement analogous to the that-clause in *I consider that Burgess is reliable.*

Items (27a–e) are Old English constructions with adjective phrases serving as verbal complements. The verb is *tellan* 'consider' in (27a–c); *talian* in (27d) has similar meaning. Item (27e) is analogous to expressions like *I knew him honest,* which are idiomatic in some varieties of English. With (27f) compare *they found him dead.*

(27) (a) *nē his / **līf-dagas** lēoda / **ǣngum***   SO/Io/PjV

         ***nytte** / tealde* (793a–94a)

         'and (he) by no means considered his (Grendel's) life-days useful to any (one) of the people'

    (b) *swā hyne / **Gēata bearn** gōdne / (ne) tealdon* (2184)   oS/PjV

         'since the Geats did not consider him strong'

    (c) *þȳ ic / **Heaðo-beardna** hyldo / (ne) telge,*   s/OV/IoPj

         ***dryht**-sibbe / **dǣl Denum** / unfǣcne* (2067–68)

         'for that reason I do not consider the friendship of the Heathobards, (their) part in the alliance, free of deceit towards the Danes'

    (d) *nō ic mē an / **here**-wæsmum hnāgran / talige,*   so/PjV

         ***gūþ**-ge- / weorca, þonne / **Grend**el hine* (677a–78a)

         'I by no means consider myself more lacking in martial vigor, in respect of battle-deeds, than Grendel (considers) himself'

    (e) *syðþan hē / **aldor-þegn un**- / lifigendne,*   sO/Pj/V

         *þone / **dēorestan dēadne** / wisse* (1308–9)

         'after he knew the most beloved senior thane unresponsive, dead'

    (f) *syððan hīe ge- / **fricgeað frēan** / ūserne*   sV/O/Pj

         ***eal**dor- / lēasne* (3002a–3a)

         'after they learned our lord dead'

Constituents sharing a verse observe normative SO, OV, and PjV orders. In (27c) the heavy predicate adjective is displaced beyond the verb to the right periphery.

In some dialects of Modern English, *think* has the same syntax as *consider* and the Old English verbs in item (27). In these dialects *I thought him honest* would be idiomatic. Old English *þyncan* differs from *think* in having a nominative object of perception as subject and an optional experiencer in the dative case, like Modern English *seem*. The Old English construction backgrounds the experiencer and foregrounds the thing perceived, suggesting that the thing would probably be perceived in the same way by others. This construction minimizes the major difference between seeming and being: the element of uncertainty.

(28) (a) *swā him ge-* / **met** *ðūhte* (3057b)   (s)ioPjV

        'as (it) seemed appropriate to him'

   (b) *ne þynceð mē ge-* / **rys**ne (2653a; cf. 1748a)   (s)vio/Pj

        '(it) does not seem reasonable to me' (anticipating a that-clause)

   (c) *ðǣr him* / **fold**-*wegas* **fægere** / *þūhton,*   ioS/PjV

        cystum / **cū**ðe (866a–67a)

        'where the earthen paths seemed fair to them, known for good qualities'

   (d)   *þūhte him* / **eall** *tō rūm*   vioPj/S

        wongas / *ond* **wīc**-*stede* (2461b–62a)

        'the fields and the dwelling-place seemed all too spacious to him'

   (e) *hȳ on* / **wīg**-*ge*tawum **wyr**ðe *þinceað*   s/PjV

        eorla / *(ge)*æhtlan (368a–69a)

        'in (their) combat equipment they seem worthy of the esteem of earls'

   (f)   *nō his* / **līf**-*gedāl*   S/PjV/Io

        sārlic / *þūhte* **sec**ga / *ǣn(e)gum* (841b–842b)

        'his parting from life seemed by no means painful to any (one) of men'

In (28e) the subject is unstressed. Stressed constituents share a verse in (28a, c, e, f), observing normative PjV order. In (28d) a very heavy compound subject is shifted to the right periphery. An unstressed verb is fronted to an unoccupied C position in (28b, d) and the unstressed indirect object follows.

§6.13. Retrospect

As in predicate adverbial clauses, 'be' verbs in predicate adjective clauses are more often fronted to an unstressed position than left in archaic stressed position. There are 234 unstressed instances as compared with 197 stressed instances. Of 43 clauses with a stressed 'be' verb and a stressed predicate adjective, verb and adjective share a verse in 30 instances, always in normative PjB order and always with the 'be' verb in normative line-final position (121b, 149b, 203b, 228b, 282b, 299b, 555b, 561b, 682b, 860b, 945b, 1255b, 1255b, 1269b, 1670b, 1831b, 1941b, 2066b, 2161b, 2187b, 2199b, 2332b, 2378b, 2467b, 2480b, 2491b, 2682b, 2696b, 2838b, 3174b). The subject shares a verse with the 'be' verb in two instances (435b, 1814a) and with the predicate adjective in four instances (817a, 2137b, 2170b, 2483b). These six instances observe normative SB and SPj orders. The remaining clauses have each stressed constituent in a separate verse (opening verses: 393a, 544a, 789a, 1110a, 1243b, 2730b, 2911b).

Like the OV verb phrases in chapter three, the PjB verb phrases in this chapter are normative in a language with SOV typology. The frequency with which stressed constituents of the verb phrase share a verse (30 out of 43 possible instances) provides further evidence that the poet uses verb phrases with OV typology as formulaic building blocks. The corresponding verb phrases of predicate adverbial constructions are similar, though the fact that they typically use prepositional phrases as adverbials can make it harder to fit the whole verb phrase into a single verse. Stressed constituents of the verb phrase always share a verse in normative order if the prepositional phrase is small enough, however, and the stressed verb always occupies normative line-final position (§5.8).

CHAPTER 7

PREDICATE NOMINATIVE CLAUSES

§7.0 Introduction

These constructions encode an equation between a subject noun and a pre-dicate noun (Pn, pn). In mathematics, equation has a huge role to play. In heroic discourse, this relation between arguments needs to be mentioned less often than characteristics encoded by adjectives, many of which express core generic concepts. The number of predicate nominative clauses in *Beowulf* is predictably smaller than the number of predicate adjective clauses. In §7.6 verb phrases with stressed predicate nouns and 'be' verbs will be com-pared with the corresponding verb phrases in predicate adjective and predi-cate adverbial clauses.

§7.1 Instances with all major constituents stressed

In *Beowulf* the subject of a predicate nominative construction is usually rea-lized as an unstressed pronoun and the 'be' verb is usually fronted to an unstressed position. Full realizations with stressed subjects, verbs, and pre-dicate nominatives represent a tiny fraction of the small total. There are no one-verse examples like *ecg* / *īren wæs* 'the edge was iron.' Though such examples are easy to construct, the constituents would usually have to be arranged as heavy type D verses with a word group in a complex Sxs or Sxxs foot. As with the corresponding predicate adjective constructions (§6.1), the poet prefers to rearrange the major constituents as a type A1 verse like *ecg wæs* / *īren* (item 6c below), with the verb on an unstressed position at me-trical location x2.

Items (1a, b) are multi-verse examples with the verb at normative location s4. In the cited instances a subordinating conjunction blocks verb fronting.

(1) (a) *gyf þonne / **Frȳs**na hwylc   **frē**cnen / spræce*   S/PnB

        *ðæs / **morþ**(o)r-hetes   **mynd**giend / wære* (1104–5)

        'then if (anyone) whoever of the Frisians by dangerous speech should be a

        reminder of the deadly hatred'

    (b)   *seopðan / **Gren**del wearð,*   SB/Pn

        *eald-ge- / winna,   **in**-genga / mīn* (1775b–76b; cf. 1349b–51a)

        'since Grendel, the old adversary, became my invader'

Item (1a) has normative SPnB order and normative grouping of the major constituents, with the subject in one verse and the constituents of the verb phrase in a following verse. In the instances like (1b) a modified predicate nominative has been shifted to the right periphery.

§7.2   Instances with arguments that are unexpressed or restricted to initial position

Items (2a–c) are one-verse instances with relativized predicate nominatives.

(2) (a) *hwæt / **syn**don gē[,]   **searo**- / hæbbendra,*   wpnBS

        *byr**num / <u>werede</u>* (237a–38a)

        'what (kind of people) are you, oh wearers of armor, protected by mailcoats?'

    (b) *hwæt þā / **men** wǣron* (233b)   wpnSB

        'what (kind of people) the men were'

    (c) *swylc / **Æschere** wæs* (1329b)   wpnSB

        'such (a man) Æschere was'

In (2a) the predicate nominative is realized as a relative interrogative pronoun and the verb is routinely fronted before the stressed subject. In this unusual instance the 'be' verb alliterates at location s1b as the most prominent word in the verse. Item (2b) is similar but with the stressed verb at normative location s4. In (2c) subject and verb observe normative SB order in a b-verse with the predicate nominative realized as *swylc*, the second of two identical correlative pronouns. The first correlative would translate as *what* in a corresponding Modern English sentence like *what a man should be, such a man Asher was.* The stressed verb stands at normative metrical location s4.

Items (3a–d) are the multi-verse instances. Stressed constituents sharing a verse observe the normative orders PnB, SB, IoB, and SPn. The stressed verbs occupy normative metrical location s4.

(3) (a) *þām ðāra **māðma** **mund**-bora wæs*   ws/PnB

      ***long**e / hwīle* (2779a–80a)

      'who was the protector of those treasures for a long while'

  (b) *hwylce / **Sǣ**-Gēata **sī**ðas / wǣron* (1986; cf. 233b)   wpn/SB

      'what the Sea-Geats' adventures were'

  (c)   *Ēadgilse / wearð*   (s)IoB/Pn

      *fēa-sceaftum / **frēond*** (2392b–93a)

      '(he) became a friend to ill-fated Eadgils'

  (d)   *þām æt / **sæcce** wearð,*   wioB/SPn

      *wræccan / **wine**-lēasum[,] **Wēoh**stān / bana*

      mēces / ecgum (2612b–14a)

      'to whom — to that friendless exile — Weohstan became a slayer with the edges of a sword'

Items (3a, b) are syntactically complete one-line clauses. In (3a) the relative pronoun *þām* does double duty as oblique dative object of the verb in the preceding clause and subject of the predicate nominative construction. In (3b) the predicate nominative is represented by a relative interrogative pronoun. In (3c) a subject with the same referent as the subject of a preceding clause is unexpressed. In this instance *fēasceaftum* is too large to share a verse with *Ēadgilse,* its modified proper noun, and *frēond wearð* is too short to qualify as a verse. The poet creates acceptable verse patterns by splitting *Ēadgilse* from its modifier with the verb in a typical instance of hyperbaton. The heavy two-word verse containing the predicate nominative is displaced to the right periphery. In (3d) an indirect object in the dative of disadvantage is relativized. This clause is similar to the archaic construction *tō banan weorðan.* In (3d), however, we have predicate nominative *bana* rather than the predicate adverbial *tō banan.* The archaic deverbative root persists but the syntax has been modernized.

§7.3 Instances with unstressed arguments

Items (4a, b) are one-verse clauses with an unstressed subject.

(4) (a) *hȳ* / **bēnan** *synt* (364b; cf. 352b, 3140b)   sPnB

      'they are petitioners'

  (b)   *nō þæt* / **lǣsest** *wæs*   sPnB

      hond-ge- / **mōta** (2354b–55a)

      'that was not the least (one) of hand-to-hand combats'

The other examples like (4a) all have *bēna* as the predicate nominative, with minor variation in person and number. All constituents are in normative syntactic order and the unstressed subject occupies normative metrical position x1. In (4b) the predicate nominative is the zero-converted adjective *lǣsest*, which also functions as the noun in a partitive genitive construction.

Items (5a–c) are multi-verse examples with the the stressed verb at normative location s4. Item (5b) has a simple past-tense form where a present perfect form would be idiomatic in Modern English.

(5) (a) *þæt hē* / **Heardr**ēde **hlā**ford / wǣre (2375)   sIo/PnB

      'that he should be lord to Heardred' (subjunctive verb)

  (b)   *ic* / **hwīle** *wæs*   sB/Pn

      ende- / sǣta (240b–41a; cf. 881b–82b, 3098b–99a)

      'I was (I have been) a coast guard for some time'

  (c)   *þæt ðām* / **gōdan** *wæs*   sIoB/Pn

      hrēow *on* / **hreð**re, **hyge**-sorga / mǣst (2327b–28b; cf. 2709b–11a)

      'for the good (man) that was misery in the breast, greatest of heart-sorrows'

Item (5a) is a one-line clause with all constituents in normative syntactic and metrical positions. In (5b, c) the modified predicate nominative is displaced to the right periphery.

§7.4 Instances with unstressed verbs

The high frequency with which 'be' verbs are fronted to unstressed positions shows up dramatically in this section, which includes the largest number of predicate nominative clauses.

§7.4a One-verse instances

In (6a–c) the subject and predicate nominative are stressed.

(6) (a) *ne wæs / **ecg** bona* (2506b; cf. 1266b–67a)   bSPn

  'the sword was not the killer'

  (b) ***Bēowulf** is / (mīn) nama* (343b)   PnbS

  'my name is Beowulf'

  (c) ***ecg** wæs / īren* (2778a)   SbPn

  'the edge was iron'

In (6a) the negated verb is fronted to an available C position as usual. In (6b) the verb occupies extrametrical location x3 in the simplest compound foot, Ssx, situated as the first foot in type E (Ssx/S). The verb follows the predicate nominative for metrical reasons. Even with a change in alliteration, the alternative with normative word order, **(mīn) **nama** / Bēowulf is,* would be an unacceptable realization of type D3 with a pronoun in avoidable anacrusis. Verse-initial placement of the predicate nominative in (6b) avoids unacceptable placement of the verb in anacrusis at metrical location x5. In (6c) placement of the verb on an unstressed position at metrical location x2 avoids ***ecg** / īren wæs,* with the complex D3 pattern S/Sxs. As we observed (section §7.1), the poet prefers to arrange such constituents as a type A1 verse like (6c).

In a few clauses like item (7) the subject is unexpressed.

(7) *wæs / **þēaw** hyra* (1246b)   (s)bPn

  '(it) was their custom'

Other examples: 771a, 1008b, 1495b, 2209b, 2657a.

All unstressed verbs in these clauses occupy normative metrical position x1. In verses 2209b and 2657a the pronoun subject has an antecedent in the immediately preceding clause. The other four instances are straightforward examples of null-subject constructions in which the only information about the subject is provided by the person, number, and case of the finite verb.

In most one-verse instances the subject is expressed by a pronoun.

(8) (a) *þæt wæs / **gōd** cyning* (11b)   sbPn

'that was a good king'

   (b) *ne wæs þæt ge- / **wrixle** til* (1304b)   bsPn

     'that was not a good bargain'

   (c) *eart þū se / **Bēowulf*** (506a)   bsPn

     'are you that (person named) Beowulf?'

Other examples like (8a): 134b, 178b, 348b, 454b, 765b, 833b, 863b, 1039a, 1075b, 1458a, 1463b, 1559b, 1607b, 1611b, 1812b, 1885b, 2390b, 2441a, 2813a, 2999a, 3056a; like (8b): 249b, 716b, 734b, 1372b, 1455a, 2532b, 2541b, 2586b.

The most common arrangement is represented by (8a), where the unstressed constituents observe normative 'sb' order. Routine verb fronting of the negated verb occurs in (8b). Pithy one-verse clauses like (8a, b) call attention to the reportability of something in the narrative, either directly as in (8a) or indirectly through ironic negative understatement, as in (8b), where the bad bargain is feud, a trade of lives on one side for lives on the other. In (8c) the verb is routinely fronted in an interrogative construction.

§7.4b Multi-verse instances

In (9a–c) the only unstressed constituent is the verb. The inanimate possessive dative in (9a) is excluded from the notation as an adjunct STP. The animate and personified datives in (9b, c) are interpreted as indirect objects. The unstressed verb in (9a) moves to an available C position and the adjunct modifier supplies the alliteration. In (9b, c) the adverb stands before the verb as usual.

(9) (a) *wæs þǣm / **hæft**-mēce **Hrun**ting / nama* (1457)   b/PnS

     'the name to that hilted sword was "Hrunting"'

   (b)   *þā wæs / **forma** sīð*   (s)bPn/Io

     ***geon**gan / cempan* (2625b–26a)

     'then (it) was the first time for the young warrior' (anticipating a that-clause)

   (c)   *ðā wæs / **forma** sīð*   (s)bPn/Io

     ***dēo**rum / mādme* (1527b–28a)

     'then (it) was the first time for the precious treasure' (anticipating a that-clause)

In (9a) the subject and predicate nominative are out of normative SPn order for metrical reasons. As it stands the b-verse is an acceptable realization of type A3 (Ss/Sx), with an unresolved short syllable on the second S position. Even with the required change of alliteration, the SPn alternative would be *nama* / Hrunting (*S/Sx: SO2), with obligatory resolution of *nama* on the first S position. In (9b, c) the subject is unexpressed and the modified indirect object is displaced to the right periphery, where it provides an ideal two-word verse of type A1. In (9c) use of the construction in (9b) personifies a precious sword as a combatant.

In (10a–e) the unstressed verb shares location x1 with an unstressed argument. Each stressed constituent occupies a separate verse.

(10) (a)   *wē synt **Higel**āces*   sb/Pn

      ***bē**od-ge-* / *nēatas* (342b–43a)

      'we are Hygelac's table-companions'

(b) *þæt wæs* / ***Hrōð**gāre **hrē**owa* / *tornost*   sbIo/Pn

      (2129; cf. 1296a–98a, 2817a–18a)

      'that was the greatest of miseries for Hrothgar'

(c) *þæt wæs* / ***wr**æc micel **wine*** / *Scyldinga,*   sbPn/Io

      ***mō**des* / *brecða* (170a–71a; cf. 290b–91a, 1691b–92a)

      'that was a great misery for the friend of the Scyldings, a disruption of the mind'

(d) *wes þū* / ***mund**-bora mīnum* / ***mago**-þegnum,*   bsPn/Io

      ***hond**-ge-* / *sellum* (1480a–81a)

      'be thou a guardian for my kindred thanes — (my) close companions'

(e)   *wæs him* / ***Bē**owulfes sīð,*   bioS/Pn

      mō**dges* / *mere-faran, **micel / *æfþunca* (501b–2b)

      'Beowulf's exploit — the seafaring of the bold (man) — was a great annoyance to him'

Opening verses in other examples like (10a): 260a, 335b, 407b, 2406a, 2611a.

In (10a–c) the unstressed constituents observe normative 'sb' order. In (10b) an indirect object too short to fill a verse stands in normative position before the predicate nominative. The modified indirect objects in (10c, d) fill a verse and are displaced as usual to the right periphery. The unstressed imperative verb in (10d) is routinely fronted and occupies an unstressed position due to its low prominence. In (10e) the unstressed argument is an indirect object and the verb is fronted to an unoccupied C position, marking the transition to a new topic, Unferth's attempt to belittle *Beowulf*'s accomplishments.

§7.5 Other constructions with predicate nominatives

Two instances are closely related to predicate adjective clauses with *talian* 'consider.' The unexpressed objects are specified in a a following that-clause.

(11) **sōð** ic / _talige_ (532b; cf. 1845b)   (o)PnsV

    'I consider (that) the truth'

Verse 1845b has *wēn* 'expectation' rather than *sōð* but is otherwise identical. In such cases one might posit a verbless predicate-noun phrase *(þæt) sōð* analogous to predicate adjective phrases like *Burgess reliable* or *mē hnāgran* (§6.12). The verb would take the predicate-noun phrase as its accusative complement. There would be no need to posit an underlying 'be' verb.

    OE *talian* functions similarly in (12a, b).

(12) (a)   *þæt ic mē* / **ǣ**nigne   sioO/PnV

      under / **swegl**es begong   (ge)**sacan** ne tealde (1772b–73b)

      'that I did not consider anyone a threat to me'

    (b) *þē hē ūsic* / **gār**-wīgend   **gōde** / tealde,   soPn/V

      hwate / **helm**-berend (2641a–42a)

      'because he considered us good spear-fighters, keen helmet-wearers'

Nominative and accusative forms of stressed arguments are often identical in Old English. Item (5a) provides an example in which both constituents of the predicate-noun phrase are marked unambiguously as accusative (*ǣnigne, gesacan*). In (5b) the first term of the equation is an unambiguously accusative form of a personal pronoun.

§7.6. Retrospect

As in chapters five and six, unstressed 'be' verbs preponderate, with 53 instances as compared with 29 stressed 'be' verbs. Stressed constituents of the verb phrase share a verse in seven instances (352b, 364b, 1105b, 2354b, 2375b, 2779b, 3140b). All have normative order (PnB) and all have the verb in normative line-final position. These are characteristics we observed in the corresponding predicate adverbial and predicate adjective constructions.

CHAPTER 8

PARTICIPIAL CLAUSES

§8.0 Introduction

English participial constructions are complements of auxiliary *have* or *be*. Government by the auxiliary is marked by assignment of participial form to the verbal head of the complement. Past tense is typically marked on participles with a suffixed *-ed* or *-en*. Present tense is typically marked with the suffix *-end*, which does the work of Modern English *-ing*. The past participle (Pt, pt) was inflected as an adjective in the Germanic precursor of Old English. The present participle (Pr, pr) originally had nominal inflection but was later inflected as an adjective (Braune 1966: 84). A few present participles continued to function as nouns and differentiated from the new adjectival forms. OE *fēond* 'enemy' is an archaism of this kind, as shown by the old noun formative *-nd*. The original meaning of the word was 'a hating one, a hater.' By the Old English period, *fēond* had adopted inflections used for root nouns and was no longer inflected like an Old English participle (OEG: 257).

The participle functions as an attributive adjective in Old English constructions like *fǣted wǣge* 'ornamented cup' (2253b). Passive constructions like *they were wearied* or *they were dampened* mean more or less the same thing as predicate adjective constructions like *they were weary* or *they were damp*. In these respects it makes sense to describe participles as verbal adjectives. A contrast with adjectives becomes conspicuous, however, when a participle is modified by an adjunct phrase encoding an expressed cause or agent. It is not acceptable to say *they were weary by the effort* or *they were damp by the rain*. The word governed by the finite 'be' verb in such phrases must be transparently derived from a verb. In acceptable passive constructions like *they were wearied by the effort* or *they were dampened by the rain,* the adjectival root is followed by a verbal suffix and may also be extended with a verbal formative like the *-en-* in *dampened.*

The verbal character of participles is acknowledged in traditional grammar by classifying them as principal parts of verbs, along with finite verbs and infinitives. As with verbs that govern infinitives, verbs that govern participles are called auxiliaries (notated as A, a) rather than copulas or linking verbs. The auxiliary and its governed participle form a closely bound constituent that I will refer to as the VERBAL COMPLEX. Transitive participles can take direct objects in active constructions like *they are encountering a problem,* with the present participle governed by auxiliary *be,* or *they have encountered a problem,* with the past participle governed by auxiliary *have.* Neither **they are aware a problem* nor **they were aware a problem* is acceptable, though we can say *they are / were aware of a problem,* with an adjunct phrase in the genitive case.

It is a commonplace of rhetoric that using a by-phrase for the cause of an event is a de-emphasizing technique. When responsible entities are especially vulnerable to the limelight a legal or public relations advocate can leave those entities unspecified in passive constructions like *some laws were allegedly violated* (by guilty agents) or *a few deaths were apparently caused* (by a noxious commercial product). I attribute the effect of de-emphasis to demotion of the responsible entity from subject — a major sentence constituent — to optional adjunct modifier of a verbal adjective. By-phrases are excluded from the syntactic notations, as with adjunct prepositional phrases that modify finite verbs or infinitives.

In Old English a dative-instrumental inflection frequently does the work of Modern English 'by,' e.g. in *hond<u>um</u> gebrōden* 'woven by hands' (1443b). For consistency I will use a single term, BY-PHRASE, for these constructions and also for participial constructions like *mēce geþinged* 'settled with a sword' (1937b), where the dative-instrumental inflection on the inanimate noun translates most idiomatically with a preposition other than 'by.' Though somewhat more prominent than 'be' verbs, auxiliaries like *habban* have extremely low prominence.

§8.1 Instances with all major constituents stressed

§8.1a Imaginable one-verse instances

Verses like (1a, b) would have normative SPtA syntax but do not appear in *Beowulf*.

(1) (a) **Bēow** / *(ge)bolgen wæs* (constructed)   SPtA

 'Beow was enraged'   S/Sxs (D3 with extrametrical syllable)

 (b) **Bēow** *ge-* / **boren** *wæs* (constructed)   SPtA

 'Beow was born'   Sx/Ss (A2 with two words in the second foot)

Since most past participles have unstressed prefixes, a participial construction like (1a) would have a complex type D3 pattern with an extrametrical syllable and a word group in the second foot. The only such verse in the poem is *Beowulf* 1539a, **brægd** / *(þā)* **beadwe** *heard*. When the participle is resolvable, as in (1b), the result would be a rare type A2 variant that contravenes OE 3.4. Given a set of constituents like those in (1a, b), the poet prefers to place the finite verb on an unstressed position after the first stress in a verse of type A1, the least complex type and the one most tolerant of complex realizations. For examples see §8.5a. Compare the analogous preference for type A1 in predicate adjective and predicate nominative constructions with three stressed constituents (§§6.1, 7.1).

§8.1b Multi-verse instances

Items (2a–i) have finite 'be' verbs as auxiliaries and past participles that encode perfective aspect. Item (2e) is an Old English active intransitive clause that has *wæs* as the auxiliary with a verb of motion. The remaining examples are passive constructions. Stressed constituents sharing a verse observe normative orders (PtA, SA, SPt, IoA). The poet uses *wæs* in (2f) where the subjunctive mood would be preferable in Modern English. The note in K4 considers proposals that allow for indicative meaning but concludes that *wæs* must mean 'would have been.'

(2) (a)   *siððan* / **æfen-lēoht**   S/PtA

 under / **heofenes haðor** *be-* / **holen** *weorþeð* (413b–14b; cf. 219–20)

 'after the evening light becomes concealed under the enclosure of heaven'

 (b)   *forðām* / **Offa** *wæs*   SA/Pt *geofum* ond / *gūðum,* *gār-cēne* / *man,*

wīde / *(ge)weorðod* (1957b–59; cf. 1838b–39a)

'therefore Offa — that spear-keen man — was widely honored'

(c) **Heorot** / *innan wæs* SA/Pt

*frēon*dum / *(ā)fylled* (1017b–18a)

'Heorot was filled inside by friends'

(d) *þæt ðes* / **eorl** *wære* SA/Pt

ge- / **boren bete**ra (1702b–3a; cf. 3061b–62a)

'that this man was very well born'

(e) *þæt his* / **aldres** *wæs* **ende** / *(ge)gongen,* A/SPt

dōgera / **dæg**-*rīm* (822a–23a)

'that the end of his life, the numbered times of (its) days, was come'

(f) **æt-rihte** / *wæs* A/SPt

gūð *ge-* / *twǣfed* (1657b–58a; cf. 2175b–76b)

'the battle was (would have been) decided right away'

(g) **Bīowulfe** / *wearð* A/S/Pt

dryht-māðma / **dæl** **dēa**ðe / *(for)golden*

(2842b–43b; cf. 2423b–24b, 2676b–77a)

'the share of noble treasures was paid for by Beowulf with death'

(h) **Bēowulfe** / *wearð* IoA/SPt

gūð-*hrēð* / *gyfeþe* (818b–19a; cf. 823b–24b)

'fighting fame was granted to Beowulf'

(i) **Higelāce** / *wæs* IoA/S/Pt

sīð / *Bēowulfes* **snūde** / *(ge)cȳðed* (1970b–71b)

'Beowulf's arrival was quickly reported to Hygelac'

Item (2a) has normative syntactic order, with the subject in one verse and constituents of the verb phrase in a later verse. In all but one instance the stressed auxiliaries are placed at normative metrical location s4. In the exception, item (2e), placement at metrical location s2 allows for expression of the major constituents in a single line. The core syntactic position of the participle is clause-final when not followed by an auxiliary. In (2d) the participle fronted to metrical location s1a for metrical reasons. If *boren* were resolved in an alternative with normative order, we would have **betera geboren,* with the unacceptable pattern **Sxx/S (O6); without resolution, we would have an otherwise unattested A1 variant with an extrametrical prefix and a short syllable on the second lift (K4: 330). In (2b–d, g) the heavy modified participles are displaced to the right periphery. In (2e–i) the auxiliary is fronted before the subject to a subordinate lift in the opening verse, preceded by a more prominent constituent that provides the alliteration.

Bēowulfe in (2h) may look like an indirect object at first glance but the context makes it clear that death is a price paid for the treasure by Beowulf, not a price paid by an unexpressed agent to Beowulf as a beneficiary. Though skeptical about a dative of human agency distinct from instrumental and indirect object function, Mitchell (OES 1: 577) acknowledges that (2h) is one of the most plausible examples. I interpret *dēaðe* as an inanimate instrument and *Beowulfe* an animate agent, setting aside the question of whether the agent would have been dative or instrumental when these cases had distinct forms. In (2c), similarly, it seems simplest to interpret the friends as filling the hall of their own agency rather than positing some unspecified agent to fill the hall by means of friends. I interpret the dative constituents in these verses as adjuncts and exclude them from the notation.

Items (3a–e) are active constructions with transitive participles. In all instances the stressed auxiliary occupies normative location s4. Major constituents sharing a verse observe the normative orders PrA, SA, OPt, and PtA.

(3) (a) *ac se / **ǣglǣca** **ēh**tende / wæs,*   S/PrA/O

      *deorc / **dēaþ**-scua, **dugu**þe / (ond) <u>geogoþe</u>* (159–60; cf. 3028a–29a)

      'but the awe-inspirer — that dark death-shadow — was persecuting the old fighters and the young ones'

   (b)   *nū / **scealc** hafað*   SA/OPt

      *þurh / **driht**nes miht **dǣd** ge- / <u>fremede</u>* (939b–40a; 2453b–54b)

      'now the man has performed a deed'

   (c)   *bealo-cwealm / hafað*   SA/O/Pt

      fela / feorh-cynna forð on- / sended (2265b–66b)

      'evil killing has has sent forth a great number of human beings (to death)'

   (d)   *þēah ðe / **win**tra lȳt*   O/PtA/S

      *under / **burh**-locan ge- / **biden** hæbbe(,)*

      Hǣreþes / dohtor (1927b–29a)

      'though Haereth's daughter may have experienced a small number of winters within the fortress wall' (subjunctive verb)

In (3a) a past-tense form of *wesan* governs a present participle with imper-
fective aspect marked by the suffix *-end*. The past-tense auxiliary and the
present participle combine in (3a) to form a PAST IMPERFECT clause, which
focuses on a span of past time within which an action continued. Old English
present participles have lower frequency than in Modern English, partly because Old English employs the simple present where Modern English employs *-ing* forms in participial constructions like *I'm leaving now* or *I'm going
to the theater next Saturday*. In (3b–d) a present-tense form of *habban* governs a participle with perfective aspect in a PRESENT PERFECT clause that
focuses on a point in present time after an action is completed.

§8.2   Instances with arguments that are unexpressed or re-
stricted to initial position

There are no one-verse instances. Items (4a–f) are multi-verse instances with
unexpressed subjects. In these instances the referent of the unexpressed subject can easily be understood from a following that-clause, from an antecedent in the immediately preceding clause, or by an antecedent in a clause
followed by an unbroken series of other clauses with the same subject unexpressed. Items (4a–c) are passive constructions with intransitive participles. In these constructions a past-tense form of the 'be' verb combines with
a perfective participle to form a PAST PERFECT construction that focuses on
a point in past time when an action is completed. Items (4d–f) are active
constructions with transitive participles. Item (4e) is a present perfect clause
with a present-tense auxiliary. The other clauses are PLUPERFECT clauses
with a past-tense auxiliary, translated as *had*. Pluperfect clauses focus on a
point in past time after an action is completed and before some other action
occurs. In (4e) *gē* is a conjunction rather than the identically spelled second-
person pronoun.

(4) (a)   *syððan / ǣrest wearð*   (s)A/Pt

         *fēasceaft / fun*den (6b–7a; cf. 1937b–38b)

         'after (he) was previously found destitute'

    (b)   **un**synnum *wearð*   (s)A/Pt

         *be- / **loren lēo**fum   æt þām / **lind**-plegan*

         ***bearn**um / (ond) **brōð**rum* (1072b–74a)

         '(she) was blamelessly deprived of beloved children and brothers at the shield-
         play (fighting)'

    (c)   *syððan / ǣrest wearð*   (s)A/Pt/Io

258

gyfen[,] / *gold*-hroden[,] *geon*gum / cempan,

æðelum / *dīore* (1947b–49a)

'after (she) was previously betrothed, adorned with gold, to the young champion, dear to people'

(d)   *sōna* / *hæfde*   (s)A/OPt

un- / *lyfigendes* *eal* ge- / feormod,

fēt ond / *folma* (743b–45a)

'soon (he) had eaten all of the lifeless one, (including) feet and hands'

(e) *gē* / *feor* hafað *fǣhð*e / (ge)stǣled (1340)   (s)A/OPt

'and (she) has thoroughly settled the feud'

(f)   *gearwor* / *hæfde*   (s)A/O/Pt

āgendes / *ēst* *ǣr* ge- / scēawod (3074b–75b)

'rather, (he) had previously expected the favor of the owner'

In (4e) placement of the stressed auxiliary at metrical location s2 makes it possible to realize the major constituents as a single line. In all other instances the stressed auxiliary occupies normative metrical location s4. In (4d–f) the participle remains in core syntactic position at the end of the clause, as often when the auxiliary is fronted, and at metrical location s4. In (4a) the participle stands at metrical location s2 in core syntactic position. In (4b, c) the participle occupies its least favored metrical location, on metrical location s1a before a more prominent noun that alliterates in accord with the rule of precedence. Item (4b) avoids **lēofum / (be)loren,* which scans as *Sxx/S (O6) or as a rare type A1 variant. Compare (2d) above for avoidance of the same two patterns. Item (4c) avoids **gold-hroden / gyfen.** This constructed variant does not scan as Ss/Sx (A3), since resolution of *-hroden* on the s position of the first foot would violate Kaluza's Law. It does scan as a rare variant of type E (Ssx/S), with unresolved *-hroden* occupying the s and x positions of the first foot and *gyfen* resolved on the subordinate S position. The only comparable example in *Beowulf* is 1009b, **Healfdenes / sunu.** Occupation of the Ssx foot by a short syllable in this unique example contravenes OE 8.3. Item (4c) as it stands is a variant of type D2 (S/Ssx), with the compound foot in normative final position, normative resolution of a short syllable with primary stress on the most prominent lift, and normative nonresolution of a short syllable with subordinate stress on the least prominent lift. There are 38 verses of this kind in the poem, including **sunu** / *Healfdenes,* which occurs seven times (268a, 344b, 645a, 1040b, 1652b, 1699a, 2147a) and **maga** / **Healfdenes,** which occurs five times (189b, 1474b,

1867a, 2011b, 2143b). **_Healfdenes_** / <u>_sunu_</u> looks like an opportunistic reversal of a familiar pattern to obtain alliteration on [h].

Items (5a, b) have relativized objects. Stressed constituents sharing a verse observe normative SPt and PtA orders and the auxiliaries occupy normative location x4.

(5) (a)   _hwām þæt_ / **_sweord_** _geworht,_   wioSPt/A

    īrena / _cyst,_   **_ǣrest_** / _wǣre_ (1696b–97b)

    'for whom that sword, choicest of steels, was perhaps first made'

(b)   _swylce on_ / **_horde_** _ǣr_   wo/S/PtA

    nīð-hēd(i)ge / _men   ge-_ / **_numen_** _hæfdon_ (3164b–65b)

    'such as people with envious minds had taken previously in the hoard'

Item (5a) has a relativized indirect object in a clause with a subjunctive auxiliary. In (5b) _swylce_ functions as the relativized direct object of the participle.

§8.3 Instances with unstressed subjects

§8.3a One-verse instances

The clauses in item (6) are passive constructions in the past tense with normative syntactic order. The auxiliary varies between _wæs_ and _wearð_ in these clauses for no apparent reason.

(6) (a) _ðā hē ge-_ / **_bolgen_** _wæs_ (723b, 1539b, 2550b)   sPtA

    'when he was enraged'

  (b) _hit geond-_ / **_brǣded_** _wearð_   **_bed_**_dum_ / _(ond)_ **_bol_**_strum_

    (1239b–40a; cf. 2692b)   sPtA

    'it was overspread with beds and cushions'

Like (6a): 693b, 1239b, 1293b, 2220b.

All instances are b-verses of type B1 (x/Sxs) with the finite auxiliary in its normative syntactic and metrical position. The participles alliterate appropriately as the most prominent constituents. All have unstressed prefixes after the unstressed subject at normative metrical location x1. The three identical instances of (6a) highlight the ferocious determination of a mighty combatant attacking a hated adversary. This formulaic phrase is used for the hero Beowulf (1539b, 2250b) and also for the monster Grendel (723b). The similar instance in 2220b, used for the dragon, is identical except for having *þæt* instead of *ðā.*

§8.3b Multi-verse instances

Wesan, weorðan, and *habban* serve as auxiliaries in (7a–f). All instances have the finite verb at normative location s4. Items (7b, c) are intransitive active constructions; the rest are passives.

(7) (a) *þēah ðe hē / **slǣ**pende   be- / **syred** wurde*   s/PtA
      þēofes / cræfte (2218–19a)
      'though (while) sleeping he might have been tricked by the skill of a thief'
      (subjunctive)

  (b) *syððan hīe tō- / **gædre**   ge- / **gān** hæfdon* (2630; cf. 2104)   s/PtA
      'after they had come together'

  (c)   *swā hit ā- / **gan**gen wearð*   sPtA/Io
      eorla / manegum (1234b–35a)
      'as it was gone (had gone) for many (a one) of earls'

  (d)   *ac hē þæs / **fæste** wæs*   sA/Pt
      *in**nan** / (ond) ūtan   īren- / bendum*
      searo-þoncum** / (be)**smiþod (773b–75a)
      'but it was firmly enough constructed by clever techniques with iron bands inside and outside'

  (e)   *swā hyt / **lun**gre wearð*   sA/Pt
      *on hyra / **sinc**-gifan   **sāre** / (ge)endod* (2310b–11a; cf. 902b–4a)
      'just as it was quickly ended on (to the disadvantage of) their treasure-giver'

  (f)   *sīo ge- **hā**ten [is],*
      ***geong, gold**-hroden,   **gladum** suna Frōdan* (2024b–25b)   sPtA/Io
      'young, adorned with gold, she is pledged to the gracious son of Froda'

Items (7a, b) are one-line clauses with the unstressed subject at normative metrical location x1 and stressed constituents of the verb phrase sharing a later verse in normative order. In (7c, f) a heavy indirect object is displaced to the right periphery and stressed constituents of the verbal complex share the opening verse in normative order. In (7d, e) a heavy modified participle is displaced to the right periphery and a modifier of the verb supplies the required alliteration on the first lift of the opening verse.

In (8a–c) auxiliary *hæfde* governs transitive participles in pluperfect constructions. Stressed constituents sharing a verse observe normative orders (PtA, OA).

(8) (a) *þæt hē / **dæg**-hwīla   ge- / **drogen** hæfde,*   sO/PtA

      eorðan / wynne (2726a–27a; cf. 2397–99, 3147a–48a)

      'that he had enjoyed his daytimes, delights of earth'

  (b) *nealles ic ðām / **lēanum**   for- / **loren** hæfde,*   sO/PtA

      *mægnes / **mēde*** (2145a–46a, dat. obj; cf. 804a–05b, acc. obj.)

      'by no means had I lost (done without) recompense, the reward of strength'

  (c) *hraðe hēo / **æþelinga**   **ānne** / hæfde*   s/OA/Pt

      *fæste / (be)**fangen*** (1294a–95a)

      'at once she had firmly seized one of the athelings'

In (8a, b) all major constituents appear in normative syntactic order. The stressed objects provide alliteration for the opening verses and the midline caesura separates these objects from the verbal complex. In (8c) a heavy modified participle is shifted to the right periphery. Alliteration for the first line is provided by an object and its modifier in noun-adjective order, with enjambment before the second verse as usual.

§8.4 Instances with unstressed objects

There are no one-verse instances. In (9a–d) the unstressed argument is a direct or indirect object at normative metrical location x1. Stressed constituents sharing a verse observe normative PtA and SA orders.

(9) (a)   *hū hit / **Hring**-Dene*   oS/PtA

      *æfter / **bēor**-þege   ge- / **būn** hæfdon* (116b–17b; cf. 106a–7a, 1599)

      'how the Ring-Danes had occupied it after the beer-drinking'

  (b)   *ac hyne / **sār** hafað*   oSA/Pt

      *in / **nīð**-gripe   **nearwe** / (be)fongen,*

      balwon / **ben**dum (975b–77a)

      'but pain has wound him tightly with baleful bonds in a hostile grip'

  (c) *ðǣm **eafera** wæs   **æfter** / cenned*   ioSA/Pt

      geong in / **gear**dum (12a–13a; cf. 1356a–57a)

      'in the dwellings a young heir was born to him afterwards' (hyperbaton)

(d)   *þā him ā- / **lumpen** wæs*   ioPtA/S

*   **wist**-fylle / **wēn** (733b–34a; cf. 140b–42a)

'when the expectation of a plentiful meal was come (had come) to him'

In (9a) the stressed subject supplies alliteration for the opening verse and stressed constituents of the verbal complex share a following verse. In (9b, c) the participle is modified by an alliterating adverb in a verse displaced to the right periphery. In (9d) a modified subject is displaced. In (9a, b, d) the stressed auxiliary occupies normative metrical location s4. In the verses like (9c) the auxiliary is placed at metrical location s3, making it possible to arrange the major constituents in a single line. In the cited example hyperbaton removes the adjunct modifier *geong* from the syntactically complete clause. In the other example a partitive genitive modifier of the subject is removed by hyperbaton.

In item (10) the subject and direct object are both unstressed and alliteration for the opening verse is provided by an adjunct. Constituents of the verbal complex share a verse in normative order, with the auxiliary at normative location s4.

(10) *syðþan hē hine tō / **gūðe** ge- / **gyred** hæfde* (1472; cf. 2707a–8a)   so/PtA

'after he had prepared himself for combat'

Both instances are pluperfect clauses with participles governed by past-tense forms of *habban*. All major constituents are in normative order.

§8.5 Instances with unstressed auxiliaries and no unstressed arguments

As expected, these auxiliaries are often fronted to unstressed positions due to their low prominence. The 'be' auxiliaries with the lowest prominence are fronted most often.

§8.5a One-verse instances

In (11a–e) a 'be' auxiliary is used with verbs of motion that take abstract subjects and encode movement through time rather than space. The 'be' auxiliaries are fronted to unstressed positions at normative location x1 and the stressed constituents observe normative SPt order. All instances are of type C2 or C4.

(11) (a) *ðā wæs / **wint(e)r** scacen* (1136b)   aSPt

        'then winter was (had) departed'

   (b) *on ðǣm wæs / **ōr** writen* (1688b)   aSPt

        'on which (a sword) the origin was inscribed'

   (c) *wæs hira / **blǣd** scacen* (1124b; cf. 2913b)   aSPt

        'their glory was (had) departed'

   (d) *ðā wæs / **hord** rāsod* (2283b)   aSPt

        'then the hoard was explored'

   (e) *nū is se / **dæg** cumen* (2646b)   aSPt

        'now the day is come'

Other examples like (1a): 223b, 1151b, 2306b, 2727b (hyperbaton).

In these types non-resolution is normative on the s position, which provides a favorable site for unresolved short syllables (OE 8.5). Most participles in item (11) have a short root syllable on the s position. The exception is *rāsod* in (11d). In (11a, d, e) a fronted verb is preceded by an adverb, with *ðā* 'then' being the most common adverb. In (11b) the adverbial constituent that begins the clause is a light prepositional phrase with a relative pronoun object.

Items (12a, b) have prefixed participles with long root syllables. For these clauses type A1 is most appropriate. Stressed constituents observe normative SPt order. Sudden transitions from joyful peacetime to disastrous conflict, a conspicuous feature of the narrative from beginning to end, are highlighted in verses like (12a). Verses 1176b, 1303b, 1703b, and 2287b perform the same function.

(12) (a) ***wrōht** wæs / (ge)nīwod* (2287b)   SaPt

        'strife was renewed'

   (b) ***sōð** is / (ge)cȳþed* (700b)   SaPt

        'the truth is well known'

Other examples like (12a): 1107a, 1159b, 1303b, 2554a; like (12b): 1176b, 1703b, 3084b.

If the unstressed auxiliary in (12a, b) occupied normative location x1, the result would be an unacceptable A1 variant with verbal anacrusis. The poet avoids this problem by placing the unstressed verb at location x2. The prominence of verbal SPs normally restricts them to location x1. Exceptions occur only with the least prominent verbs, once with *sceal* (1060b), once with *wearð* (1302a), and thirty times with a form of *wesan*, the least promi-nent of all. All 32 instances occur in type A1. The auxiliary is a form of *wesan* in all ten instances like (12a, b).

§8.5b Multi-verse instances

The unstressed verb occupies normative metrical location x1 in all examples but (13f), where placement of the verb at location x2 avoids unacceptable anacrusis. Stressed constituents sharing a verse observe normative IoPt and SPt orders.

(13) (a) *þæt wæs / **ȳð**-geblond **eal** ge- / menged* (1593)   aS/Pt

    'that the surging wave was all mingled (polluted)'

 (b)   *is his / **eafora nū***   aS/Pt

    ***heard** / **hēr** cumen* (375b–76a; cf. 476b–77a)

    'his strong son is now come here' (hyperbaton)

 (c) *wǣron / **ȳð**-gebland **eal** ge- / fǣlsod,*   aS/Pt

    ēacne / eardas (1620a–21a)

    'that the vast domains, the surging waves, were all cleansed'

 (d)   *þā wæs / **ende**-dæg*   aS/IoPt

    *gōdum / (ge)**gong**en* (3035b–36a)

    'then the final day was come (had come) for the good (man)'

 (e) *ðā wæs / **gylden** hilt **game**lum / rince,*   aS/Io/Pt

    *hārum / **hild**-fruman, on / **hand** gyfen,*

    *enta / **ǣr**-geweorc* (1677a–79a)

    'then the golden hilt, ancient work of the giants, was given in hand to the old warrior, that leader in combat'

 (f)   ***sorh** is / (ge)nīwod*   SaPt/Io

    ***Deni**gea / lēodum* (1322b–23a)

    'sorrow is renewed for the people of the Danes'

Opening verses in other examples like (13a): 36b, 917b, 1300a, 2961a, 3051a, 3134a; like (13c): 262a, 330b, 349a, 997a, 3040b.

Item (13a) is an unusual example of verb fronting after a C position occupied by the complementizer *þæt* (§1.8). In (13b, c) the C position is unoccupied and the verb moves to it. In (13d, e) adverbial *ðā* precedes the unstressed verb as usual. In (13e) a modified indirect object occupies a verse of its own in a clause with all stressed constituents in normative order. The modified indirect object in (13f) is displaced to the right periphery.

In (14a–f) stressed subjects and participles share a verse in normative SPt order. Item (14b) is the only instance with a present participle.

(14) (a) *þā wæs æfter / **wiste wōp** / up āhafen,*   a/SPt

      *micel / **mor**gen-swēg* (128–29a)

      'then after prosperity weeping was raised up, great lamentation in the morning'

  (b) *ðær wæs on / **blōde brim** / weallende* (847)   a/SPr

      'there the sea was welling in blood'

  (c) *þæs wǣron mid / **Ēotenum ecge** / cūðe* (1145)   a/SPt

      'of this (sword) the edges were known among the Jutes'

  (d) *wæs / **mere**-fixa **mōd** on- / hrēred* (549)   a/SPt

      'the temper of the sea-fishes was provoked'

  (e) *þā wæs / **Hrōðgāre hors** ge- / bǣted,*   aIo/SPt

      *wicg / **wun**den-feax* (1399a–1400a; cf. 64a–65a, 491–92, 2324a–25a)

      'then a horse — a steed with braided mane — was bridled for Hrothgar'

  (f) *wæs þām / **yldestan un**-ge- / dēfe*   aIo/SPt

      *mǣges / **dǣ**dum **mor**þ(o)r-bed / strêd* (2435–36)

      'then a death-bed was unfittingly prepared for the oldest (one) by the deeds of a kinsman'

Opening verses in other examples like (14a): 642a, 856b, 1288a, 1310a.

In (14d, f) the C position is available and the verb moves to it. In (14a, b, e) the unstressed verb is preceded by an adverb. In (14c) fronting of *þæs* brings it closer to its antecedent in the preceding clause. Interpreting *þæs* as 'of which' would be problematic because relative pronouns normally block fronting of the verb before the subject. In (14d) alliteration is supplied by an adjunct genitive modifier split by the caesura from the noun it modifies. As usual, the enjambment is situated between the first two verses. In (14e, f) alliteration for the opening verse is provided by an unmodified indirect object fronted before the subject.

Items (15a, b) are the remaining intransitive clauses with the subject and participle in normative order. All instances have unstressed *wæs* after clause-initial *þā*.

(15) (a)   *þā wæs / **æht** boden*   aSPt/Io

           Swēona */ lēodum* (2957b–58a)

           'then chase was given to the people of the Swedes'

     (b) *þā wæs on / **gange** **gifu** / Hrōðgāres*   a/S/Pt

           oft ge- / æhted (1884a–85a; cf. 1629a–30a, 1896a–98a)

           'then on the path Hrothgar's gift (a horse) was often admired'

In (15a) subject and participle share the opening verse in normative order and a heavy indirect object is displaced to the right periphery. In the clauses like (15b) each major constituent occupies a verse of its own.

In (16a–c) the stressed major constituents occupy separate verses out of normative order.

(16) (a) *wæs ðā ge- / **bolgen** **beor**ges / hyrde* (2304)   aPt/S

           'then the guardian of the barrow was enraged'

     (b) *hraðe wæs ge- / **rȳmed**, swā se / **rīca** bebēad,*   aPt/Io/S

           *fēðe- / gestum **flet** / innanweard* (1975–76)

           'the hall was promptly cleared inside for the guests on foot, as the great man ordered'

     (c) *þā wæs be / **feaxe** on / **flet** boren*   a/Pt/S

           ***Grendl**es / hēafod(,) þǣr / **guman** druncon,*

           *eges**līc** / (for) **eorlum** ond þǣre / **ide**se mid,*

           ***wlite**-sēon / **wrǣt**lic* (1647a–50a; cf. 1437a–40a)

           'then Grendel's head was borne by the hair onto the hall floor where people were drinking — an awesome (thing) before the men and the noblewoman present (Queen Wealhtheow), an amazing, spectacular sight'

Opening verses in other examples like (16a): 361a, 1550a (with *hæfde*), 2063a, 2450a.

A heavy modified subject is displaced to the right periphery in (16a, c). In (16a) the auxiliary is fronted to its less usual position before *ðā*, marking a transition to a phase of the narrative. In (16b, c) the adverb precedes the auxiliary as usual and these clauses represent actions within the same phase of the narrative.

Items (17a–d) have transitive participles. Stressed constituents sharing a verse observe normative OPt order.

(17) (a) *hæfde / **æghwæ**ðer en*de / *(ge)fēred*   aS/OPt

        lænan** / **līfes (2844a–45a; cf. 205a–6a, 665b–67a, 2301a–2a)

        'each one had reached the end of transitory life'

    (b)   *hæfde / **East**-Denum*   aIo/S/OPt

        ***Gēat**-mecga / lēod   **gilp** ge- / læsted* (828b–29b)

        'the man of the Geats had fulfilled his boast to the East-Danes'

    (c) *hæfde / **līg**-draca **lēoda** / fæsten,*   aS/O/Pt

        *ēalond / ūtan, **eorð**-weard / ðone[,]*

        ***glēdum** / (for)**grun**den* (2333a–35a)

        'the fire-dragon had destroyed the fortress of the people with flames (and)
        the ancestral land outside — that whole region of the earth'

    (d) *wæs se / **grimma gæst   Gren**del / hāten,*   aS/OPt

        ***mære** / **mearc**-stapa* (102a–3a; cf. 373)

        'the grim demon was called Grendel, a famous stalker of the borderland'

Items (17a–c) are pluperfect active constructions with auxiliary *habban*. Item
(17a) has the most common pattern, with the subject in the opening verse
and stressed major constituents of the verb phrase sharing a later verse in
normative order. In (17b) an indirect object too small to fill a verse is fronted
beyond a heavier subject verse to the left periphery, where it supplies alliteration for the opening verse. Placement of the subject phrase in the opening
verse would create *(hæfde) Gēatmecga / lēod,* with unacceptable anacrusis in
type E (Ssx/S). In the verse as it stands the transitive participle shares a verse
with its inanimate object in normative OPt order and the animate indirect
object is more distant. In (17c) the stressed constituents observe normative
order, as in (17a), but the participle and its object occupy separate verses.
Item (17d) is the passive equivalent of an active construction with two objects, a primary argument referring to an inanimate name and a secondary
argument referring to an animate humanoid. The active construction would
translate as 'they called the grim demon Grendel.' In the passive equivalent
the inanimate argument is governed by a participial form of the verb, which
shares a verse with its object in normative order.

§8.6 Instances with an unstressed verb and an unexpressed or relativized argument

§8.6a One-verse instances

Items (18a, c) have unexpressed subjects and (18b) also has an unexpressed object.

(18) (a) *wæs in / **feorh** dropen* (2981b)   (s)aPt

    '(he) was struck into the life' (fatally)

  (b) *hæfde þā ge- / **frūnen*** (2403a)   (so)aPt

    'then (he) had learned (that)' (anticipating an indirect question)

  (c) ***Wīglāf** / (wæs) hāten, **Wēox**stānes / sunu,*   (s)OaPt

    *lēoflic / **lind**-wiga, **lēod** / Scylfinga,*

    ***mǣg** / Ælfheres* (2602a–4a)

    '(he) was called Wiglaf, son of Wistan, an admirable shield-fighter, a man of the Scylfings, kinsman of Ælfhere'

Item (18a) is a passive construction. Item (18b) is an active construction with a transitive participle. The verb is fronted before the adverb in (18b) to mark a digression from the main narrative line that provides background information. Like (17d), (18c) is the passive equivalent of a double-object construction with an inanimate name as primary object. The unstressed auxiliary in (18c) occupies metrical location x4 for metrical reasons. If this auxiliary stood at normative location x1 it would create verbal anacrusis in a verse of type A3 (Ss/Sx), a pattern in which no kind of anacrusis is acceptable (OE 9.7).

§8.6b Multi-verse instances

Items (19a–c) are passive constructions with past-tense auxiliaries. There is no antecedent for the unexpressed subject in (19b), which seems to be understood from ***flet**sittendum* as 'the hall.' In (19c) most of the semantic content of the verb phrase is concentrated in the adverb, somewhat as in predicate adverbial constructions.

(19) (a)   *wǣron / **hēr** tela*   (s)a/Pt

    ***willum** / (be)wenede* (1820b–21a; cf. 1694–95, 1745–47)

    'here (we) were well hosted with delights'

(b) *þā wæs / **eft** swā **ǣr** **ellen**- / rōfum*   (s)a/Io/Pt

*flet- / sittendum **fæge**re / (ge)reorded*

nīowan / stefne (1787a–89a)

'then again as before, on a new occasion, (it) was courteously prepared for the valor-bold ones sitting in the hall'

(c) *ðā wæs ge- / **gongen** **guman** / unfrōdum*   (s)aPt/Io

earfoð- / līce (2821a–22a)

'that (it) was gone (had gone) badly for the young man'

In (19a) the unstressed auxiliary is fronted to normative metrical location x1 and the following adverb is stressed. In (19b, c) the auxiliary is preceded as usual by unstressed adverbial *ðā*. The stressed participle occupies its core position as the last major constituent in (19a, b). In (19c) the heavy indirect object is displaced to the right periphery.

Items (20a–d) are active constructions with transitive participles. The unstressed auxiliaries occupy normative location x1. Items (20a–c) have unexpressed subjects. The referent of the subject in (20c) is specified in a parenthetical relative clause. The object is unexpressed in (20d).

(20) (a) *hæfde / **eorð**-scrafa **en**de / (ge)nyttod* (3046; cf. 2952a–53a)   (s)a/OPt

'(he) had used the last one of (his) earth-caves'

(b) *hæfde / **land**-wara **līge** / (be)fangen,*   (s)aO/Pt

*bǣle / (ond) **bron**de* (2321a–22a; cf. 883a–84a)

'(he) had enveloped the land-dwellers in flame, in fire and conflagration'

(c) *hæfde þā ge- / **fǣlsod** sē þe ǣr / **fēor**ran cōm,*   (s)aPt/O

*snotor ond / **swȳð**-ferhð, **sele** / Hrōðgāres* (825a–27a)

'the one who came from afar, wise and great-hearted, had purified Hrothgar's hall'

(d) *hæfde / **āg**-lǣca **el**ne / (ge)gongen* (893)   (o)aS/Pt

'the awe-inspirer had attained (that) with courage' (anticipating a that-clause)

In (20a) the stressed object and its governing participle share a verse in normative order. Item (20b) has the same order of major constituents with the object and participle in separate verses. In (20c) a modified object is displaced beyond the parenthetical relative clause to the right periphery. Item

(20d) is a one-line clause with the stressed constituents occupying separate verses in normative order.

§8.7 Instances with an unstressed argument and an unstressed auxiliary

There are no instances with relativized arguments. Item (21) is the only one-verse instance with an unstressed argument.

(21) *him wæs / **ful** boren* (1192a)   ioaSPt

    'A cup was brought to him'

The stressed constituents are in normative SPt order and the unstressed constituents are in normative ioa order.

Items (22a–c) are multi-verse instances with the unstressed subject and the unstressed auxiliary at normative location x1. Item (22a) is a passive construction. Items (22b, c) are active constructions with transitive participles and stressed objects.

(22) (a) *sīo wæs / **orðoncum**   **eall** ge- / gyrwed*   sa/Pt

        *dēofles / cræftum ond / **dracan** fellum* (2087–88)

        'it was all made by clever techniques with the skills of a demon and with

         skins from a dragon'

    (b)   *hæbbe ic / **mǣrða** fela*   asO/Pt

        *(on)**gun**nen / (on) **geogoþe*** (408b–9a)

        'I have undertaken many (a one) of famous deeds in youth'

    (c) *hæfdon hȳ for- / **healden**   **helm** / Scylfinga,*   asPt/O

        *þone / **sēlestan**   **sǣ-** / cyninga*

        *þāra ðe in / **Swīorīce**   **sinc** / brytnade,*

        mǣrne / þēoden (2381a–84a)

        'they had opposed the lord of the Scylfings, the highest-ranking (one) of

         the sea-kings who dealt treasure in Sweden, a famous lord'

In (22a) subject and auxiliary observe normative order. Unstressed *sīo* stands appropriately close to its lexical noun antecedent in the previous clause and is hard to distinguish from a relative pronoun. Items (21b, c) provide good examples of presentative fronting — fronting of an unstressed verb to mark

271

the beginning of a new discourse unit (Luraghi 1995: 364). These clauses initiate multi-line narrative digressions that provide background information for something just introduced in the narrative foreground. Departure from normative placement of the participle in (22b) avoids *(on) geogoþe /* *(on)gunnen,* with a much less desirable form of anacrusis. As it stands the verse has ordinary prefixal anacrusis. In (22c) displacement of the modified subject makes it possible to arrange all the major constituents in a syntactically complete one-line clause, followed by an appositional phrase, a parenthetical relative clause, and a variation of *helm Scylfinga* that is displaced beyond the parenthesis.

Items (23a, b) are multi-verse instances with unstressed indirect objects.

(23) (a)   *ūs wæs / ā syððan*   ioa/SPt

Mere / *-wīoingas* **milts** *un-* / *gyfeðe* (2920b–21b)

'the favor of the Merovingians was denied to us us ever afterwards'

(b)   *mē wearð* / **Grendl**es *þing*   ioaS/Pt

on mīnre/ ēþel-tyrf **un**dyrne / *cūð* (409b–10b)

'the affair of Grendel became openly known to me on my home turf'

The stressed constituents observe normative order. The stressed participles remain in core syntactic position at metrical location s4, their preferred location when the auxiliary is moved. Unstressed constituents in the opening verses observe normative 'ioa' order.

§8.8   Instances with an unstressed argument and an unexpressed or relativized argument

§8.8a   One-verse instances

Items (24a, b) have unexpressed subjects and unstressed indirect objects. The stressed constituents observe normative PtA order.

(24) (a) *ðā him ge- / rȳmed wearð* (2983b; cf. 1103b, 3088b)   (s)ioPtA

'when (that) was granted to them'

(b) *swā ūs ge- / worden is* (3078b)   (s)ioPtA

'as (it) is come to pass for us'

In these clauses clauses the C position is occupied by a subordinating con-junction and fronting of the auxiliary is blocked. In (24b) *weorðan* 'become' behaves like a verb of motion through time, taking auxiliary 'be' rather than 'have' as in Modern English.

Items (25a, b) are active constructions in which the object of a transitive participle is unexpressed.

(25) (a) *ac hīe hæfdon ge-* / *frūnen* (694a; cf. 595a)   (o)saPt

          'for they had learned (that)'

      (b) *hafast þū ge-* / *fēred* (1221a, 1855a; cf. 433a)   (o)asPt

          'you have attained (that)'

These compact main clauses are followed by that-clauses that specify the reference of the unexpressed object. All are of a-verses of type A7 (xx/Sx), with the participle alliterating on the only available lift as the most promi-nent constituent. In (25a) the C position is occupied by a subordinating conjunction and the subject precedes the verb in normative order. In (25b) the C position is available and the verb moves to it. The clauses in (25a) introduce summaries of relevant information that characters have acquired by asking questions. The two identical instances like (25b) introduce sum-maries of Beowulf's accomplishments by Queen Wealhtheow. The third in-stance, verse 433a, summarizes information that the speaker has acquired by asking questions.

§8.8b Multi-verse instances

Items (26a–c) are present perfect clauses. The direct object is unexpressed in (26a) and relativized in (26b, c).

(26) (a)   *þū þē* / *self hafast*   (o)sioA/Pt

         dǣdum / *(ge)fremed* (953b–54a)

         'you yourself have accomplished (that) for yourself with (your) deeds'

      (b) *þāra þe ic on* / *fold*an   *ge-* / *frægen hæbbe* (1196)   wos/PtA

          'which I have learned about on earth'

      (c)   *hwæt mē* / **Gren***del hafað*   woioSA/Pt

         hȳn*ðo* / *(on)* **Heoro***te*   *mid his* / **hete***-þancum,*

         fǣr*-nīða[,]* / *(ge)fremed* (474b–76a)

'what (kinds) of humiliations in Heorot, of surprise attacks, Grendel has caused for me with his malicious schemes'

Item (26a) is followed by a that-clause specifying the reference of the unexpressed object. Reflexive *þē* is the indirect object. The modified participle is displaced to the right periphery and the unstressed constituents observe normative order. In (26b, c) the fixed initial position of the relative pronoun determines the order of unstressed constituents. Stressed constituents sharing a verse observe normative PtA and SA orders. The second line in (26c) provides a good example of semantically inessential detail that is relevant to immediate context and has clearly been added to vivify the narrative. This line could be removed without a trace and serves no metrical purpose. The surprise attacks mentioned by Hrothgar are carried on by night, which adds to the gravity of a crime in ancient Germanic culture.

§8.9 Instances with unexpressed auxiliaries

There are several instances with an expressed participle and an expressed argument.

§8.9a One-verse instances.

In (27a, b) clauses with unexpressed auxiliaries follow an initial clause in which the auxiliary is expressed (included for clarity below). The appropriate tense, person, and number features are easily understood from the first clause.

(27) (a)   *ðā wæs /* **heal** *roden*   (a)SPt (twice)

        *fēon*da */ fēorum,   swilce /* **Fin** *slægen,*

        cyning *on / corþre,   ond sēo /* **cwēn** *numen* (1151b–53b)

        'then the hall was reddened with the life-blood of foes, likewise Fin (was) slain, the king amid his troop, and the queen (was) taken'

   (b) *ðā wæs /* **hord** *rāsod,*   (a)PtS

      *(on)***boren** */* **bēa**ga *hord* (2283b–84a)

      'then the hoard was explored (and) the hoard of rings (was) diminished'

Other examples with normative SPt order as in (27a): 999a, 1065a, 1065b, 3089b, 3135b.

The second and third b-verses in (27a) cannot be interpreted as variations of the opening b-verse because they express different propositions in a sequence of narrative actions expressed by the participles. In (27b), similarly, exploring the hoard is distinct from taking rings away from it. Departure from normative SPt order in (27b) is required because *$b\bar{e}aga$ $hord$ / $(on)boren$ would have the unacceptable pattern *Sxs/S (M1).

§8.9b Multi-verse instances

In (28a–d) subject and participle observe normative SPt order. In (28d) a heavy indirect object has been displaced to the right periphery.

(28) (a) **atol** / $\bar{y}ða$ $geswing$ **eal** ge- / $menged$ (a)S/Pt

         hāton / **heol**fre (848a–49a; cf. 486a–87b)

         'the terrifying agitation of the waves (was) all polluted by hot blood'

    (b)   ond / **frēond**-laþu   (a)S/Pt

         wordum / (be)**wæg**ned (1192b–93a; cf. 1193b–95b)

         'and friendship (was) offered by means of words'

    (c)   **sīd**-rand / **man**ig   (a)S/Pt

         hafen / **han**da fæst (1289b–90a; cf. 1107b–8a)

         'many a broad shield (was) taken firmly by hand'

    (d)   **bēne** / (ge)**tī**ðad   (a)SPt/Io

         fēasceaftum / men (2284b–85a)

         '(some) grace (was) granted to the unfortunate man'

Item (28a) is a one-line clause followed by a heavy by-phrase displaced to the right periphery. In (28b) the clause begins with the subject in a b-verse and is concluded in the following a-verse, which is constructed by modification of the participle with an adverbial noun. In (28d) the grammatical subject has inherent genitive case rather than the usual nominative case (see §3.1a for discussion). Such passive constructions occur when the verb assigns oblique case rather than accusative case to a direct object (Blake 2001: 59). As the note in K4 observes, the oblique subject remains an object in the descriptivist analysis of these constructions as 'impersonal' (OES 1: 355–57), which assumes that the grammatical subject is unexpressed 'it.'

§8.10. Other constructions with participles

These remaining participial clauses have low frequency and more than the usual number of major constituents. There are no instances that fit within a single verse. Item (29) is a passive construction with an unexpressed infinitive auxiliary.

(29) *sceal se / hearda helm   hyr*sted- / *golde,*   (i)aS/Pt

     fǣtum[,] / (be)feallen (2255a–56a)

     'the hard helmet shall (be) deprived of gold decoration (and) ornaments'

An infinitive with null phonological content must be posited in (29) because *sceal* needs to have a syntactic feature checked against a governed infinitive.

Items (30a–d) have participial phrases analogous to adjective phrases without a 'be' verb (§6.12). Constituents sharing a verse observe normative OV, OPt, and PtV orders. An unstressed indirect object occupies normative metrical location x1 in (30c, d). In (30a–c) a verb of knowing employs a syntactic structure more often employed with a verb of seeing.

(30) (a)   *ic þā / lēode wāt*   sOV/Pt

     gē wið / fēond gē wið frēond   fæste / (ge)worhte,

     ǣghwæs / untǣle   ealde / wīsan (1863b–65b)

     'I see (know) those people firmly bound against foe and with friend, blameless in respect of everything after the old fashion'

    (b)   *wiste þǣm / āhlǣcan*   (s)V/OPt

     tō þǣm / hēah-sele   hilde / (ge)þinged (646b–47b)

     '(he) saw (knew) battle planned at the high hall by the awe-inspirer'

    (c) *ac him / wæl-bende   weotode / tealde*   (s)ioO/PtV

     hand-ge- / wriþene (1936a–37a)

     'but (he) saw (knew) hand-tied death-cuffs decreed for him'

    (d) *gedēð him swā ge- / weald(e)ne   worolde / dǣlas,*   (s)v.ioPt/O

     sīde / rīce (1732a–33a)

     '(he) makes regions of the world, a broad kingdom, subjugated to him'

    (e) *ðā wæs / hāten hreþe   Heort / innanweard*   aPt[1]/S/Pt[2]

     *fol*mum / *(ge)frætwod* (991a–92a)

     'then Heorot was ordered decorated inside by hands'

In (30a–d) the participial phrase is the complement of a finite verb, as in MnE active sentences like *I consider that subject closed.* In (30e) the head of the participial phrase has been moved to subject position in a passive clause, as in MnE passives like *that subject was considered closed.*

§8.11 Retrospect

When used as auxiliaries, 'be' verbs are distributed like the 'be' verbs in the previous three chapters, which are used as linkers. Unstressed usage of these verbs again preponderates, with 75 instances as compared with 43 stressed instances. When we turn to lower-frequency *habban,* however, we find 21 unstressed instances as compared with 28 stressed instances. The proportions of stressed and unstressed usage are sensitive to fine distinctions of prominence due to differences in frequency. Stressed constituents of the verb phrase share a verse in 36 total instances, always in normative order. There are 18 instances with a past participle and an auxiliary 'be' verb in PtA order (140b, 414b, 693b, 723b, 733b, 1103b, 1234b, 1239b, 1293b, 1539b, 2024b, 2218b, 2220b, 2550b, 2692b, 2983b, 3078b, 3088b). An additional 16 instances with PtA order have *habban* as the auxiliary (106b, 117b, 220b, 804b, 1196b, 1472b, 1599b, 2104b, 2145b, 2397b, 2630b, 2707b, 2726b, 2983b, 3147b, 3165b). There are two instances with present participles in PrA order (159b, 3028b).

CHAPTER 9

CLAUSES WITH UNINFLECTED INFINITIVES

§9.0 Introduction

The verse clauses in this chapter contain infinitive constructions that are complements of auxiliary verbs. These complements are headed by infinitive main verbs or by infinitive auxiliaries that take their own infinitive complements. Government by an auxiliary is marked by assignment of infinitive form to the verbal head of the complement. Old English infinitives are derived from Proto-Germanic verbal nouns (OEG: 299). They originally had inflectional endings for the nominative, genitive, dative, instrumental, and accusative cases. Inflections for these cases survive in Gothic and in prehistoric inscriptions. The Old English infinitives in this chapter are descendants of accusative forms that had lost their accusative inflection. Infinitives of intransitive verbs can govern indirect objects (as defined in §4.0). Infinitive forms of transitive verbs are transitive and govern the same kinds of direct objects. As with auxiliaries and participles, an auxiliary and its governed infinitive form a closely bound verbal complex. Constituents of a verbal complex with an intransitive infinitive typically share a b-verse in normative IA order, with the finite auxiliary at normative location s4. Transitive infinitives often share a verse with their governing infinitives but still more often with their governed objects, as a transitive main verb would do.

I will use the term CORE AUXILIARY for Old English verbs that typically govern infinitives: the pre-modals *agan* 'ought,' *cunnan* 'can,' *durran* 'dare', *magan* 'may', *sculan* 'shall' and *willan* 'will'; plus *mōtan* 'may,' *þurfan* 'need,' and indeclinable *uton* 'let us,' which has the force of a plural imperative or hortative subjunctive with a basic meaning similar to *sculan*. The Old Eng-

lish pre-modals are analyzed in detail by Mitchell (OES 1: 415–27). A pe-
culiarity of these verbs is that they sometimes occur independently without
an infinitive, expressed or understood, and sometimes govern object nouns
or pronouns, unlike the Modern English modals descended from them (OES
1: 419). The pre-modals have special meanings when used independently,
as for example with *agan* 'possess,' *cunnan* 'know,' *magan* 'be strong,' and
sculan 'owe.' OE *willan* can take a direct object, like Modern English *want*.

I refer to verbs that sometimes govern infinitives but routinely occur
without them as PERIPHERAL AUXILIARIES. Transitive verbs that function as
peripheral auxiliaries can govern direct object nouns and pronouns in addition to the infinitives that they govern. Intransitive peripheral auxiliaries of
motion govern infinitives in constructions that would have present participles in Modern English, as for example in *gangan cwōmon* 'came walk' =
'came walking' (Pascual 2021). I will translate such constructions in the for-
mat 'came walk(ing).'

The verse clauses surveyed in this chapter have as many as six major
constituents. To construct large verse clauses with infinitive constructions
the poet makes conspicuous use of two-word verse phrases as useful building
blocks. We will find rich samples of two-word type II verses shared in normative order by a variety of major constituents. Ways of arranging the larger
number of constituents in these clauses are correspondingly numerous in
relation to the total number of instances within a given set of metrically
defined constituents. For obvious reasons of space, the larger number of
possibilities to be discussed requires a more concise discussion. I must assume that the reader has acquired familiarity with the principles at work in
previous chapters.

As verbal nouns that can govern objects, infinitives combine the higher
prominence of lexical nouns with the lower prominence of lexical finite
verbs. The result is an intermediate prominence. Like finite verbs, infinitives
are attracted to normative metrical location s4 but less strongly. When an
infinitive competes with a finite verb for placement at the end of a line, the
finite verb usually prevails. Placement of infinitives on metrical location s1a
before a more prominent noun or adjective is dispreferred, but less strongly
so than with finite verbs; and fronting of infinitives to unstressed positions
is rare. See item (47) and §9.10 for the handful of examples from *Beowulf*.

§9.1 Instances with stress on all major constituents

For the reasons given in §8.1 there are no examples with all three stressed constituents in a single verse. Items (1a–e) are multi-verse examples with core auxiliaries and intransitive infinitives. Constituents sharing a verse observe normative IA and SI orders.

(1) (a) *þæt se / **byrn**-wiga **bū**gan / sceolde* (2918)   S/IA

       'that the mailed warrior should fall'

  (b)   *þonne / **scyld**-freca*   S/IA

     *on- / **gēan gra**mum   **gan**gan / scolde* (1033b–34b)

     'that the shield-warrior should go against foes'

  (c) *nealles / **folc**-cyning **fyrd**-ge- / steallum*   S/Io/IA

     *gyl**pan / þorfte* (2873a–74a)

     'the folk-king by no means needed to boast to (his) army comrades'

  (d)   *lof-dǣdum / sceal*   A/SI

     *in / **mǣg**þa (ge)hwǣm **man** ge- / þêon* (24b–25b)

     'by praiseworthy deeds one shall prosper in each (one) of tribes'

  (e)   *lond-rihtes / mōt*   A/S/I

     *þǣre / **mǣg**-burge **mon**na / ǣghwylc*

     īdel / hweorfan (2886b–88a)

     'each of the people of that kindred must wander deprived of a right to land'

Opening verses in other examples like (1a): 910a, 1523a; like (1b): 84a, 242a, 737b, 1066a, 1069a, 2081a.

The instances like (1a) are one-line clauses. Those like (1b) have adjunct verses between the subject verse and constituents of the predicate. In (1c) the indirect object stands in normative position between subject and infinitive and the verbal complex follows in an a-verse. In (1d, e) the auxiliary is fronted beyond the subject to normative metrical location s4 at the end of an opening b-verse, preceded by a semantically inessential adjunct that provides the alliteration. In (1d) the fronted auxiliary leaves a trace in the clause with the subject and infinitive, which remains psychologically complete (§1.8). Item (1e) has the same word order with each major constituent in a separate verse.

    In (2a–c) the intransitive infinitives are peripheral.

(2) (a) *þǣr* / **swīð**-*ferhþe* **sit**tan / *ēodon,*   S/IA

     þrȳðum / **dealle** (493a–94a; cf. 739)

     'there (or 'where') stout-hearted (people) went to sit, famous for (their) abili-
     ties'

  (b) *oþ ðe* / **nī**pende   **niht** *ofer* / *ealle,*   S/IA

     scadu-*helma* / *(ge)***sceapu**[,]   **scrī**ðan / *cwōman*[,]

     wan *under* / **wol**cnum (649a–51a)

     'until darkening night, the shape of the shadow–helmet, came slip(ping) over
     all things, colorless beneath the clouds'

  (c) *nō hēr* / **cūð**licor   **cuman** *on-* / *gunnon*   IA/S

     lind- / **hæb**bende (244a–45a)

     'shield-bearing (people) did by no means come here more openly' (have by
     no means come here more openly, in a less suspicious manner)

Constituents of the verb phrases in (2a–c) share a verse in normative order,
with the auxiliary in normative metrical location s4. Item (2a) is a syntactically complete one-line clause followed by an adjunct phrase. In (2b) the
poet adds stressed adjuncts before the subject phrase, before the verb phrase,
and after the verb phrase. The enjambment between *niht* and its modifier
nīpende comes as usual in the earliest possible location, at the end of the
opening verse. Below the reader will encounter many such examples of early
enjambment in accord with the principle of closure (§1.19). In (2c) the
heavy subject is displaced beyond the verb phrase.

    In (3a–d) the subject and auxiliary precede the infinitive. The most
common arrangement is that in (3a), with the subject and auxiliary sharing
a b–verse in normative syntactic order and the infinitive in a later verse.

(3) (a)   *þæt ðæt* / **fȳr** *ongon*   SA/I

     sweðrian / **syð**ðan (2701b–2a)

     'that the fire began to to subside afterwards'

  (b) *þanon* / **eft** ge<u>witon</u>   **eald**-ge- / **sī**ðas,   A / S / I

     swylce / **geong** *manig* *of* / **gomen**-*wāþe*

     fram / **mere mōd**ge   **mēa**rum / *rīdan,*

     beornas / *(on)* **blan**cum (853a–56a; cf. 1640a–42a)

     'from there the old retainers, many young ones too, went rid(ing) on steeds
     (back) from the successful expedition, warriors on horses'

  (c) **myn**te / *(se)* **mǣ**ra,   *hwǣr hē* / **meah**te *swā,*   AS/I *wīdre* / *(ge)win*dan   *ond on* / *weg* þanon

flēon on / *fen*-hopu (762a–64a)

'the notorious one intended — if he could (do) so — to turn outward and flee away from there into concealing marshlands'

(d) þæt ðǣr on / *worð*ig   *wīg*endra / hlēo,   S/A/I

   lind-ge- / stealla,   *lif*igende / cwōm,

   heaðo-lāces / hāl[,]   tō / *hofe* gongan (1972–74)

   'that there in the homeland the protector of warriors, of shield-companions, hale from the battle-play, came walk(ing) alive to the court'

Opening verses in other examples like (3a): 1605b, 2210b, 2552b, 2711b, 2914b, 2944b.

The stressed auxiliaries occupy normative metrical location s4 in (3a). In (3b) the major constituents occupy separate verses. The auxiliary is fronted to metrical location s3 in the opening verse, preceded by a semantically in-essential adverb that provides the alliteration. Constituents in the opening verse are out of normative SA order in (3c), where the auxiliary alliterates at metrical location s1a, followed by a more prominent constituent that al-literates in accord with the rule of precedence. Departure from normative SA order avoids *(se) *mǣra* / *mynte,* which has unacceptable anacrusis (OE 9.6). Item (3d) is similar to (3a) but with the major constituents in separate verses.

   In (4a–g) a core auxiliary and a transitive infinitive share a verse in nor-mative order. The object of the infinitive is marked with a superscript 'i.'

(4) (a) nē hūru / *Hildeburh*   *heri*an / þorfte   S/IA/Oi

   *Ēot*ena / trēowe (1071a–72a)

   'Indeed, Hildeburh needed by no means praise the fidelity of the Jutes'

   (b)   *bēah*-hordum / leng   Oi/S/IA

   wyrm / *wōh*-bogen   *weald*an / ne mōste (2826b–27b, dat. obj.)

   'the twisted, perverse serpent could not keep the ring-hoard longer'

   (c) ðonne / *sweor*da gelāc   *sun*u / Healfdenes   Oi/S/IA

   *efn*an / wolde (1040a–41a)

   'when Halfdane's son would (wanted to) perform the play of swords'

   (d)   ðǣr ā- / *bīd*an sceal   IA/S/Oi

   *mag*a / *mān*e fāh   *micl*an / dōmes (977b–78a, gen. obj.)

'there the man stained with crime shall await the great judgment'

(e) *swā be-* /*gylpan ne þearf* **Gren***deles* / *māga*   IA/S/O^i

   ǣnig / *(ofer)* **eor***ðan*   **ūht**-*hlem* / *þone* (2006–7)

   'so any of Grendel's kindred need not praise (boast about) the uproar at dawn'

   (so none of Grendel's kindred, etc.)

(f) *þæt se* / **mǣ***ra*   **maga** / *Ecgðēowes*   S/O^i/IA

   grund-*wong þone*   *of-* / **gyfan** *wolde* (2587–88)

   'that the famous son of Ecgtheow would relinquish the earth beneath (would
   die)'

(g) *þæt ðām* / **hring**-*sele*   **hrī***nan* / *(ne) mōste*   O^i/IA/S

   gum*ena* / *ǣnig,* (3053a–54a, dat. obj.)

   'that any (one) of men might not touch that ring-hall' (that no one might
   touch, etc.)

Opening verses in other examples like (4a): 644b, 1276b, 2963a; like (4b):
801b, 2314b.

In (4a) the modified object occupies a whole verse and is displaced to the
right periphery. In (4b, c) a smaller object suitable for emphasis is fronted
to metrical location s1a in the opening verse, where it provides the alliteration. In (4d, e) the subjects and objects fill type II verses displaced to the
right periphery, where they maintain normative SO order. Item (4f) has similar subjects and objects but they remain in their core positions. In the
complex (4g) the subject fills a type II verse displaced to the right periphery
and a fronted object smaller than a verse provides alliteration for an opening
verse of type C. Item (4g) contrasts with (4b, c), where object fronting emphasizes an important concept that is not the focus of preceding discussion.
In (4g) the ring-hall and its contents have been discussed in a sequence of
previous clauses and fronting links the object to semantically related material in accord with the 'iconicity of distance' principle, which applies to
stressed constituents as well as to unstressed pronouns and their antecedents.

    In (5a–e) the subject shares the opening verse with the auxiliary in nor-
mative SA order. Objects sharing a verse with a transitive infinitive observe
normative OI order.

(5) (a)   *oððæt his* / **byre** *mihte*   SA/O^{i}I

   eorl-*scipe* / **efnan** *swā his* / **ǣr**-*fæder* (2621b–22a; cf. 1468b–69b)

   'until his child could perform the duties of a man like his late father'

284

(b)   **byrne** *ne / meahte*   SA/Io/OʲI

geongum / **gār**-wigan **gēoce** / (ge)fremman (2673b–74b)

'the mailcoat could not provide help to the young spear-fighter'

(c)   **God** / *ēaþe mæg*   SA/Oⁱ²/Oⁱ¹I

þone / **dol**-sceaðan **dǣ**da / (ge)twǣfan (478a–79b)

'God can easily deny the foolish attacker (heroic) accomplishments'

(d)   **sinc** / *ēaðe mæg,*   SA/Oⁱ/I

gold on / **grun**de, **gum**-cynnes / (ge)_hwone_

ofer- / **hī**gian (2764b–66a)

'treasure — gold in the ground — may easily escape any one of human kind'

(e) *ūre / **ǣ**ghwylc sceal   ende / (ge)bīdan*   SA/OʲI

worolde / **lī**fes (1386a–87a)

'each of us shall experience an end of the life of this world'

The auxiliary occupies normative line-final position in (5a–d). In (5e) place-ment of the stressed auxiliary at metrical location s3 makes it possible to arrange the major constituents in a single line. In (5b) the inanimate direct object shares a verse with the finite verb and the animate indirect object is more remote, as usual. Item (5c) is a double-object construction with an inanimate primary object in the genitive case and an animate secondary object in the accusative case. The inanimate object is in closer construction with the finite verb, even though it has genitive case, and the animate object is more remote, even though it has accusative case.

Instances requiring more than one change in word order are predictably less common. Constituents sharing a verse observe normative SA, OA, and SI orders.

(6) (a)   **fēower** / *scoldon*   SA/I/Oⁱ

on þǣm / **wæl**-stenge **weor**cum / (ge)_ferian_

tō þǣm / **gold**-sele **Gren**dles / hēafod (1637b–39a)

'four (people) had to carry Grendel's head to the gold-hall on that spear-shaft — with difficulties'

(b)   **sibb'** / *ǣfre ne mæg*   OʲA/SI

wiht on- / **wen**dan (2600b–01a)

'anything cannot ever change kinship' (nothing can ever change kinship)

In (6a) a modified infinitive is displaced to the right periphery and a modified object is displaced beyond it. In (6b) the auxiliary is fronted to location s3 in the opening verse, preceded by an object suitable for emphatic fronting that provides the alliteration.

Items (7a–d) have transitive peripheral auxiliaries and intransitive infinitives. The object of the auxiliary is marked by a superscript 'a.' Stressed constituents sharing a verse observe normative IA, OA, and SA orders.

(7) (a) **hwīlum / heaþo-rōfe hlēapan / lēton,**   S/IA/O[a]

       on ge- / flit faran[,] fealwe / mēaras (864–65)

       'at times the battle-bold (ones) let their glossy horses leap, run in competition'

   (b) *þæt ðā / **līðende land** ge- / sāwon,*   S/O[a]A/I

       brim-<u>clifu</u>[,] / **blīcan, beor**gas / stēape,

       sīde / **sǣ**-næssas (221a–23a)

       'that the voyagers saw land shin(ing), sea-cliffs, steep eminences, great sea-nesses'

   (c)   **hord-**wynne / fond   O[a]A/S/I

       eald / ūht-sceaða opene / standan (2270b–71b)

       'the old attacker at dawn found the hoard-joy (treasury) stand(ing) open'

   (d) *syððan / **orwearde ǣnigne / dǣl**   O[a]/SA/I

       sec*gas / (ge)sē*gon on / **sele** <u>wunian</u>(,)

       lǣnne / licgan (3127a–29a)

       'after men saw any portion remain in the hall to lie decrepit without a guardian'

In (7a) the heavy modified object has been displaced to the right periphery. In (7b) a heavy type II verse occupied by the infinitive and a variation of the object is displaced rightward, followed by two more variations of the object. In (7c) a modified subject and a modified infinitive have been displaced to the right periphery, where they maintain normative SI order. Here *standan* resembles the 'be' verb in a predicate adjective construction with *opene* as the adjective. The phrase *lǣnne licgan* in (7d) is similar. Here the transitive auxiliary governs infinitive *wunian*. Klaeber's comma after the second line, retained in K4, suggests interpretation of *lǣnne licgan* as a variation of the preceding verse, which is certainly plausible. It also seems possible, however, to interpret infinitive *wunian* as the governor of infinitive *licgan* in a double-infinitive construction, as suggested in the translation. We will encounter several double-infinitive constructions below. See items (15), (47), and (58) for examples.

An auxiliary precedes a transitive infinitive in (8a–h). In (8b–g) the auxiliary is peripheral. Stressed constituents sharing a verse are out of normative order in the instances like (8b). In the remaining instances stressed constituents sharing a verse observe normative OI, SI, SA, and OA orders.

(8) (a)   *ǣghwæþres / sceal*   A/S/Oⁱ I

    scearp / **scyld**-*wiga*   *ge-* / **scād** *witan,*

    worda / *(ond)* **wor**ca   (287b–89a; cf. 3064b–65b)

    'a sharp (-witted) shield-warrior should know differentiation in respect of each of two things: words and deeds' (how to judge both words and deeds)

(b)   **myn**te / *(se)* **mān**-*scaða*   **man**na / *cynnes*   AS/Oⁱ I

    sumne / *(be)***syr***wan*   *in* / **sele** *þām hēan*   (712–13; cf. 839a–41a, 3031–32)

    'the criminal attacker intended to ensnare some (one) of men's kindred in the high hall'

(c)   *hwīlum* / **eft** *ongan,*   **el**do / *(ge)bunden,*   A/S/Oⁱ I

    gomel / **gūð**-*wiga*   **giogu***ðe* / **cwī***ðan,*

    hilde- / *strengo* (2111a–13a)

    'sometimes, bound with old age, the elderly battle-fighter began to lament (his) youth, (his) strength in combat'

(d)   *him of* / **hræ***ðre gewāt*

    sā*wol* / **sē***cean*   **sōð**-*fæstra* / **dōm** (2819b–20b)   A/SI/Oⁱ

    'the soul went out of his breast to seek the judgement of the righteous'

(e)   *ða se* / **gǣst** *ongan*   **glē***dum* / **spī***wan* (2312, dat. obj.)   SA/Oⁱ I

    'then the creature began to spew flames'

(f)   **Higel***āc on-* / *gan*   SA/Oⁱ/I

    sīnne / *(ge)***sel***dan*   *in* / **sele** *þām hēan*

    fæg*re* / **fric***gcean* (1983b–85a; cf. 871b–72b)

    'Hygelac began to question his comrade courteously in the high hall'

(g)   *þæt him* / **hilde**-*grāp*   **hreþ***re* / *(ne) mihte,*   S/Oⁱ A/I

    eorres / **in***wit-feng,*   **ald***re[,]* / *(ge)***sceþ***ðan* (1446–47)

    'so that the battle-grip, the malicious grasp of the angry (one), might not harm his breast, his life'

Opening verses in other examples like (8e): 2073b (gen. obj.), 2365b (gen. obj.), 2669a (gen. obj.).

The auxiliary is fronted before the subject to normative location s4 in (8a, d). Departure from normative SA order occurs for metrical reasons in the clauses like (8b). In the cited example AS order avoids *(se) **mān**-_scaða_ / **myn**te, with anacrusis in type A3 (Ss/Sx), an unacceptable violation of OE 9.7. The SA alternative 3031a would be ***unblīðe** / ēodon, with the unacceptable pattern *Ssx/Sx (H5). The SA alternative to 839a, ***folc**-_togan_ / **fēr**don, would also have the unacceptable H5 pattern. Since -_togan_ has a closed final syllable, Kaluza's law blocks resolution and the verse cannot be scanned as Ss/Sx (A3). In (9g) _aldre,_ a variation of the object _hreþre,_ shares a displaced type II verse with the infinitive. If there were no coreferential antecedent like _hreþre, aldre_ would be a major constituent rather than a variation and **aldre** / (ge)_sceþðan_ would be one of the many two-word verses that have normative OI order. The type II verse **eorres** / **inwit**-feng, a modified variation of the subject, is displaced to the a-verse of the last line. If there were no antecedent for the subject and object variations (8g) would have A/S/O^iI structure, as in (8a, c). A general-case strategy for maximizing the utility of a two-word verse is to use it whether or not there is a corefer ential antecedent, expressing a major constituent, adding vivid detail, glossing an intricate figure of speech, or filling a metrical gap as desired.

§9.2. Instances with an unexpressed or relativized subject

Item (9), the only one-verse example, has a peripheral auxiliary.

(9) **byr**gean / þenceð (448b)   (s)IA

   '(he) thinks to dine'

Item (9) is a reduced two-word realization of the S/IA structure in item (1a). It is the third of three clauses with the same subject, which is expressed in the first clause.

   Items (10a–d) are multi-verse examples with unexpressed subjects and intransitive infinitives. Constituents sharing a verse observe normative IA order.

(10) (a) þæs þe / **þin**cean mæg **þeg**ne / _monegum_ (1341)   (s)IA/Io

      'as (it) may seem to many a thane'

(b)   *nō on / **wealle** læng*   (s)/IA

   bīdan / wolde (2307b–8a)

   '(he) would not wait longer on the wall'

(c) *wið ðām / āglæcean* **elles** */ meahte*   (s)A/I

   gylpe / (wið)grīpan (2520a–21a)

   '(I) might otherwise come to grips with the awe-inspirer successfully'

Item (10a) is a one-line clause with a modified indirect object displaced to the right periphery. In (10b) the opening verse is filled out by a semantically inessential phrase. The emphatic negative in the opening verse is essential for interpretation of the verb phrase and I interpret (10b) as a multi-verse clause. Placement of the major constituents in the opening verse would create an otherwise unattested instance of emphatic *nō* in anacrusis. In (10c) the verb occupies normative metrical location s4 and a modified infinitive is displaced to the right periphery.

In (11a, b) the subject is relativized.

(11) (a)   *þā him / **mid** scoldon*   wsA/I

      *on / **flōdes** ǣht* **feor** *ge- / wītan* (41b–42b)

      'which had to go with him far into the realm of the sea'

   (b) *ðā ne / **dorston** ǣr* **dareð**um */ lācan*   wsA/I

      *on hyra / **man-dryhtnes** **miclan** / þearfe* (2848–49)

      'who durst not previously fight with spears in their earthly lord's great need'

In (11a) the verb occupies normative metrical location s4 in the opening b-verse and the modified infinitive is displaced to the next b-verse, where the infinitive also occupies location s4, its favored location when not followed by an auxiliary. In (11b) placement of the auxiliary at location s1a makes it possible to arrange the major constituents as a one-line verse. The verb alliterates appropriately as the most prominent constituent in the opening verse and alliteration on the adverb is not required by the rule of precedence. The modified infinitive is displaced to location s4 in the right periphery.

Items (12a–f) have unexpressed subjects and transitive infinitives. Constituents sharing a verse observe normative IA, OI, and OA orders. In (12a–e) the auxiliary occupies normative location s4; in (12f) a verse-final auxiliary alliterates on the only lift in a type A7 verse at location s1b.

(12) (a) *oððe þone /* **cyne**dōm   **cī**osan */ wolde*   (s)Oⁱ/IA

        (2376; cf. 1493b–94a, gen. obj.)

        'or (he) would choose the kingdom'

   (b)   *ðǣr ge- /* **lȳ**fan *sceal*   (s)IA/Oⁱ

        dryhtnes */* **dō**me (440b–41a, dat. obj.; cf. 1004a–6b)

        'there (he) must expect god's judgment'

   (c) *nō ðȳ ǣr /* **suna sī**num   **syl**lan */ wolde,*   (s)Io/IA/Oⁱ

        hwatum */* **Heoro**-wearde,   *þēah hē him /* **hold** *wǣre,*

        brēost-ge- */ wǣdu* (2160a–62a)

        '(he) would none the sooner give the breast-armor to his son, bold Heoro-
weard, though he may have been loyal to him' (subjunctive finite verb)

   (d)   *ond swā tō /* **ald**re *sceall*   (s)A/Oⁱl

        sæcce */ fremman* (2498b–99a; cf. 2464b–65b, 2904b–6a)

        'and (I) will always perform combat in this way'

   (e)   **frēo**de */ (ne) woldon*   (s)OⁱA/I

        ofer / **heafo heal**dan (2476b–77a)

        '(they) would not keep peace across the sea'

   (f) *þēah þe ne /* **meah**te   *on /* **mere** *drīfan*   (s)A/I/Oⁱ

        hringed- */* **stef**nan (1130a–31a; cf. 424b–25b)

        'though (he) could not drive the curved prow (boat) on the sea'

Item (12a) is a one-line clause with all constituents in normative order. Whole-verse objects that fill category II verses are displaced to the right periphery in (12b, c, f). A modified infinitive is displaced to the right periphery in (12e). In (12f) the same kind of modified infinitive is displaced to the right periphery, followed out of normative order by the displaced object. These departures from syntactic norms are mitigated by placement of each stressed constituent in a separate verse (OE 2.3).

Items (13a–e) have peripheral auxiliaries. In (13d, e) the auxiliary is transitive. Items (13a, d, e) have intransitive infinitives; items (13b, c) have transitive infinitives. In (13c) *geongum cempan* is excluded from the notation as a possessive dative adjunct. Constituents sharing a verse observe normative OI, OA, and IA orders. The metrically peculiar opening verse in (13e) is attributable to scribal modernization of archaic *unmet* (Goering 2020).

(13) (a)   *þanon /* **eft gewāt**[,]   (s)A/I

hūðe / hrēmig[,]   *tō / hām faran*   (123b–24b)

'from there (he) went journey(ing) towards home, proud of the plunder'

(b)   *nyðer / eft gewāt*   (s)A/O^{i}I

dennes / nīos(i)an (3044b–45a, gen. obj.; cf. 2878b–79b, gen. obj.)

'(he) went back down to seek (his) den'

(c) *(on)ginneð / geōmor-mōd*   *geongum / cempan*   (s)A/O^{i}I

þurh / hreðra gehygd   *higes / cunnian* (2044–45, gen. obj.)

'(he) begins to tempt the young man's mind with the meditations of his heart'

(d)   *fȳr-lēoht ge- / seah,*   (s)O^{a}A/I

blācne / lēoman[,]   *beorhte / scīnan* (1516b–17b)

'(they) saw fire-light, a brilliant flame, shine brightly'

(e)   **Gēat**   */ unigmetes wēl,*   (s)O^a/IA

rōfne / rand-wigan,   *restan / lyste* (1792b–93b)

'(it) pleased the Geat, that bold shield-fighter, exceedingly well to rest'

In (13a) a modified infinitive is displaced to the right periphery; in (13b) the infinitive and its object share a displaced type II verse. All instances have the auxiliary at metrical location s4 except for (13c). Here verse-final placement of the auxiliary would create **geōmor-mōd / (on)ginneð* (*Sxs/Sx: MH1). Double alliteration is provided and the rule of precedence is satisfied. In (13d) a modified infinitive is displaced. At first glance it may look as if the infinitive in (13e) is functioning as a verbal noun subject, but transitive infinitives in such constructions can take objects and there are rare but persuasive examples of *lystan* with a pronoun subject (OES 1: 434–35). It seems best to view (13d) as an analogue to instances in which *lystan* governs a that-clause and no anticipatory pronoun subject is expressed in the main clause. I accordingly interpret (13e) as a verse clause in which *lyste* takes *restan* as an infinitive complement rather than as a subject and the subject is unexpressed. Under this interpretation all major constituents observe normative order.

Unlike a that-clause, an infinitive complement has lost its its status as a logical proposition, but the infinitive still functions like a finite verb in important syntactic respects. The rarity of examples with anticipatory pronoun subjects is attributable to the fact that infinitives are so thoroughly integrated into the domain of a finite verb. The logical subjects of infinitives are often raised into the main clause (*Frankie told Brett to race her Maserati*). Under government by the auxiliary, infinitives undergo a change in form that differentiates them from finite verbs in that-clauses, which routinely take noun subjects as well as pronoun subjects. The semantic content of the verbal complex is concentrated in the infinitive and can sometimes be paraphrased by a single verb with subjunctive inflection. A clause with a finite auxiliary and an infinitive looks more like a single sentence with a compound verb and less like two sentences in need of two subjects.

In (14a–e) the subject is relativized. Item (14b) is the only instance with a peripheral auxiliary. Constituents sharing a verse observe normative IA and OI orders.

(14) (a) *sē ðone / gomelan grētan / sceolde* (2421)   wsO^i/IA
       'which should confront the old (man)'

    (b)   *þē þus / brontne cēol*   wsO^i/IA
       ofer / lagu-stræte lǣdan / cwōmon,
       hider ofer / holmas (238b–40a)
       'who thus come guid(ing) a tall ship here over the seas, over the water-street'

    (c)   *þæt ðæs / āhlǣcan*   ws/O^i/IA
       blōdge / beadu-folme on- / beran wolde (989b–90b)
       'that would harm the awe-inspirer's bloody battle-hand'

    (d) *sē þe / secgan wile sōð æfter / rihte* (1049)   wsIA/O^i
       'who will speak truth according to what is right'

    (e)   *hwæðer / sēl mæge*   wsA/O^{i}I
       æfter / wæl-rǣse wunde / (ge)dȳgan
       uncer / twēga (2530b–32a)
       'which of us two will better survive wounds after the bloody conflict'

Opening verses in other examples like (14a): 230a, 704a, 1260a, 1445a (dat. obj.), 1449a, 1462a, 2257a.

Most instances are like (14a), with normative syntactic order and the major constituents arranged in a single line. In (14b) the clause opens in the b-verse, an adjunct prepositional phrase fills the next a-verse, and the verbal complex occupies the following b-verse, with the auxiliary at normative metrical location s4. In (14c) the possessive modifier *āhlǣcan* provides alliteration for the opening verse. The enjambment between *āhlǣcan* and its modified noun phrase occurs before the second verse as usual. In (14d) the heavy type II verse containing the object is displaced to the right periphery. In (14e) the auxiliary occupies normative metrical location s4 in the opening verse, where its adverbial modifier provides the alliteration. A two-word type II verse shared by the infinitive and its object is displaced to the right periphery, along with modified adjuncts that fill metrical gaps.

In item (15) a transitive infinitive (I^1) governs a second transitive infinitive (I^2). The logical subject of the second infinitive is the syntactic object of the first infinitive. The verbal complex in the second verse observes normative order, with the core auxiliary in normative location s4.

(15) *þæt* / **heal**-*reced*   *hā*tan / *wolde,*   (s)$O^{i2}/I^1A/O^{i1}I^2$

   medo-*ærn* / **micel,**   **men** *ge*- / *wyrcean* (68–69)

   'that (he) would order men to build a hall-dwelling, a great mead-house'

The orders OIA and OI are normative but the object of the second infinitive has switched places with the object of the first infinitive. No other arrangement of the major constituents would be metrically acceptable.

Items (16a–e) have transitive peripheral auxiliaries and transitive infinitives. The accusative object of the auxiliary is the logical subject of the infinitive. All these instances have the finite auxiliary before the infinitive rather than in absolute final position.

(16) (a)   *tō ðæs ðe* / **eorla** *hlēo,*   (s)$O^a/A/O^iI$

         bonan / *Ong(e)nþeoes*   **bur**gum / *(in) innan,*

         *geong*ne / *gūð-cyning*   *gōd*ne / *(ge)frūnon*

         hringas / **dǣ**lan (1967b–70a)

         'to where in the dwellings they understood the protector of earls,

         Ongentheow's bane, that powerful young fighting king, to distribute rings'
         (learned where Hygelac was distributing rings to his retainers)

   (b) **hā**tað / **heaðo**-*mǣre*   **hlǣw** *ge*- / *wyrcean*   (s)AO^a/O^iI

      beorhtne / *(æfter)* **bǣ**le   *æt* / **brimes** *nosan* (2802–3)

      'order the battle-famous (men) to build a splendid barrow at the promontory by the sea'

   (c)   **bearhtm** *on*- / *gēaton(,)*   (s)O^iA/O^aI

      gūð-horn / **ga**lan (1431b–32a)

      'they heard the battle-horn sing a bright note'

   (d)   *sē æt* / **Heorote** *fand*   ws$A/O^a/O^iI$

wæccendne / *wer*   *wīges* / *bīdan* (1267b–68b, gen. obj.)

'who found a waking man await(ing) combat at Heorot'

(e) *þāra þe of* / *wealle*   *wōp* ge- / *hȳrdon*,   ws/O^{i}A/I/O^a

gryre-*lēoð* / *ga*lan   *godes* / *ondsacan*,

sige-*lēasne* / *sang* (785a–87a)

'who through the wall heard God's adversary sing a terror-chant, a song without victory'

In verses shared by a verb and an object, the object is the one governed by the verb in (16a, b, d). In (16c) each verb shares a verse with the other verb's object. In (16e) the auxiliary shares a verse with the object of the infinitive and the heavy object of the auxiliary is displaced to the right periphery. In the opening verse of (16b), departure from normative order by routine fronting of an imperative avoids **heaðo-mǣre* / *hātað* (*Ssx/Sx: H5). The more prominent object alliterates as required by the rule of precedence.

§9.3 Instances with objects that are unexpressed or relativized

Items (17a, b) are one-line clauses with subject and object unexpressed and constituents of the verbal complex in normative IA order. Item (17b) has a peripheral auxiliary. The conjunction *ond* links these clauses overtly to preceding clauses in which the arguments are expressed.

(17) (a) *ond for* / *þrēa-nȳdum*   *þolian* / *scoldon* (832)   (so)IA

'and out of dire necessity (they) had to suffer (that)'

(b) *ond on* / *healfa gehwone*   *hēawan* / *þōhton* (800)   (so)IA

'and on every side (they) tried to hew (him)'

The opening a-verses are completed by prepositional phrases that supply the alliteration and add concrete detail.

Items (18a–c) are multi-verse instances. Constituents sharing a verse observe normative IA and SA orders.

(18) (a)   *þonne ǣnig* / *mon ōðer*   (o)S/IA

tō beadu-lāce   *æt-* / *beran* meahte,

gōd ond / *geato*lic,   *gīganta* / *(ge)weorc* (1560b–62b; cf. 2373–74)

'than any other man might carry (it) to battle-play, strong and richly equipped, the work of giants'

(b)   *swylce / þȳ dōgor*   woS/IA

heaþo- / *liðende*   **hab**ban / *scoldon* (1797b–98b)

'such as seafaring soldiers should have in that era'

(c)   **men** *ne / cunnon*   (o)SA/I

*sec*gan / *(tō)* **sō**ðe,   **sele**- / *rædende,*

hæleð *under /* **heofe**num (50b–52a)

'men — hall counselors, heroes under heaven — cannot say (that) in truth'

The object is unexpressed in (18a, c) and relativized in (18b). The verses like (18a) have the subject in one verse and stressed constituents of the verb phrase sharing a later verse in normative order, with the auxiliary in normative metrical position s4. In (18b) relativization of the object makes it possible to arrange the stressed major constituents in a single line with the caesura at the natural point of division between the subject and constituents of the verbal complex. In (18c) a modified infinitive is displaced to the right periphery. Displacement of the modifier beyond the infinitive avoids *(tō) *sōðe* / *secgan,* two-word type A1 with easily avoidable anacrusis (OE 9.6).

Unexpressed objects have higher than usual frequency in this chapter due to their employment with high-frequency verbs of speaking that govern infinitives, especially *hātan* 'to order, command.' Items (19a–g) have transitive peripheral auxiliaries and transitive infinitives. The unexpressed objects of the auxiliaries refer to minor characters who carry out orders by major characters and are normally out of focus.

(19) (a) *ond ge*- / **heal**dan **hēt**   **hil**de- / *geatwe* (674)   (soᵃ)IA/Oⁱ

'and (he) ordered (him) to guard the combat equipment'

(b)   *ond þone /* **æn**ne *heht*   (soᵃ)OⁱA/I

golde / *(for)*gyl*dan* (1053b–54a)

'and (he) ordered (someone) to pay for that one with gold'

(c) **heht** *þā / (se)* **hear**da   **Hrun**ting / *beran*   (oᵃ)AS/OⁱI/Io

sunu / *Ecglāfes* (1807a–8a)

'the hardy (one) then commanded (someone) to bring Hrunting to the son of Ecglaf'

(d) **hēt** / *(ðā)* **Hil**de-burh   *æt /* **Hnæf**es *āde*   (oᵃ)AS/Oⁱ/I

hire / **sel**fre **sunu**   *sweolo*ðe / *(be)*fæstan (1114–15)

'Hildeburh then commanded (someone) to commit her own son to the flames at Hnaef's funeral pyre'

(e) *þā of / wealle geseah   weard / Scildinga*   (oᵃ)A/S/I/Oⁱ

beran ofer / bolcan   beorhte / randas,

fyrd-searu / fūslic(u) (229a–32a)

'then from the wall a watchman of the Scyldings saw (people) carry bright shields (and) well-prepared armor over the gangplank'

(f) *mǣre / māðþum-sweord   manige / (ge)sāwon*   (oᵃ)Oⁱ/SA/I

beforan / beorn beran (1023a–24a)

'many (people) saw (someone) bring a bright treasure-sword before the man'

(g) *heht ðā þæt / heaðo-weorc   tō / hagan bīodan*   (soᵃ)AOⁱ/I

up ofer / ecg-clif (2892a–93a)

'(he) told (someone) to announce that deed of battle at the enclosure up over the shore-cliff'

(h) *þā ic / Frēa-ware   flet- / sittende*   woⁱ¹sOⁱ²/Oᵃ/IA

nemnan / hȳrde (2022a–23a)

'whom I heard those sitting in the hall call Freawaru'

Heavy modified objects of infinitives are displaced to the right periphery in (19a, e). A heavy indirect object of the infinitive is displaced in (19c), where the inanimate object shares a verse with its governing infinitive and the animate object is more distant as usual. In (19b, f) the displaced constituent is a heavy modified infinitive. Metrical constraints explain why constituents sharing a verse depart from normative orders in (19c, d, g). In (19c) normative SA order would require alliteration on a weakly stressed finite verb occupying a subordinate s position, which is strongly dispreferred (OE 7.5). In (19d) SA order would create the unacceptable verse pattern *Sxs/S (M1). In (19g) OA order would create the unacceptable B1 variant *ðā þæt / heaðo-weorc heht*, an unacceptable type B variant with prominent secondary stress on an x position (OE 4.3).

§9.4 Instances with unstressed subjects

The only one-verse instance is item (20).

(20) *gif hē / wealdan mōt* (442b)   sIA

'if he can manage'

The K4 glossary represents (20) as an 'absolute' use of *wealdan,* which would not require an expressed or unexpressed object. The stressed constituents observe normative metrical and syntactic order.

Items (21a–f) are multi-verse clauses with intransitive infinitives and unstressed subjects at normative location x1.

(21) (a) *þæt hē* / **blōde** *fāh*   **bū***gan* / *sceolde* (2974a)   s/IA

        'that he should fall, stained with blood'

  (b)   *þā hīe tō* / **sele** *furðum*   s/IA

       in hyra / **gryre**-*geatwum*   **gan***gan* / *cwōmon* (323b–24b)

       'when they first came walk(ing) to the hall in their intimidating combat gear'

  (c) *ðǣr hē þȳ* / **fyr***ste*   **for***man* / *dōg(o)re*   s/IA

       weal*dan* / *mōste* (2573a–74a; cf. 541b–43a, 1671b–74a)

       'if he might manage on that occasion — on the first day'

  (d)   *ac ic mid* / **grā***pe sceal*   sA/I

       fōn *wið* / **fēon***de* (438b–49a)

       'but I shall struggle against the enemy with (my) grasp' (fight hand-to-hand)

  (e) *þæt hē for* / **mund**-*gripe*   **mī***num* / *scolde*   s/A/I

       lic*gean* / **līf**-*bysig* (965a–66a)

       'that because of my hand-grip he should lie struggling for life'

  (f)   *nō ðū ymb* / **mī***nes ne þearft*   sA/I

       līces / *feorme*   **leng** / *sorgian* (450b–51b)

       'by no means need you care longer about the nourishment of my body'

  (g)   *þæt hīe him* / **tō** *mihton*   sA/I

       geg*num* / **gan***gan* (313b–14a)

       'that they might go towards it together'

Opening verses in other examples like (21a): 1305a, 1350a, 2400a, 3108b.

In the verses like (21a) the constituents of the verb phrase share a b-verse in normative order and in their normative metrical locations, either in an opening b-verse or in the b-verse of a subsequent line. Item (21b) is a similar example with a peripheral auxiliary. The verses like (21c) have constituents of the verb phrase in normative order and in normative syntactic positions but the stressed auxiliary is at metrical location s1b. In (21d) verb-final order would place an alliterating infinitive on the s position of a type B verse. Infinitives are more prominent than finite verbs but the type A1 variant in (21d) is the same one used to avoid violation of OE 7.5 in verses with alliterating finite verbs. Whether infinitives are subject to OE 7.5 is difficult to determine because item (21d) is one of just three verses with this syntactic pattern that might imaginably qualify as type B if the order of stressed constituents were reversed (cf. 2842a, 2878a). The verb-final alternative for (21e), *līf-bysig / licgean, scans as *Ssx/Sx (H5). Resolution of -bysig is blocked by Kaluza's law. Items (21f, g) have heavy modified infinitives displaced to the right periphery. In (21f) the possessive pronoun is split by hyperbaton from its governed noun līces. In (21g) alliteration for the opening verse is supplied by a stressed postposition that alliterates before the verb as the cognate adverb would do in a quasi-compound.

Items (22a–d) have core auxiliaries and transitive infinitives. Item (22e) has a transitive peripheral auxiliary and an intransitive infinitive. In all instances the infinitive and auxiliary share a b-verse in normative order.

(22) (a) þæt ic / **sǣ**-næssas ge- / **sēon** mihte, sO^i/IA

windige / weallas (571a–72a)

'so that I might see the sea-bluffs, the windy walls'

(b) oþþæt hȳ / **sæl** timbred sO^i/IA

geatolic / (ond) **gold**-fāh, on- / **gyton** mihton (307b–8b)

'until they could see the timbered hall, stately and adorned with gold'

(c) þæt hē / **lȳtel** fæc **long**-ge- / strēona s/O^i/IA

brūcan / mōste (2240a–41a, gen. obj.; cf. 2371a–72a)

'that he could enjoy the long-accumulated treasure for little time'

(d) nalles hē ðā / **frætwe** **Frēs**- / cyninge, sO^i/Io/IA

brēost- / weorðunge, **bringan** / mōste (2503–4)

'he could by no means bring the treasures (and) the breast-ornament to the Frisian king'

(e) oþ þæt hē / **fǣringa** **fyrgen**- / bēamas s/O^a/IA

ofer / **hārne** stān **hleonian** / funde

wyn-lēasne / **wudu** (1414a–16a; cf. 267a–69a)

'until suddenly he found forest-trees lean(ing) over grey stone, a joyless wood'

Opening verses in other examples like (22a): 168a, 182a, 648a, 656a, 880a, 894a (gen. obj.), 1140a, 1464a, 1496a, 1504a, 1628a, 1877a, 1911a, 2038a (dat. obj.), 2466a, 2636a, 2770a, 2954a (dat. obj.), 2984a (dat. obj.), 3100a (gen. obj); like (22b): 1025b (gen. obj.), 1087b, 1093b, 2626b.

In the instances like (22a) the major constituents are arranged in a one-line clause with normative syntactic order and the caesura at the natural point of syntactic division between the direct object and the verbal complex. In those like (22b) the clause opens in a b-verse and constituents of the verbal complex occupy a later b-verse. In (22c) the subject shares a verse with an adverbial adjunct that provides the alliteration, a modified object fills the b-verse, and the verbal complex is situated in a following a-verse. In (22d) a heavy indirect object is displaced beyond a simplex direct object that supplies alliteration for the opening verse. In (22e) the object of the transitive auxiliary occupies its normative syntactic position.

In (23a–f) a heavy direct object has been displaced to the right periphery. Items (23d–f) have peripheral auxiliaries.

(23) (a)   *gyf þū* / **heal***dan wylt*   sIA/O^i

        mā*ga* / *rīce* (1852b–53a)

        'if you will govern the domain of the kinsmen'

(b) *þæt hīe in* / **bēor**-*sele*   **bī***dan* / *woldon*   s/IA/O^i

        Grend*les* / **gū***þe*   *mid* / **gryr***um ecga* (482–83, gen. obj.)

        'that they would await Grendel's attack in the beer-hall with the terrors of swords'

(c) *nū ic* / **suna** *mīnum*   **syl***lan* / *wolde*   sIo/IA/O^i

        gūð-*ge-* / *wǣdu* (2729a–30a)

        'now I would give my son the battle-garment (corslet)'

(d) *þonne hē æt* / **gū***ðe* *ge-* / **gān** *þenceð*   s/IA/O^i

        long-*sumne* / **lof** (1535a–36a; cf. 1597a–98a)

        'when he thinks to earn long-lasting fame in combat'

(e) *swylce hē* / **siomi***an geseah* **segn** / *eall gylden*   sIA/O^a

        hēah *ofer* / **hor***de*, **hond**-*wundra* / *mǣst*,

        *(ge)***locen** / **leoðo**-*cræftum* (2767a–69a)

        'also, he saw hang(ing) high over the hoard a banner all golden, greatest of hand-wonders, intertwined with skills of limbs'

(f) *hwīlum hē on* / **lufan** **lǣ***teð* / *hworfan*   s/AI/O^i

*mon*nes / *mōd-geþonc* **mǣ**ran / *cynnes* (1728–29)

'at times he allows the mind of a man of famous lineage to wander'

Opening verses in other instances like (23a): 636b, 684b, 1378b, 1674b, 2275b; like (23b): 157a (gen. obj.), 1078a.

In (23a–e) the stressed constituents of the verbal complex share a verse in normative order. In (23b) alliteration for the opening verse is supplied by an adjunct and the verbal complex follows in a later verse. In (23c) alliteration for the opening verse is supplied by an indirect object. Item (23d) is like (23b) except that the auxiliary is peripheral. In (23e) the displaced constituent is the object of the peripheral auxiliary. Except for (23e, f), all instances have the stressed auxiliary in normative metrical location s4. The departure from normative placement in (23e) makes it possible to arrange all major constituents in a single line, reducing complexity (OE 1.1). Item (23f) is the only line in *Beowulf* with such unusual meter in both verses. The a-verse is a rare variant of type A7 with an unresolved Sx foot (K4: 330); the b-verse is a rare instance in which an alliterating auxiliary and an infinitive share a verse out of normative IA order (K4: 335). This anomaly could be corrected by placing the auxiliary before the prepositional phrase to create *hwīlum hē* / **lǣ**teð *on* / **lu**fan *hworfan,* which has unremarkable verses of type A7 (cf. 2665a) and type C2 (cf. 1130b).

In (24a–e) an infinitive and its object observe normative order in a two-word type II verse displaced to the right periphery. All instances have core auxiliaries.

(24) (a)   *ic tō* / **sǣ** *wille(,)*   sA/OI

         wið / **wrāð** **we**rod   **wearde** / *healdan* (318b–19b)

         'I will keep guard by the sea against a hostile troop'

(b) *gif ic æt* / **þearfe** **þī**nre / *scolde*   s/A/OI

     aldre / *linnan* (1477a–78a. dat. obj.; cf. 365a–66a)

     'if I should lose life at your need (in your service)'

(c) *swā hē ne* / **mih**te — *nō hē þæs* / **mō**dig *wæs* —   s A / O I

     wǣpna / *(ge)*weal*dan* (1508a–9a, gen. obj.)

     'so that he could not wield weapons, no matter how brave he was'

(d)   *ic þǣm* / **gō**dan *sceal*   sIoA/OI

     for his / **mōd-þræce** **mād**mas / *bēodan* (384b–85a)

     'I shall offer treasures to the mighty (one) for his courageous initiative'

(e) *þæs ðe ic* / **mōste** **mīnum** / *lēodum* sA/Io/OI

    ǣr / **swylt**-*dæge* **swylc** *ge-* / *strȳnan* (2797–98)

    'That I could gain such (a thing) for my people before (my) death-day'

Opening verses in other examples like (24a): 251b, 445b, 588b, 683b, 1179b, 1371b (dat. obj.), 1733b, 2512b, 2535b, 2654b, 2657b, 2739b, 3176b; like (24e): 365a (dat. obj.), 1822a (gen. obj.).

The most common arrangement is the one in (24a), with the stressed auxiliary in normative location s4 and the other stressed constituents sharing a verse in normative OI order. Subject and auxiliary occupy the opening verse in all instances except (24b), where alliteration for the line is provided by *þearfe* and its postpositional modifier *þīnre,* with the enjambment between the first two verses as usual. In most cases the auxiliary stands in normative metrical position at the end of a line. The exceptions are (24c, e), where an auxiliary at location s1b alliterates on the only lift of a type A7 verse. The added indirect objects in (24d, e) observe normative syntactic position before the direct objects and are more distant from the governing infinitives. The heavy indirect object in (24e) is displaced beyond the auxiliary; the lighter indirect object in (24d) remains in normative syntactic position before the auxiliary.

    Similar examples with peripheral infinitives are shown in (25a–e).

(25) (a)   *ic ðǣr* / **furðum** *cwōm* sA/OI

    tō ðām / **hring**-*sele* **Hrōðgār** / *grētan* (2009b–10b)

    'next I came to greet Hrothgar there at the ring-hall' (a hall where rings are given)

(b)   *þæt ðū ne ā-* / **lǣte** *be ðē* / **lifi**gendum,* sA/OI

    dōm *ge-* / **drēo**san (2665a–66a)

    'that with you living (while you were living) you would not let glory decline'

(c)   *þæt wē* / **fun**diaþ sA/OI

    Higelāc / **sē**can (1819b–20a)

    'that we desire to seek out Hygelac'

(d)   *þæt ic* / **ǣ**nigra *mē* sIo/A/OI

    wēana / *(ne)* **wēn**de *tō* / **wīdan** <u>*feore*</u>

    bōte / *(ge)***bīdan** (932b–34a)

301

'that I did not expect to experience a remedy of any woes for myself throughout life'

(e) *hē / fēara sum   be- / foran gengde*   s/A/OI

wīsra / monna   wong / scēawian (1412–13; cf. 1988a–90a)

'he went ahead to inspect the place as one of a few wise men (with a few wise men)'

(f) *meaht ðū, / mīn wine,   mēce / (ge)cnāwan* (2047)   As/OI

'can you identify that sword, my friend?'

Opening verses in other examples like (25a): 100b, 1263b, 1274b, 1585b, 2743b.

Item (25a), the most common arrangement, has the unstressed subject in normative location x1 and the stressed auxiliary in normative location s4. In (25b) the stressed auxiliary alliterates at location s1b in an a-verse of type A7; in (25c) the stressed auxiliary alliterates at location s1b in a b-verse of type C1. In (25d) the direct object shares a verse with its governing infinitive and the indirect object is more distant as usual. The unstressed subject in (25e) is the only major constituent in the opening verse. The auxiliary is routinely fronted in (25f), an interrogative clause, putting unstressed *ðū* in location x2 rather than location x5 and avoiding pronominal anacrusis. Possessive adjectives like *mīn* seem to be more prominent than most function words and can alliterate in preference to a following noun, as here.

In (26a, b) the unstressed subject occupies normative location x1 and a core auxiliary shares a verse with the object, observing normative OA order. Item (26c) is a similar instance with a peripheral auxiliary.

(26) (a)   *þæt hē þā / geogoðe wile*   sOA/I

ārum / healdan (1181b–82a; cf. 527b–28b, gen. obj.; 595b–97b)

'that he will maintain the youths with honors'

(b) *þæt hē / mā mōste   manna / cynnes*   sOA/I

ðicgean / (ofer) þā niht (735a–36a)

'that he might eat more of mankind beyond *that* night'

(c) *gif hē / wæccende   weard on- / funde*   s/OA/I

būon on / beorge (2841a–82a)

'if he found a waking guardian dwell(ing) in the barrow'

302

The auxiliary in (26a, c) occupies normative metrical location s4. In (26b) it alliterates on an s position in a type I verse, contravening OE 7.5. In this instance the departure from normative verb placement avoids enjambment between *mā* and the other constituents of a partitive genitive construction. Interposition of constituents like *mā* provides a more prominent syntactic break for alignment with the major internal boundary of the line. The infinitive occupies location s2 in (26a); in (26b, c) it occupies location s1a, followed by a more prominent lexical noun that alliterates as required by the rule of precedence. Placement of the less prominent infinitive on the more prominent lift avoids otherwise unattested variants with anacrusis in types A3 (Ss/Sx) and A1 (Sx/Sx). The enjambment in (26c) occurs between the first two verses as usual.

In (27a–g) the stressed major constituents occupy separate verses. The unstressed subject in (27g) also occupies a separate verse. In three instances with hyperbaton modified constituents are split from their modifiers — *mīn* in (27b), *wlitig* in (27d), and *lāðne* in (27f). There is no violation of Kuhn's Laws in (27c) because *mē* is a possessive dative STP rather than an indirect object SP.

(27) (a) | *þæt hē* / **þanon** *scolde* | sA/O/I

eft / *eard*-*lufan* **ǣfre** / *(ge)sēcean,*

folc oþðe / **frēo**-*burh* (691b–93a)

'that from there he could only seek out the beloved homeland, the people and the noble fortress'

(b) | *þæt ic ðȳ* / **sēft** *mæge* | sA/I/O

æfter / **māðð(u)m**-*welan* **mīn** *ā*- / *lǣtan*

līf ond / **lēod**scipe (2749b–51a)

'so that I may the more pleasantly relinquish my life and my people amidst a wealth of treasure'

(c) | *nū ic,* / **Bēowulf,** *þec,* | sO/A/I

secg / *betesta,* *mē for* / **sunu** *wylle*

frēogan / *(on)* **ferh**þe (946b–48a)

'now, Beowulf, best of warriors, I will love you in (my) heart as a son to me (my son)'

(d) *þæt ic on* / **wāge** *geseah* **wlitig** / *hangian* sA/I/O

eald-*sweord* / **ēacen** (1662a–63a)

'that I saw hang(ing) on the wall a splendid antique sword'

303

(e)   *þæt hē on / **eorð**an geseah*   sA/O/I

*þone **lēo**festan **lī**fes / (æt) ende*

***blēa**te / (ge)**bæ̆**ran* (2822b–24a)

'that he saw the most beloved (one) on the ground at the end of life be hav(ing) pitiably'

(f) *ǣr hī þǣr ge- / **sē**gan **syl**licran / wiht,*   sA/O/I

***wyrm**[,] on / **won**ge **wi**ðerrǣhtes / þǣr[,]*

***lāð**ne[,] / **lic**gean* (3038a–40a; cf. 1082–83)

'earlier they saw that strange loathly creature, the dragon, ly(ing) right be-side (Beowulf) there on the ground'

(g) *gif ic þonne on / **eor**þan ōwihte / mæg*   s/A/O/I

*þīnre / **mōd**-lufan **mā**ran / <u>til</u>ian,*

***gumen**a / dryhten, **gūð**-ge- / weorca* (1822–25)

'then if I can in any way earn more of your heart's love with respect to achievements in combat, lord of men'

In (27a–c, e, g) the auxiliary stands in normative location s4; in (27d) it occupies location s3 and an adjunct prepositional phrase supplies the alliteration; and in (27f) it alliterates at location s1b as the only stressed constituent in a type A7 verse. In (27c, e) an infinitive in a type II verse is displaced to the right periphery.

Old English *oððe* translates best as 'and' when exclusive 'or' would be too restrictive, as in (27a), where it seems odd to suppose that the visitor must choose between visiting his people and visiting his fortified hometown. A common metonym for a homeland in *Beowulf* is a defensible refuge for people and valuable resources (cf. 1127a, *hāmas ond hēaburh*; 912b–13b, *folc gehealdan, hord ond hlēoburh, hæleþa rīce*). As noted in the K4 glossary (s.v.), the similar conjunction *ac* alternates between 'but' and 'and' in *Beowulf*. This is the sort of ambiguity that philosophers avoid by using three logical operators to distinguish among selections from the set that includes A, B, and no other member: 'and' for A + B, 'exclusive or' for A or B but not A + B, and 'inclusive or' for A, B, or A + B.

Items (28a, b) have intransitive core auxiliaries and infinitives that take double objects.

(28) (a)   *ic þæs / **Hrōð**gār mæg*   sO^{i2}A/O^{i1}I

*þurh / **rū**mne <u>sefan</u> **rǣd** ge- / **lǣ**ran* (277b–78b)

'In respect of this I can teach Hrothgar advice with a generous heart'

(b)   *ac hē /* **hraþe** *wolde*   sA/O^{12}I/O^{i1}

Gren*dle / (for)***gyl***dan* **gūð**-*r$\bar{æ}$sa /* <u>fela</u> (1576b–77b)

'but he wished promptly to remunerate Grendel many aggressive attacks'
(to pay Grendel back for his attacks)

In (28a) both objects are accusative. The animate secondary object of the infinitive provides alliteration for the opening verse. As usual the inanimate primary object is in closer construction with its governing verb, observing normative order with the infinitive in a type II verse displaced to the right periphery. In (28b) a heavy modified object is displaced to the right periphery from its normative syntactic position immediately before the verb and provides the b-verse for the line. As a result the lighter animate object and the infinitive share an a-verse of type A1 in normative order.

In (29a–e) the subject shares the opening verse with a transitive peripheral auxiliary that governs a transitive infinitive. Item (29a), with OE *sēon*, a transitive auxiliary of direct perception, translates straightforwardly into ordinary English. The other examples have OE *gefrīgnan* 'to learn by diligent questioning.' Heroic poets use this term to assert that the deeds they celebrate have been been validated and handed down by an unbroken succession of experts, beginning with a poet who judged those deeds on the basis of contemporary evidence. OE *gefrīgnan* denotes acquisition of reliable knowledge about something not directly perceived, like Modern English *learn, discover, ascertain, verify,* and *determine.* As (29b–e) show, *gefrīgnan* can represent what is discovered with an infinitive clause, unlike the Modern English verbs. We now say *I learned that one kinsman avenged the other* but not *I learned one kinsman to avenge the other.* In (29b–d) the adverbials *on morgne, snūde,* and *on hlǣwe* are moved from normative position before the infinitives they modify to a position before the stressed auxiliary. The adverbials clearly do not modify the auxiliaries here, since the poet cannot have been in the barrow and cannot have heard about an event in the remote past quickly or by the next day. This kind of long-distance fronting occurs in early English but is no longer permissible in Modern English, with its stricter constraints on word order (§1.8).

(29) (a) *þæt hīe ge- /* **sāw***on* **swylce** */ twēgen*   sA/O^{a}/O^{i}I

        mic*le /* **mearc**-*stapan* **mōr***as / healdan,*

        el*lor- / g$\bar{æ}$stas* (1347a–49a)

'that they saw two such gigantic border-prowlers — alien spirits — rule the moors'

(b) *þā ic on / **morgne gefrægn** **mǣg** / ōðerne* sA/OᵃOⁱ/I

   *bil**les** / ecgum   on / **bonan** stǣlan* (2484–85; cf. 2694a–96a)

   'then I heard one kinsman to avenge the other on the killer in the morning (that one kinsman avenged the other)'

(c) *ðā ic / **snūde gefrægn** **sunu** / Wīhstānes* sA/Oᵃ/Oⁱ/I

   *æfter / **word**-cwydum   **wun**dum / dryhtne*

   *hȳran / **heaðo**-sīocum* (2752a–54a)

   'then I heard the son of Wistan promptly to obey the wounded chieftain, injured in combat' (that the son of Wistan promptly obeyed, etc.)

(d) *ðā ic on / **hlǣwe gefrægn** **hord** / rēafian,* sA/OⁱI/Oᵃ

   *eald / en**ta** geweorc,   **ānne** / mannan* (2773–74)

   'then I heard one man to rifle the hoard in the barrow, old work of giants' (that one man rifled, etc.)

(e) *(ne ge)**frǣgn** ic / **frēond**-licor   **fēower** / mādmas* As/Oᵃ/Oⁱ/Io.I

   *gol**de** / (ge)**gyrede**   **gum**-manna / ꞁ̲e̲l̲a̲*

   *in / **ealo**-ben**ce**   ōð̲r̲u̲m̲ / (ge)sellan* (1027–29)

   'I did not hear many (a one) of mortal men to give four treasures adorned with gold to another' (I have not heard that many men have given, etc.)

In (29b) the two objects share a verse in normative OᵃOⁱ order, with the logical subject of the infinitive before its logical object. Items (29a, c) have the same word order but the objects are in separate verses. In (29d) the heavy object of the auxiliary is displaced to the right periphery and the infinitive shares a verse with its object in normative order. In (29e) a negated stressed verb is fronted to initial position and the unstressed subject SP occupies location x2. With the subject in normative location x1 an otherwise unattested form of anacrusis would be created. In (29e) as we have it the disyllabic anacrusis is of the usual kind, consisting of a negative particle and an unstressed prefix. The modified direct objects of the auxiliary and the infinitive fill whole verses and the indirect object shares a verse with the infinitive in normative Io.I order.

   Items (30a–c) are the remaining examples with transitive auxiliaries and transitive infinitives.

(30) (a) *hwæþere hē his / **fol**me forlēt* sOᵃA/OⁱI

    *tō / **līf**-wraþe **lāst** / weardian,*

    earm *ond* / **eaxle** (970b–72a)

    'however, he left his hand, arm, and shoulder to guard (his) track as a life-protection'

(b) *swylce ic* / **magu**-*þegnas* **mīne** / *hāte*   sO^a/A/O^i/I

    wið / **fēon**da ge<u>hwone</u> **flotan** / *ēowerne,*

    nīw- / *tyrwydne* **nacan** *on* / *sande*

    ārum / *healdan* (293a–96a)

    'also, I will order my kindred thanes to honorably protect your newly-tarred boat against each one of enemies (against every enemy)'

(c) *ond þū* / **Unferð** *lǣt* **ealde** *lāfe,*   sO^{a}A/O^i/I

    wrǣtlīc / **wǣg**-*sweord,* **wīd**-cūðne / *man*

    heard-ecg / **hab**ban (1488a–90a)

    'and you let Unferth, the widely-known man, have the old heirloom, that splendid wave-patterned sword, hard-edged'

All three verses have the same word order. In (30a) each verb form shares a verse with its object in normative order. Item (30b) has the same word order with each stressed major constituent in a separate verse. In (30c) the imperative verb is not fronted as usual to absolute initial position. Multiple variations of the heavy object separate it from its governing infinitive. The second line could be omitted without a trace and its obvious function is to supply concrete detail relevant to the immediate context.

§9.5 Instances with unstressed objects (including instances that also have an unstressed subject)

§9.5a One-verse instances

In item (31) both arguments are unstressed, making it possible to fit a construction with four major constituents into a single verse.

(31)   *þæt hē mec* / **fremman** <u>wile</u>   soIA

    wordum / *(ond)* **weor**cum (1832b–33a; cf. 446b–47a)

    'that he will support me with words and deeds'

In these instances with syntactically complete opening verses all major constituents observe normative syntactic order and the auxiliary stands in normative metrical position at line end.

§9.5b Multi-verse instances

Items (32a, b) have unstressed arguments and all major constituents in normative order, as in item (31).

(32) (a) *þæt wē hine swā / **gōdne**   **grētan** / mōton*

        (347; cf. 679, 961–62, 1998)   so/IA

        'so that we may greet him, so powerful (a man)'

    (b) *hē mec þǣr on / **in**nan[,]   **un**- / synnigne,*   so/IA

        *dīor / **dǣd**-fruma[,]   ge- / **dōn** wolde*

        *mani**g**ra / sumne (2089a–91a; cf. 963–64)*

        'he — that bold doer of deeds — wanted to put me in there — guiltless, one of many'

    (c)   *wit unc wið / **hron**-fixas*   so/IA

        *weri**a**n / þōhton (540b–41a)*

        'we thought to protect ourselves against whale-fishes'

The examples like (32a) have the major constituents arranged in a single line. Line 679 has the contract negative auxiliary *nelle* 'don't want' in line-final position. In the examples like (32b) adjunct verses separate the arguments from the verbal complex, which occupies a b-verse in the following line. The cited instance in (32b) represents an unsettling moment for Beowulf when he realizes that Grendel plans to put him in a gigantic game bag to be eaten later, along with everyone not already eaten in Hrothgar's hall. In (32c) alliteration for the opening b-verse is supplied by an adjunct prepositional phrase and the verbal complex occupies the following a-verse, with the auxiliary in location s2. The prepositional phrase is semantically functional in the immediate context.

In (33a–d) the object is the only unstressed argument. Stressed constituents of the verbal complex share a b-verse in normative IA order, with the auxiliary in normative line-final position.

(33) (a) *þæt hit / **sceā**den-mǣl   **scȳ**ran / mōste (1939)*   oS/IA

        'that the patterned sword must settle it'

(b)   *nē hyne on **medo**-bence   **mic**les wyrðne*   oS/IA

   ***dryh**ten Wedera   ge- / **dōn** wolde* (2185–86; cf. 9–10, 461b–62b)

   'nor would the lord of the Geats do him honor much on the mead-bench'

(c)   *þæt hine / **syð**þan nō*   o/S/IA

   ***brond** / (nē) beado-mēcas   **bī**tan / (ne) meahton* (1453b–54b)

   'that afterwards (neither) brands nor battle-swords could not in no way cut
   him'

(d)   *þæt hīe / **seoð**ðan nō   ge- / **sēon** mōston(,)*   o/IA/S

   ***mō**dige / (on) me**þ**le* (1875a–76a; cf. 1515a–16a, dat. obj.)

   'that they, the bold ones, could by no means see each other afterwards in
   conversation'

Opening verses in other examples like (33a): 812a (dat. obj.), 979a (dat.
obj.), 988a (dat. obj.), 2340a; like (33b): 779a, 3161b.

Items (33a, b) have all stressed constituents in normative SIA order and the
auxiliary in normative location s4. Item (33a) has the most common arrangement, with all major constituents expressed in a single line. In (33c)
the pronoun object is fronted to normative location x1 and the heavy subject
follows in a line with all stressed major constituents in normative order. Item
(33d) is a one-line clause followed by a heavy type II verse with a variation
and an adjunct phrase relevant to immediate context. Item (33b) has the
kind of multiple negation employed in African American Vernacular English expressions like *It ain't no cat can't get in no coop,* the widely-cited example in Labov (1972a). In such expressions every negatable element of the
clause is negated to provide a more emphatic alternative to simple negation.
The AAVE example has the same meaning as *there is no cat that can get into
any (pigeon) coop.* Item (33b) translates more idiomatically as 'that in no way
could brands or battle-swords cut him afterwards.'

   Items (34a–f) have unstressed indirect objects. The infinitives share a
verse with an auxiliary or a direct object, observing normative IA or OI
order. The reflexive dative pronouns in (34d–f) are indirect object beneficiaries coreferential with the subject. The personified boat in (34a) has a
reflexive indirect object in the dative of disadvantage.

(34) (a)   *þȳ lǣs hym / **ȳ**þa ðrym*   ioS/O/IA

   ***wudu** / **wyn**suman   for- / **wrecan** meahte* (1918b–19b)

'lest the power of waves might break up the fine wood (boat) for itself (to its disadvantage)'

(b) *ðā ic ðē, / **beorn**-cyning,   **bring**an / wylle,*   osio/IA

ēstum / (ge)ȳwan (2148a–49a)

'those I will bring to you, king of men, display with good wishes'

(c)   *þæt þū ðē for / **sunu** wolde*   sioA/OI

***here**-rinc / **hab**ban* (1175b–76a)

'that you would take the fighting man as a son for you'

(d) *ond him / **eft** gewāt   **Ong**(e)nðioes / bearn*   ioA/S/OI

***hā**mes / nīosan* (2387a–88a, gen. obj.)

'and Ongentheow's child went to visit (his) home for himself'

(e) *(ge)**witon** him / (ðā) **wīg**end   **wī**ca / nēos(i)an,*   AioS/OI

frēondum / (be)feallen (1125a–26a, gen. obj.)

'then warriors went to visit (their) dwellings for themselves, bereft of friends'

(f) *(ge)**wāt** him / (þā tō) **waro**ðe   **wic**ge / rīdan*   Aio/OI/S

***þegn** / Hrōðgāres* (234a–35a, dat. obj.)

'then Hrothgar's thane went rid(ing) to the shore for himself on a horse'

In (34a) the unstressed indirect object occupies normative metrical position x1 and the stressed constituents observe normative order. In (34b) all three arguments are unstressed pronouns. Fronting the unstressed direct object brings it closer to its core generic antecedent *māðmas* 'treasures' in the immediately preceding clause. In (34c) the unstressed arguments share location x1 in normative order and the stressed auxiliary occupies normative metrical position s4. In (34d) the stressed auxiliary occupies a subordinate lift in the a-verse, its preferred location when it does not alliterate and is not in line-final position. In (34e, f) the stressed auxiliary occupies metrical location s1a, the prominent subject noun alliterates in accord with the rule of precedence, and the unstressed pronoun occupies metrical location x2. These departures from normative placement avoid *him ðā / **wīgend** gewiton* and *him þā tō / **waroðe** (ge)wāt*, which violate OE 7.5. The violations would be especially anomalous here because the low prominence of these finite verbs is lowered further by their very high frequency. The verb-final alternative to (34e) would be even more anomalous because the alliterating auxiliary *gewiton* would also have to be resolved (OE 8.5). In (34e, f) as they stand verb fronting marks a transition to a new topic.

In (35a–d) other pairs of stressed major constituents share a verse, observing normative SA, OA, and SI orders. Items (35a–c) have core auxiliaries; item (35d) has a peripheral auxiliary. The unstressed arguments are fronted to normative location x1. In (35b, c) the indefinite adjectives *ǣnige* 'any' and *nǣnig* 'not any' are split from the constituents they modify by hyperbaton.

(35) (a) *þæt him / īrenna   **ecge** / mihton*   o/SA/I

   ***hel**pan / (æt) **hil**de* (2683a–84a, dat. obj.)

   'that iron edges might help him in battle'

(b)   *ond hē him / **helpe** ne mæg,*   sioOA/I

   ***eald** ond / in**frōd**,   **ǣnige** / (ge)fremman* (2448b–49b)

   'and he, old and greatly smitten with age, cannot provide any help to him'

(c) *nǣnig þæt / **dor**ste   **dēor** ge- / nēþan*   oA/SI

   *s**wǣs**ra / (ge)**sīð**a(,)   nefne / **sin**-frêa* (1933–34)

   'not any bold (man) of (her) own companions dared to risk that except the eminent lord'

(d) *him ðā / **Scyld** gewāt   tō ge- / **scæp**-hwīle*   ioSA/I

   ***fela**-hrōr / **fē**ran   on / **frēan** wǣre* (26–27)

   'then at the appointed time Scyld, (still) very vigorous, went journey(ing) for himself into the protection of the lord'

The auxiliaries occupy normative location s4 in (35a, b), location s1b in (35c), and location s3 in (35d). Modified infinitives are displaced to the right periphery in (35a, d). In (35b) the split indefinite *ǣnige* provides alliteration for a displaced type II verse that contains the infinitive. In (35c) hyperbaton makes it possible to arrange the major constituents in a single line. In (35d) a semantically inessential constituent completes the first line and the modified infinitive occupies location s2 in the following a-verse.

Items (36a–f) have core auxiliaries. Each stressed constituent occupies a separate verse. There are no instances with the stressed constituents in normative order and none with the core auxiliary in its normative syntactic location at the end of the clause. Here as generally departures from normative order become more tolerable when the poet avoids placing major constituents in the same verse, something that can be achieved with semantically inessential adjuncts. The parenthesis in item (36b) has a contract negative verb on a stressed position at location s4. Contract negatives usually appear unstressed in initial position, always when the contract form is monosyllabic. This disproportion is not surprising, since contraction is more likely to occur when both constituents are unstressed.

(36) (a) *nōðer hȳ hine ne / **mōston,** syððan / **mergen** cwōm,*   soA/I

       dēað- / wērigne, **Denia** / lēode,*

       bron**de / (for)**bærnan (2124a–26a)

       'nor could they, the people of the Danes, burn him, death-weary, with fire after morning came'

   (b) *þæt hīe ne / **mōste,** þā / **metod** nolde,*   oA/S/I

       *se / **scyn-scaþa** under / **sceadu** bregdan* (706a–7b)

       'that the demonic foe could not draw them under the shadows, since the creator didn't want (that)'

   (c) *þæt him / **fēola lāf** <u>**frēcne**</u> / (ne) meahte*   oS/A/I

       <u>**scūr**-heard</u> / **sceþðan** (1032a–33a, dat. obj.)

       'so that the storm-hard leavings of the files (swords durable in the storm of battle) could not severely damage it (a helmet)'

   (d) *gyf him / **ed**-wenden **ǣfre** / scolde*   ioS/A/I

       <u>***bealuwa bisigu***</u>, ***bōt**[,] / eft cuman* (280–81)

       'if a remedy— a reversal of affliction from attacks — should ever come for him'

   (e)   *ac ic him / <u>**Gēata**</u> sceal*   sioA/O/I

       ***eafoð** ond / **ellen** **un**gēara / nū,*

       gūþe** / (ge)**bēodan (601b–03a)

       'but quite soon now I shall offer him combat, the strength and valor of the Geats'

   (f) *ic him / **līf**-wraðe **lȳtle** / meahte*   sioO/A/I

       *(æt)**gifan** æt / **gūðe*** (2877a–78a)

       'I could give him little life-protection in battle'

In (36a) the fronted auxiliary occupies location s1b in the opening a-verse and the auxiliary in the parenthesis occupies normative location s4. In (36b–f) the auxiliary in the larger clause occupies normative location s4. In (36c–e) the underlined modifiers are split by hyperbaton from their modified constituents *fēola lāf, sceþðan, edwenden,* and *eafoð ond ellen.*

In (37a–c) there are two objects, one stressed and one unstressed. Constituents of the verbal complex share a verse in normative IA order.

(37) (a) 　　　　　*nē inc / **ǣnig** mon,* 　　　　　　$o^{i2}S/IA/O^{i1}$

*nē / **lēof** nē **lāð**, be- / **lēan** mihte*

sorhfullne / **sīð** (510b–12a, unstressed dat. obj.)

'nor could any man, loved or loathed, deny you (dissuade you from) the wretched adventure'

(b) *forðām mē / **wītan** ne ðearf **waldend** / fīra* 　　　$o^{i2}IA/S/O^{i1}$

morð(o)r-bealo / **māga** (2741a–42a, with unstressed dat. obj.)

'therefore the ruler of men need not blame the murder of kin on me'

(c) 　　　　　*ic / **þē** nū ðā,* 　　　　　　　　$so^{i1}/IA/O^{i2}$

brego / **Beorht**-dena, **bid**dan / wille,

eodor / Scyldinga, **ān**re / bēne

(426b–28b, unstressed dat. obj., inanimate gen. obj.)

'now then, I will ask you one favor, chief of the Bright-Danes, protector of the Scyldings'

(d) *Ic þæt / **lond**-būend, **lēode** / mīne,* 　　　　$so^{i}O^{a}/IA$

sele- / **rǣ**dende, **secgan** / **hȳrde**

(1345–46; cf. 350b–53b, unstressed gen. obj.)

'I heard the inhabitants of the land — my people, hall-councilors — say that'

In (37a–c) the infinitive governs both objects and a heavy modified object is displaced to the right periphery. In (37d) the infinitive governs an unstressed object and a peripheral auxiliary governs a stressed object smaller than a verse. The auxiliary follows both objects in absolute final position. The stressed auxiliary occupies location s4 in (37a, c, d) and location s3 in (37b). With normative word order in (37b) the opening verse would be **(for ðām) **waldend** / fīra,* type A1 with anacrusis avoidable by rearrangement of constituents at line level. I cannot provide an exact syntactic equivalent for (37b) in Modern English. We now say 'he need not blame that on me' or 'he need not blame me for that' but not 'he need not blame me that.'

In (38a–c) the infinitive shares a verse with its primary object in normative order and the unstressed secondary object occupies normative location x1. In (38a) the auxiliary of a parenthetical clause occupies normative location s4 and the auxiliary in the larger clause occupies metrical location s1b in the opening verse.

(38) (a) *ic hine ne / **mih**te, þā / **metod** nolde,* 　　　$so^{2}A/O^{1}I$

*gan*ges / *(ge)twǣman* (967a–68a, gen. inanimate obj.)

'since the creator didn't want (that), I could not deny him departure' (prevent him from escaping)

(b) *hwæþer him* / *alwalda* *ǣfre* / *wille*   o²S/A/O¹I

æfter / *wēa*-*spelle* *wyrpe* / *(ge)fremman* (1314–15)

'whether the all-ruler will ever grant him a reversal (of fortune) after a time of woe'

(c)   *hē hine* / *eft ongon*   so²A/O¹I

*wǣte*res / *weorpan* (2790b–91a, gen. inanimate object)

'he then began to sprinkle water onto him / to sprinkle him with water'

The primary inanimate objects share a verse with their verbal governors in normative OI order, whether they are accusative, as in (38b), or genitive, as in (38a, c). A Modern English translation for (38c) requires expression of one object as a prepositional phrase. A double-object construction like 'began to sprinkle him water' would be unacceptable.

§9.6 Instances with an unstressed argument and an unexpressed argument.

Instances with unexpressed objects are particularly numerous in this section due to their employment with high-frequency verbs of commanding like *hātan*.

§9.6a One-verse instances

Items (39a–c) have core auxiliaries. Items (39d, e) have transitive peripheral auxiliaries.

(39) (a) *hwæt, þæt* / *secgan mæg* (942b)   (s)o/IA

'lo, (she) may say that' (anticipating a relative clause that identifies the subject)

(b) *him be-* / *beorgan ne con* (1746b, dat. obj.)   (s)ioIA

'(he) cannot protect himself'

(c) *gif hē ūs ge-* / *un*nan <u>*wile*</u> (346b)   (o)s.ioIA

'if he will grant (it) to us'

(d) *ond ēowic* / *grētan hēt* (3095b)   (soᵃ)oIA

314

'and (he) told (me) to greet you'

(e) *lēte* / *(hyne)* **licgean**   *þǣr hē* **longe** *wæs,*   (s)Ao^{a}I^1/O^{2}I^2

   wīcum / **wunian**   *oð* / **woruld**-*ende*   (3082a)

   '(he should) let him lie where he was for a long time to inhabit those pre-
   cincts until the end of the world'

In (39a–d) auxiliary and infinitive observe normative IA order and the auxiliary occupies normative location s4. In (39e) the hortative subjunctive
auxiliary is routinely fronted, as with imperatives. In this example *hine,* the
object of the peripheral auxiliary, occupies metrical location x4 for metrical
reasons. Placement of *hine* at normative location x1 would create easily
avoidable anacrusis, contravening OE 9.6. The first auxiliary, *licgean,* governs a second auxiliary, *wunian,* which shares a verse with its inanimate
object in normative order.

§9.6b Multi-verse instances

Items (40a–c) have core auxiliaries and unstressed subjects. Constituents
sharing a verse observe normative IA order. The object is unexpressed in
(40a) and relativized in (40b, c). The auxiliaries occupy normative location
s4.

(40) (a) *nū wē* / **sǣ**-*līðend*   **secgan** / *wyllað[,]*   (o)s/IA

   feorran / <u>cumene</u>[,] (1818a–19a)

   'now we seafarers, having come from afar, wish to say (that)'

   (b) *þone þe ðū mid* / **rih**te   **rǣ**dan / *sceoldest*

   (2056; cf. 1156a–57a, 2735a–36a)   wos/IA

   'which you should wield by right'

   (c) *ðē wē* / **ealle**   **ǣr** *ne* / *meahton*   wos/A/I

   snyttrum / *(be)***syr**wan* (941a–42a)

   'which we all could not contrive with (our) wits'

Items (40a, b) are syntactically complete one-line clauses. In (40c) a heavy
modified infinitive has been displaced to the right periphery in the next line.

Items (41a–e) have peripheral auxiliaries in constructions with two objects.

(41) (a) *ðē mē se* / **gō**da   *ā*- / **gifan** *þenceð* (355)   wo.ioS/IA

315

'which the worthy (man) thinks to give me'

(b) *þæt hē fram /* **Sige**-*mundes* **sec**gan / *hȳrde*   (o^a)wo^{i}s/IA

    ellen- / *dǣdum, uncūþes /* <u>*fela*</u>,

    Wǣlsinges / (ge)win, wīde / sīðas (875–77, as emended)

'that he heard (someone) say about Sigmund's brave deeds — the Volsung's hardship (and) wide-ranging adventures, many unfamiliar'

(c)   *nō ic /* **wiht** *fram þē*   (o^a)sO^i/IA

    swylcra / **searo**-*nīða* **sec**gan / *hȳrde,*

    billa / **brō**gan (581b–83a, gen. infinitive obj.)

'I by no means heard (anyone) speak (about) such armed conflicts — of such terror of swords — with regard to you'

(d) *swā wē /* **sōþ**līce **sec**gan / *hȳrdon* (273)   (o^{i}o^a)s/IA

'as we truly heard (someone) say (that)'

(e) *ðā ic /* **wī**de gefrægn **weorc** ge- / **ban**nan   (o^a)sA/O^{i}I/Io^i

    manigre / **mǣg**þe geond þisne / **middan**geard,

    folc-<u>stede</u> / **frætw**an (74a–76a)

'then I heard (someone) to assign to many a tribe widely throughout this middle-earth the work to build the folk-hall' ('that someone assigned to many a tribe the work,' etc.)

In (41a–d) expressed constituents are placed in the usual way, with the movable unstressed SPs at location x1, the stressed constituents in their normative syntactic positions, and the stressed auxiliary in normative metrical location s4. In (40b–e) the object of a transitive auxiliary is unexpressed. In (40d) the object of the infinitive is unexpressed as well. The infinitive in (40e) governs two objects. As expected, its inanimate direct object shares a verse with this infinitive while its indirect object is more remote. The auxiliary in (40e) has been fronted to metrical location s3, preceded by a stressed adverb that provides the alliteration. Although the adverb *wide* modifies *gebannan* in the infinitive construction, it undergoes long-distance fronting to a stressed position before the auxiliary. Compare (29b–d) and the note to line 575 in K4. In (41b) *Sigemundes,* emended from *Sigemunde* in K4, is split from *ellendǣdum* by hyperbaton. As the note in K4 observes, some textual critics regard the emendation as too distant from normal prose usage, but hyperbaton is well attested in poetry and the alternative explanations seem less persuasive.

§9.7 Instances with unstressed auxiliaries and all arguments stressed.

All the unstressed auxiliaries in this section occupy normative metrical location x1.

§9.7a One-verse instances

The only examples are like item (42). Stressed constituents observe normative SI order.

(42) *swā sceal / **man** dôn* (1172b, 1534b; cf. 2166b)   aSI
    'so should one do'

Only the most compact clauses are realized as a single verse. Those in item (42) have the minimum number of major constituents: subject, infinitive, and auxiliary. All instances are b-verses with the unmoved infinitive in core syntactic position and at metrical location s4, its preferred location when not followed by an auxiliary.

§9.7b Multi-verse instances

Items (43a–f) are intransitive multi-verse clauses with the same word order as in item (42). Item (43g) is the only instance with a different word order. There are core auxiliaries in (43a, c). The other examples have the peripheral auxiliary *cōm*. All auxiliaries occupy unstressed positions at normative location x1.

(43) (a) *swā sceal / **geong** guma   **gōde** / (ge)wyrcean,*   aS/I
        ***fromum** / **feoh**-giftum   on / **fæder** bearme*
        (20–21; cf. 2260b–62a, 2508b–9a)
        'thus should a young man work with goods, with splendid treasure-gifts, in the keeping of his father (while still a youth)'

   (b)   *ðā cōm / **beorht** lēoma*   aS/I
        *ofer / **sceadwa sca**can* (1802b–3a, as emended)
        'then a bright light came glid(ing) over the shadows'

   (c)   *ne scel / **ānes** hwæt*   aS/I
        ***mel**tan / (mid þam) **mōd**(i)gan* (3010b–11a)

'by no means shall (only) one part (of the treasure) melt (be cremated) with the brave (one)'

(d) *cōm þā tō* / *recede*   *rinc* / *sīðian,*   a/SI
drēamum / *(be)dǣled* (720a–21a)

'then the man came journey(ing) to the hall, bereft of joys'

(e) *ðā cōm of* / *mōre*   *under* / *mist-hleoþum*   a/SI
Grendel / *gongan* (710a–11a)

'then from the moor under the mist-hills Grendel came walk(ing)'

(f) *cōm þā tō* / *lande*   *lid-manna* / *helm*   a/S/I
swīð-mōd / *swymman* (1623a–24a; cf. 640b–41b)

'then the great-hearted protector of the seafaring men came swim(ming) to land'

(g)   *cōm on* / *wanre niht*   a/IS
scrīðan / *sceadu-genga* (702b–3a)

'the shadow-walker came glid(ing) through the black night'

In (43a, d) the infinitive occupies core syntactic position at metrical location s4. In (43b, e, f) the infinitive occupies a subordinate lift in the a-verse. In (43c, g) the alliterating infinitive occupies metrical location s1a in the clause-final a-verse, followed by a more prominent noun that also alliterates in accord with the rule of precedence. In (43g) this puts constituents sharing a verse out of normative SI order. Placement of the infinitive at location s1a avoids *(mid þam) mōd(i)gan* / *meltan* in (43c), with easily avoidable anacrusis (OE 9.6), and *sceadu-genga* / *scrīðan* in (43g), an unacceptable verse with the pattern *Ssx/Sx (H5).

In (44a–e) a stressed object shares a verse with a transitive infinitive. Items (44a–d) have core auxiliaries; item (44e) has a peripheral auxiliary.

(44) (a) *wolde* / *self cyning*   *symbel* / *þicgan* (1010)   aS/OI

'the king himself would (wanted to) enjoy the feast'

(b)   *ne mihte* / *snot(o)r hæleð*   aS/OI
wēan on- / *wendan* (190b–91a; cf. 3077a–78a)

'the wise man could not avert the misfortune'

(c)   *sceolde* / *hwæðre swā þēah*   a/S/OI
æðeling / *unwrecen*   *ealdres* / *linnan* (2442b–43b, gen. obj.)

'nevertheless the atheling had to lose life unavenged'

(d)   *swā sceal / **ǣghwylc** mon*   aS/IO

     *(ā)**lǣ**tan / **lǣn**-dagas* (2590b–91a)

     'since each man must relinquish transitory days (of life)'

(e)   *ēode / **scealc** monig*   aS/OI

     ***swīð**- / hicgende   tō / **sele** þām hēan*

     searo**-wundor / **sēon (918b–20a)

     'many a strong-minded man went to the high hall to see the impressive wonder'

Opening verses in other examples like (44a): 664a, 1443a, 1791a (gen. obj.), 2855a; like (44c): 1805b (gen. obj.), 2341b, 2401a, 2550a.

Most instances are like (44a, c), with the infinitive in core position at the end of the line. In (44b, e) the infinitive occupies a subordinate lift at the end of the a-verse. Departure from normative OI order in (44d) avoids **lǣn-dagas / (ā)lǣtan* (*Ssx/Sx: H5). This cannot be scanned as Ss/Sx (A3) because resolution of *dagas* is blocked by Kaluza's law (OE 8.6). As the verse stands it has ordinary prefixal anacrusis.

In the remaining instances with object and infinitive in the same verse an additional major constituent has been added. Items (45a–c) have core auxiliaries; item (45d) has a peripheral auxiliary. The unstressed auxiliaries occupy normative location x1. Stressed constituents sharing a verse observe normative OI order.

(45) (a) *ne meahte se / **snella**   **sunu** / Wonrēdes*   a/S/Io/OI

     *eal**dum** / ceorle   **ond**slyht / **giofan*** (2971–72)

     'the brave son of Wonred could not give a counter-stroke to the old man'

   (b) *wolde / **dōm** Godes   **dǣ**dum / rǣdan*   aS/OI/Io

     ***gum**ena / (ge)hwylcum* (2858a–59a, dat. obj.)

     'God's judgment would control deeds for each one of men'

   (c) *nū sceal / **sinc**-þego ond / **swyrd**-gifu,*   aS/Io/I

     ***eall** / ēðel-wyn[,]   ēowrum / cynne,*

     ***lufen**[,] ā- / **lic**gean* (2884a–86a)

     'now the receiving of treasure and the giving of swords — pleasure, all joy of home — shall cease for your kindred'

   (d) *ðā cōm / **in** gân   **ealdor** / ðegna,*   aI¹/S/OI²

     ***dǣd**-cēne / mon   **dōme** / (ge)wurþad,*

hæle / *hilde-dēor,* **Hrōðgār** / *grētan* (1644–46)

'then the leader of thanes, a man bold in deeds honored by fame, a battle-brave hero, came walk(ing) in to greet Hrothgar'

The added constituent is a stressed indirect object in (45a–c) and a second infinitive in (45d). In (45a) a negated auxiliary moves to an available C position. The C position is also available in (45b) and the auxiliary moves to it. In (45c, d) the auxiliary follows a clause-initial adverb. In (45a) the indirect object occupies its normative syntactic position, before the direct object and more distant from the governing infinitive. The heavy indirect object in (45b) is displaced to the right periphery and is distanced to the right of the verse shared by the direct object and the governing infinitive. In (45c) the stressed major constituents occupy separate verses in normative order. The peripheral finite auxiliary in (45d) governs a peripheral infinitive auxiliary, which in turn governs the second infinitive. The heavy modified subject in (45d) is displaced to the right of its associated verbal complex, stopping short of the second infinitive construction.

In (46a, b) each stressed constituent occupies a verse of its own. In (46b) the object of the peripheral auxiliary is separated by a parenthetical clause from the infinitive, which follows its own object in normative order.

(46) (a) *nolde* / **eorla** hlēo **ǣnige** / *þinga*   aS/O/I

      þone / **cwealm-cu**man **cwicne** / *(for)lǣtan* (791–92)

      'the protector of earls wouldn't let the murderous visitor depart alive for any one of things (for any consideration)'

   (b) *lēt se* / **hearda** **Higelāces** / *þegn*   a/S/Oᵃ/Oⁱ/I

      brādne / *mēce,* *þā his* / **brōðor** *læg,*

      eald-*sweord* / **eotonisc** **en**tiscne / *helm*

      brecan *ofer* / **bord**-*weal* (2977a–80a)

      'when his brother lay low, the hardy thane of Hygelac caused the broad blade, the ancient giant-made sword, to break the giant-made helmet over the shield-wall'

Stressed constituents observe normative syntactic order in (46a). In the last verse of (46b) an infinitive occupies metrical location s1a and a more prominent noun on a subordinate lift alliterates in accord with the rule of precedence. Normative order in this verse would create *ofer* **bord**-*weal* **brecan**, which has two possible interpretations. With *ofer* interpreted as extrametrical the result would be *(xx)Ss/Sx, an unacceptable variant of type A3 with anacrusis (OE 9.7). With *ofer* interpreted as a light foot the result would be *ofer / **bord**-weal **brecan,*** an unacceptable variant of xx/Sxs (type B3) with the secondary constituent of a poetic compound on the internal x position of the Sxs foot (OE 4.3). As it stands the verse is an unremarkable instance of Sxx/Ss (A6).

Items (47a–d) are the remaining instances. In (47d) the finite auxiliary *scolde* governs *flêon,* a infinitive auxiliary of motion that governs infinitive *sēcean* in a double-infinitive construction.

(47) (a)   *ā mæg /* **God** *wyrcan*   aSI/O

       wun*der / (æfter)* **wun***dre,* **wul***dres / hyrde* (930b–31a; cf. 3114b–15b)

       'may God, guardian of glory, always work wonder after wonder'

    (b) *sceal /* **hring**-*naca ofer /* **heafu** *bringan*   aS/I/O

       lāc *ond /* **luf**-*tācen* (1862a–63a; cf. 2291a–92a, 2305a–6a)

       'a ring-prowed ship shall bring gifts and love-tokens over the sea'

    (c) *ongunnon þā on /* **beorge** **bǣl**-*fӯra / mǣst*   a/O/SI

       wī*gend /* **wec***can* (3143a–44a)

       'then on the barrow warriors began to awaken (ignite) the greatest of funeral pyres'

    (d)   *scolde /* **Gren***del þonan*   aS/I^1/I^2O

       feorh-*sēoc /* **flê***on under /* **fen**-*hleoðu*

       sēcean / **wyn***lēas /* **wī***c* (819b–21a)

       'from there Grendel had to flee mortally wounded beneath the fen-cliffs to seek a joyless home'

Fronting of the auxiliary is routine in hortative subjunctive constructions like (47a), as in imperative constructions with similar force. Heavy objects are displaced to the right periphery in (47a, b, d). Heavy modified arguments are rarely fronted but in (47c) a whole-verse modified object that could not share a verse with the infinitive is moved before the lighter subject to fill a b-verse. Item (47d) contains one of the rare unstressed infinitives in *Beowulf.* Fronting of the infinitive avoids ***wyn**lēas **wī**c / sēcean (*Sxs/Sx: MH1). Use of an unstressed infinitive avoids *sēcean / wynlēas wīc,* which would not scan normally even if it were followed by a b-verse alliterating on s-. Prominent alliterating constituents like *wīc* and *wynlēas* never share a verse in *Beowulf* unless they contribute to the obligatory alliteration and occupy metrical locations where such alliteration is permissible.

§9.8 Instances with an unstressed auxiliary and an unexpressed or relativized argument

High-frequency peripheral auxiliaries can be fronted to unstressed rather than stressed positions in imperative constructions. There are several such instances in this section.

§9.8a One-verse instances

Items (48a, b) have an unstressed core auxiliary, an unexpressed subject, and an intransitive infinitive.

(48) (a) *wolde on /* **heol**ster *flēon* (755b)   (s)aI

   '(he) wanted to flee into shadow'

   (b) *ne mihte ðā for- /* **hab**ban (2609a)

   '(he) could not hold back then'

In (48a) the infinitive stands in normative position at the end of the clause and the line. In (48b) the infinitive alliterates at metrical location s1b in type A7, which is restricted to the a-verse.

   Items (49a–d) have transitive infinitives. Stressed constituents sharing a verse observe normative OI order.

(49) (a) *wolde hire /* **mǣg** *wrecan* (1339b)   (s)aOI

   '(she) wanted to avenge her child'

   (b) *sē ðe wyle /* **sōð** *specan* (2864b)   wsaOI

   'who will speak truth'

   (c)   *heht his /* **sweord** *niman,*   (soᵃ)aOⁱI

   lēoflic */ īren* (1808b–9a)

   '(he) told (him) to take his sword, the admirable iron (implement)'

   (d) *lēton /* **holm** *beran* (48b)   (soⁱ)aOᵃI

   '(they) let the sea take (him)'

Like (49a): 1060b, 1546b, 2294b, 3171a (as emended).

In (49a) the subject is unexpressed and the stressed constituents follow the unstressed auxiliary. Item (49b) is a similar verse with a relativized subject. In (49c) the object of a transitive auxiliary is unexpressed. In (49d) the object of the infinitive is unexpressed and the object of the auxiliary becomes adjacent to the infinitive.

§9.8b Instances in multi-verse clauses

Item (50a) has an intransitive peripheral auxiliary and an intransitive infinitive. Stressed constituents sharing a verse in (50b–d) observe normative order, with the object before its governing transitive infinitive.

(50) (a) *gewāt ðā* / ***byrn**ende ge-* / ***bogen** scrīðan,* (s)a/I

    tō ge- / ***scipe scyn**dan* (2569a–70a)

    'fiery (and) sinuous, toward (his) fate (he) came glid(ing), rush(ing)'

  (b) *þǣr mæg* / ***nih**ta gehwǣm **nīð**-wundor* / *sēon,* (s)a/OI

    ***fȳr** on* / ***flō**de* (1365a–66a; cf. 796a–97a, 2589)

    'there (one) can see a dreadful wonder — fire in the water'

  (c) *ac sceal* / ***geō**mor-mōd, **gol**de* / *(be)rēafod,* (s)a/OI

    oft[,] nalles / ***ǣ**ne[,] **el**-* / *land* / *tredan* (3018–19)

    'but (each one) shall tread foreign land often, by no means once, bereft of gold'

  (d)   ***gēong** sōna* / *tō* (s)a/OI

    ***set**les* / ***nēo**san* (1785b–86a)

    '(he) went promptly off to find a seat'

  (e) *geseah ðā be* / ***wealle** sē ðe* / ***worna** fela,* (s)a/IO

    ***gum**-cystum* / ***gōd, gū**ða* / *(ge)dīgde,*

    ***hil**de-* / ***hlem**ma, þonne/ ***hni**tan fēðan,*

    ***ston**dan* / ***stān**-bogan* (2542a–45a)

    'then by the wall (the one) who survived a great number of combats, of battle-crashes when foot-troops clashed, strong in manly virtues, saw stone arches stand(ing)'

Opening verses in other examples like (50d): 1292b (dat. obj.), 2408b, 2547b, 2666b.

Item (50a) is a one-line intransitive clause followed by a variation. The instances like (50b) have all major constituents in a single line. In (50c) the verses with major constituents are separated by semantically inessential verses and the infinitive occupies normative location s4 in the second line. The clauses like (50d) begin with a b-verse and the infinitive occupies a subordinate lift in the following a-verse. Within the last verse of (50e) the heavy object is shifted beyond the infinitive. Departure from normative OI order here avoids *__stānbogan__ / __ston__*dan,* which violates Kaluza's law if *-bogan* is resolved and is also unacceptable if scanned without resolution as *Ssx/Sx (H5). This is the same ambiguous pattern avoided in (44d).

In (51a–d) the stressed constituents occupy separate verses. Items (51a, c, d) have transitive infinitives; item (51b) has a transitive peripheral auxiliary. In (51c) an imperative peripheral auxiliary is fronted to an unstressed position.

(51) (a)   *ne meahte / **wǣ**fre mōd*   (s)aO/I
             *(for)**hab**ban / (in) **hre**þre* (1150b–51a)
             '(he) could not restrain that restless impulse in (his) heart'

     (b) *fand þā ðǣr / **in**ne   æþelinga / (ge)driht*   (s)a/O^a/I
         *__swefan__ æfter / **sym**ble* (118a–19a)
         'therein he found a troop of athelings sleep(ing) after the feast'

     (c)   *gewītaþ / **forð** beran*   (s)aI/O
         *__wǣ__pen / (ond ge)**wǣ**du* (291b–92a)
         'go forth bear(ing) weapons and corslets'

     (d) *gewāt ðā / **nēo**sian,   syþðan / **niht** becōm,*   (s)aI/O
         *__hêan__ / **hū**ses* (115a–16a, gen. obj.)
         'then after night came (he) went to visit the high house (hall)'

Items (51a, b) have the stressed major constituents in normative order. In both instances a prepositional phrase in the final verse has been displaced beyond the infinitive to the right periphery and the infinitive occupies metrical location s1a. With normative word order these verses would have a preposition in anacrusis. In (51a) as it stands we have ordinary prefixal anacrusis. In (51b) displacement of the prepositional phrase eliminates an anacrusis with a disyllabic preposition, something unattested in *Beowulf*. In (51c, d) heavy objects are displaced to the right periphery.

Items (52a–d) have transitive peripheral auxiliaries and transitive infinitives. Constituents sharing a verse observe normative OI order.

(52) (a)   *geseah his / **mon**-dryhten*   (s)aOᵃ/OⁱI

    *under / **here**-grīman   **hāt** / þrōwian* (2604b–5b)

    'he saw his human lord suffer heat under the battle-mask' (a faceplate for a helmet)

(b) *gesāwon ðā æfter / **wætere**   **wyrm**-cynnes / fela,*   (s)a/Oᵃ/OⁱI

    sellice / sǣdracan,   **sund** / cunnian* (1425–26; cf. 3033a–34a)

    'then they saw strange sea-dragons try swimming through the water'

(c)   *lēton / **wēg** niman,*   (s)aOᵃI/Oⁱ

    *flōd / **fæð**mian,   **frætwa** / hyrde* (3132b–33b)

    '(they) let the wave take — the flood embrace — the guardian of treasures'

(d) *lēt ðone / **brego**-stōl   **Bīowulf** / healdan*   (s)aOⁱ/OᵃI

    (2389; cf. 3166a–37a)

    '(he) let Beowulf have the chieftain's throne'

(e) *lǣtað / **hil**de-bord   **hēr** on- / bīdan,*   (s)aOᵃ/I/Oⁱ

    wudu[,] / **wæl**-sceaftas[,]   **worda** / (ge)þinges* (397–98, gen. obj.)

    '(you) let battle-shields (and) wooden spears — battle-shafts — await the exchange of words'

In (52a, b) the infinitive shares a verse with its governed object. In (52c) the heavy modified object of the infinitive is displaced to the right periphery and the infinitive shares a verse in normative order with its logical subject, the object of the auxiliary. In (52d) an infinitive object smaller than a verse is fronted to complete the opening verse. Here too the infinitive shares the verse with its logical subject in normative order. The unstressed auxiliary in (52e) is routinely fronted in an imperative construction. The stressed constituents occupy separate verses and the heavy modified object of the infinitive is displaced to the right periphery.

In (53a–c) the finite auxiliary *(w)uton* 'let us, we should' governs an infinitive auxiliary of motion that governs a second infinitive. The first and second infinitives are in normative order. Verb fronting is routine in hortative constructions with *(w)uton*, as with imperatives.

(53) (a)   *uton / (h)**raþe** fēran*   (s)aI¹/OI²

    Grendles / māgan   **gang** / scēawigan* (1390b–91b)

    '(we) should go at once to examine the track of Grendel's kinswoman'

(b)   *wutun / **gon**gan tō,*   (s)aI¹/I²O *hel*pan / *hild*-*fruman* (2648b–49a)

'(we) should go forth to help the battle-leader'

(c) **uton** *nū* / **efstan** *ōðre* / *sīðe*,   (s)AI^1/I^2/O

 sēon *ond* / **sēcean** **searo**-*gimma* / *(ge)þræc*,

 wundur / *(under)* **wealle** (3101a–3a)

'(we) should hasten a second time to identify (look for) and seek out the
heap of wrought gems, that wonder below the wall'

In (53a) the second infinitive and its object share a verse in normative OI
order. Departure from OI order in (53b) avoids ***hild*fruman / **help**an,* the
kind of H5 variant avoided in (44d) and (50e). The heavy modified object
in (53c) is displaced beyond its governing infinitive constituent, which is
followed in the same verse by a variation.

As in other constructions, infinitive constructions with unexpressed objects have relatively low frequency because objects tend to be less well established than subjects in previous discourse. The major constituents in item
(54), the only instance in a single-object construction, are arranged in a one-
line clause followed by variations of the subject and infinitive. The reference
of the unexpressed object is specified in a following that-clause.

(54) *mæg þonne on þæm* / **golde on*gitan** *Gēa*ta / *dryhten*,   (o)aI/S

 *(ge)*s**ēon** / **sunu** *Hrædles* (1484a–85a)

'then by the gold the lord of the Geats, Hrethel's son, can understand (that) —
see (that)'

The heavy modified subject is displaced to the right periphery, where it provides a normative A1 verse to complete the line. The modifier provides the
required alliteration for the b-verse. The third verse is a good example of a
multi-term variation that does not express a distinct idea of its own and
therefore does not qualify for discussion as a verse clause.

In (55a–d) the infinitive and the peripheral auxiliary are both transitive.
The auxiliary, *hātan,* is fronted to an unstressed position at metrical location
x1. As usual in *Beowulf,* the unexpressed object of *hātan* refers to an unspecified retainer.

(55) (a) *heht ðā* / *eorla hlēo* **eah**ta / *mēaras*   (o^a)aS/O^1/I

 *fǣ*ted- / *hlēore* *on* / **flet** *tēon*,

in under / *eode*ras (1035a–37a)

'the protector of earls told (someone) to lead eight steeds with cheek-plates onto the floor, in under the ceilings'

(b) *hēt ðā* / *eorla hlēo*   *in* ge- / _fetian,_   (oᵃ)aS/I/Oⁱ

heaðo-rōf / *cyning,*   *Hrēðles* / *lāfe[,]*

*gol*de / *(ge)gyrede* (2190a–92a)

'the protector of earls — that battle-bold king — told (someone) to fetch in Hrethel's heirloom, adorned with gold'

(c) *hēt þā* / *up* beran   *æþelinga* / *(ge)strēon,*   (soᵃ)aI/Oⁱ

frætwe / *(ond) fǣt-gold* (1920a–21a; cf. 2152a–54a)

'(he) told (someone) to take up the wealth of athelings, the treasures and plated gold'

(d)   *hāt* / *in* gân   (soᵃ)aI1/I²Oⁱ²

sēon / *sib*be-gedriht   *samod æt-* / _gædere_ (386b–87b)

'(you) tell (him) to come in to see the troop of friends gathered together'

                                           (imperative)

(e) *hēt ðā* ge- / *bēodan*   *byre* / *Wīhstānes,*   (oᵃoⁱ)aI/S/Io

hæle / *hil*de-dīor,   *hæleða* / _monegum,_

bold- / *āgendra* (3110a–12a)

'Wistan's son, that battle-bold hero, told (someone) to announce (that) to many a one of heroes, of hall-owners'

In (55a, b) the infinitive occupies core position at metrical location s4. The infinitive occupies a subordinate a-verse lift in (55c). As with placement of finite verbs at the end of the a-verse, this departure from line-final placement of the infinitive makes it possible to arrange the major constituents in a single line. The heavy displaced object fills the b-verse. In (55d) an imperative peripheral auxiliary is fronted to an unstressed position in the opening b-verse, followed by a line-final infinitive in core syntactic position. Alliteration is supplied by a semantically essential adverb that forms a quasi-compound with the infinitive. The second infinitive and its stressed object share an a-verse out of normative order, avoiding **sibbe-gedriht* / *sēon*, with the unacceptable pattern *Sxxs/S (M2).

§9.9 Instances with an unstressed auxiliary and an unstressed argument (including instances with an additional argument that is unexpressed)

§9.9a One-verse examples

In (56a–f) the unstressed argument and auxiliary occupy normative location x1. Items (56a–d) have core auxiliaries; items (56 e–g) have peripheral auxiliaries.

(56) (a)   *ic sceal / **forð** sprecan*   s a I
gēn *ymbe / **Grendel*** (2069b–70a)

'I shall speak out further concerning Grendel'

(b)   *þā sceall / **brond** fretan*   oaSI
***ǣ**led / þeccean* (3014b)

'the flame shall consume — the fire shall enfold — those (things)'

(c) *þæt, lā, mæg / **sec**gan* (1700a, 2864a)   (s)oaI

'indeed, (one) may say that,' anticipating a that-clause

(d)   *nolde ic / **sweord** beran,*   asOI
wǣ**pen[,] / (tō) **wyrme (2518b–19a)

'I wouldn't take a sword, a weapon, to the dragon'

(e) *hēt hine / **wēl** brūcan* (1045a)   (so[i])ao[a]I

'(he told) him to enjoy (it) well'

(f) *hēt hyne / **brū**can well* (2812b)   (so[i])ao[a]I

'(he) told him to enjoy (it) well'

(g) *gewiton him þā / **fē**ran* (301a)   (s)a.ioI

'then (they) went walk(ing) for themselves'

In (56a) the unstressed subject and auxiliary share location x1 in normative 'sa' order. In (56b, c) the unstressed constituents observe normative 'oa' order. In (56d) the contract negative auxiliary is attracted to a C position and the unstressed subject follows. A C position is also available in (56e–g) and the unstressed auxiliaries move to it. The infinitive occupies metrical location s4 in (56a, b, d). In (56c, g) the infinitive occupies metrical location s1b in type A7, which is restricted to the a-verse. Items (56e, f) exploit alternative placements for semantically inessential *wēl* to use traditional phraseology in differing alliterative environments. In (56e) the adverb subordinates the verb it modifies and takes the alliteration. In (56f) the adverb is subordinated and the verb alliterates. The uniquely movable adverb provides a very useful component for the formulaic poet. Alliteration provides good metrical evidence for subordination of simplex adverbs when they follow the verb. If the adverb had the same prominence relative to the verb in (56f) as in (56e), the rule of prominence would require double alliteration in verses with the structure of (56e). We would then expect type I verses like (56e) to have double alliteration in the a–verse and much lower frequency in the b– verse. In fact all the type I a–verses of this kind have single alliteration in *Beowulf* (34a, 620a, 740a, 1408a, 1870a, 2345a, 2516a, 3156a). The number of corresponding b–verses is higher, not lower (136b, 538b, 748b, 762b, 797b, 1218b, 2091b, 2208b, 2395b, 2519b, 2656b, 2855b, 2878b, 2968b, 2990b).

§9.9b Multi-verse examples

The unstressed subject shares a verse with an unstressed core auxiliary in (57a–c), which have transitive infinitives. Items (57d–f) have intransitive infinitives and transitive peripheral auxiliaries. Item (57g) has a core auxiliary and an intransitive infinitive. Stressed constituents sharing a verse observe normative OI order.

(57) (a) *þæt ic mōte / **āna**,   mīnra / **eorla** gedryht,*   sa/OI

        *ond þes / **hearda hēap**,   **Heorot** / fǣlsian* (431–32)

        'that I personally, the retinue of my earls, and this band of bold (people) may purify Heorot'

    (b)   *hē mæg / **þǣr** fela*   saO/I

        *frēonda / **fin**dan* (1837b–38a)

        'he can find a multitude of friends there' (if not elsewhere)

    (c)   *nelle ic / **beor**ges weard*   asO/I

        *(ofer)**flēon** / **fō**tes trem* (2524b–25a)

        'I won't flee the space of a foot from the guardian of the barrow'

    (d)   *ne hȳrde ic / **snot**(o)rlicor*   as/OI

        *on swā / **geon**gum <u>feore</u>   **guman** / þingian* (1842b–43b; cf. 1659a–60a)

        'I never heard a man negotiate more wisely at such a young age'

    (e) *ne gefrægen ic þā / **mæg**þe   **mā**ran / <u>weorode</u>*   asO/I

        *ymb hyra / **sinc**-gyfan   **sēl** ge- / **bǣ**ran* (1011–12)

        'I never knew people in a greater troop to behave better around their trea– sure-giver'

(f) *geseah hē in* / *recede* **rin**ca / *manige(,)*   as/O/I

   swefan[,] / **sibbe**-gedriht **samod** *æt-* / *gæ̱dere,*

   mago-rinca / *hēap* (728a–30a)

   'in the hall he saw many (a one) of men sleep(ing), a band of friends gathered together, a heap of kindred heroes'

(g) *sē scel tō ge-* / **myn**dum **mī**num / *lēodum*   sa/Io/I

   hēah / **hlī**fian *on* / **Hrones** *Næsse* (2804–5)

   'which shall tower high for my people on Whale's Ness as a memorial'

In (57a) the C position before the subordinate clause is filled by a *þæt* complementizer and fronting of the auxiliary before the subject is blocked. Placing the subject first in (57b, g) brings it closer to its antecedent in the preceding clause. It is difficult to distinguish (57g) from an independent
sentence with a pronoun subject. Placement of *sē* keeps it closest to its antecedent whether *sē* is a relative pronoun, as the punctuation in K4 implies,
or a fronted pronoun subject. The C position is empty in (57c-f) and the
unstressed auxiliary moves to it. Negation of the verb promotes fronting in
(57c–e). In (57a, d, e), the infinitive remains in core position at metrical
location s4. In (57b, g) the infinitive occupies metrical location s2. In (57c,
f) the infinitive occupies metrical location s1a before a more prominent
noun, with double alliteration as required by the rule of precedence. In (57c)
this avoids **fōtes trem* / *(ofer)flēon* (*Sxs/S: M1); in (57f) it avoids ***sibbe**-
gedriht / **swefan** (*Sxxs/S: M2).

   Items (58a–d) are the remaining instances with the subject and auxiliary
as the only unstressed constituents.

(58) (a) *wille ic ā-* / **sec**gan **sunu** / *Healfdenes,*   asI/Io/O

   mæ̱rum / *þēodne,* **mīn** / *æ̱rende,*

   aldre / *þīnum* (344a–46a)

   'I want to speak my message to the son of Halfdane, the famous chieftain,
   your lord'

(b) *ne meahton wē ge-* / **læ̱ran** **lēof**ne / *þēoden,*   asI/O^{i2}/O^{i1}

   rīces / *hyrde,* **ræ̱d** / *æ̱nigne* (3079–80)

   'we could not teach the beloved lord, guardian of the kingdom, any advice'

(c) *ne hȳrde ic* / **cȳm**licor **cēol** ge- / *gyrwan*   (o^a)as/O^{i}I

   hilde- / *wæ̱pnum* *ond* / **heaðo**-wæ̱dum,

   billum / *(ond) byrnum* (38a–40a)

330

'I never knew (anyone) to equip a boat more splendidly with fighting wea-
pons and combat armor, with swords and mail-coats'

(d) *nū gē mōtan* / **gangan**   *in ēowrum* / **gūð**-*ge*- / <u>*tawum*</u>   saI[1]/OI[2]

under / **here**-*grīman*   **Hrōðgār** *ge*- / *sēon* (395–96)

'now you may go see Hrothgar in your combat gear under battle-helmets'

In (58a, b, d) the stressed infinitive provides alliteration for the opening
verse at location s1b in type A7, a type restricted to the a-verse. Type A7
leaves good room for the multiple unstressed SPs at normative location x1.
In (58c) fronting the peripheral auxiliary to an unstressed position makes it
possible to arrange the major constituents in a single line with the stressed
infinitive in core syntactic position at metrical location s4. The unstressed
auxiliary moves to an available C position in (58a–c), with negation promoting movement in (58b, c). In (58d) a clause-initial adverb precedes the
verb. In (58a) both heavy objects are displaced beyond the infinitive to the
right periphery, with the indirect object maintaining normative order before
the direct object. In (58b) the infinitive takes an inanimate primary object
and an animate secondary object, both in the accusative case. As in (58a),
both objects are realized as two-word verses and displaced to the right periphery, where they maintain normative order, with the animate object before the inanimate object.

In (58d), a double-infinitive construction, the core auxiliary *mōtan* governs *gangan*, an infinitive peripheral auxiliary that governs *gesēon*, the second infinitive. Transitive *gesēon* shares a verse with its object *Hrōðgār*, observing normative OI order. No double-infinitive clauses in *Beowulf* have
the auxiliary in absolute final position, the normative position for finite verbs
in most verse clauses. I could not find examples in other Old English poems
by consulting entries for common transitive infinitives in glossaries or con-
cordances, nor could I find prose examples by consulting the indexes in
OES 2. If examples exist they do not seem to have attracted much attention.
Double-infinitive clauses with the finite verb in absolute final position are
well known to be unacceptable in standard German. They seem to have been
unacceptable in Old English as well.

Unstressed objects share location x1 with the unstressed auxiliary in
(59a–c). Items (59b, c) have indirect object beneficiaries coreferential with
the subject.

(59) (a) *mæg þæs þonne of*- / **þyn**can   **ðēod**(*e*)**n** / *Heaðo-Beardna*   aoI/S

ond / *þegna gehwām* *þāra* / *lēoda* (2032–33, genitive object)

'then the lord of the Heathobards and all the thanes of that people may resent it'

(b) *gewāt him ðā se* / *gōda*   *mid his* / *gædelingum,*   aioS/OI

frōd, / *fela*-geōmor,   *fæsten* / *sēcean* (2949–50; cf. 1963a–65a)

'the powerful (man), old and very unhappy, went for himself with his companions to seek the stronghold'

(c)   *gewāt him* / *on naca*   aioS/IO

drēfan / *dēop wæter* (1903b–4a)

'the boat went onward for itself to traverse deep water'

In all three instances the unstressed auxiliary is fronted past the unstressed object to an available C position. The note to (59a) in K4 recommends against emending nominative *ðēoden,* so I have interpreted it as a modified subject displaced to the right periphery. In (59b) the stressed constituents sharing a verse observe normative OI order. Constituents sharing a verse in (59c), a typical instance of personification, depart from OI order to avoid **dēop wæter* / *drēfan,* with the unacceptable H5 pattern avoided by IO order in (50e) and several preceding instances.

Items (60a–d) have unexpressed arguments as well as unstressed arguments. Stressed constituents occupy separate verses. In (60a, c) the object of *hātan* refers to an unnamed retainer and is unexpressed, as usual in third-person narration. In (60b) the object refers to *Beowulf,* an important named person. Here the object is expressed. Wulfgar is a high official of Hrothgar's, an important named person famous for his valor and wisdom (348a–50a). In (60d), however, Wulfgar is delivering a message from his lord to Beowulf, an important visitor. In this role Wulfgar is concise and businesslike, omitting as irrelevant the pronoun that refers to him.

(60) (a)   *hēt him* / *ȳð-lidan*   (so[a])a.ioO[i]/I

gōdne / *(ge)gyrwan* (198b–99a)

'(he) told (someone) to make a sturdy wave-roamer for him'

(b) *hēt hine mid þǣm* / *lācum*   *lēode* / *swǣse*   (s)ao[a]/O[i]/I

sēcean / *(on ge)syntum* (1868a–69a)

'(he) told him to seek out his own people with those gifts in good health'

(c) *heht him þā ge-* / *wyrcean*   *wīgendra* / *hlēo*   (o[a])a.ioI/S/O[i]

eall īrenne,   eorla / dryhten,

wīg-bord / wrǣtlic (2337a–39a)

'the protector of warriors told (someone) to make a remarkable shield for him entirely out of iron'

(d) *ēow hēt / secgan sige-drihten / mīn,* (oⁱoᵃ)ioaI/S

aldor / Ēast-Dena (391a–92a)

'my victory-lord, leader of the East-Danes, told (me) to say (that) to you' (anticipating a that-clause)

In (60a–c) unstressed *hātan* is fronted beyond an unstressed object pronoun to an available C position. In (60d) Wulfgar fronts the pronoun referring to *Beowulf*, perhaps in acknowledgement of *Beowulf*'s status. Compare the fronting of *mē* by Wealhtheow in (1175a). In (60a, b) the stressed constituents observe normative OI order. In (60c) the heavy subject and object are displaced to the right periphery, where they maintain normative SO order. In (60d) the heavy subject is displaced. In (60a) the infinitive occupies metrical location s4. In (60b) the infinitive occupies metrical location s1a and a more prominent following noun alliterates in accord with the rule of precedence. Departure from verse-final placement of the infinitive avoids **(on ge)syntum / sēcean,* an unacceptable two-word A1 variant with anacrusis (OE 9.6). In (60c, d) the infinitive is the most prominent constituent in the opening verse and alliterates at location s1b in type A7, which is restricted to the a-verse.

§9.10 Instances with unexpressed verbs

Due to their predictability and extremely low information content, infinitive forms of 'be' are routinely unexpressed in some Old English constructions even when there is no expressed antecedent in a preceding clause (OES 1: 419–21). Similar instances in which a modal auxiliary appears without an infinitive verb of motion are not uncommon in Old English and can still be found in Early Modern English (OES 1: 421). In such instances the concept of motion is typically implicit in an adverb like *away* or a prepositional phrase like *to London.* Most unexpressed verbs in *Beowulf* are understood from an expressed antecedent in a preceding clause, however. The more fully expressed clause may be followed by a single reduced clause or by a sequence of reduced clauses in which all unexpressed verb forms are understood from the same antecedent. When auxiliaries are unexpressed, an expressed antecedent must provide the appropriate features of mood, tense, person, and number for every unexpressed auxiliary in the sequence. The antecedent of an unexpressed infinitive must have the appropriate meaning but the expressed antecedent need not be an infinitive form of the verb.

§9.10a One-verse instances

There is one instance with an unexpressed core auxiliary and an intransitive infinitive.

(61) (a)   *ond / **sacu** restan,*   (a)SI

           ***in**wit- / nīþas* (1857b–8a)

           'and strife — malicious attacks — (shall) cease'

The expressed constituents are in normative order and the second verse is a semantically inessential variation of *sacu*. The immediately preceding clause has expressed *sceal*.

The verse clauses with unexpressed auxiliaries in (62a–c) have transitive infinitives and unexpressed subjects. The instances in (62d) have intransitive infinitives.

(62) (a) ***wrǣtte** / (giond)**wlītan*** (2771a)   (sa)O^{i}I

         '(he could) survey the treasures'

     (b) *sēcan / **dēofla** gedrǣg* (756a)   (sa)iO^i

         '(he would) seek the company of devils'

     (c) ***sēcean** / **sāwle** hord* (2422a; cf. 1450a–51a)   (sa)IO^i

         '(it would) seek the treasury of the soul' (attack life)

     (d)   *orcas / stondan*   (sa)O^{a}I

       *fyrn-manna / **fatu** feormend- / lēase,*

       *hyrstum / (be)**hrorene*** (2760b–62a; cf. 1427)

       '(he saw) cups stand(ing), goblets of long-vanished people lacking a polisher, with ruined ornamentation'

Like (62a), in a-verse: 11a, 801a, 874a (dat. obj.), 911a (dat. obj.), 1470a, 1524a (dat. obj.), 1940a, 2046a, 2313a, 2514a, 2758a, 3083a (dat. obj.), 3172a; in b-verse: 125b, 185b (gen. obj.), 188b, 911b, 1126b, 1278b, 2655b, 2754b, 2857b, 3171b.

The most common arrangement by far is the one in (62a), with the stressed constituents sharing a verse in normative OI order. Some unexpressed auxiliaries in these instances have peripheral auxiliary antecedents. Item (62b) has one of the rare unstressed infinitives. Since unstressed infinitives have greater prominence than the vast majority of other SPs, they are predictably assigned to normative location x1, the only permissible unstressed location for prominent verbal SPs. The same infinitive is stressed as usual in (62c). In (62b, c) the verse-internal foot boundary must fall at the major syntactic break that separates the infinitive from its modified object. If the modified objects preceded the infinitives in normative syntactic order, the unacceptable result in (62b) would be *Sxxs/Sx (MH3). In the verses like (62c) the result would be *Sxs/Sx (MH1).

Items (63a–b) have a transitive infinitive at location s2 and an unexpressed direct object.

(63) (a) *ǽled / þeccean* (3015a)   (oa)SI

'the fire (shall) devour (it)'

(b) **earne** / *secgan* (3026a)   (soa)Io.I

'(he shall) say (that) to the eagle' (anticipating a relative 'how' clause)

In (63a) stressed constituents observe normative SI order. In (63b) the subject is unexpressed. Stressed constituents observe normative Io.I order. The line is completed in the following b-verse by a relative clause with its finite verb at normative location s4.

Items (64a–c) have an unexpressed subject, a stressed object, and an unexpressed object. The expressed constituents observe normative OI order. The first verse in (64a) is a syntactically complete one-verse clause. The b-verse is a good example of a construction with only one expressed major constituent that does not qualify for discussion as a verse clause.

(64) (a) **bān-fatu** / **bærnan**   ond on/ **bǽl** dôn   (sao^a)O^{i}I

   $\bar{e}$ame / (on) **eaxle** (1116a–12b)

   '(she ordered someone) to burn the bone-container and place (it) on the pyre at the shoulder of the maternal uncle'

(b) **aldre** / (be)nēotan   (sao^2)O^{1}I

   (680a, dat. inf. obj.; cf. 2390a, dat. inf. obj.)

   '(I will not) deny (him) life' (deprive him of life)

The unexpressed object in (64a) is the object of the unexpressed transitive auxiliary. In (64b) the infinitive governs two objects. The animate accusative object is unexpressed and as a result the dative inanimate object shares the verse with its governing infinitive.

Items (65a–c) have unexpressed infinitives.

(65) (a) *swā hē hyra / **mā** wolde* (1055b)   (i)sOA
          'as he would (kill) a greater number of them'

      (b) *(nū) **hæleð** ne / mǣston* (2247b)   (oi)SA
          'now that men cannot (do that)'

      (c) *ic him / **æfter** sceal* (2816b; cf. 543b, 594b, 2585b–86a)   (i)sA
          'I shall (go) after them'

In (65a, b) the unexpressed infinitive has an antecedent in the immediately preceding clause but the antecedent verb does not have infinitive form. The antecedent for (65b) is an imperative. In (65c) there is no antecedent for the unexpressed infinitive verb of motion.

§9.10b Multi-verse instances

In (66a, b) both constituents of the verbal complex are intransitive.

(66) (a)   *ond se / **ell**or-gāst*   (a)S/I
          *on / **fēon**da geweald   **feor** / sīðian* (807b–8b)
          'and the alien spirit (had to) journey far away'

      (b) *symle ic him on / **fēð**an   be- / **foran** wolde,*   (i)s/A
          *āna / (on) **or**de* (2497a–98a)
          'always I would (go) before him alone on foot in the vanguard'

In (66a) an antecedent for the unexpressed auxiliary is expressed as *scolde*. The stressed infinitive occupies core syntactic position at metrical location s4, as usual when the auxiliary is moved or unexpressed. In (66b) the unexpressed infinitive verb of motion has no antecedent. The unstressed subject occupies normative location x1, preceded by a sentential adverb. The stressed auxiliary occupies normative metrical location s4. Constituents of the postpositional phrase *him beforan* are split by hyperbaton.

In (67a–d) a direct object shares a verse with its governing infinitive, observing normative OI order. The adjacent examples in (67a) have a parallelistic rhetorical effect, highlighting the contrast between joyful peacetime and sorrowful wartime.

(67) (a)   *nalles / **hear**pan swēg*   (a)S/OI

       wīgend / **wec**cean (3023b–24a; cf. 3024b–25b)

       'by no means (shall) the music of the harp awaken warriors'

    (b) **heaðo**- / *līð*endum   **hord** *for-* / *standan,*   (sa)Io/OI

       bearn *ond* / **brȳ**de (2955a–56a)

       '(he could) deny the attacking sailors hoard, child, and wife' (protect his treasury, child, and wife from the attacking sailors)

    (c)   **dēa**ð / *rē*nian   (sa)OI/Io

       hond-*ge*- / *steallan* (2168b–69a; cf. 71–73)

       '(he should not) prepare death for a close companion'

    (d)   **sār** / *wā*nigean   (sa)O[i]I/O[a]

       helle / **hæf**ton (787b–88a)

       '(they heard) the captive of hell bewail the wound'

In (67a) the stressed subject observes normative order with the object and infinitive. The boundary between verses falls at the natural point of syntactic division. In (67b) an indirect object in the dative of disadvantage occupies its normative syntactic position before a direct object and farther from the governing verb. In (67c) the heavy indirect object is displaced beyond the infinitive to the right periphery. In (67d) the heavy direct object of an unexpressed transitive auxiliary is displaced.

In (68a–c) other combinations of stressed constituents share a verse, observing normative SI, SO, and Io.I orders. The form *bregdon* in (68b) is a variant spelling of infinitive *bregdan*.

(68) (a)   *nalles / **eorl** wegan*   (a)SI/O

       māððum / *(tō ge)***myn**dum (3015b–16a)

       'by no means (shall) an earl wear a treasure as an honor'

    (b)   **manig** / *ō*þerne   (a)SO/I

       gōdum / *(ge)***grē**tan   *ofer* / **gano**tes bæð (1860b–61b)

       'many a one (shall) greet another with gifts over the gannet's bath (ocean)'

    (c) *nealles* / **in**wit-net   **ōð**rum / *bregdon*   (sa)O/Io.I

       dyrnum / *cræfte* (2167a–68a)

'(one should) by no means weave a net of malice for others'

The infinitives occupy core position at metrical location s4 in (68a) and in (68c), a syntactically complete one-line clause. The type II verse that contains the object is displaced to the right periphery in (68a). In (68b) the infinitive occupies a subordinate lift at metrical location s2. The light object *ōþerne* shares the opening verse with the subject in normative SO order. In (68c) a direct object smaller than a verse is fronted to the opening verse from its core position after the indirect object. Departure from normative IoO order makes it possible to arrange the major constituents in a single line. If these constituents were arranged as a single line with normative order, the b-verse would be *inwit-net / bregdon,* with the unacceptable pattern Sxs/Sx (MH1).

In (69a–g) each stressed constituent occupies a separate verse. In (69a) the possessive pronoun is postposed and split from the noun it modifies by hyperbaton.

(69) (a)   *oþðe / ende-dæg*   (sa)O/I

     on þisse / meodu-healle mīnne / (ge)bīdan (637b–38b; cf. 1084a–85a)

     'or (I will) live to see my final day in this mead-hall'

  (b)   *strēam / ūt þonan*   (sa)O/I

   brecan[,] of / beorge (2545b–46a)

   '(he saw) a stream burst out from there, from the barrow'

  (c) *ond þē þā / andsware ǣdre / (ge)cȳðan* (354)   (sa)ioO/I

   'and (I shall) promptly report the answer to you'

  (d)   *nē / mægð scȳne*   (a)S/I/O

   habban / (on) healse hring- / weorðunge (3016b–17b)

   'nor (shall) a beautiful woman wear a ring-adornment on (her) neck'

  (e) *ond on / spēd wrecan spel ge- / rāde* (873; cf. 2775a–76a)   (sa)I/O

   'and (he began) to recite an appropriate tale with skill'

  (f) *ond þonne ge- / ferian frēan / ūserne,*   (sa)I/O

   lēofne / mannan (3107a–8a)

   'and then (we should) carry our lord, that beloved man'

  (g)   *sundur / (ge)dǣlan*   (sa)I/O

   līf wið / līce (2422b–23a; cf. 2126b–27a)

   '(it would) divide life from the body'

In (69a–c) the stressed constituents observe normative order. In (69d–g) the object occupies a heavy verse displaced to the right periphery. The infinitive occupies metrical location s4 in (69a, c, g). In (69e) it occupies location s3 and in (69f) it occupies location s1b in a type A7 verse. In (69b, d) the infinitive occupies location s1a and the more prominent noun alliterates in accord with the rule of precedence. In (69b) verb-final order would place a resolved and alliterating infinitive on the s position of a type I verse. This is an instance in which the infinitive seems to follow the rules for finite verbs that occupy s positions (OE 7.5, OE 8.5). In (69d) verse-final placement of the infinitive would create a type A1 verse with easily avoidable anacrusis, contravening OE 9.6.

§9.11 Retrospect

In this chapter we have considered a variety of core and peripheral auxiliaries that have relatively high frequencies but lower frequencies than 'be' verbs. These auxiliaries are fronted less often than 'be' verbs to unstressed positions due to their higher prominence. Core auxiliaries provide the larger sample, with 271 instances (68%), as compared with 128 instances for peripheral auxiliaries (32%). Among the core auxiliaries 204 are stressed (75%) and 67 are unstressed (25%). Among the peripheral auxiliaries 83 are stressed (64%) and 46 are unstressed (36%). Unlike 'be' verbs, these auxiliaries have a majority of stressed instances. The peripheral auxiliaries have somewhat lower frequency than the core auxiliaries but do not show a higher percentage of stressed instances. What significance this might have is difficult to assess. The 'have' and 'be' auxiliaries in chapter eight are easy to compare because both appear in the same kinds of constructions and these constructions are relatively simple. Comparison is less straightforward with core auxiliaries, which are rarely transitive, and peripheral auxiliaries, which are often transitive and appear in entirely different kinds of constructions. To make matters more difficult, infinitive constructions tend to be quite complex, as the reader will have noticed. Focused research on this topic in a larger corpus would be welcome.

Fortunately, stressed major constituents sharing a two-word type II verse are less difficult to analyze. A special feature of this chapter is its transitive infinitives. The position of verbs relative to their arguments can be studied with transitive infinitives as well as transitive finite core and peripheral auxiliaries. The following summaries are for two-word verses with subjects, direct objects, auxiliaries, and infinitives.

Total stressed core auxiliaries: **204**

     Following infinitive in normative IA order: **132**

     (No two-word examples with AI order)

     Following object of infinitive in normative OA order: **8**

     (No two-word examples with AO order)

     Following subject in normative SA order: **6**

     (No two-word examples with AS order)

     Remainders in verses without arguments or infinitives: **58**

     (One example with A/I order that is not a two-word example)

More than half of the stressed core auxiliaries share a verse with their governed infinitives in the IA order that is normative for SOV languages. The closely-bound verbal complex with a stressed finite verb in clause-final position seems to be well established in *Beowulf* as a formulaic building block. The unique example with AI order has a hortative auxiliary that is routinely fronted. Normative SOV order is also strictly observed by less closely bound constituents when they share a two-word verse with a core auxiliary, but instances of this kind have far lower frequency.

Total stressed peripheral auxiliaries: **96**

     Following infinitive in normative IA order: **20**

     Preceding infinitive in AI order: **1 (1728b)**

     Following object in normative OA order,

         with its own object: **5**

         with object of infinitive: **2**

     (No two-word examples with AO order)

     Following subject in normative SA order: **6**

     (No two-word examples with AS order)

     Remainders   **34**

Of the 96 stressed peripheral auxiliaries 21% share a verse with a stressed infinitive, a significant frequency but lower than that for core auxiliaries. Less closely bound constituents share a verse with the stressed auxiliary more often, though the effect of close binding is observable among the examples with normative OA order, most of which involve the object of the auxiliary rather than a more remote object. The IA building block seems to be less well established with peripheral auxiliaries than with core auxiliaries. Since peripheral auxiliaries have lower frequency than core auxiliaries, what we observe follows from a fundamental principle of oral-formulaic theory: that the most frequently used constituents have the most fixed or stable form (Parry 1928, 1933; Lord 1960).

Total stressed transitive infinitives:	**388**
With core auxiliaries:	**70**
With peripheral auxiliaries:	**16**
Following object in normative OI order,	
with its own object:	**132**
with object of another verb form:	**11**
Preceding object in IO order:	**5** (non-reversible)
Following subject in normative SI order:	**10**
Preceding subject in IS order:	**1** (703a)
Remainders	**143**

Although many transitive infinitives are found with their governing auxiliaries in IA building blocks, they share a type II verse more often with their governed objects. Like two-word OV verses with finite verbs, these two-word OI verses seem to be well established as building blocks with object-verb order. Metrical constraints of the highest rank are responsible for reversal of normative order in the five IO verses (387a, 1450a, 2591a, 2649a, 2754a). It is not surprising to find that the object-verb order in the typologist's representative SOV sentence should compete successfully with infinitive-auxiliary order for inclusion of transitive infinitives in two-word verses.

CHAPTER 10

REMAINDERS

§10.0 Introduction

Some of the constructions in this chapter are sufficiently complex to interest researchers who explore the outer limits of syntactic coherence. Their complexity has the expected inhibiting effect on their frequencies in *Beowulf* and these frequencies are sometimes so low that Sievers's evaluations of metrical acceptability have limited statistical significance. As we have seen (§1.14), this limitation of Sievers's system shows up with particular clarity in type D5. The universalist theory evaluates metrical acceptability by identifying departures from a wider variety of metrical norms and summing the additive complexities. The norms used for evaluation apply to every relevant verse in the poem and are properly grounded statistically.

§10.1 Clauses with conjoined verbs

In (1a–e) I interpret the two finite verbs as conjoined occupants of a single head position. On that analysis the clauses like (1e) have only one major constituent.

(1) (a)　　　　　　　*ond hē þā / **forð**-gesceaft*　　　　　　　sO/V&V

　　　　*(for)**gyteð** ond / (for)**gȳ**með* (1750b–51a)

　　　　'and he forgets and neglects the future state of things'

　　(b)　***hafa** nū / (ond ge)**heald**　**hū**sa / sēlest* (658)　　　(s)V&V/O

　　　　'maintain and protect the best of halls now'

　　(c)　*oð þæt him on / **in**nan　**ofer**-hygda / dæl*　　　　　S/V&V

　　　　***weax**eð / (ond) **wrī**dað* (1740a–41a; cf. 1766b–67a)

343

'until within him the degree of overconfidence grows and flourishes'

(d) **hēold** *mec / (ond)* **hæfde   Hrēðel** / *cyning* (2430)   Vo&V/S

'King Hrethel protected and maintained me'

(e) **wīston** / *(ond ne)* **wēndon** (1604a; cf. 161a, 600a, 2057a–58a)   (so)V&V

'(they) wished and did not expect' (anticipating a that-clause)

Stressed constituents in (1a, c) observe normative order. Displaced to the right periphery are a heavy modified object in (1b) and a heavy modified subject in (1d). In (1d) the unstressed object occupies metrical location x2 for metrical reasons. Placement of this object in location x1 would create unusual and unnecessary anacrusis. No clause pattern can be deduced from the evidence of the instances in (1e), which do not meet the requirements for discussion as verse clauses. The example at *Beowulf* 600a has the verbs paratactically juxtaposed rather than linked by an overt conjunction.

§10.2 HYBRID instances in which a short main clause with a finite verb of speaking, hearing, or thinking is followed in the same verse by the opening of a subordinate clause with its own finite verb

In (2a–g) a main clause shares a verse with the opening of a subordinate transitive clause. The boundary between clauses is marked by a colon in the notations. The reference of the unexpressed object in the main clause is specified in the subordinate clause. In (2a, f, g) the subject of the main clause is unexpressed, leaving more room for constituents of the subordinate clause.

(2) (a) *cwæð þæt se* / **ælmiht(i)ga   eorðan** / *worhte,*   (so)v:S/OV

  wlite-*beorhtne* / **wang** (92a–93a)

  '(he) said that the Almighty created earth, the beautiful bright plain'

  (b)   *ic ne* / **wāt** *hwæder*   (o)sV:S/OV

  atol / **æse** *wlanc* **eft**-*sīðas* / *tēah*

  fylle / *(ge)***frēcnod** (1331b–33a)

  'I do not know whither the horrid (one), emboldened by feasting, took his return pathways'

  (c) *hȳrde ic þæt þām* / **frætwum   fēower** / **mēaras**   (o)vs:Io/S/OV

  lungre, / *(ge)***līce** ,   **lāst** / *weardode,*

  æppel- / *feal(u)we* (2163a–65a)

344

'(I) heard that four horses, apple-fallow, swift, matched, guarded the rear for those treasures' (followed as the last items in a parade of splendid gifts)

(d) *wēn' ic* / *(þæt gē for) wlen*co,   nalles for / *wræc-sīð*um,   (o)Vs:s/OV

ac for / *hige-þrymmum* *Hrōð*gār / *sōhton* (338–39)

'I think that you sought out Hrothgar because of high spirits, by no means because of a journey into exile, rather because of great-heartedness'

(e) *hȳrde ic þæt hē ðone* / *heals-bēah* *Hygde* / *(ge)sealde,*   (o)Vs:sO/IoV

wrǣtlicne / *wund(u)r-māðð(u)m,* ðone þe him / *Wealhðēo geaf,*

*ðēod*nes / *dohtor,* *þrīo wicg* / *somod*

*swan*cor / *(ond) sadol-beorht* (2172a–75a)

'I heard that he gave that neck-ring to Hygd — the splendid wonder-treasure that Wealhtheow, a king's daughter, gave to him — three horses as well, supple and saddle-bright' (equipped with a splendid saddle)

(f) *mynte þæt hē ge-* / *dǣlde,* ǣr þon / *dæg cwōme*   (so)v:sV/O

atol / *āg-lǣca,* *ān*ra / *(ge)hwylces*

līf wið / *līce* (731a–33a; cf. 3096a–98a)

'(he) thought — that dire awe-inspirer — that he might divide the life of each of the individuals from the body before daytime should come'

(g) *cwæð þæt hyt* / *hæfde* *Hioro*gār / *cyning,*   (so)v:oV/S

lēod / *Scyldunga* *lange hwīle* (2158–59)

'(he) said that King Heorogar, a man of the Scyldings, had it a long time'

In (2a–d) stressed constituents of the verb phrase in the subordinate clause share a verse in normative order and the stressed verb stands at normative metrical position s4. In (2c) a cargo of treasure seems to be personified as a wealthy traveler with a rear guard of horses. I interpret the treasure as an indirect object beneficiary. Fronting of the direct object before the indirect object in (2e) makes it possible to express all major constituents as a single line. The major constituents are followed by variations of the arguments and a parenthetical relative clause with the finite verb at normative location s4. In (2f, g) the stressed constituents occupy separate verses. In (2f) a type II verse containing the object is displaced to the right periphery. In (2g) displacement of the heavy subject makes it possible to express the major constituents as a single line. In (2c–e) the main verb has been fronted before an unstressed subject to an available C position. Fronting of the stressed verbs in (2d, e) avoids placement of the pronouns in unusual and unnecessary anacrusis.

In items (3a, b) the main verb introduces an intransitive clause.

(3) (a) *cwæð þæt* / **wilcuman Weder**a *lēodum*   (s)v:/S/V

         scaþan / *scīr-hame* *tō* / *scipe fōron* (1894–95)

         '(he) said that the mailcoated warriors went to ship welcome to the people of

         the Geats' (that the Geats would be glad the warriors were sailing home)

   (b)   *þū* / **wāst** *gif hit is*   sV:V

         swā wē / **sōþlīce secgan** / *hȳrdon* (272b–73b)

         'you know if it is as we actually heard (someone) say'

In (3a) *cwæð* shares the opening verse with part of an adjunct phrase in the subordinate clause. The stressed subject and verb in the subordinate clause occupy separate verses in normative order, with the verb in metrical location s4. It may be appropriate to interpret *wilcuman* as an adjective zero-converted to an adverb, translating as 'agreeably' (cf. K4: cxlix). In either case *Wedera lēodum* would be an adjunct modifier of *wilcuman*. For other interpretations of this construction see the textual note in K4. In (3b) the 'be' verb is modified by the following subordinate clause, which functions as a predicate adverbial. Single alliteration does not contravene the rule of precedence in the opening verse because the 'be' verb is less prominent than the preceding verb.

     In (4a, b) the subordinate clause has a predicate adjective. Constituents sharing a verse observe normative SPj and PjV orders. No subordinating conjunction is expressed in (4b). The comma after *cwæð* in K4 provides a useful way to prevent misunderstanding of the first two words as 'said he,' with *hē* interpreted as subject of *cwæð* rather than of *tealde*.

(4) (a)   **frægn** *gif* / *(him) wǣre*   (s)V:ioB/SPj

         æfter / **nēod**-*laðum* **niht** *ge-* / *tǣse* (1319b–20b)

         '(he) asked if the night had been agreeable to him according to his desire'

   (b) *cwæð, hē þone* / **gūð**-*wine* **gōd**ne *tealde,*   (s)v:sO/PjV

         wīg- / *cræftigne* (1810a–11a)

         '(he) said he considered the war-friend (sword) strong, mighty in battle'

In both instances the verb of the subordinate clause occupies normative location s4. In (4a) the stressed verb is fronted beyond the subject to the opening verse. The verse with the subject and predicate adjective contains a trace of the moved verb and is a coherent syntactic construction rather than a pair of extraneous constituents. The subordinate clause in (4b) has the same syntax as the other instances with *tellan* in §6.12.

Items (5a, b) are predicate nominative constructions with the stressed constituents in separate verses. In (5a) unstressed *hyrde* has been moved before the unstressed subject to an available C position.

(5) (a) *hȳrde ic þæt / **Yrse** wæs / **Onelan** cwēn,*   vs:S/bPn

       ***Heaðo**-Scilfingas   **heals**-ge- / bedda* (62–63)

       'I heard that Yrse was Onela's Queen, the dear bedfellow of that Battle-Scylfing'

  (b) *cwǣdon þæt hē / **wǣre**   **wyruld**-cyninga*   (s)v:sB/Pn

       *man**na** / **mild**ust   ond / **mon**-ðwǣrust,*

       *lēodum / **līð**ost   ond / **lof**- / geornost* (3180–81)

       '(they) said that he was the kindest (one) of men, of earthly kings, most gracious to the people and most eager for praise'

As the note to (5a) in K4 explains, the emendation printed in the text has the unstressed SP *wæs* in the second verse of the clause, violating Kuhn's Laws and the SPMR. Further emendation may be required to make sense of this example. The very heavy predicate nominative in (5b) is elaborated in five verses displaced to the right periphery. This list of Beowulf's heroic virtues provides a conclusion for the poem, linking his desire for fame to his love for the people.

§10.3 Hybrid constructions with a clause-initial verb and a short subordinate clause

In (6a–e) the only expressed constituent of the main clause is an imperative or hortative subjunctive. Non-expression of the subject is routine in these instances. All examples have the verb of the subordinate clause at normative metrical location s4.

(6) (a)   ***wes** þenden / (þū) <u>lifige</u>,*   (s)B:sV/Pj

      ***æþeling**, / **ēa**dig* (1224b–25a)

      '(you) be blessed while you live, atheling'

  (b)   ***brūc** þenden / (þū) **mōte***   (s)V:sA:/O

      ***mani**gra / **mēd**o* (1177b–78a)

'(you) enjoy the rewarding of many while you have the ability'

(c) *sēc gif / (þū) dyrre* (1379b)   (so)V:sA

'(you) seek (it) if you are daring'

(d) *frem*me */ (sē þe) wille* (2766b cf. 1003b, 1394b)   (so)V:wsA

'(one should) try (it) who feels the desire'

(e)   *wyrce / (sē þe) mōte*   (s)V:wsA

*dōm*es */ (ǣr) dēaþe* (1387b–88a, gen. obj.)

'(one) who is capable should seek glory before death'

The alliterating main verb is imperative in (6a–c) and hortative in (6d, e). To situate the finite verb at normative location s4 in the subordinate clauses of (6a, b, e), major constituents of the main clause are delayed until the next line. If the verbs designated as 'A' in (6b–e) were Modern English auxiliaries they would require a following infinitive, expressed or unexpressed. The Old English antecedents of these auxiliaries "show only inchoate grammaticization," however, and can retain independent meaning, especially in the era of *Beowulf* (K4: cli). I retain the designation 'A' for these verbs to distinguish them from ordinary main verbs but they do not function as auxiliaries here. The translations are meant to approximate the independent meanings of the verbs.

In (7a–d) the first verb is declarative. All instances have the verb of the subordinate clause in line-final position. The core auxiliary *mōtan* seems to be used independently in (7c, d), as in (6b). In (7e) the infinitive governed by auxiliary *sceal* is understood from the infinitive in the immediately preceding clause.

(7) (a) *nāh hwā / sweord wege* (2252b)   (s)v:wsOV

'(I) do not have (anyone) who might bear a sword' (subjunctive verb)

(b)   *hēold þenden / lifde,*   (s)V:(s)V/O

gamol ond / gūð-rēouw, glæde / Scyldingas (57b–58b)

'while (he) lived, old and fierce in combat, (he) ruled the gracious Scyldings'

(c) *brēac þonne / mōste* (1487b)   (so)V:(s)A

'(I) enjoyed (it) while (I) had the ability'

(d)   *gǣþ eft sē / (þe) mōt*   Vs:wsA

tō / medo mōdig (603b–04a)

'he who has the ability goes high-spirited to mead' (simple present tense for future)

(e) *gǣð ā / **wyrd** swā hīo scel* (455b)   vS:sA

  'fate always proceeds as it must (proceed)'

In (7a) stressed constituents of the subordinate clause share the opening
verse in normative OV order. In (7b) line-final placement of *lifde* is achieved
by delaying the object of the main clause to a following verse, as in (6b).
Fronting of *gǣþ* to an alliterating position in (7d) avoids **eft sē (þe) / mōt
gǣþ*, with two stressed words in the second foot, which would be unacceptable whether or not *eft* alliterated (OE 3.4). In (7e) the same verb is fronted
to an available C position but without metrical stress. The unstressed pronoun SP *hēo* in (7e) occupies location x3 in the Sxxs foot, contravening OE
9.3. This is a very rare event within the poem as a whole but likelier to occur,
of course, in a verse with two clauses.

§10.4 Mixed constructions with two finite verbs and an unin-flected infinitive

In (8a–d) a short main clause introduces a clause with an infinitive construction. Stressed constituents sharing a verse observe normative IA order.

(8) (a)   *cwæð, hē / **gūð**-cyning*   (s)v:sO/IA

  *ofer / **swan**-rāde **sē**cean / wolde,*

  ***mǣrne** / þēoden* (199b–201a)

  '(he) said he would seek out the fighting king — that famous chieftain — over
  the swan-road (sea)'

 (b) *wēne ic þæt hē mid / **gōde** **gyl**dan / wille*   vs:s/IA/O

  ***un**cran / **eaferan** (1184a–85a)

  'I expect that he will repay our sons with good (things)'

 (c) *cwæð, hē on / **mergenne** **mē**ces / ecgum*   (s)v:s/IA/o?

  ***gē**tan wolde,   sum' on **galg**-trēowum*

  ***fug**lum / (tō) gamene* (2939a–41a)

  '(he) said in the morning he would kill some (enemies) with the edges of a
  sword on a gallows-tree as a joy to the birds'

 (d) ***wēn'** ic þæt hē / **wille**,   gif hē / **wealdan** mōt,*   Vs:sA/O/I

  *in þǣm / **gūð**-sele **Gēa**tena / lēode*

  ***etan** / **un**-forhte* (442a–44a)

'if he can prevail, I expect that he will eat people of the Geats without fear in the martial hall'

(e)   ***sæg****de / (sē þe) cūþe*   (s)V:wsA/O/I

frum*-sceaft / fīra* ***feor****ran / reccan* (90b–91b)

'(someone) spoke who could narrate the first creation of men from long ago'

The stressed auxiliary occupies normative metrical position s4 in (8a, b). In (8d, e) each stressed constituent occupies a separate verse. The syntax of (8c) is difficult to interpret. Unstressed *sum'*, a contracted form of accusative plural *sume,* appears to supply an object for *gētan;* but placement of this unstressed SP in the fourth verse of a clause would be a spectacular violation of Kuhn's first law and the SPMR. One or more verses may be missing here. See the note in K4 for various conjectures. In (8b, d) the two clauses sharing the verse create an unusually long string of unstressed syllables. The abbreviated form *wēn'* in (8d) shortens the string and might originally have been present in in (8b) as well. In both instances *wēn(e)* is fronted before the unstressed subject to an available C position. Placement of stressed *wēn'* in (8d) avoids unnecessary anacrusis.

In (9a, b) *þǣm* functions as relativized indirect object of the main verb and the following pronoun functions as relativized subject of the subordinate clause. Item (9a) is the ancestor of a construction that survives into archaic Modern English expressions like *woe is me!*

(9) (a)   ***wā*** *bið þǣm / (ðe) sceal*   PnBwio:wsA/OI

þurh / ***slīð****ne nīð* ***sāw****le / (be)scūfan*

in / ***fȳ****res* ***fæþm*** (183b–85a)

'(it) is a misery for one who must throw the soul into the fire's embrace through dire necessity'

(b)   ***wēl*** *bið þǣm / (þe) mōt*   Pdwio:wsA/OI

æfter / ***dēað****-dæge* ***drih****ten / sēcean* (186b–87b)

'(it) is well for one who may seek the lord after the day of death'

Items (9a, b) are adjacent in the poem and have a parallelistic rhetorical effect, highlighting the binary opposition of joy and sorrow that pervades the poem. In (9a) I interpret *wā* as a predicate nominative. In (9b) the adverb *wēl* forms a predicate adverbial construction with the 'be' verb. In the K4 glossary entry for *wā,* the editors cite an alternative interpretation of *wā* as an adverb. Under that interpretation, (9a) and (9b) would have the same clause pattern. In both instances the finite verb occupies normative metrical location s4 in the opening b-verse and its governed infinitive occupies location s4 in a following line. The infinitives share the b-verse with their objects in normative OI syntactic order.

Items (10a–d) are the remaining instances. In (10a) *wolde* appears to function independently, with no understood infinitive.

(10) (a)   *nefne* / **god** *sylfa,*   S/Awio:sA:/OI

         sigora / **sōð**-*cyning,*   **seal**de *(þām ðe hē)* / *wolde*

         hord / **ope**nian (3054b–57a)

         'unless God himself, truth-king of victories, allowed to open the hoard whomever he selected'

     (b)   *ne sceal þǣr* / **dyrne** *sum*   aPjS/I:/sV

         wesan, *þæs* / *(ic)* **wē**ne (271b–72a)

         'any particular thing shall not be secret there, as I suppose' (nothing shall be secret, etc.)

     (c) **wesan,** *þenden* / *(ic)* **wealde**   **wī**dan / **rī**ces,   (a)I:sV/O:/SPj

         māþmas / *(ge)***mǣ**ne

         (1859a–60a, gen. obj. in interjected subordinate clause)

         'treasures (shall) be shared while I rule the spacious kingdom'

     (d) **drun**cne / **dryht**-*guman*   **dōð** *swā* / *(ic) bidde* (1231)   S/V:sV

         'supplied with drink, the male retainers do as I bid'

In (10a, d) the main verb shares a b-verse with a short subordinate clause and the verb in the short clause occupies normative location s4. In the poem as a whole placement of a finite verb at location s1a in the b-verse is rare but in (10a, d) both stressed constituents of the b-verse are finite verbs and the first one must provide the mandatory alliteration. Since the verbs have comparable prominence there is no violation of the rule of precedence. Stressed constituents sharing a verse in (10a, c) observe normative OI and SPj orders. The predicate adjective *dyrne* in (10b) is out of normative order with the subject *sum,* which bears phrase-final stress in a verse of type B1 (x/Sxs). If *sum* preceded *dyrne* here it would lack stress and the result would be a verse of type A7 (xx/Sx), a type unacceptable in the b-verse. Interposition of *sum* between the predicate adjective and its governing verb also avoids enjambment in this case. Item (10c) appears in a long, unbroken sequence of clauses with unexpressed auxiliaries. The expressed antecedent is *sceal* in *Beowulf* 1855b. Within the interjected subordinate clause the modified object is displaced beyond its governing finite verb. Within the discontinuous main clause the infinitive 'be' verb is fronted to metrical location s1a in the opening verse, while subject and predicate adjective follow the interjected clause in a type II verse. Although 'be' verbs like *wesan* have lower prominence than corresponding forms of main verbs like *wealdan*, there is no clear infraction of the rule of prominence in (10d) because the 'be' verb is an infinitive and the main verb is finite.

§10.5 The remaining hybrid constructions with an uninflected infinitive

The infinitive governs a predicate adverb in (11a), a predicate adjective in (11b), a predicate nominative in (11c), and the participle of a passive construction in (11d). The subject in (11d) is split from its adjectival modifiers by hyperbaton. Stressed constituents sharing a verse observe normative PdI, PjI, and SI orders. In (11d) *gār* is split by the verb from its modifying adjective *monig* in a typical instance of hyperbaton.

(11) (a) *ne mæg ic hēr / **leng** wesan* (2801b)   as/PdI

        'I cannot be here longer'

    (b)   *scolde his / **ald(o)r-gedāl***   aS/PjI

        *on / **ðǣm** dæge **þysses** / līfes*

        ***earm**līc / wurðan* (805b–7a)

        'his death had to be wretched on that day of this worldly life'

    (c)   *swylc sceolde / **secg** wesan,*   pna/SI

        þegn** æt / **ðearfe (2708b–9a; cf. 1328b–29a)

        'such (a one) should a man be — a thane at need'

    (d)   *forðon sceall / **gār** wesan*   aSI/Pt

        ***monig** / **morgen**-ceald **mundum** / bewunden,*

        hæfen** on / **handa (3021b–23a)

        'therefore shall many a morning-cold spear be wound with palms, taken in hand'

In (11a) the negated auxiliary is attracted to a C position in the left periphery. In (11a, c, d) the infinitives occupy metrical location s4, as usual when not followed by a finite verb. In (11b) the infinitive occupies metrical location s2. The other instance like (11c) has a similar opening verse, with *eorl* rather than *secg* for alliteration.

Items (12a–c) are existential constructions with infinitives. The 'be' verbs have their common meanings 'be present' and 'occur.' Constituents sharing a verse observe normative IA and SA orders.

(12) (a) *mǣl is/ (mē tō) fēran* (316a)   SbioI

      'the time to go is present for me' (it is time for me to go)

  (b) *þurh hwæt his / **worulde gedāl**   weorðan / sceolde* (3068)   S/IA

      'by what (cause) his separation from the world should occur' (what would cause his death)

  (c)   *ac unc **feohte** sceal*   ioSA/I

      weorðan** æt **wealle (2525b–26a)

      'but for us two combat shall occur at the wall'

In (12a) *fēran* is governed by *tō*, like *fērenne*, the inflected form. Mitchell (OES 1: 408) observes that inflected and uninflected infinitive forms sometimes alternate in otherwise similar constructions. Here the infinitive phrase functions as adjunct modifier of a noun, as an inflected infinitive phrase would do. In this unusual instance the subject noun does not alliterate and occupies metrical location x1, as with prominent SPs like finite verbs. A few similar verses can be found in Old Norse poetry (Russom 1987: 111). Item (12b) is a one-line clause with the caesura in the ideal location, between a subject and constituents of the verb phrase. In (12c) the stressed auxiliary occupies normative metrical location s4 and the existential infinitive occupies location s1a in the following a-verse, with alliteration on the more prominent noun as required by the rule of precedence. If the infinitive occupied its more usual location at the end of the verse we would have **(æt) **wealle** / **weorðan***, with easily avoidable anacrusis (OE 9.6).

In items (13a, b) a predicate adjective phrase functions as the object complement of an infinitive verb. The similar item (13c) has a predicate adverbial phrase as complement of *wiste*. More idiomatic Modern English translations would have *to be* before the complement but there is no need to posit an unexpressed infinitive in a minimalist analysis of such Old English verses (§6.12).

(13) (a)   *þāra þe hē / cēnoste*   wosPj/IA

*fin*dan / *mihte* (206b–7a; cf. 2869b–70b)

'of those whom he could find bravest'

(b) **bæd** hine / **blīðne** *æt þǣre* / **bēor**-*þege,* (si)AoPj

lēodum / **lēof**ne (617a–18a)

'(she) ordered him happy at the beer-feast — (a man) dear to the people'

(c) *wiste his* / **fin**gra geweald (s)vO/Pd

on / **grames grā**pum (764b–65a)

'he knew the power of his fingers in his enemy's grasp'

In (13a) the object is relativized from an underlying clause equivalent to *he could find them bravest,* where both constituents in *them bravest* receive accusative case from the transitive infinitive *findan.* The stressed constituents share a verse in normative order. I interpret the syntax in (13b) as analogous to *she made him happy.* Placement of the unstressed pronoun SP in metrical location x2 creates a verse of type A5 (Sxx/Sx). The verb-final alternative, *hine* / **blīðne bæd**, has alliteration on a weakly stressed constituent occupying a subordinate s position, contravening OE 7.5. The unstressed verb in (13c) occupies normative metrical location x1 and the stressed constituents are in normative syntactic order. I interpret the syntax as analogous to *he saw his fingers in the enemy's grip.*

In (14a–c) an infinitive 'be' verb is unexpressed. Stressed constituents sharing a verse observe normative PjA , IoA, and SPj orders.

(14) (a) *nealles* / **Het**ware **hrēm**ge / *þorfton* (i)S/PjA

fēðe- / *wīges* (2363a–64a)

'the Hetware by no means needed (to be) proud of the battle on foot'

(b) *þæt þām* / **fol**cum sceal, (i)IoA/SPj

Gēata / *lēodum ond* / **Gār**-denum[,]

sib ge- / **mǣ**nu (1855b–57a)

'that for those populations, the people of the Geats and the Spear-Danes, peace shall (be) mutual'

(c) *unc sceal* / **worn** fela (i)ioaS/Pj

māþma / *(ge)***mǣn**ra (1783b–84a; cf. 2659b–60b)

'for us two a great many treasures shall (be) mutual' (we shall share many treasures)

The stressed auxiliaries occupy normative metrical location s4 in (14a, b). In the syntactically complete first line of (14a) the caesura falls in the ideal location between the subject and major constituents of the verb phrase. In (14b) a type II verse with the subject and predicate adjective is displaced to the right periphery. In a minimalist analysis the auxiliary would be represented by a trace and the unexpressed 'be' verb would be represented by a null auxiliary with no phonological content (cf. Radford 1997: 137). On that analysis *sib gemǣnu* is a psychologically complete two-word verse appropriate for placement at the end of the clause. In (14c) the unstressed auxiliary and the unstressed pronoun share normative location x1 in normative order.

In (15a–c) a core auxiliary appears without an expressed infinitive. I include (15b, c) for illustrative purposes although they do not qualify for discussion as verse clauses, since their only expressed major constituents are arguments rather than verbs.

(15) (a) *ðǣr hīe / **meah**ton swā*   (797b; cf. 762b, 2091b)   s A

   'if they were sufficiently capable'

   (b) *swā nū / **gȳt** dêð*   (1134b)   (s)A

   'as (it) still does now'

   (c) *nō þȳ ǣr / **fram** meahte*   (754b)   (si)A

   'no sooner for that might (he go) away'

In (15a) *magan* can be used with its independent meaning 'be capable' and there is no need to posit an unexpressed infinitive (OES 1: 424). No unexpressed infinitive is posited in (15b) because OE *dōn* did not yet govern infinitives as the Old English pre-modals did (OES 1: 264). The construction in (15c), with an unexpressed infinitive verb of motion, survives into the Early Modern era.

§10.6 Constructions with impersonal *geweorðan*

These constructions are particularly challenging.

(16) (a) *lēte **Sūð**-Dene   sylfe / (ge)weorðan*   aO/I?

   *gūðe / (wið) **Grend**el*   (1996a–97a)

   'in respect of the feud with Grendel (you) let be (give over) to the South-Danes themselves'

   (b) *þā ðæs / **monige** gewearð*   (1598b)   OV?

'then in respect of this (it) struck many' (anticipating a that-cause)

(c) *hafað þæs ge- / **worden** **wine** / Scyldinga,*   aPt/O?

rīces / hyrde (2026a–27a)

'(it) has struck the friend of the Scyldings in respect of this (the friend of the Scyldings has agreed to this)'

The imperative construction in (16a) seems to anticipate Modern English *let be,* used to discourage someone from unwise involvement in a hopeless situation. As Mitchell observes (OES, 1: 436), *geweorðan* means something like 'strike' in clauses like (16b), where it governs an accusative object. It is as if the dative argument in a construction like 'it occurred to many' had been changed to accusative to represent a thought as plausible enough to compel acceptance by an impartial experiencer. If so this construction would provide another example of an accusative animate object functioning as indirect — in this case, as indirect object of an intransitive verb. Mitchell goes on to equate 'it struck them' with 'they agreed' in instances like (16c). Like many of the constructions in this chapter, those like (16b, c) are topics for further linguistic research. For our purposes the metrical facts are clear enough. The unstressed peripheral auxiliary in (16a) is fronted to metrical location x1 and the infinitive stands at the end of the line, its normative metrical position when not followed by an auxiliary. Stressed constituents occupy their normative locations in (16b). In (16c) the heavy accusative argument is displaced to the right periphery.

§10.7 Manuscript verses with an inflected infinitive (In)

The Old English inflected infinitive developed from a dative verbal noun and retained a dative inflection after the infinitive suffix (Campbell 1959: 299). Inflected infinitives are preceded by *tō,* which governs the dative case when used as a preposition. Like all infinitives, the inflected ones are more prominent than finite verbs. Infinitive phrases like *tō **healdanne*** in (17d) have the same weight as two-word prepositional phrases, which are often displaced to the right periphery.

In (17a–d) the inflected infinitive has a Modern English translation as a dative noun in a prepositional phrase. In these instances the infinitive is not governed by an auxiliary and functions as the adjunct modifier of a predicate adjective, as in (17a, b); of a predicate noun, as in (17c); or of a direct object noun, as in (17d). In (17c) an adjective is split from its modified object noun by hyperbaton. For comprehensive analysis of inflected infinitives I will include them in the notation but parenthesize them when they function as adjuncts to show that they are not part of basic sentence structure. Sievers and some researchers who use his evaluative techniques argue for deletion of the dative inflection in (17b) and four other type D verses (K4: 328). The other type D verses are (18c–e) and (21b) below.

(17) (a) *wǣron / **æþelingas*** *eft tō / lēodum*　　　　　　　　bS/Pj(In)

　　　　*fūse / (tō) **faren**ne* (1804a–5a)

　　　　'the athelings were eager for a journey back to their people'

　　(b) *(tō) **lang** ys /(tō) **reccen**(ne)* (2093a)　　　　　　　　Pjb(In)

　　　　'(it) is too long for narration'

　　(c) *þæt þe / **Sǣ**-gēatas　**sēl**ran / næbben*　　　　　　　S/V/(In)/O

　　　　*tō ge- / **cēo**senne　**cyning** / ǣnigne,*

　　　　***hord**-weard / **hæle**þa* (1850a–52a)

　　　　'that the Sea-Geats will not have for a choice any better king, hoard-guardian of heroes'

　　(d) *seleð him on / **ēþle**　**eor**þan / wynne*　　　　　　　(s)Vio/O/(In)

　　　　*tō / **heal**danne,　**hlēo**-burh wera* (1730–31)

　　　　'(he) gives him in his homeland an earthly delight for a possession, a fortress of men'

In (17a, b) the inflected infinitive follows the more prominent predicate adjective that it modifies. In (17d) a syntactically complete one-line clause is followed by an adjunct inflected infinitive that modifies the object. In (17c) the subject split by hyperbaton is *sēlran cyning ǣnigne*. Unstressed finite verbs occupy normative metrical location x1 in (17a, d). The contract negative finite verb in (17c) is not fronted and remains at metrical location s4. Unstressed *ys* in (17b) is placed at location x2 for metrical reasons. Placement of *ys* at location x1 would create an unacceptable type II verse with a verb in anacrusis.

In (18a–f) the inflected infinitive has evolved farther from its nominal origin and is more difficult to translate as the object of a preposition. In (18a, b) the infinitives are governed by finite peripheral auxiliaries, like many uninflected infinitives. In (18c) the infinitive is governed by a participial auxiliary, as in Modern English sentences like *This employee was found to exceed expectations.* The inflected infinitives are major sentence constituents in these instances. See Mitchell (OES 1: 408) on occasional use of inflected infinitive forms for uninflected ones and vice versa. In (18d–f) the infinitive is not governed by an auxiliary and is parenthesized in the notation.

(18) (a)   *ōðres ne / **gȳme**ð*   (s)V/In/O

                *tō ge- / **bī**danne **burg**um / (in) innan*

                yrfe- / weardas (2451b–53a, gen. obj.)

                '(he) does not expect to see another heir in the dwellings'

    (b)   *þēah ðe / **hlā**ford ūs*   SIo/O/A/In

                *þis / **ellen**-weorc **ā**na / (ā)ðōhte*

                *tō ge- / **frem**manne, **folc**es / hyrde* (2642b–44b)

                'though (our) lord, guardian of the people, intended to perform this work of valor by himself for us'

    (c)   *ðā wæs / **hring**-bogan **heor**te / (ge)fȳsed*   b/S/Pt/OIn

                *sæcce / (tō) **sē**cean(ne)* (2561a–62a)

                'then the heart of the curve-twisted (serpent) was aroused to seek combat'

    (d)   *wund(o)r is / (tō) secgan(ne)*   (s)Pnb(In)

                *hū / **mih**tig god **man**na / cynne*

                *þurh / **sī**dne sefan **snyt**tru / bryttað,*

                *eard ond / **eorl**scipe* (1724b–26b)

                '(it) is a wonder to relate how mighty God distributes wisdom, land and lordship to the kindred of men'

    (e) *sorh (is mē tō) secgan(ne) on / **sefan** mīnum*   PnbioS

                *gume**na / æ**ngum* (473a–74a)   where S = (o)In

                'to say (that) to any (one) of men is a sorrow to me in my heart' (anticipating a relative clause)

    (f)   *ofost is / **sē**lest*   (o)SbPj/(In)

                *tō ge- / **cȳ**ðanne* (256b–57a)

                'haste to reveal (that) is best' (anticipating a clause)

In (18a) the adjectival modifier *ōðres* has been split by hyperbaton from the whole-verse compound object *yrfeweardas*, a variant spelling of genitive singular *yrfeweardes*. In normal syntactic position after *ōðres*, *yrfeweardas* would overburden the opening verse. Since it takes a direct object, the infinitive in (18c) cannot be translated as a noun unless its object argument is changed to object of an adjunct prepositional phrase, as for example in *the serpent was aroused for the pursuit of vengeance*, which seems unidiomatic though arguably grammatical. *The serpent was prepared for the pursuit of vengeance*, though more idiomatic, does not quite express the same meaning. The referent for the unexpressed subject in (18d) is specified by the subordinate how-clause and the infinitive is an adjunct modifier of the predicate nominative *wundor*. Compare *that is a tale for the telling,* used to assert that a narrative has the reportable content that it ought to have. If the infinitive governed the clause, (18d) would assert that telling how God distributes wisdom is a wonder, but the wonder is what God does rather than the report of it. In (18e), on the other hand, the misery for Hrothgar is *saying* that he has been unsuccessful in defending his people. Here the infinitive phrase functions as subject. In (18f) the infinitive phrase is an adjunct modifier of the subject, from which it is split by hyperbaton. Instances like (18d–f) test the limits of the notation and are obvious candidates for deeper syntactic analysis. The metrical facts are clear enough, however. The stressed peripheral auxiliaries in (18a, b) occupy normative metrical location s4. Whole-verse infinitive phrases are displaced to the right periphery in (18a–c, f). Placement of an unstressed 'be' verb after the first stress rather than in normative location x1 avoids unacceptable anacrusis in (18d, e).

In (19a, b) inflected infinitives are in close construction with adverbs.

(19) (a)   *næs him* / *feor þanon*   (s)bioPd/(InO)

              tō ge- / *sēcanne*   *sinces* / *bryttan,*

              Higelāc Hrēþling (1921b–23a)

              'from there for him (it) was not far to seek the distributor of treasure'

    (b)   *Denum eallum* / *wæs,*   IoB/S

              winum / *Scyldinga*   *weorce* / *(on) mōde*

              tō ge- / *þolianne*   *ðegne* / <u>*monegum,*</u>

              oncȳð / *eorla gehwǣm* (1417b–20a)

              'to suffer painfully in the mind, a distress for each (one) of earls, came to pass for all the Danes, for the friends of the Scyldings, for many (a one) of thanes'

In (19a) the infinitive phrase is an adjunct modifier of a predicate adverb. In (19b) I interpret the infinitive as a verbal noun subject modified by an adjunct adverbial phrase. The indirect object is varied three times, emphasizing that the ghastly death of Æschere was deeply felt by everyone who knew him. The unstressed contract negative 'be' verb comes first as usual in (19a).

In (19b) the stressed 'be' verb occupies normative metrical position s4 and the whole-verse inflected infinitive is displaced to the right periphery.

In (20a–c) the logical object of an inflected infinitive is the subject of a predicate adjective construction and the infinitive is an adjunct modifier of the predicate adjective. These instances are textbook examples of TOUGH MOVEMENT, so called with an eye to expressions like *Baker is tough to discourage* (Crystal 1985: 312; Rezac 2006). Mitchell (OES 1: 641–46) discusses similar constructions in Old English prose. The translations in parentheses are for alternative constructions with a phrasal subject in which the logical object of the inflected infinitive is its direct object.

(20) (a)   *nō þæt ȳðe byð*   sPjB/(In)

                *tō be- / **flēonne*** (1002b–3a)

                'that is by no means easy to escape' (cf. 'to escape that is by no means easy')

     (b) *hwæt / **swīð**-ferhðum   **sēlest** / wære*   sIo/PjB/(In)

                *wið / **fær**-gryrum   tō ge-**frem**manne* (173–74)

                'what might be best to do for stout-hearted (men) against sudden attacks' (cf. 'to do that against sudden attacks might be best for stout-hearted men')

     (c) *swā bið / **geō**morlīc   **gome**lum / ceorle*   (s)bPj/Io/(In)

                *tō ge- / **bī**danne* (2444a–45a)

                '(that) is so sad to endure for an old man' (cf. 'to endure that is so sad for an old man')

All major constituents observe normative order in (20a, b). In (20c) the unstressed 'be' verb is fronted to normative metrical location x1. The major constituents, which do not include the inflected infinitive, are arranged as a syntactically complete verse in (20a) and as a syntactically complete line in (20b, c). The whole-verse infinitive adjuncts are displaced to a following line.

In (21a, b) the logical object of an inflected infinitive functions as a predicate noun modified by an adjective. OE *þæt* and *swylc* function as pronoun subjects in these predicate nominative constructions. I interpret *gumena ænigum* and *idese* as semantically inessential adjuncts. The parenthesized translations are for alternative constructions with a predicate adjective instead of an adjectival modifier and a direct object instead of a predicate noun.

(21) (a)   *næs þæt / ȳðe cēap*   bsPn/(In)

tō ge- / ***gangenne*** ***gume***na / *ǣnigum* (2415b–16b)

'that wasn't an easy purchase to obtain for any man' (cf. 'to obtain that purchase wasn't easy for any man')

(b)   *ne bið swylc* / ***cwēnlīc*** / *þēaw*   bsPn/(In)

idese / *(tō) efnan(ne)* (1940b–41a)

'such a thing is not a queenly thing to do for a lady' (cf. 'to do such a thing is not queenly for a lady')

Items (21a, b) have very complex syntax but it is not particularly difficult to see how the metrical constraints apply. The negated verbs are fronted to available C positions as usual. In (21a) the infinitive and its modifier occupy separate verses. The modified noun adjunct is heavier than the infinitive adjunct and is displaced beyond it. In (21b) semantically inessential *idese* fits within the same verse as the infinitive. No matter how we analyze the syntax here, the infinitive must follow *idese* to avoid unacceptable anacrusis, in type A if we omit the dative inflection or in type E if we include it.

§10.8 Metrical complexity in groups of examples too small to be reliably analyzed by Sievers's methods

Inflected infinitives provide a good opportunity to show how the universalist theory analyzes some variants that are regarded as unacceptable by Sievers because they are rare realizations of his verse types, which he represents as a pattern of stress and vowel length. Verse 1941a in item (21b) is an instance of Sievers type D* (Sx/Ssx). Other D* verses with inflected infinitives are 473a (item 18e), 1724b (item 18d), 2093a (item 17b) and 2562a (item 18c). I classify instances of type D* as type D6 when the verse begins with a trochaic word but as type D2 with an extrametrical syllable when the first word is a stressed monosyllable followed by one or more unstressed words. I exclude from consideration verses 1125b, 2671b, and 1663b, which might be analyzed as type D5 (Sx/Sxx). Verses classified as type D* are complex on any analysis and most of them appear in the a-verse with double alliteration. From Sievers's perspective other realizations of type D* look like anomalies to be emended if possible (K4: 331). Removal of the inflection from the infinitives creates a variant of type A1 that is acceptable to Sievers and emendation is suggested even for items (21b) and (18c, e), which are a-verses with double alliteration (K4: 328). What makes makes type D* anomalous within Sievers's system is the unstressed syllable after the first stress, which violates Sievers's four-position rule. Type D* contrasts with type Da

(S/Ssx), which has four metrical positions as scanned by Sievers and is not regarded as an anomalous candidate for emendation.

Evaluation of verses with inflected infinitives is quite different in a theory that defines verse types as word patterns bound by OE 6.2, a metrical equivalent of the rule for stress subordination in a language with SOV syntax. This rule plays a crucial role in placement of type D verses with an Ssx foot in second position. Within an a-verse of type D, an S position in an Ssx foot is subordinated to an S position in the first foot. Since it is subordinated only once, the S position of the Ssx foot is eligible for alliteration. If its s position is occupied by a prominent noun or adjective, or by the secondary constituent of a poetic compound, the S position in the Ssx foot must alliterate in order to create the required strong-weak prominence contour (OE 7.3, RP 7). Alliteration on the S position of an Ssx word group is not required if the s position is occupied by a less prominent constituent (K4: 334). In such word groups the prominence contour is strong-weak either way and alliteration is optional. The prominence of every lift is reduced when type D occupies the b-verse. Here the second S position is doubly subordinated and is no longer eligible for alliteration.

Let us take a closer look at the determinants for placement of Sievers's types D* and Da, notating all unstressed syllables between the S positions as constituents of the first foot in accord with Sievers's scansion system. Four-position type Da occurs a total of 388 times in *Beowulf*, 195 times in the a-verse and 193 times in the b-verse. Among the 195 a-verses, the second foot is occupied 73 times by a poetic compound and two times by a word group with a prominent second constituent (896a, 1485a). Double alliteration is obligatory for these 75 instances and they comprise 19% of the 388 total instances. Five-position type D* occurs 132 times in *Beowulf*, 122 times in the a-verse and 10 times in the b-verse. Among the 122 a-verses there are 99 with an Ssx poetic compound and three with a prominent sx constituent in an Ssx word group. All 102 of these a-verses require double alliteration and they comprise 77% of the 132 total instances. Type D* shows such a strong preference for the a-verse in part because the percentage of instances requiring double alliteration is nearly four times as high as in type Da. If we scan according to the manuscript and restrict attention to instances that do not require double alliteration, type Da appears 113 times in the a-verse and 188 times in the b-verse. Type D* appears 24 times in the a-verse and ten times in the b-verse.

The prominence of subordinate constituents in Ssx feet also influences verse placement in type D verses that are not categorically restricted to the first half of the line. As with unstressed constituents, there is a gradation of meaningful prominence among syllables with subordinate stress. The most prominent have significant information content and have not undergone significant changes in form. Several are adjectives and participles subordinated to the stressed prefix *un-* (Campbell 1959: 31–32). Such constituents occur in nine Da verses like *torn unlȳtel* 'no little pain' (833a), five times in the a-verse and four times in the b-verse (cf. 444a, 498a, 960a, 3012a; 120b, 127b, 2413b, 2821b). The two comparable instances in type D* are split evenly between a-verse and b-verse: *æðeling / **unwrecen*** 'unavenged atheling' (2443a) and ***seah** on / unlēofe* 'he looked on the unloved (men)' (2863b). Secondary constituents of non-poetic compounds also retain significant stress, as shown by the fact that they are spelled like independent words. The only example in type Da is *fēond / man-cynnes* 'enemy of mankind' (164b). In type D* there are six examples like ***him** on / andsware* 'to him in answer' (1840b), two in the b-verse and four in the a-verse (cf. 689a, 1002a, 1351a, 1453a, 2432b). Forms used as suffixes also retain significant prominence if their resemblance to independent words is easy to recognize. Suffixes in type D include *-līc* (6X), *-sum* (612a), *-full* (3099a), *-lēas* (2613), and *-scipe* (1727a, 2751a). These occupy the s position in two Da verses like *(ge)sægd / sōðlīce* 'stated truly,' both with anacrusis (141a; cf. 3062a). The two b-verses are ***un** / -murnlīce* 'not regretfully' (449b) and ***un-*** / *wāclīcne* 'not sparingly' (3138b), both with stressed *un-*. There are 9 a-verses of type D* like ***wīgend** / **weorðfullost*** 'a most worthy combatant' (3099a; cf. 356a, 612a, 1027a, 1727a, 2136a, 2613a, 2646a, 2751a). No b-verse examples occur. In all there are fourteen Da verses with wordlike secondary constituents. They are split evenly between the two halves of the line, with 7 a-verses and 7 b-verses. They comprise 5% of 301 total instances that are permissible in the b-verse and have higher frequency there, with 188 instances (62%) as compared with 113 instances in the a-verse (38%). The seventeen type D* verses with wordlike secondary constituents have higher frequency in the a-verse, with fourteen instances (82%) as compared with three in the b-verse (18%). They comprise 50% of 34 total instances that occur 24 times in the a-verse (71%) and ten times in the b-verse (29%). Although these wordlike secondary constituents are acceptable in the b-verse they create an attraction to the a-verse. This attraction affects only a small percentage of Da verses but half of the D* verses.

Suffixes that do not correspond to independent words can be divided into two groups, heavy and light. A HEAVY SUFFIX ends in two consonants. Heavy suffixes occupy s positions primarily when followed by an unstressed word-final syllable but occasionally when they appear in word-final position (K4: 330). The number of word-final instances is significant but relatively small compared to the number of instances with a noun or adjective root in final position. This can be attributed to the principle that relative prominence is most sharply delineated at word-level, in the smallest prosodic domain (Kiparsky 2018). In word-medial position a heavy suffix contrasts with the immediately preceding primary stress and the immediately following zero stress. In word-final position there is no contrast with zero stress and the stress on the heavy suffix is less conspicuous. There are 127 type Da verses with a heavy suffix on the s position, comprising 42% of the Da verses that are permissible in the second half of the line. Once again these are evenly distributed between the two halves of the line, with 63 a-verses like *hæleð* / *hīofende* 'sighing heroes' (3142a) and 64 b-verses like *lond* / *Bron-dinga* 'land of the Brondings' (521b). The seven type D* verses with heavy suffixes comprise 22% of those permissible in the b-verse. Given their inherent complexity and the influence of the heavy suffix, it is not surprising to find that all seven instances are a-verses like *þēoden* / *Scyldinga* (1675a, 1871a; cf. 906a, 913a, 1154a, 2439a, 2734a).

We now turn to constituents that create an attraction to the b-verse when they occupy an s position in type D. There is a good sample of Da verses with Ssx proper names that have subordinate nouns as secondary constituents. The nouns are spelled correctly in these proper names but they are used without regard for their meanings and seem to be less prominent than wordlike constituents with significant information content. There are 67 Da verses with a noun root in the secondary constituent of an Ssx proper name, comprising 22% of instances permissible in the b-verse. Of the 67 Da verses, 24 are a-verses like *bearn* / *Healfdenes* 'Halfdane's child' (469a) and 43 are b-verses like *sweord* / *Bīowulfes* 'Beowulf's sword' (2681b). There are only four corresponding verses of type D*, comprising 13% of instances permissible in the b-verse. Type D* seems to be confined to the a-verse in part because it has a lower percentage of proper names attracted to the b-verse. The attraction to the b-verse is evident in these four instances. The only a-verse is *eaforum* / *Ecgwelan* 'descendants of Ecgwela,' dat. sg. (1710a). The b-verses are *dohtor* / *Hrōðgāres* 'Hrothgar's daughter' (2020b), *ðēoden* / *Heaðo-Beardna* 'lord of the Heathobards' (2032b), and *dēad is* / *Æschere* 'Aeschere is dead' (1323b). As the editors make clear (K4: 331–32), these instances in the b-verse cannot be eliminated by uncontroversial techniques of emendation based on a sizable number examples in *Beowulf* — techniques like those used by Sievers for emendation of contract forms or epenthetic vowels, for example (Russom 1998: 60–63). Scansion of 1710a or 1323b as Sx/Ss would posit two otherwise rare violations of the rule of the coda in an independently defined set of four verses. Reduction of 2020b and 2032b to

S/Ssx would add two otherwise rare instances of unetymolo-gical parasiting in *dohtor* and *ðēoden,* contrary to the prevailing trend in *Beo-wulf* toward correct metrical employment of archaisms (Fulk 1992).

In a few old Ssx compounds, lexicalization proceeded so far that the secondary constituent lost its independent meaning entirely, underwent phonological reduction, and was no longer spelled like the corresponding independent word. Such compounds appear five times in type Da, always in the b-verse (153b, 1498b, 1769b, 2620b, and the secondary constituent of the triple compound at 2778b). In four of these instances the Ssx word is *missere* (possibly *missēre*). The only instance in type D* is an a-verse, *yrre / ōretta* 'angry warrior' (1532a).

Realization of the Ssx foot as a word group creates metrical complexity in type D and promotes employment in the a-verse, all other things being equal. When the sx constituent of the word group is a finite verb or a function word, however, its weakly stressed syllable is strongly attracted to the least prominent lift at the end of the line, promoting employment in the b-verse. In type Da there are two instances with sx function words, both b-verses: **strēam** / *ūt þonan* 'a stream (flowed) out from there' (2545b) and **bēah** / *eft þonan* '(he) fled back from there' (2956b). The instances in type D* are **ðolode** / *ǣr fela* 'previously he suffered much' (1525b), **fērdon** / **forð** *þonon* 'they fared forth from there' (1632a), and **oft** *sceall* / **eorl** *monig* 'many an earl shall (endure exile) often' (3077a). Here as in other cases the complexity of verses analyzed by Sievers as type D* creates a strong attraction to the a-verse but the constituent on the s position can counteract this influence. Emending **ðolode** / *ǣr fela*, the instance of type D* in the b-verse, requires an unusual form of elision between the last syllable of *ðolode* and *ǣr,* which must bear stress for normal scansion. Elision is securely attested in Germanic alliterative meters, with many instances required in compound feet that would otherwise scan as Sxxxs, a pattern that does not occur in Old English compounds (Russom 1998: 139–44). In the securely attested instances, however, both of the elided syllables are unstressed.

The SOV norm strongly promotes placement of finite verbs at the end of the line. All instances of type Da that end in finite verbs are b-verses. Five are like like **weras** / *on sāwon* 'the men looked on' (1650b), with a finite verb at the end of an Ssx word group (cf. 215b, 572b, 1422b, 3131b). One additional b-verse has an Ssx finite verb derived from a compound: **guman** / *ōnetton* 'the men hastened' (306b). The only instance of type D* also stands at the end of the line: **gode** *ic* / *þanc secge* 'I say thanks to God' (1997b). As we have seen, non-finite verb forms are attracted to line-final position but more weakly than finite verbs. There is one a-verse instance in type Da:

heard / hēr cumen 'the bold (man) having come here' (376a). The other three instances are b-verses like *gid / oft wrecen* 'a poem (was) often recited' (1065b; cf. 281b, 2551b). The one example in type D* is line-final: *snūde / eft cuman* 'to come back quickly' (1869b). Elimination of this instance would require the same unusual elision as the one required to eliminate *ðolode / ǣr fela*. Elision might be less problematic in *gode ic / þanc secge,* where *ic* and the final syllable of *gode* are both unstressed. Here, however, the same unstressed syllable would have to be resolved with the preceding vowel as well as elided with the following vowel and that kind of elision is not securely attested. Elision is a good topic for further research in a larger corpus.

A LIGHT SUFFIX has a short vowel followed by a single consonant. Light suffixes can occupy an s position when immediately followed by the initial consonant of an inflectional ending but metrical stress is not securely attested for these suffixes in verse-final position. The only putative instance in *Beowulf* is *Hrēðel / cyning* 'King Hrethel' (2430b). In generative phonology the difference between light and heavy suffixes is explained by a rule of FINAL CONSONANT EXTRAMETRICALITY, abbreviated as FCE (Dresher and Lahiri 1999: 707; Russom 2001). In languages with an FCE rule, word-final consonants become invisible to rules that are sensitive to syllable weight. Hayes (1982) provides examples of FCE effects in Hopi and Classical Arabic as well as in Modern English. In Old English, a word-final consonant is extrametrical and is disregarded by the rule that assigns stress to closed non-root syllables in subordinate constituents. FCE has no effect on a heavy suffix ending in two consonants because the first consonant after the vowel remains visible and the stress rule treats the suffix as a closed syllable with the appropriate weight for stress. When the only final consonant of a light suffix is removed, however, the result is treated as a short syllable that is too light to bear stress. The light suffixes that appear in type D are *-an* (4X) *-en* (10X), *-er* (9X), *-ig* (12X), and *-yd* (1X). These include the infinitive suffixes of inflected infinitives. The consonant-initial inflections that follow them are *-ne* (35X) and *-ra* (2X). The *-ne* ending of inflected infinitives is included in the large group of instances with final *-ne*. Unlike heavy suffixes, light ones create a strong attraction to the b-verse. In type Da there are eight a-verse instances like *nīw- / tyrwydne* 'newly tarred' (295a; cf. 1021a, 1586a, 1625a, 1637a, 1811a, 2125a, 2338a). These are considerably outnumbered by the 23 b-verse instances like *hring / gyldenne* 'golden ring' (2809b; cf. 47b, 216b, 294b, 312b, 652b, 746b, 962b, 1518b, 1780b, 1851b, 1860b, 2089b, 2259b, 2484b, 2537b, 2720b, 2889b, 2985b, 3002b, 3080b, 3091b, 3107b). The a-verses of type D* are *idese tō / efnanne* (1941a: item 21b), *brōðor / ōðerne* 'one brother (shot) the other' (2440a), *sæcce tō / sēceanne*

(2562a: item 18c), **sorh** *is mē tō* / **secganne** (473a: item 18e), and *tō* **lang** *ys tō* / *reccenne* (2093a: item 17b). There is one b-verse, **wundor** *is tō secganne* (1724b: item 18d). As in other instances, the inherent complexity of type D* creates a strong attraction to the a-verse. As in other instances, this attraction can be overcome by a constituent on the s position that creates a strong attraction to the b-verse. From the perspective of the universalist theory there is nothing anomalous about b-verse instances of type D* in the *Beowulf* manuscript.

The inflected infinitive is an archaic construction that was replaced by our modern construction with *to* followed by a bare infinitive. The proposed emendations for type D* replace the archaic construction with the more modern construction. An outstanding accomplishment of Fulk (1992) was to show that *Beowulf* is among the earliest narrative poems in Old English, along with *Genesis A* and *Daniel*. Although there are occasional exceptions, the distinction between inflected and uninflected infinitives is observed pretty consistently in prose during most of the Old English period (OES 1: 408). We would not expect to find five exceptions among the sixteen verses in *Beowulf* that contain inflected infinitives.

Within Sievers's system, an additional eight of the sixteen instances would scan normally with or without the word-final inflection. All eight of these are a-verses like *tō ge-* / *cȳðanne* 'to reveal' (257a), with *tō* and an unstressed prefix as the only unstressed constituents before the first stress. Sievers's system would allow a verse like *tō ge-* / *cȳðan* to be scanned as his type A3, redefined as type A7 in the universalist classification system. On closer inspection the emendations turn out to be very anomalous realizations of the A7 pattern xx/Sx. As we have observed (§1.14), the *Beowulf* poet makes a conspicuous effort to avoid confusion between xx feet and anacruses, which normally consist of unstressed prefixes and never extend beyond two metrical syllables, the maximum length of an Old English unstressed prefix (Russom 1998: 49–52). The pattern xx/Sx occurs more than 290 times in *Beowulf*. In all but eight instances the xx foot is differentiated from an anacrusis by addition of one or more extrametrical syllables. Each of the eight exceptional instances has two non-prefixal words in the xx foot, at least one of which is an unstressed SP that rarely or never occurs in anacrusis. Such instances are also well differentiated. The verbal SPs are *wæs* (262a), *hēt* (391a), and *lēt* (2977a). The personal pronoun SPs are *ēow* (391a), *ic* (632a), *þæt* (632a), *wē* (941a), *man* (1175a), and *him* (2036a). The fixed SPs are the relative pronoun *ðē* (941a) and the complementizer *þæt* (2587a). It seems quite unlikely that eight supposedly acceptable emendations like *tō ge-* / *cȳðan,* with an unstressed prefix and no SP, would have the same frequency as the the four-syllable instances in the manuscript that contain one or more SPs. Since the pattern xx/Sx is unacceptable in the b-verse, Sievers's system requires the inflected infinitive in *tō ge-* / *fremmanne* 'to do, perform' (174b). The supposedly ambiguous examples in the a-verse have exactly the same linguistic structure as verse 174b and emending them to otherwise unattested realizations of their type seems unreasonable. Since metrically correct archaisms are the general rule in *Beowulf*, it seems more likely that a late scribe is responsible for the one manuscript instance in which *tō* governs an uninflected infinitive: *mǣl is mē tō* / *fēran* 'it is time for me to go' (316a).

Sievers discovered rules of language and meter that are still valid today. His rule of resolution made it possible to reconstruct Old English vowel length, which is quite different from Modern English vowel length due to drastic changes that occurred during the Middle English period. His rules for metrical interpretation of contract and epenthetic forms provided exemplary scientific explanations for their varying metrical values. He used his discoveries with remarkable insight to identify the stress patterns that were acceptable in Old English verses. The fact that so many apparent examples of other patterns could be explained by resolution, decontraction, or epenthesis provided very strong independent support for his system of scansion. He was not able, however, to provide a rule system that applied in the same way to every verse in *Beowulf* and explained why his unacceptable patterns were unacceptable. His system makes it possible to prove beyond a reasonable doubt that apparent exceptions are merely apparent when a sizeable number of them can be reinterpreted in the same linguistically rigorous way. The system reaches its limits, however, when confronted with a relatively small number of exceptions that have similar linguistic structure. As we have seen, this problem becomes particularly severe when we try to explain placement within the line of a low-frequency subtype like type D*. To deal with the most challenging problems of textual criticism in an Old English poem, rules that apply to all of its verses in the same way are required. To discover such rules we must go beyond classification of verse patterns based on stress and length to consider gradations of prominence in all kinds of syllables, morphological patterns, and rules based on SOV syntactic structure.

CHAPTER 11

CONCLUSIONS

§11.0 The main line of argument

My core hypothesis is that the syntax of *Beowulf,* insofar as it differs from Old English prose syntax, can be explained by a theory of meter based on universal principles of verse construction. I take subject-object-verb order as the starting point for metrical and linguistic evolution of English, following Smith (1971), Antonsen (2002), and Lehmann (2005–7), who argue that Proto-Germanic retained the SOV structure of early Indo-European languages (§1.3). Departure from strict SOV order was permissible in these languages under certain conditions. Since the Indo-European accent was not a strong expiratory stress, fronting to clause-initial position was the most effective way to emphasize a constituent, and this technique could be applied to unstressed syllables as well as stressed ones. Fronting of verbs for emphasis was routine in imperative, hortative subjunctive, and interrogative constructions. Verb fronting was also used for presentative clauses that marked a transition to a new topic (Luraghi 1995). A rich inflectional system avoided confusion about the syntactic role of a noun or pronoun argument when it was fronted for emphasis.

Tendencies observable in languages of all types had predictable effects on early Germanic word orders (§1.4). Iconicity of distance, a tendency to identify close semantic relations with close placement of the related constituents, served to clarify the relation between an antecedent and a pronoun fronted to initial position. Processing was facilitated by two important techniques: placement of light, predictable constituents toward the beginning of a clause and of heavy constituents with new information toward the end. When we turn to *Beowulf* we also find systematic constraints on word order

369

with no parallels in prose texts. These are the departures to be explained by the universalist theory of Old English meter.

§11.1 Generative linguistics and generative metrics

Kiparsky (1977: 239–40) observes that the optional rules of elision in iambic pentameter, which allow assignment of adjacent vowels to one metrical position, correspond to optional linguistic rules that allow adjacent vowels ordinarily pronounced as two syllables to be pronounced as one syllable in casual speech. What is metrical about the pentameter rules is that they permit monosyllabic interpretation of elidable sequences even in formal poems like Shakespeare's sonnets, which are unlikely to be performed with casual pronunciations. Such relations between language and meter are expected in the universalist theory of Old English meter, which abstracts metrical entities from linguistic entities and metrical norms from linguistic norms. The *Beowulf* poet's rule for resolution corresponds to a phonological rule that requires length under primary word stress but not under subordinate word stress (OE 8.6). The rule of metrical subordination (OE 6.2) corresponds to a rule for phrasal stress in SOV Proto-Germanic. The universalist theory also abstracts metrical rules from syntactic rules. The SPMR is abstracted from an optional fronting rule based on the universal tendency to place light, easily processed constituents toward the beginning of a clause. What is metrical about this rule is that it applies in a quasi-obligatory way, with very rare exceptions. Since verses are abstracted from normative phrases, the normative verse is a natural syntactic constituent with its sub-constituents in normative order. Syntactic complexity causes metrical complexity and has the expected inhibiting effect on departure from normative word order in verses shared by stressed major constituents, as shown in the retrospect sections for chapters 3–9. The metrical principle of closure restricts syntactic complexity toward the end of a metrical unit. Enjambment normally occurs at the earliest location, between the first and second verses of a verse clause. The quasi-obligatory application of the SPMR is attributable to the fact that it concentrates metrical complexity in the first verse of the clause (§1.19).

The syntax of *Beowulf* is affected by metrical rules based on phonology and morphology. A finite main verb with a short root syllable is often fronted from its normative syntactic position to avoid violation of OE 8.5. Similar fronting occurs with alliterating finite verbs to avoid violation of OE 7.5. Violation of these rules usually avoids violation of higher-ranking rules, especially the rules for verse patterns (§1.13), which restrict departure from a verse norm of two feet with the simplest morphological pattern (Sx/Sx).

The verse pattern rules have highest rank. They are never violated and their categorical application is not peculiar to Old English poetry. Such rules provide the continuity of form that makes the line identifiable as a metrical unit — the metrical constant of Jakobson (1960: 257). The flexibility required for poetic narration is provided by rule-governed mismatch to permissible patterns and, in poems with very strict mismatch rules, by making a rule-governed choice of patterns available.

Given a set of words with specified grammatical forms, minimalist theory considers how they can be ordered to provide an intelligible syntactic structure (§1.8). Here I begin with a set of words that have specified metrical values as well as specified grammatical forms and consider how they can be ordered to provide a metrically acceptable verse clause. Departure from SVO typology in Modern English is quite strictly limited. During the transitional period between SOV and SVO the *Beowulf* poet could usually employ either order in a phrase of two stressed words and many verse patterns were acceptable with the order of feet reversed. The relative freedom of word order in the earliest available texts is what has prompted the debate about which order, if any, might have been basic in Proto-Germanic (§1.3).

§11.2 Oral-formulaic theory, discourse analysis, and literary interpretation

Formulaic poems like *Beowulf* provide linguistic evidence of special importance for historical linguists. Their traditional technique resists change and preserves archaic features that can be rare or absent in prose. One such feature in *Beowulf* is the postpositional phrase, which is characteristic of SOV languages and becomes steadily less common as English moves toward SVO typology (§1.6). The trend from postposed to preposed constituents also affected 'be' verbs in *Beowulf* and a few high-frequency main verbs were fronted as well, sometimes to unstressed positions, as generally with 'be' verbs, and sometimes to stressed positions, as shown by the fact that they alliterated (§1.5). Fronting of stressed verbs with progressively higher prominence would have accelerated the trend away from verb-final syntax in the typologist's diagnostic sentence with stress on all major constituents.

To construct absorbing narrative action, oral storytellers use paratactic, chronologically ordered sequences of the simplest clause structures (Labov 1972b). These syntactic structures create no impediments to understanding of fast-paced oral narration and facilitate the kind of memorization required for cultural continuity in a pre-literate era. In *Beowulf*, however, narrative clauses can be disrupted by metrical requirements. Placement of constituents

371

that would normally precede the verb is affected by use of semantically in-essential modifiers to provide alliteration, fill out a verse, and facilitate re-positioning of semantically essential constituents that would cause metrical problems if left in core position. As with heavy constituents generally, mo-dified arguments are usually displaced beyond the finite verb to the right periphery, often to a clause-final a-verse that makes the most convenient location available for the opening of the next clause (§2.5). Modified con-stituents are far more common in *Beowulf* than in early prose of similar con-tent (§2.0). Their effects have to be factored out for assessment of basic word order. Unmodified arguments, on the other hand, provide weighty statistical evidence for basic order in the poem. As we have seen, an unmodified direct object often shares a verse with the finite verb, almost always in normative OV order, and is rarely displaced beyond the verb.

The generic concepts of a formulaic tradition provide an indispensable starting point for literary interpretation. In *Beowulf* the idealized generic king is a competent administrator and general who is admired only insofar as he cares effectively for the *lēode* 'people.' The poet makes no significant attempt to define *lēode* more narrowly. The main characters are powerful individuals and their retinues, to be sure, but these hall-dwellers are never contrasted with farmers or tradesmen in a social hierarchy. The *þēo(w)* 'servant, at-tendant, slave' who is mentioned in line 2223 seems less likely to be a slave than a member of someone's retinue who has committed a crime. If *þēow* always meant 'slave' it would be hard to explain names for important cha-racters like Ecgtheow, Wealhtheow, or Ongentheow. The most conspicu-ously differentiated kinds of people in the poem are sociable truth-tellers and sociopathic schemers.

Focusing on the heroic hall and its inhabitants can be interpreted as a specialization of the genre for discussion of power, physical as well as poli-tical. The proper exercise of power is defined by contrasting an idealized king, queen, or hero with a binary opposite — Hrothgar with Heremod, Hygd with Fremu, Beowulf with Grendel. The gigantic Grendel takes abuse of physical power to a spectacular extreme, disregarding laws meant to con-trol violence (lines 149–58) and building up his strength by devouring peo-ple. The poet's superhero, on the other hand, is scrupulously deferential to elders like Hrothgar and Wealhtheow even as he defends their people single-handed from his sociopathic antitype. The earliest heroic narratives in Norse tradition provide conspicuous analogues for Heremod, an abusive, grasping antitype of the loving and generous Hrothgar. Icelandic and Norwegian sto-rytellers represent powerful bullies like Attila and Ermanaric as sadistic monsters who die appropriately miserable deaths. In *Beowulf,* similarly, Heremod, a terrible disappointment to the wise elders of his people, dies friendless far from home (902b–4a).

The appropriate use of political power is preservation of a space where the arts of peace and prosperity can be cultivated. When he becomes King, Beowulf provides such a space for fifty years (2209b–10a). Good kings are diplomats who settle feuds if possible. War is an unmitigated disaster and those who initiate conflict are treated with systematic contempt. Invasion of another country by Hygelac is evaluated as foolish and ends with the death of the invader. The ideology of the poem is thoroughly interwoven with its narrative content, most obviously through regular use of semantically inessential constituents with generic function. From a formal point of view, *Beowulf* is an old-fashioned story with good guys, bad guys, and poetic justice. All this may seem rather naïve, of course, but we cannot hope to instruct a dead poet in more advanced techniques of political analysis or literary composition. A more productive approach will compare what we observe in *Beowulf* with our own state ideologies and our own popular hero-tales.

Beowulf provides important material for reconstruction of Indo-European poetic tradition, as undertaken by Watkins (1995), but the poem cannot be reduced to its Indo-European or Proto-Germanic roots. The heroic epic had to adjust time and again as Indo-European migrants encountered new cultures and changing historical conditions, which included changes in their own languages. Watkins's small-scale example of such evolution is the replacement of an obsolete verb in an Indo-European dragon-slaying formula with the cognate Germanic noun *bana* (§1.0).

English kingdoms in the era of Beowulf, though by no means nation-states of the modern type, were larger and more stratified than kingdoms in the era when the meter was born. By 700 CE only the power centers of a legendary past could still be represented as stockades with a great hall and some outbuildings. Moreover, as Foley (1995) emphasizes, a skilled formulaic poet can use a traditional form for a personal agenda. The positive treatment of the elderly in *Beowulf* would be hard to duplicate in the earliest heroic narratives from Iceland or Norway. We should expect to find departure from tradition as well as conspicuous adherence. As he integrates an imported religious outlook with oral tradition, the poet shows great skill in linking the core Christian concept of charity to pre-Christian concepts of generosity and affectionate social relations; and the murderous Grendel is Christianized very effectively indeed by linking him to Cain, who initiates the sad history of violence with an act that was doubly outrageous in native tradition because the victim was Cain's own brother and because Cain attempted to conceal the crime. Not all aspects of traditional culture could be rehabilitated, however. As Neidorf has shown (2022: 12), the *Beowulf* poet elides some traditional elements inconsistent with Christian morality, for example the heroic character who chooses to fulfill a duty of vengeance by committing an abominable act. More work of this kind is needed to explain the interweaving of oral tradition, Christian literacy, and individual talent in poems like *Beowulf*.

§11.3 Application of general principles in a metrically and grammatically specified set of words

For analysis of many linguistic, stylistic, and editorial problems the ideal starting point is a group of examples that differ only with regard to the feature of special interest. The numbered sets of clauses in this book have been assembled with that ideal in mind. They differ primarily with regard to word order, the special feature of interest in the main line of argument, and are kept as similar as possible otherwise. Assembling the sets of examples was a burdensome preliminary. I hope that comprehensive presentation of the metrical evidence will make it unnecessary for an interested linguist, formulaic theorist, discourse analyst, or textual scholar to do all that kind of work over again. I have tried to devise an interdisciplinary style of presentation useful to all these potential users of the book and have occasionally pointed out features of possible interest outside the main line of argument, but readers who explore the sets of examples for evidence relevant to their projects will find much more interesting material than I have been able to discuss.

The main line of argument deals directly with problems in English historical linguistics. In clauses with a stressed subject, a stressed object, and a stressed finite verb, the evidence for SOV typology is unmistakable (§3.11). There are eighty instances with SOV order. SVO order has the next highest frequency, with 48 instances, and there are 23 instances with VSO order. The remaining instances correspond to uncommon typological orders and have predictably lower frequencies. SVO order does have significant total frequency and at first glance it might seem possible to interpret this as somehow related to verb-second order in Proto-Germanic. The strength of the metrical evidence is understated, however, by total frequencies for SOV and SVO. Ten of the instances with SOV order are one-verse clauses. There are no one-verse clauses with SVO order. Of the 70 multi-verse instances with SOV order, 55 have S/OV structure, with the subject in one verse and constituents of the verb phrase sharing a later verse in OV order. This is the same structure we observed in the earliest known line of Germanic alliterative verse (§1.11). Among the 48 multi-verse clauses with SVO order, only four have S/VO structure, with the verses divided at the natural syntactic boundary between subject and verb phrase. The predominant clause structure, with 34 instances, is SV/O, where the verse boundary between major constituents corresponds to the least natural point of syntactic division, splitting the constituents of the verb phrase. The high frequency for SV/O clearly results from rightward displacement of heavy objects in a clause with SOV typology. All 34 SV/O examples have the object in a heavy verse. Of these 22 are modified objects consisting of two stressed simplexes and in three additional instances the modified object is a whole-verse compound equally suitable for displacement. Many of the modifiers are semantically inessential. To review the verse list see chapter three, item (7a). The remaining 10 instances have S/V/O structure, with the major constituents in separate verses. As we have frequently observed in chapters 3–10, this arrangement of constituents is typical of clauses with unusual word orders. The two clause patterns with the lowest total frequencies, OSV and VOS, have even higher frequencies of instances with each major constituent in a separate verse. The metrical evidence for SOV typology is much stronger than the kind of evidence available for analysis of word order in prose texts.

One-verse clauses with unstressed subjects provide equally strong metrical evidence. The influence of the SPMR can be disregarded in such clauses because the normative position of the subject would be clause-initial whether the basic order was SOV or SVO. The basic order should therefore be identifiable as a significantly higher frequency of one-verse clauses with sOV structure. The difference in frequency is very significant indeed, with 43 instances for sOV as compared with three instances for sVO. It seems unreasonable to suppose that a preference for verb-second order in late Proto-Germanic would have left so little trace in an early poetic text with archaic diction.

It takes longer to discuss the evidence provided by clauses in which word order is disrupted for several reasons. This evidence is no less decisive, however. The chapter sections have strikingly consistent profiles. When we factor out irrelevant influence from the SPMR and displacement of heavy arguments, instances that stay closest to the SOV norm generally have the highest frequency, very obviously so in the sections with the largest numbers of examples. The most common departures from SOV order are those that avoid violation of widely recognized constraints on verse form (K4: 330–35). Other common departures avoid violation of less familiar constraints imposed by the universalist theory of Old English meter. Any doubt that these departures are due to metrical constraints should be dispelled by attention to what does *not* occur in two-word type A1 verses, where the order of feet can be changed without changing the metrical pattern and no irrelevant constraints can interfere with word placement. In the constructed A1 verse *bǣdon / bēagas* '(they) asked for rings,' departure from OV order would conform to all relevant metrical constraints but such verses never appear in *Beowulf*. When OV order creates a two-word type A1 verse, the poet never chooses VO order (§1.17).

Most of the remaining departures from SOV order are of a kind also employed in languages with SOV typology. Interrogative, imperative, and hortative subjective verbs are routinely fronted for emphasis. Less routine fronting for emphasis is verifiable because the fronted constituents are 'robustly lexical,' with low frequency in ordinary speech and correspondingly high prominence (Getty 2000, Griffith 2016). Campfire tales in Modern English achieve this effect with stress rather than fronting. A constructed example with capitalization of the emphatic constituents: "the RUSTLING sound went away and everything seemed okay again when a GRIZZLY BEAR came out of the trees." Other predictable departures from SOV order include unstressed object pronouns placed before an unstressed subject for more effective linkage to their antecedents and finite verbs fronted to mark the beginning of a new phase in the narrative.

Ries (1880: 91–111) summed up the evidence available in his era by saying that the basic word order in Common Germanic was subject first, verb last and everything else in between. Minimalist research has added evidence for the ordering of direct and indirect objects, the major constituents between subject and verb in an SOV language. One crucial distinction in this research is between structural case of the usual kind and inherent case assigned by a particular verb to one or more objects (§3.1a). In non-Indo-European languages like Kalkatungu, structural case differs from inherent case in several kinds of constructions (Blake 2001: 55–62). An object with inherent oblique case can function as a structural subject in Modern German passive constructions and such constructions also occur in Old English (OES 1: 355–57).

A second crucial distinction is between case and thematic role (§1.8). In double-object constructions with non-prepositional objects, the verb is in closer syntactic composition with an inanimate theme than with an animate recipient. The closer relation between object and theme shows up with particular clarity in languages that require agreement between a verb affix and an affix on one of two non-prepositional objects (Bárány 2024). Bárány's minimalist derivations for double-object constructions begin with the verb

376

in the same lower-level constituent with the inanimate object, a configuration in which feature checking can take place. Since the verb and inanimate object are normally adjacent in SOV languages, no movement is required to obtain normative order in an SOV double-object construction. The expected arrangement for SOV typology is represented by *Beowulf* 1725–26, an example with all major constituents stressed: *hū mihtig god / manna cynne / þurh sīdne sefan / snyttru bryttað* — literally, 'how mighty God / to mankind / with his great heart / wisdom gives.' The finite verb shares a verse with the inanimate theme as usual and the animate recipient stands outside this closely-bound construction. In Modern English double-object constructions with SVO typology, the verb is raised after checking to the beginning of the verb phrase (Bárány 2024: 398–99). The change from SOV to SVO did not require object movement so the indirect object still comes first in double-object constructions like *Speedo gave the traffic cop a donut,* in contrast to *Speedo gave a donut the traffic cop.* The Old English order of objects still distinguishes the theme from the recipient in these non-prepositional constructions after loss of dative inflections from the language. The indirect object normally follows, however, in innovating constructions like *Speedo gave a donut to the traffic cop,* where the lost dative inflection on indirect objects is replaced by a preposition. In this prepositional-object construction the theme can be brought closer to the verb in accord with iconicity of distance and overt marking of the recipient by the preposition prevents confusion with marking by word order in double-object constructions.

§11.4 Metrical theory

Old English Meter and Linguistic Theory concluded with the observation that "further progress in our understanding of language will undoubtedly suggest ways to improve the theory proposed here" (Russom 1987: 149). Not long afterward, *A History of Old English Meter* (Fulk 1992) provided a complete survey of the metrical constraints observed by Sievers and associated developments in English historical linguistics. Among the general principles greatly clarified in this book were Kuhn's laws, Kaluza's law, and Fulk's own rule of the coda. These are incorporated into the universalist theory as the SPMR, OE 8.6, and OE 8.2. Fulk's observations about linguistic and metrical history greatly facilitated extension of the generative theory to alliterative meters in cognate Germanic languages (Russom 1998). A major initiative in generative linguistics, Optimality Theory, was underway by 1993, when an earlier version of Prince and Smolensky (2004) was widely circulated and soon began to be cited in books by other researchers (e.g. Croft

2003: 308). Optimality Theory showed that it was possible to analyze complex linguistic rules for a particular language as the result of interaction among simpler rules that performed obviously necessary functions and could be formulated as linguistic universals. As I worked with Prince and Smolensky's methodology I found that rules of Old English meter could also be explained by interaction of simpler rules. In Russom (2017) I showed how some of the same simple rules applied in Middle English alliterative meter, in Modern English iambic meters, and in a sample of world meters. Here I have refocused on *Beowulf* to show how a complete system of metrical rules can be created from universal principles of verse form that interact with a given language to produce what we observe.

The universalist approach to Old English meter integrates metrical constraints on syntax, morphology, and phonology into a single generative system. This provides a straightforward methodology for analysis of departure from syntactic norms, syllabic norms, and norms of word formation, which interact to determine the frequencies of metrical patterns and placement of smaller metrical constituents within larger metrical constituents. Interpreted as departure from normative metrical form in verses, lines, and clauses, syntactic complexity is subject to the principle of closure, making it possible to explain Kuhn's first law and constraints on enjambment as avoidance of metrical complexity toward the end of a metrical unit (§1.19, §1.20). Constraints on placement of foot boundaries and verse boundaries can be expressed straightforwardly as violable rules favoring realization of these metrical boundaries as natural syntactic boundaries, for example the boundary between a subject in an a-verse and constituents of the verb phrase in a following b-verse. Important constraints on placement of unstressed words within the opening verse, many of which were not explained by Kuhn, turn out to be phonological rather than syntactic. They can be expressed as rules for matching of unstressed syllables with varying prominence to the varying prominence of metrical x positions that correspond to unstressed words, unstressed syllables of stressed words, and extrametrical syllables. These phonological constraints interact with syntactic constraints in the opening verse but apply to all verses in the clause (§1.4). The relevant distinctions of prominence in unstressed constituents were identified in recent work on close binding by Kiparsky (2018) and in work on meaningful versus mechanical prominence by Anttila, Dozat, Galbraith & Shapiro (2020).

Taking the verse clause seriously as a metrical unit also led to the discovery that placement of verse types within the clause depends on the extent to which they deviate from the Sx/Sx norm (§1.19). On a smaller scale, taking the verse seriously as a syntactic unit explained the strength of constraints on word order in verses shared by stressed major constituents (OE 2.3). These discoveries amply validated the insight that general principles can sometimes be detected as strong tendencies that enhance or inhibit one another (Prince and Smolensky 2004). Many rules of the universalist system are validated by gross statistical discrepancies in the distribution of metrical patterns but do not apply categorically. Such rules can explain how Old English meter actually works but they are unlikely to be detected if we confine attention to what does and does not occur. We also need to distinguish among what happens routinely, what happens less often, what happens rarely, and what happens so seldom that it might be due to scribal error.

APPENDIX

A. Abbreviations

Below are abbreviations for major sentence constituents in notations for syntactic patterns, with those for stressed constituents in caps and those for unstressed constituents in lower case. Boundaries between verses are marked with a forward slash (/). In chapter ten, verse-internal clause boundaries are marked with a colon (:). In citations and verse lists, grammatical cases are specified by the standard abbreviations *nom.* (nominative), *gen.* (genitive), *dat.* (dative), and *acc.* (accusative).

A, a	=	auxiliary verb
B, b	=	finite 'be' verb used in existential constructions and as a linker
I, i	=	infinitive verb
$\mathbf{I^1, i^1}$	=	infinitive governed by higher-level verb
$\mathbf{I^2, i^2}$	=	infinitive governed by lower-level verb
Io, io	=	indirect object in dative case
O, o	=	direct object in accusative case
$\mathbf{O^1, o^1}$	=	primary object (inanimate, in accusative or oblique case)
$\mathbf{O^2, o^2}$	=	secondary object (animate, in any case but nominative)
$\mathbf{O^a, o^a}$	=	object of an auxiliary verb
$\mathbf{O^i, o^i}$	=	object of an infinitive verb
Pd, pd	=	predicate adverbial (adverb, adpositional phrase, or instrumental noun)
Pj, pj	=	predicate adjective
Pn, pn	=	predicate nominative

Pt, pt	=	participle
V,v	=	finite main verb
S, s	=	subject

Below are abbreviations for important reference works. The standard abbreviation 's.v.' refers to information under a given headword in a dictionary.

K3	=	Klaeber (1950)
K4	=	Fulk, Bjork & Niles (2008)
OED	=	Oxford English Dictionary, 2nd edn. (1989)
OEG	=	Campbell (1959)
OES 1	=	Mitchell (1985), vol 1
OES 2	=	Mitchell (1985), vol 2
CV	=	Cleasby & Vigfusson (1957)

B. Notational conventions for metrical features in citations

Extrametrical syllables are parenthesized. The verse-internal boundary between feet is represented by a forward slash (/). Alliterating constituents are in boldface. When an alliterating constituent is resolved, the whole resolvable sequence is in boldface. When a non-alliterating constituent is resolved, the whole resolvable sequence is underlined. When sounds and letters are in one-to-one correspondence, the rightward boundary of a long stressed syllable or an equivalent resolvable sequence is marked in accord with the major constraints on syllable division: (1) the onset of the syllable (the part before the vowel) must correspond to a possible onset in the first syllable of a word; (2) the coda of the syllable (the part after the vowel) must correspond to a possible coda in the last syllable of a word; and (3) when more than one syllable division conforms to (1) and (2), the preferred division is the one that maximizes onsets. Applying these principles can be difficult when consonants undergo sound change word-internally, as for example when the consonant cluster [þr], which appears word-initially in words like *þrym* 'power,' is voiced to [ðr], which is not permissible word-initially. For consistency I assume that the phonetic realization is the domain of application for the rules of syllable division. A form like *broðrum* 'brothers' (dat. sg.) will accordingly be represented as ***broðrum*** when it alliterates. I implement

382

the rules in their simplest form not with any dogmatic intention but to facilitate discussion of the many interesting problems that arise. Metrical evidence can shed light on some of these problems.

C. General principles of relative prominence

RP 1. The prominence of an important constituent is enhanced at the expense of one or more other constituents, which are backgrounded.

RP 2. The relative prominence of a constituent is directly proportional to the amount of information it provides.

RP 3. The relative prominence of a constituent is inversely proportional to its frequency of occurrence and predictability.

RP 4. Governors generally have higher frequency and lower prominence than the constituents they govern.

RP 5. Prominence can be enhanced by movement to clause-initial position.

RP 6. In stress-based languages, prominence can be enhanced by stress.

RP 7. Prominence can be enhanced by sound echoes like rhyme and alliteration, which are metrical equivalents of stress.

When RP 5–7 do not interfere, RP 2–4 create a regular gradation of prominence for the parts of speech.

Prominence gradations for stressed constituents, from most to least prominent: *nouns and adjectives* > *infinitives* (verbal nouns) and *participles* (verbal adjectives) > *finite main verbs* > *finite modal auxiliaries* > *finite 'be' verbs* > *pronouns* > *STPs*. In Old English a defining adverb forms a verbal compound with an immediately following verb and the verb is subordinated to the adverb. When a defining adverb follows the modified verb the verb is more prominent and the adverb is stressed like a postposition. Root suffixes derived from major-category words are more prominent than non-root suffixes that bear no resemblance to words. Non-root suffixes ending in a consonant are more prominent than non-root suffixes that end with a short vowel (§10.7).

Prominence gradations for unstressed constituents, from most to least prominent: *Nouns in predicate nominative constructions* and *adjectives* *in predicate adjective constructions* (rarely unstressed) > *infinitives* (rarely un-stressed) > *finite main verbs* > *finite auxiliaries* > *finite 'be' verbs* > *pronouns* > *conjunctions* > *prepositions* > *other wordlike STPs* > *prefixes and negative particles.* Sentential adverbs are often cognate with conjunctions and have similar prominence when placed early in the sentence.

D. Universal principles of traditional verse form

UM 1. Metrical constituents are abstracted from linguistic constituents (metrical positions from syllables, metrical feet from words, metrical verses from phrases, metrical lines from sentences, etc.).

UM 2. Norms for a metrical constituent are abstracted from norms for the corresponding linguistic constituent. Departure from metrical norms creates metrical complexity, restricting the frequency of a metrical constituent and its placement within a larger metrical constituent.

UM 3. Metrical complexity is additive. Each departure from a norm increases complexity.

UM 4. Metrical complexity is restricted with increasing severity toward the end of a metrical unit (the principle of closure).

UM 5. When a metrical constituent such as a verse or clause contains sub-constituents of unequal weight, the lighter constituent normally precedes the heavier constituent. This constraint has been observed in other Indo-European meters and in Finnish alliterative poetry, where it is called winnowing (Behaghel 1924–32: IV, 3–9; Leino 1986: 133–34). Winnowing is a metrical analogue of the ordering norm for linguistic constituents that differ in weight and complexity (§1.4).

UM 6. When metrical norms conflict, those at higher levels of metrical structure exert more influence than those at lower levels (Youmans 1989). This rule applies when all the conflicting norms are violable and there is no conflict with a high-ranking norm that applies without exception at the relevant lower level.

UM 7. When smaller metrical constituents must occur some fixed number of times within a larger metrical constituent, it must be possible for the audience to enumerate the smaller constituents intuitively under normal conditions of reception. To make this possible, metrical constituents of different sizes must be kept distinct from one another and from extrametrical constituents.

E. Rules of Old English Meter (introduced in §1.10)

OE 1. The normative Old English line is abstracted from a clause with the major constituents in SOV order (UM 1). The line is composed of two verses, the first called the a-verse and the second called the b-verse.

OE 1.1. The normative line is realized as a verse clause. Arrangement of the major clausal constituents in a single line reduces metrical complexity (UM 2). When a clause is too small to fill a line, arrangement of its major constituents as a single verse reduces its complexity.

OE 1.2. The normative location for a boundary between verses is at the major syntactic break in the clause. In a line that corresponds to an SOV clause the major syntactic break lies between the subject and the verb phrase (the two major sub-constituents of the clause). Significant enjambment occurs when closely bound constituents are split by the boundary between verses and one of these constituents shares a verse with an extraneous constituent. Due to the influence of UM 4, enjambment normally occurs at the earliest possible location within the verse clause (between the first verse and the second).

OE 1.3. The normative metrical position for a finite verb is at the end of the line, the metrical equivalent of clause-final position (the normative syntactic position for a finite verb in an SOV language). Clause-final placement of a finite verb reduces metrical complexity.

OE 1.4. The principle of closure (UM 4) inhibits all kinds of complexity in the b-verse, including syntactic complexity (OE 5.3).

OE 2. An Old English verse has two metrical feet, as defined in OE 3.1. Verses are abstracted from natural syntactic constituents below the level of the sentence that have two words and normative word order (UM 1). The first stressed word of a verse phrase is normally the most prominent one, as in the corresponding phrases of an SOV language. Archaic postpositions are subordinated to the more prominent lexical nouns they govern and bear subordinate stress. In the era of *Beowulf,* function-word governors such as articles and adpositions are usually fronted to an unstressed position before the governed word.

OE 2.1. The foot boundary must coincide with a well-marked boundary between constituents: with a word boundary, with the boundary between word-like constituents in a compound, or with the boundary between an unstressed prefix and the stressed word to which it is attached.

OE 2.2. In a verse with three stressed words, the foot boundary must fall at the natural point of syntactic division and the compound foot must be occupied by a natural syntactic constituent.

OE 2.3. SOV typology is strongly preferred in verses shared by stressed major constituents. The poet departs from normative order in such verses primarily to avoid violation of higher-ranking rules. SOV typology is somewhat preferred — not strongly preferred — when major constituents occupy separate verses.

OE 2.4. The normative verse consists of two words with the normative word pattern, Sx (OE 3.1). This two-word realization of the type A1 pattern Sx/Sx establishes a verse norm of two x positions occupied by unstressed syllables and two S positions occupied by syllables with primary word stress. Departure from these norms causes metrical complexity (UM 2).

OE 2.5. Some combinations of feet are unacceptable as verse patterns. The criteria for acceptable verse patterns are provided in §1.13. Lists of acceptable and unacceptable foot pairings are provided in §1.14, with a compact abbreviation for each pairing.

OE 3. The Old English foot is abstracted from an Old English word and is normally realized as a word. There is a foot pattern for every native word pattern, function words and compounds included, except for large compounds that fill an acceptable verse pattern, with one constituent in each foot. Instead of being realized as a word with a given pattern, a foot can be realized as a word group with a similar stress contour. Realization of a foot as a word group causes metrical complexity (UM 2).

OE 3.1. The normative Sx foot is abstracted from the normative Old English word, which has a stressed root syllable followed by an unstressed inflection. Other foot patterns are complex to the extent that they differ from the Sx norm (UM 2).

OE 3.2. Since Old English compounds have the most prominent stress on the first constituent, falling rhythm is strongly preferred in compound feet occupied by word groups.

OE 3.3. When the first foot of a category II verse is realized as a word group, alliteration on the following S position is strongly preferred to mark the leftward boundary of the second foot.

OE 3.4. The additive complexity due to realization of a foot as a word group is restricted in complex verse patterns (UM 3). Realization of the Ss foot as a word group is strongly dispreferred in the type A2 pattern Sx/Ss, with just four possible instances in *Beowulf* (736a, 2509a, 2638a, 3105a). The extreme complexity of type A8 (xx/Ss) is shown by the fact that it is restricted to the a-verse and realization of the Ss foot as a word group is unacceptable in this type.

OE 3.5. The most complex heavy feet (Sxs and Sxxs) are restricted categorically to verse-final position, the normative position for heavy feet (UM 5).

OE 3.6. The most complex foot with normative weight, Sxx, normally precedes the least complex foot, Sx, in accord with the principle of closure (UM 4). The reverse order in type D5 (Sx/Sxx) is almost entirely restricted to an ancient pan-Germanic formula for introducing speeches (§1.14).

OE 3.7. Feet must be kept distinct from verses and from extrametrical syllables (UM 7).

OE 4. Old English metrical positions are abstracted from syllables (UM 1). Strong positions abstracted from stressed syllables are called lifts.

OE 4.1. The S position is abstracted from a long syllable with primary word stress. A syllable is long if it contains a long vowel, as with OE *sǣ* 'sea,' or a short vowel followed by a consonant, as with OE *scip* 'ship.'

OE 4.2. The s position is abstracted from a long Old English syllable with subordinate word stress, for example the secondary constituent in a compound like *man-cynnes* 'of mankind.' Vowels become more susceptible to shortening and reduction when their prominence is reduced (Bugge and Sievers 1890: 391–411). The length requirement for syllables with primary word stress applies less strictly to syllables with subordinate word stress. A short syllable with subordinate stress creates a permissible mismatch to an s position.

OE 4.3. The x position is abstracted from an unstressed constituent. Unstressed constituents are the ones most vulnerable to vowel reduction and long vowels are normally shortened in such constituents. The normative occupant of an x position is an unstressed constituent with a short vowel. Constituents with prominent secondary stress are excluded from x positions. Placement of reduced secondary stress on an x position is inhibited by OE 4.3 but occurs occasionally (Russom 1987:34–35). For further discussion of Germanic syllable structure see Russom (2001, 2002).

OE 5. The verse clause is a metrical constituent abstracted from a grammatical proposition, as defined in §1.2.

OE 5.1. The normative realization of the verse clause is as a line (OE 1.1), but there is no strict limit on the number of verses in the clause. Semantically inessential constituents often extend the clause beyond two verses. Pithy one-verse clauses are used in *Beowulf* for surprising narrative events and emphatic value judgments.

OE 5.2. Like other high-frequency constituents with low prominence, SPs with predictable information content are often fronted to unstressed syntactic positions (§1.3). In *Beowulf* this requires leftward movement from core positions of the verse clause where SPs bear subordinate stress. Leftward movement of these SPs is also promoted by the universal tendency for light, easily processed constituents of a clause to appear before heavier, more complex constituents (§1.4).

OE 5.3. Syntactic complexity causes metrical complexity within a verse clause and is subject to the principle of closure (UM 4).

OE 5.4. Conspicuous enjambment causes syntactic complexity and normally occurs between the first two verses, the earliest possible location in the clause.

OE 5.5. Unstressed SPs cause complexity in the verses to which they have been fronted. They normally occur as early in the clause as possible, before the first stress in an opening verse of category I (at metrical location x1). Placement of constituents at metrical locations x2–x5 is subject to constraints on prominence (OE 9.1–9.5). OE 5.5 retains all the valid predictions of Kuhn's first law and explains additional facts about word placement in *Beowulf*.

OE 5.6. In *Beowulf*, as in languages generally, heavy phrases are often displaced toward the end of a clause (§1.7). An important formulaic technique in the poem removes excess constituents from an opening verse by adding a stressed modifier that supplies the mandatory alliteration or fills out an acceptable pattern in verse-final position (chapter two). Two-word verses of normative type A1 are ideal candidates for displacement, since they have no inherent metrical complexity and may appear late in the clause without interference from the principle of closure (UM 4). The principle of closure inhibits late placement of two-word type II verses with the most complex heavy patterns (§1.21). Two-word verses of types B and C, which are metrically lighter than type A1, are displaced less often and are occasionally fronted.

OE 6. Patterns of linguistic prominence normally match patterns of metrical prominence (see RP 1–7, UM 2). Prominence mismatches cause complexity.

OE 6.1. When stressed constituents are of unequal prominence, the more prominent constituent normally occupies the more prominent lift. This captures some constraints imposed by Sievers's rule of precedence. See also OE 7.2.

OE 6.2. At all levels of metrical structure within the line, the first lift subordinates any following lift. This rule is abstracted from the rule for stress subordination in a typical SOV language.

OE 6.3. A constituent must have metrically significant stress to be eligible for alliteration or resolution. Constituents occupying x positions cannot alliterate and cannot be resolved. Matching in the initial onsets of metrically unstressed constituents does not count as alliteration and is not rule-governed.

OE 6.4. Metrical subordination by OE 6.2 makes a lift less appropriate for alliteration and resolution.

OE 6.5. The normative resolved or alliterating constituent has prominent phrasal stress and occupies the first S position of the verse.

OE 6.6. The constraints on alliteration are very similar to the constraints on resolution. On subordinate lifts where alliteration is dispreferred, resolution is also dispreferred. Where resolution of subordinate linguistic constituents is dispreferred, alliteration is also dispreferred.

OE 6.7. Linguistic and metrical subordination interact to produce additive effects (UM 3). Alliteration and resolution are strongly dispreferred on weakly stressed linguistic constituents occupying subordinate s positions.

OE 7. Every verse must have an alliterating lift. In verses with more than one lift the probability of alliteration is directly proportional to metrical and linguistic prominence.

OE 7.1. Alliteration is obligatory on the first and most prominent lift in a verse.

OE 7.2. Alliteration is quasi-obligatory on the most prominent linguistic constituent in a verse. When an alliterating constituent on the first lift of an a-verse is significantly less prominent than a constituent on a following lift, the more prominent constituent normally alliterates as well. This rule captures additional constraints imposed by Sievers's rule of precedence. See OE 6.1.

OE 7.3. Departure from normative falling rhythm in a compound foot occupied by a word group becomes more acceptable when the prominence of the first stressed constituent is enhanced by alliteration. When the s position of a compound foot is occupied by a prominent noun or adjective root, alliteration is obligatory on the preceding S position.

OE 7.4. Alliteration is unacceptable on a doubly subordinated lift. Such lifts include an s position in a type D verse and any lift after the first lift of a b-verse.

OE 7.5. In types B, C, and E the s position is subordinated by one preceding lift. Prominent nouns and adjectives alliterate with some frequency on the s position in types B and C. Placement of an alliterating finite verb on an s position is strongly dispreferred, however. When finite verbs alliterate, they appear primarily on the first S position, where the added metrical prominence makes alliteration more appropriate. Due to the additive effects of constraints on resolution, an alliterating finite verb on an s position is very rarely resolved (see OE 8.3, OE 8.5). Alliteration and resolution also seem to be dispreferred on finite verbs occupying the second S position in complex verse patterns, though the number of crucial cases is not very large.

OE 8. The probability of resolution for a given constituent is directly proportional to its metrical and linguistic prominence.

OE 8.1. In verses with more than one lift, resolution is obligatory on the first and most prominent lift, which also alliterates obligatorily. Resolution is obligatory or quasi-obligatory on the S position of a verse type with a single lift, where alliteration is obligatory because no other lift is available.

OE 8.2. Non-resolution is quasi-obligatory on a doubly subordinated lift, where alliteration is unacceptable. A short syllable on the s position is almost always unresolved in the second foot of type D2 (S/Ssx) and type D6 (Sx/Ssx). In most instances this rule has the same effect as the rule of the coda (Fulk 1992: 201).

OE 8.3. In type A3 (Ss/Sx), the s position of the first foot is subordinated only once. A short stressed syllable on this s position is resolvable and must always be resolved with the following unstressed syllable to avoid the unacceptable pattern *Ssx/Sx. Resolution and non-resolution both create mismatches to an s position, which is abstracted from a single long syllable with subordinate stress. Any short syllable, resolved or unresolved, creates problematic additive complexity on the s position in the first foot of type E (Ssx/S), which is more complex than type A3 because both of its feet depart from the normative length of two metrical positions. The poet avoids placement of short syllables on the s position in type E, and when short syllables do appear there, non-resolution is required more often than resolution, especially when the resolvable constituent has low prominence. Due to additive effects of constraints on alliteration, a resolved constituent on an s position in type E is especially unlikely to alliterate (OE 7.5). The only example in *Beowulf* is verse 2478a.

OE 8.4. An unresolved short syllable is permissible on the second S position in type A3 but strongly dispreferred on the subordinate S position in type A1 (K4: 330; Russom 2022d).

OE 8.5. The s position in category I verses is subordinated once. Most instances with resolved constituents on the s position appear in type B, where resolution avoids conflict with higher-ranking constraints. Non-resolution on the s position of type B always creates the pattern *(xx)Sx/Sx or *(xx)Sxx/Sx, with unnecessary anacrusis. The situation is very different in type C, which can be constructed with a resolved or unresolved constituent on the s position. Resolution of finite verbs with relatively low prominence is strongly dispreferred on the s position of type C. Since there is no interference from higher-ranking constraints, this metrical fact is entirely attributable to the additive effects of low linguistic prominence and subordinate metrical prominence, both of which inhibit resolution. Due to constraints on alliteration (OE 7.5), a resolved finite verb on an s position is very unlikely to alliterate. The only example in *Beowulf* is 2008a.

OE 8.6. A phonological domain equivalent to one long syllable or two short syllables is required for primary stress in Old English (Dresher and Lahiri 1991). Under primary stress, a short stressed syllable must be resolved with the following syllable to provide adequate length. When stress is subordinated, the energy of articulation is reduced and a smaller phonological domain may be adequate. When the energy is sufficiently reduced to be contained within a short syllable, resolution is opposed by the universal preference for one-to-one correspondence between stresses and syllables, which is violable only under special conditions like those created by the strong expiratory stress of early Germanic languages (Russom 2022d). In *Beowulf* this preference promotes non-resolution of two short syllables under subordinate stress but allows resolution as an option. When the unstressed second syllable of a resolvable sequence is long, the preference for one-to-one correspondence exerts stronger influence. The *Beowulf* poet avoids resolution of a resolvable sequence on a secondary lift when the second vowel retains archaic length or lies within a syllable closed by a consonant (Kaluza's Law).

OE 9. A metrical x position inherits its meaningful prominence from the corresponding unstressed linguistic constituent. The most prominent x positions are those in light feet, which correspond to unstressed words at phrase level. Less prominent are x positions in stressed feet with the patterns Sx, Sxx, Ssx, Sxs, and Sxxs. These x positions correspond to unstressed syllables at word level and have low but significant prominence. Extrametrical positions have zero prominence. They cannot inherit prominence because they do not correspond to linguistic constituents.

OE 9.1. Light feet must be kept distinct from extrametrical syllables (OE 3.7). The ideal location for extrametrical syllables is before the first stress of a category I verse, where they differentiate the light foot from an extrametrical anacrusis.

OE 9.2. Since all linguistic constituents have some degree of prominence, any linguistic constituent occupying an extrametrical position creates a mismatch. Mismatch to an extrametrical position is most tolerable in unstressed prefixes and negative particles, which have the lowest prominence, and least tolerable on SPs, which have the highest prominence. The most prominent SPs, finite main verbs, never occupy extrametrical location x4 or x5 in *Beowulf*. Extrametrical positions are occasionally occupied by less prominent SPs like pronouns, adverbs, finite 'be' verbs, and finite auxiliaries. The probability of assignment to an extrametrical position is inversely proportional to prominence.

OE 9.3. Foot-internal x positions have the low prominence of the word-internal syllables from which they are abstracted, which is lower than the prominence of unstressed words. In feet occupied by word groups the x positions are normally occupied by STPs. The complexity caused by an unstressed SP on a foot-internal x position has the expected additive relation to the inherent complexity of the foot (§1.12). Nearly all instances in *Beowulf* appear on the x position of the normative Sx foot, the foot most tolerant of complexity. There are only three instances with an SP on an x position in a long heavy foot (*Beowulf* 272b, 343b, 455b).

OE 9.4. The additive complexity created by realization of a complex foot as a word group imposes morphological constraints on unstressed syllables within these groups. In the most complex heavy feet, Sxs and Sxxs, employment of unstressed constituents stays close to the morphology of the corresponding compound word. In an Sxxs foot occupied by a word group, the x positions are normally occupied by an inflectional syllable followed by an unstressed prefix, imitating the morphology of compounds like *sibbe-ge-*

driht 'kindred band.' The internal x position of an Sxs foot is normally occupied by an unstressed word-final syllable or a prefix, imitating the morphology of Sxs compounds like *bolgen-mōd* 'wrathful-minded' and *hand-geweorc* 'handiwork.'

OE 9.5. The probability that an unstressed constituent will be assigned to a light foot is directly proportional to its linguistic prominence. Light feet are normally occupied by SPs that seldom or never appear in anacrusis, such as finite verbs, pronouns, and conjunctions. Use of less prominent constituents as light feet causes complexity and is strongly dispreferred in the most complex verse patterns of category I, types A7 (xx/Sx) and A8 (xx/Ss), which are confined to the first half of the line by UM 4. A light foot can also be be differentiated from an anacrusis by addition of one or more extrametrical syllables.

OE 9.6. An alternative word order is strongly preferred if it creates a more acceptable kind of anacrusis or avoids anacrusis altogether. Anacrusis in type A1 with two trochaic words is so easily avoided that it never occurs in the poem (cf. Bliss 1967: 43).

OE 9.7. The additive complexity of anacrusis is unacceptable in heavy verse types with a compound foot out of normative final position (Types A3, A4, and E).

F. Metrical locations

To facilitate discussion of verses that are subject to a variety of constraints it is convenient to group metrical positions with similar prominence into locations with short identifiers. It is sufficient to distinguish five locations for lifts and five locations for x positions. Locations are numbered according to the prominence of the lifts that normally occupy them, with 1 highest.

Locations for lifts:

Location s1a: On the first S position of a verse with two lifts, where alliteration and resolution are obligatory.

Location s1b: On the first and last lift in type A7, C1, or C3, where alliteration is obligatory because no other lift is available and resolution is quasi-obligatory (or perhaps obligatory). Lifts in location s1b seem to be slightly less prominent than those in location s1a because they do not contrast with a less prominent lift in the same verse.

Location s2: On a subordinate S position in an a-verse, where alliteration and resolution are optional in many verse patterns.

Location s3: On an s position in types B, C, and E, where alliteration is permissible in the a-verse but never required. In type B, a short vowel on the last lift must be resolved to avoid unnecessary anacrusis. In types C and E, where there is no interference from higher-ranking rules, resolution is strongly dispreferred. The last lift in type B is somewhat more appropriate for resolution than the last lift in type C, since in type C this lift contrasts with an adjacent and more prominent S position, whereas in type B the last lift is distanced from the S position by a less prominent unstressed vowel.

Location s4: On a subordinate lift in a subordinate metrical constituent, where alliteration is unacceptable and non-resolution is quasi-obligatory. These lifts include the s positions in type D verses and any lift after the first lift of the b-verse.

Locations for x positions:

Location x1: before the first alliteration in a category I verse. This is the only permissible location for the most prominent unstressed SPs. The probability of placement at location x1 is directly proportional to meaningful prominence.

Location x2: on a metrical position in a foot with normative weight. This is a preferred location for unstressed prefixes with very low prominence. Unstressed main verbs are unacceptable at location x2 and the frequency of other constituents at this location is inversely proportional to their meaningful prominence.

Location x3: on a metrical position in a compound foot. As with location x2, the frequency of constituents at this location is inversely proportional to their prominence, but prominent unstressed constituents are even less acceptable at location x3. Unstressed SPs rarely appear at this location and there are no examples with verbal SPs. Word groups occupying the most complex compound feet (Sxs and Sxxs) normally match the unstressed syllables of the corresponding compounds as closely as possible (OE 9.4).

Location x4: on an extrametrical position before the second foot of a class II verse. This location is strongly biased toward constituents of extremely low prominence like unstressed prefixes and negative particles. No finite main verbs appear at location x4, and the very few examples with other finite verb forms strongly favor 'be' verbs over auxiliaries.

Location x5: on an extrametrical position before the first foot of a class II verse (in anacrusis). The vast majority of constituents on this extrametrical position are unstressed prefixes and negative particles. No verb of any kind appears in anacrusis and instances with SPs are extremely rare. All kinds of anacrusis are strongly dispreferred and the poet sometimes avoids anacrusis by departure from normative word order (OE 9.6).

GLOSSARY OF TECHNICAL TERMS
AS USED IN THIS BOOK

The section number after each headword refers to the place where it is first introduced. Words in unbolded small caps that appear within an entry have main entries elsewhere in the glossary.

ABSTRACT CASE (§3.1). A case that represents purely syntactic relations between words, as when accusative case is used to represent government of a direct object by a verb. See INHERENT CASE.

A-VERSE (§1.10). The first half of the alliterative line.

ADJUNCTS (§1.3). Modifiers that are ordered with respect to the constituent they modify, in contrast to MAJOR CONSTITUENTS. Typical adjunct modifiers are adjectives that modify nouns and adverbs that modify verbs.

ADPOSITION (§1.3). A category of words that includes prepositions and POSTPOSITIONS.

AGENT (§1.8). The initiator of a verbal action. See THEMATIC ROLES.

ANACRUSIS (§1.11). An EXTRAMETRICAL unstressed syllable placed before a verse-initial foot that contains a stressed constituent.

ARGUMENT (§1.2). In logic, something to which a property or relation is attributed by a PREDICATE. Logical arguments are expressed by grammatical subjects and objects.

B-VERSE (§1.10). The second half of the alliterative line.

CATEGORICAL RULE (§1.8). A rule that admits of no exceptions.

CHAIN (§1.8). See TRACE.

CHECKING (§1.8). In minimalist theory, an operation that determines whether a linguistic constituent has the required features for the syntactic position it occupies, for example whether a subject in specifier position has the features of person, number, and case required by an adjacent verbal head.

CLOSURE, PRINCIPLE OF (§1.9). The universal principle that metrical rules become stricter toward the end of a metrical unit.

COMP, C POSITION (§1.8). The head position occupied by a COMPLEMENTIZER when one is present. A finite verb can be moved to this position if there is no complementizer in the clause. This is a NON–ARGU-MENT POSITION.

COMPLEMENT (§1.8). The constituent of a phrase or clause that is governed by the HEAD, for example the object of a verbal head or a prepositional head. In minimalist theory any constituent that moves must move into a SPECIFIER or HEAD position, never into a complement position.

COMPLEMENTIZER (§1.8). In minimalist theory, a constituent placed before the subject specifier that creates a verbal complement from an independent clause. Typical complementizers are subordinating conjunctions like *that, if,* and *when.*

CORE (§1.8). In analysis of Old English meter and formulaic structure, the core consists of normative positions for all major sentence constituents of the verse clause, beginning with the normative subject position and ending with the normative position of the finite verb. See LEFT PERIPHERY, RIGHT PERIPHERY.

DATIVE OF DISADVANTAGE (§3.5). An indirect object adversely affected by the verbal action.

DATIVE OF SEPARATION (§3.5). An indirect object deprived of something rather than given something.

DEEP STRUCTURE (§1.8). In early generative grammar, an acceptable order of words with each constituent in the position where it is interpreted.

DISPLACEMENT (§1.8). Rightward repositioning of heavier constituents. Assumed in minimalist theory to result from leftward movement of other constituents that are typically lighter.

DITRANSITIVE VERB (§1.8). A verb that takes two objects.

DOUBLE-OBJECT CONSTRUCTION (§1.8). A construction that has two objects, both of which are realized as nouns rather than as prepositional phrases. See PREPOSITIONAL DATIVE CONSTRUCTION.

DUMMY (§5.6). A word used without regard for its usual meaning to occupy a required syntactic position.

ELISION (§10.8). Assignment of adjacent unstressed vowels to one metrical position. In alliterative meter elision normally (perhaps always) occurs only when both vowels are unstressed.

EMPHATIC FRONTING (§1.5). Movement of a constituent before the subject to provide a kind of emphasis that does not depend on stress and is not restricted to stress-based languages.

ENJAMBMENT (§1.22). An unexpected occurrence of a metrical boundary between words in close syntactic composition.

EXPLANATORY POWER (§1.8). Linguistic and metrical rules have explanatory power if they provide an explanation for *why* they apply as they do. A rule that does no more than to distinguish attested instances from unattested ones can provide a useful descriptive generalization but has no explanatory power.

EXTRAMETRICAL CONSTITUENTS (§1.9). In Germanic alliterative meters, constituents that lie outside the metrical pattern and occupy extrametrical positions governed by a special set of rules.

EXTRAPOSITION (§1.8). In early generative grammar, rightward movement of a heavy constituent. Not permissible in minimalist theory.

FINAL-CONSONANT EXTRAMETRICALITY (§10.8). Disregarding the final consonant by a rule that distinguishes between light and heavy syllables.

FINITE VERB (§1.2). A verb form that specifies the time within which a proposition is meant to be interpreted.

FIXED SP (§1.21). See SP.

FOOT LENGTH AND WEIGHT (§1.12). The normative foot has the trochaic pattern of the normative Old English word. Light feet correspond to unstressed words. Stressed feet include normative feet and heavy feet that correspond to compounds. Short feet correspond to monosyllabic words. Long feet correspond to words with more than two syllables.

FUNCTION WORD, FUNCTIONAL CONSTITUENT. See LEXICAL CONSTITUENT.

GOVERNMENT (§1.3). A relation between the HEAD of a phrase and its COMPLEMENT, for example between a verb and its object in a verb phrase or a preposition and its object in a prepositional phrase. A governor is typically less prominent than its governed constituent and may assign a special form to it. English verbs and prepositions assign object case to their governed nouns, for example, and auxiliary verbs assign special forms to the infinitives and participles that they govern.

GRAMMATICAL PROPOSITION (§1.2). An assertion expressed by a clause with a finite verb. The grammatical proposition is the domain within which syntactic movement usually occurs.

HEAD (§1.8). In linguistics, the constituent of a phrase or clause that determines its syntactic function. Clauses are headed by finite verbs and prepositional phrases are headed by prepositions, for example. Verb movement takes a verbal head upward and leftward to a higher-level head position. See COMP.

HYPERBATON (§1.23). A device of poetic syntax that separates two closely bound constituents with an extraneous constituent.

HYPOTAXIS (§1.8). Extensive subordination of clauses to a main clause in complex sentences below the level of the paragraph.

ICONICITY, LINGUISTIC PRINCIPLE OF (§1.4). A universal tendency toward ordering of words to imitate ordering of other entities in human experience.

ICONICITY OF DISTANCE (§1.4). Representation of close semantic relations between words by placing them close together within the discourse.

INHERENT CASE (§3.1). A case that expresses a meaning distinguishable from its purely syntactic role.

KALUZA'S LAW (§3.1b). A rule against RESOLUTION of a resolvable sequence closed by a consonant in a constituent with subordinate metrical and linguistic prominence (OE 8.6).

KUHN'S LAWS (§1.21). Rules for placement of unstressed constituents in alliterative meter. Kuhn's first law requires placement of all SPs in the first verse of a clause. The second law requires that any unstressed constituents before the first metrical stress must include an SP. See SPMR.

LEFT PERIPHERY (§1.8). A syntactic domain before the normative position of the subject. See CORE.

LEXICAL CONSTITUENT (§1.3). A word with low frequency and high information content such as a stressed English noun, main verb, or descriptive adjective, in contrast to a FUNCTIONAL CONSTITUENT with high frequency and low information content such as a pronoun, auxiliary verb, or demonstrative adjective. Functional constituents are less prominent than lexical constituents and are typically unstressed in stress-based languages like English.

LEXICON (§1.8). An internalized mental dictionary that specifies idiosyncratic semantic and syntactic features of linguistic constituents.

LIFT (§1.10). See METRICAL POSITION.

LINKER (§5.1b). A verb that links a subject to a constituent that provides most of the semantic content in the verb phrase, such as a predicate noun, a predicate adjective, or a predicate adverbial. The typical linker is a 'be' verb with minimal semantic content that provides obligatory grammatical features such as person, number, and tense.

LOGICAL SUBJECT, LOGICAL OBJECT (§1.2). An argument of a lower-level verb that has been RAISED into a higher-level constituent where it becomes the grammatical subject or object of another verb.

MATCHING (§1.19). The relation between metrical constituents and the linguistic constituents aligned with them.

MAJOR CONSTITUENTS (§1.3). Subjects, objects, verbs, predicate adjectives, predicate nouns, and PREDICATE ADVERBS. Major constituents are ordered with respect to one another, in contrast to ADJUNCTS, which are ordered with respect to the constituents they modify. The possible word orders of a language can often be predicted from the usual order of stressed major constituents.

MEANINGFUL PROMINENCE (§1.4). An attribute of unstressed constituents with relatively high information content. Lack of meaningful prominence makes an unstressed constituent vulnerable to reduction and loss.

MECHANICAL PROMINENCE (§1.4). Prominence assigned independently of meaning by stress rules based on syntax. In Germanic languages an unstressed constituent has reduced mechanical prominence when closely bound to a stressed constituent and enhanced mechanical prominence in clause-final or phrase-final position.

METRICAL AMBIGUITY (§1.21). A failure to differentiate metrical constituents at different levels of metrical structure such as metrical positions, feet, verses, and lines.

METRICAL COMPLEXITY (§1.9). The consequence of departure from metrical norms, which imposes constraints on the frequency and placement of metrical constituents

METRICAL CONSTANT (§1.9). A a metrical norm applying to every verse in a poem.

METRICAL POSITION (§1.10). In Germanic alliterative meter, an abstract position within the poetic line occupied by one syllable or by a sequence of two syllables that are RESOLVED or ELIDED. The *S position*, also called a primary lift, is normally occupied by a syllable with primary word stress. The *s position*, also called a secondary lift, is normally occupied by a syllable with subordinate word stress. The *x position* is normally occupied by an unstressed syllable.

MINIMALIST PROGRAM, MINIMALISM (§1.4). The prevailing approach in current generative syntax.

MONOTRANSITIVE (§1.8). A verb that takes only one object.

MOVABLE SP (§1.21). See SP.

NEGATIVE ATTRACTION (§1.5). Movement to clause-initial position of negative particles and any constituents to which they are bound, such as indefinite pronouns. Negative attraction is obligatory in Modern English constructions like *nobody goes* (compare **anybody doesn't go*).

NON-ARGUMENT POSITION (§1.8). A position that cannot be occupied by the subject or object of a verb. See **COMP, OPERATORS**.

NORMATIVE (§1.4). A term used for basic word orders that are sometimes disrupted by syntactic movement.

NULL-SUBJECT LANGUAGE (§3.2). A language in which subject position need not be occupied by a word and the subject is specified otherwise, for example by a verbal inflection.

OBLIQUE OBJECT (§3.1). A direct object with oblique case (genitive, dative, or instrumental).

OPERATORS (§1.8). In minimalist theory, certain constituents that occupy a higher-level specifier position before COMP. These include negative and interrogative constituents that precede an auxiliary in Modern English constructions like *never have I seen such a thing!* and *why did you do that?*, where COMP is occupied by the auxiliary. The specifier position occupied by such negative and interrogative constituents is a NON-ARGUMENT POSITION.

OPTIMALITY THEORY (§1.8). In linguistics, a theory that replaces complex, language-specific rules that may seem arbitrary with universal micro-rules that can be shown to facilitate language use in specific ways. Optimality rules are ranked in a hierarchy of influence and all but the most influential are violable rather than CATEGORICAL.

ORNAMENTAL (§1.8). A term for an element of poetic form that is not regulated by rule, such as alliteration in rhymed poetry or rhyme in alliterative poetry.

PARATAXIS (§1.8). Use of simple sentences and coordinating conjunctions to create syntactic structures below the level of the paragraph, contrasting with HYPOTAXIS.

PARTITIVE GENITIVE (§3.1). A construction that defines the referent of a noun as a member of a set of things specified by a genitive modifier, e.g. *a sample of the chocolates in the store window.* The modified noun is often ZERO-CONVERTED from an adjective, as in *the best of the bunch,* and typically distinguishes its referent from other members of the set specified by the modifier.

PREDICATE (§1.2). A logical entity that attributes properties and relations to objects of thought called ARGUMENTS. Logical predicates are typically expressed by verb phrases in ordinary language.

PREPOSITIONAL DATIVE CONSTRUCTION (§1.2). A construction in which an object is expressed as a prepositional phrase.

PRESENTATIVE SENTENCE (§1.4). A sentence that uses verb fronting to highlight a change of topic.

POSTPOSITION (§1.3). The equivalent of a preposition in a language with strict SOV typology.

PSYCHOLOGICALLY COMPLETE (§1.8). A SYNTACTICALLY COMPLETE clause in which one of the major constituents is a TRACE.

PUNCTUAL ASPECT (§2.3). Used to describe verbs that represent action at a point in time.

QUASI-AUXILIARY (§1.4). A high-frequency verb that can govern a non-finite verb but also governs noun objects routinely.

QUASI-COMPOUND (§1.14). In Old English, a constituent with a stressed adverb that subordinates a following verb.

REALIZATION (§1.4). In metrical terminology, use of linguistic constituents to fill metrical constituents, as for example when a trochaic foot is realized as a trochaic word or as a stressed monosyllable followed by an unstressed monosyllable.

RECIPIENT (§1.8). An animate object affected indirectly by a verbal action. See THEMATIC ROLE.

REPORTABLE (§2.3). Unusual enough to be worth talking about. 'Remarkable' in the literal sense of the term.

RESOLUTION (§§1.10, 1.18). Occupation of one stressed metrical position by a short stressed syllable and a following unstressed syllable.

RIGHT PERIPHERY (§1.8). A metrical domain after the normative position of the finite verb. See CORE.

RULE OF PRECEDENCE (§3.1b). A preference for placement of the most prominent constituent of the verse on the most prominent lift and for alliteration on the most prominent constituent when it follows a less prominent constituent that alliterates. See OE 6.1 and OE 7.2 in the Appendix.

SEMANTICALLY INESSENTIAL (§2.4). A constituent that is not required for sense or grammar. In formulaic poetry, semantically inessential constituents often encode major concerns of the genre, as with courage and generosity in *Beowulf*.

SEMANTICALLY FUNCTIONAL IN CONTEXT (§2.4). A term used for descriptive detail that enhances the reality effect at a particular point in a narrative.

SEMANTIC BLEACHING (§2.4). A reduction in the prominence of a word with low frequency in the language that occurs in a discourse where the word has high frequency.

SIMPLEX, SIMPLEX WORD (§1.12). A word with a unitary meaning like *bird*, in contrast to words like *blackbird* and *upswing,* which combine two simplexes into a word with a complex internal structure.

SP, MOVABLE SP, FIXED SP (§1.21). A constituent of relatively low prominence at the level of the clause, such as a pronoun, a finite verb, a sentence adverb, or a sentential conjunction. Called a *Satzpartikel* in Kuhn (1933). Movable SPs like verbs and personal pronouns can appear at various locations within a sentence. Fixed SPs like conjunctions and relative pronouns precede the subject and cannot be moved beyond it. Though they have low prominence and are often unstressed, SPs have higher prominence than unstressed words closely bound to a stressed word in a phrase below clause level, such as a preposition in a prepositional phrase. See STP.

SP MOVEMENT RULE, SPMR (§1.21). A universalist reformulation of KUHN'S LAWS based on general principles of verse construction.

SPECIFIER (§1.8). In minimalist theory, a constituent of a phrase or clause placed before the HEAD and at a higher level of syntactic structure, for example the subject of a verbal head or the adverb *totally* in a prepositional phrase like *totally in ruins.* Syntactic movement can take such a constituent upward and leftward into a higher-level specifier position.

STARRED EXAMPLES (§1.8). Unacceptable linguistic or metrical patterns constructed to show what a rule prevents from happening. Such constituents are marked with an asterisk.

STP (§1.21). A constituent of relatively low prominence in a phrase below the level of the clause, such as a preposition in a prepositional phrase. Called a *Satzteilpartikel* in Kuhn (1933).

SYNTACTICALLY COMPLETE (§1.8). The constituent formed by a finite verb and all of its arguments is syntactically complete with or without any additional constituents such as conjunctions, adjunct vocatives, and adjunct VARIATIONS.

SYNTACTIC POSITION (§1.8). In minimalist generative grammar, a position that can be occupied by a SPECIFIER, a HEAD, or a COMPLEMENT.

Syntactic positions are distinct from the linguistic constituents that can occupy them and persist when constituents are moved out of them into higher-level positions. See TRACE.

SYSTEMATIC GAP (§4.1a). Absence of a linguistic structure that might be expected to occur with significant frequency but in fact never occurs, suggesting a systematic attempt to avoid it.

SYSTEMATIC EXCEPTION (§4.1a). An apparent exception to a rule that turns out to be only apparent and testifies to the validity of a properly formulated rule.

THEMATIC ROLES, THETA-ROLES, ϴ-ROLES (§1.8). In minimalist theory, semantic roles such as AGENT, THEME, and RECIPIENT, which are assigned to arguments by verbs. Agents typically correspond to subjects, themes to direct objects, and recipients to indirect objects.

TOPICALIZATION (§1.4). Calling special attention to a constituent by moving it before the subject, as in *Pizza I like, calzones not so much.*

TOUGH MOVEMENT (§10.7). Movement of the object in a subordinate clause to an empty subject position in a sentence like *(it) is tough to discourage Baker*, which creates *Baker is tough to discourage.*

TRACE (§1.8). In minimalist theory, a constituent left behind in a position originally occupied by a constituent that is moved after CHECKING. Although surplus traces are not pronounced, they behave in other respects like ordinary constituents. Leftward movement of a syntactic constituent into progressively higher positions must follow an orderly pathway of traces called a CHAIN.

TYPOLOGICAL POLYSEMY (§1.4). A universal tendency to perform similar grammatical functions in similar ways, as with relativization and TOPICALIZATION.

VARIANT (§1.19). In Old English meter, a realization of a verse type that mismatches the normative two-word realization in some way.

VARIATION (§1.7). A constituent in apposition to a preceding constituent in the same clause. Use of variations for their metrical value is an important technique of formulaic composition. Variations are similar to Modern English epithets like *the rat* in clauses like *Heatherington tried to cheat me again, the rat!*

VERBAL COMPLEX (§9.0). The constituent formed by a non-finite verb form and its governing auxiliary.

VERSE LENGTH AND WEIGHT (§1.13). NORMATIVE verses have two trochaic feet with two primary lifts and two metrical x positions. Long verses have five or six metrical positions. Heavy verses have two primary lifts and a secondary lift. Light verses have only one primary lift.

WINNOWING (§1.9). A metrical analogue of the ordering norm for linguistic constituents that differ in weight and complexity (§1.4). See DISPLACEMENT.

WORD FOOT (§1.9). A foot abstracted from a word, as in Old Irish and Old English alliterative meters.

ZERO CONVERSION (§1.22). Derivation of one part of speech from another without a derivational affix or any other change in form.

BIBLIOGRAPHY

Andrew, Stephen Ogden. 1940. *Syntax and Style in Old English*. Cambridge: Cambridge University Press.

Andrew, Stephen Ogden. 1948. *Postscript on 'Beowulf.'* Cambridge: Cambridge University Press.

Antonsen, Elmer H. 1975. *A Concise Grammar of the Older Runic Inscriptions*. Tübingen: Niemeyer.

Antonsen, Elmer H. 2002. *Runes and Germanic Linguistics*. Berlin: Mouton de Gruyter.

Anttila, Arto, Timothy Dozat, Daniel Galbraith & Naomi Shapiro. 2020. Sentence stress in presidential speeches. In Gerrit Kentner & Joost Kremers (eds.), *Prosody in Syntactic Encoding*, 17–50. Berlin: Mouton de Gruyter.

Bacskai-Atkari, Julia. 2020. German V2 and doubly filled COMP in West Germanic. *Journal of Comparative Germanic Linguistics* 23, 125–60.

Beekes, Robert S. P. 1995. *Comparative Indo-European Linguistics: An Introduction*. Amsterdam: Benjamins.

Behaghel, Otto. 1923–32. *Deutsche Syntax: Eine geschichtliche Darstellung*, 4 vols. Heidelburg: Winter.

Bessinger, Jess B. & Philip H. Smith. 1978. *A Concordance to the Anglo-Saxon Poetic Records*. Ithaca, NY: Cornell University Press.

Blake, Barry J. 2001. *Case*, 2nd edn. Cambridge: Cambridge University Press.

Bliss, Alan J. 1967. *The Metre of 'Beowulf,'* rev. edn. Oxford: Blackwell.

Blockley, Mary. 2001. *Aspects of Old English Poetic Syntax: Where Clauses Begin*. Urbana: University of Illinois Press.

Blockley, Mary & Thomas Cable. 2000. Kuhn's laws, Old English poetry, and the new philology. In Peter S. Baker (ed.), *The 'Beowulf' Reader*, 261–79. New York: Routledge.

Brown, Roger. 1973. *A First Language: The Early Stages*. Cambridge, MA: Harvard University Press.

Bugge, Sophus and Eduard Sievers. 1890. Vokalverkürzung im Altnordischen. *Beiträge zur Geschichte der deutschen Sprache und Literatur* 15, 391–411.

Cable, Thomas. 1991. *The English Alliterative Tradition*. Philadelphia: University of Pennsylvania Press.

Campbell, Alistair. 1959. *Old English Grammar*. Oxford: Clarendon.

Cassidy, Frederic G. & Richard N. Ringler (eds.). 1971. *Bright's Old English Grammar and Reader,* 3rd edn. Fort Worth: Harcourt Brace Jovanovich.

Chomsky, Noam. 1957. *Syntactic Structures*. The Hague: Mouton.

Chomsky, Noam. 1959. Review of Skinner (1957). *Language* 35, 26–58.

Chomsky, Noam. 1965. *Aspects of the Theory of Syntax*. Cambridge, MA: MIT Press.

Chomsky, Noam. 1971. Basic principles. In John Patrick Brierley Allen and Paul Van Buren (eds.), *Chomsky: Selected Readings*. London: Oxford University Press.

Chomsky, Noam. 1993. A minimalist program for linguistic theory. In Kenneth Hale and Samuel J. Keyser (eds.), *The View from Building 20: Essays in Linguistics in Honor of Sylvain Bromberger*, 1–52. Cambridge, MA: MIT Press.

Cleasby, Richard & Gudbrand Vigfusson. 1957. *An Icelandic-English Dictionary*. Oxford: Oxford University Press.

Croft, William. 2003. *Typology and Universals*, 2nd edn. Cambridge: Cambridge University Press.

Crystal, David. 1985. *A Dictionary of Linguistics and Phonetics*. Oxford: Blackwell.

Dresher, Elan & Aditi Lahiri. 1991. The Germanic foot: Metrical coherence in Old English. *Linguistic Inquiry* 22, 251–86.

Dryer, Matthew. 2007. Word order. In Timothy Shopen (ed.), *Language Typology and Syntactic Description, Volume I: Clause Structure*, 2nd edn., 61–131. Cambridge: Cambridge University Press.

Duffell, Martin J. 2008. *A New History of English Metre*. London: Modern Humanities Research Association and Manley Publishing.

Duggan, Hoyt N. 1986. The shape of the b-verse in Middle English alliterative poetry. *Speculum* 61, 564–92.

Faulkes, Anthony. 1998. *Snorri Sturluson, Edda: Skáldskaparmál*, 2 vols. London: Viking Society for Northern Research.

Feynman, Richard. 1967. *The Character of Physical Law*. Cambridge, MA: MIT Press.

Foley, John Miles. 1995. *The Singer of Tales in Performance*. Bloomington: Indiana University Press.

Fox, Michael. 2020. *Following the Formula in 'Beowulf,' 'Örvar-Odds Saga,' and Tolkien*. Cham, Switzerland: Palgrave Macmillan and Springer Nature.

Frank, Roberta. 1978. *Old Norse Court Poetry: The Dróttkvætt Stanza*. Ithaca, NY: Cornell University Press.

Fry, Donald K. 1967. Variation and economy in *Beowulf*. *Modern Philology* 65, 353–56.

Fulk, Robert D. 1992. *A History of Old English Meter*. Philadelphia: University of Pennsylvania Press.

Fulk, Robert D., Robert E. Bjork & John D. Niles (eds.). 2008. *Klaeber's 'Beowulf and the Fight at Finnsburg,'* 4th edn. Toronto: University of Toronto Press. Abbreviated as K4.

Gade, Kari Ellen. 1995. *The Structure of Old Norse Dróttkvætt Poetry*. Ithaca, NY: Cornell University Press.

Getty, Michael. 1997. Was finite verb placement in Germanic prosodically conditioned? Evidence from *Beowulf* and *Heliand*. *Journal of English and Germanic Philology* 96, 155–81.

Getty, Michael. 2000. Differences in the metrical behavior of Old English finite verbs: Evidence for grammaticalization. *English Language and Linguistics* 4, 37–67.

Gleitman, Lila R. & Eric Wanner. 1982. The state of the state of the art. In Eric Wanner & Lila R. Gleitman (eds.), *Language Acquisition: The State of the Art*, 13-48. New York: Cambridge University Press.

Goering, Nelson. 2020. Old Saxon *unmet, Genesis B* 313b *ungemet,* and unmetrical scribal forms in Germanic alliterative verse. *Studia Neophilologica* 93, 24–33.

Greenberg, Joseph H. (ed.). 1966. *Universals of Grammar.* Cambridge, MA: MIT Press.

Griffith, Mark. 2016. Alliterating finite verbs and the origin of rank in Old English poetry. In Neidorf et al. (eds.), 103–21.

Gussenhoven, Carlos. 1992. Sentence accents and argument structure. In Iggy M. Roca (ed.), *Thematic Structure: Its Role in Grammar*, 79–106. Berlin: Foris.

Halle, Morris & Samuel J. Keyser. 1971. *English Stress: Its Form, its Growth, and its Role in Verse.* New York: Harper and Row.

Hanson, Kristin & Paul Kiparsky. 1996. A parametric theory of poetic meter. *Language* 72, 287–335.

Hartman, Megan. 2020. *Poetic Style and Innovation in Old English, Old Norse, and Old Saxon.* Kalamazoo: Medieval Institute Publications.

Hayes, Bruce. 1982. Extrametricality and English stress. *Linguistic Inquiry* 13, 227-276.

Hopper, Paul J. 1975. *The Syntax of the Simple Sentence in Proto-Germanic.* The Hague: Mouton.

Hutcheson, Bellenden Rand. 1995. *Old English Poetic Metre.* Cambridge: D. S. Brewer.

Inoue, Noriko. 2009. To/for + infinitive and the long medial dip in the a-verse. In Judith Jefferson and Ad Putter (eds.), *Approaches to the Metres of Alliterative Verse.* Leeds: Leeds Texts and Monographs.

Jespersen, Otto. 1933. Notes on metre. In Jespersen, *Linguistica: Selected Papers in English, French and German*, 249–74. Copenhagen: Levin & Munksgaard.

Kayne, Richard S. 1994. *The Antisymmetry of Syntax.* Cambridge, MA: MIT Press.

Kendall, Calvin B. 1991. *The Metrical Grammar of 'Beowulf.'* Cambridge: Cambridge University Press.

Kiparsky, Paul. 1973. The role of linguistics in a theory of poetry. *Daedalus* 59, 231–44.

Kiparsky, Paul. 1977. The rhythmic structure of English verse. *Linguistic Inquiry* 8, 189–247.

Kiparsky, Paul. 2018. Micro-parametric typology: Correspondence constraints. Paper presented at the Nordmetrik conference hosted by Stockholm University and the Swedish Academy, 13 September.

Klaeber, Friedrich. 1950. *Beowulf and the Fight at Finnsburg,* 3rd edn. with first and second supplements. Lexington, MA: D. C. Heath. Abbreviated as K3.

Krahe, Hans & Wolfgang Meid. 1967. *Germanische Sprachwissenschaft, III: Wortbildungslehre.* Berlin: de Gruyter.

Krapp, George Philip & Elliott Van Kirk Dobbie (eds.). 1931–53. *The Anglo–Saxon Poetic Records*, 6 vols. New York: Columbia University Press. Abbreviated as ASPR.

Kuhn, Hans. 1929. *Das Füllwort of-um im Altwestnordischen.* Göttingen: Vandenhoeck & Ruprecht.

Kuhn, Hans. 1933. Zur Wortstellung und -betonung im Altgermanischen. *Beiträge zur Geschichte der deutschen Sprache und Literatur* 57, 1–109.

Labov, William. 1972a. Negative attraction and negative concord in English grammar. *Language* 48, 773–818.

Labov, William. 1972b. The transformation of experience in narrative syntax. In Labov, *Language in the Inner City,* 354-96. Philadelphia: University of Pennsylvania Press.

Lehmann, Winfred P. 1969. Proto-Indo-European compounds in relation to other Proto-Indo-European syntactic patterns. *Acta Linguistica Hafniensia* 12, 1–20.

Lehmann, Winfred P. 1993. *Theoretical Bases of Indo-European Linguistics.* London: Routledge.

Lehmann, Winfred P. 2005–7. *Proto-Germanic Grammar*, ed. Johnathan Slocum. Austin, TX: Linguistics Research Center, University of Texas at Austin.

Leino, Pentti. 1986. *Language and Metre: Metrics and the Metrical System of Finnish.* Helsinki: Suomalaisen Kirjallisuuden Seura.

Lord, Albert Bates. 1960. *The Singer of Tales.* Cambridge, MA: Harvard University Press.

Lucas, Peter J. 1987. Some aspects of the interaction between verse grammar and metre in Old English poetry. *Studia Neophilologica* 59, 145–75.

Luraghi, Silvia. 1995. The function of verb initial sentences in some ancient Indo-European languages. In Pamela A. Dowling & Michael Noonan (eds.), *Word Order in Discourse,* 355–86. Amsterdam: John Benjamins.

Maling, Joan M. 1972. On 'Gapping and the order of constituents'. Linguistic Inquiry 3, 101–8.

Mallory, James Patrick. 1989. *In Search of the Indo-Europeans: Language, Archaeology, and Myth.* London: Thames and Hudson.

Mines, Rachael. 2002. An examination of Kuhn's second law and its validity as a metrical-syntactic rule. *Studies in Philology* 99, 337–55.

Mitchell, Bruce. 1985. *Old English Syntax,* 2 vols. Oxford: Oxford University Press. Abbreviated as OES.

Momma, Haruko. 1997. *The Composition of Old English Poetry.* Cambridge: Cambridge University Press.

Neckel, Gustav (ed.). 1983. *Edda: Die Lieder des Codex Regius nebst verwandten Denkmälern,* 2 vols., 5th edn rev. Hans Kuhn. Heidelberg: Winter.

Neidorf, Leonard (ed.). 2014. *The Dating of 'Beowulf': A Reassessment.* Cambridge: D. S. Brewer.

Neidorf, Leonard. 2022. *The Art and Thought of the Beowulf Poet.* Ithaca, NY: Cornell University Press.

Neidorf, Leonard, Rafael J. Pascual & Tom Shippey (eds.). 2016. *Old English Philology: Studies in Honour of R. D. Fulk.* Cambridge: D. S. Brewer.

Nunes, Jairo. 2004. *Linearization of Chains and Sideward Movement.* Cambridge, MA: MIT Press.

O'Neal, David. 2018. A syntactic basis for the distribution of metrical types in Beowulf. *Medieval Journal* 7, 29–61.

Orton, Peter. 1999. Anglo-Saxon attitudes to Kuhn's Laws. *Review of English Studies* 50, 287–303.

Parry, Milman. 1928. *L'Épithète Traditionelle dans Homère*. Paris: Belles Lettres.

Parry, Milman. 1933. Whole formulaic verses in Greek and Southslavic heroic song. *Transactions of the American Philological Association* 64, 179–97.

Pascual, Rafael J. 2021. *Beowulf* 1889b, *Andreas* 1221b and Old English poetic style. *Studia Neophilologica* 93, 12–23.

Pinker, Steven. 1999. *Words and Rules: The Ingredients of Language*. New York: Basic Books.

Pintzuk, Susan & Anthony S. Kroch. 1989. The rightward movement of complements and adjuncts in the Old English of Beowulf. *Language Variation and Change* 1, 115–43.

Pintzuk, Susan. 1999. *Phrase Structures in Competition: Variation and Change in Old English Word Order*. New York: Garland.

Pope, John C. 1966. *The Rhythm of 'Beowulf,'* 2nd edn. New Haven: Yale University Press.

Postal, Paul M. & Geoffrey K. Pullum. 1978. Traces and the description of English complementizer contraction. *Linguistic Inquiry* 9, 1–29.

Prince, Alan & Paul Smolensky. 2004. *Optimality Theory: Constraint Interaction in Generative Grammar*, 2nd edn. Malden, MA: Blackwell.

Putter, Ad, Judith Jefferson & Myra Stokes. 2007. *Studies in the Metre of Alliterative Verse*. Oxford: Society for the study of medieval languages and literature.

Radford, Andrew. 1997. *Syntactic Theory and the Structure of English: A Minimalist Approach*. Cambridge: Cambridge University Press.

Redford, Michael. 2003. Middle English stress doubles: New evidence from Chaucer's meter. In Paula Fikkert & Haike Jacobs (eds.), *Development in Prosodic Systems*, 159–95. Berlin: Mouton de Gruyter.

Renoir, Alain. 1962. Point of view and design for terror in *Beowulf*. *Neuphilologische Mitteilungen* 63, 154–67.

Rezac, Milan. 2006. On tough-movement. In Cedric Boeckx (ed.), *Minimalist Essays*, 288–325. Amsterdam: John Benjamins.

Ries, John. 1880. *Die Stellung von Subject und Prädicatsverbum im Hêliand nebst einem Anhang metrischer Excurse: Ein Beitrag zur germanischen Wortstellungslehre*. Strassburg: Trübner.

Ross, John Robert. 1970. Gapping and the order of constituents. *Actes du Xe Congrès International des Linguistes*, 842–52. Bucharest: Editions de l'Académie de la République Socialiste de Roumanie.

Russom, Geoffrey. 1976. A syntactic key to a number of *Pearl*-group cruxes. *Journal of English Linguistics* 10, 21–29.

Russom, Geoffrey. 1987. *Old English Meter and Linguistic Theory*. Cambridge: Cambridge University Press.

Russom, Geoffrey. 1998. *'Beowulf' and Old Germanic Metre*. Cambridge: Cambridge University Press.

Russom, Geoffrey. 2001. Metrical evidence for subordinate stress in Old English. *Journal of Germanic Linguistics* 13, 39–64.

Russom, Geoffrey. 2002. A bard's-eye view of the Germanic syllable. *Journal of English and Germanic Philology* 101, 305–28.

Russom, Geoffrey. 2010. Aesthetic criteria in Old English heroic style. In John M. Hill (ed.), *On the Aesthetics of 'Beowulf' and other Old English Poems*, 64–80. Toronto: University of Toronto Press.

Russom, Geoffrey. 2012. What explanatory metrics has to say about the history of English function words. In David Denison, Ricardo Bermúdez-Otero, Chris McCully & Emma Moore (eds.), *English Historical Metrics*, 15–27. Cambridge: Cambridge University Press.

Russom, Geoffrey. 2016. Metrical complexity and verse placement in Beowulf. In Neidorf et al. (eds.), 82–102.

Russom, Geoffrey. 2017. *The Evolution of Verse structure in Old and Middle English Poetry: From the Earliest Alliterative Poems to Iambic Pentameter*. Cambridge: Cambridge University Press.

Russom, Geoffrey. 2018. Optimality theory, language typology, and universalist metrics. *Studia Metrica et Poetica* 5, 7–27.

Russom, Geoffrey. 2022a. Metrical evidence for the history of Old English syntax. *English Language and Linguistics* 26, 583–601.

Russom, Geoffrey. 2022b. The word-foot theory of Old English meter, version II. *Journal of English and Germanic Philology* 121, 34–64.

Russom, Geoffrey. 2022c. On the difference between rhythm and meter in poetry: *Beowulf* as a case in point. *Journal of English and Germanic Philology* 121, 174–201.

Russom, Geoffrey. 2022d. The mystery of Old English type A2k. In Rachael A. Burns and Rafael J. Pascual (eds.), *Tradition and Innovation in Old English Metre*. Leeds: Arc Humanities Press, 233–48.

Salmons, Joe. 1992. *Accentual Change and Language Contact: Comparative Survey and a Case Study of Early Northern Europe.* Stanford, CA: Stanford University Press.

Sievers, Eduard. 1893. *Altgermanische Metrik.* Halle: Niemeyer.

Skinner, B. F. 1957. *Verbal Behavior.* New York: Appleton-Century-Crofts.

Smith, Jesse Robert. 1971. Word order in the older Germanic dialects. Urbana: University of Illinois dissertation.

Stevens, Wallace. 1957. *The Collected Poems of Wallace Stevens.* New York: Knopf.

Stockwell, Robert P. & Donka Minkova. 1994. Kuhn's Laws and the rise of verb-second syntax. In Toril Swan, Endre Mørck & Olaf Jansen (eds.), *Language Change and Language Structure: Older Germanic Languages in a Comparative Perspective*, 213–33. Berlin: Mouton de Gruyter.

Stroik, Thomas. 1996. Extraposition and expletive-movement: A minimalist account. *Lingua* 99, 237–51.

Tarlinskaja, Marina. 1984. Rhythm-morphology-syntax-rhythm: In memory of Roman Jakobson. *Style* 18, 1–26.

Traugott, Elizabeth Closs. 1992. Syntax. In Richard M. Hogg (ed.), *Cambridge History of the English Language,* vol. 3, 168–289. Cambridge: Cambridge University Press.

Travis, James. 1973. *Early Celtic Versecraft: Origin, Development, Diffusion.* Ithaca, NY: Cornell University Press.

Truckenbrodt, Hubert. 2006. Phrasal stress. In Keith Brown (ed.), *Encyclopedia of Language and Linguistics*, 2nd edn, 572–9. Boston: Elsevier.

Vennemann, Theo. 1974. Topics, subjects, and word order: From SXV to SVX via TVX. In John Anderson & Charles Jones (eds.), *Historical Linguistics: Proceedings of the First International Conference on Historical Linguistics*, 339–76. Amsterdam: North-Holland.

Wackernagel, Jakob. 1892. Über ein Gesetz der indogermanischen Wortstellung. *Indogermanische Forschungen* 1, 333–436.

Watkins, Calvert. 1995. *How to Kill a Dragon: Aspects of Indo-European Poetics*. Oxford: Oxford University Press.

Wimsatt, William K. & Monroe C. Beardsley. 1959. The concept of meter: An exercise in abstraction. *Publications of the Modern Language Association* 74, 585–98.

Youmans, Gilbert. 1983. Generative tests for generative meter. *Language* 59, 67–92.

Youmans, Gilbert. 1989. Milton's meter. In Paul Kiparsky & Gilbert Youmans (eds.), *Phonetics and Phonology, vol. I: Rhythm and Meter*, 341–79. San Diego: Academic Press.

www.ingramcontent.com/pod-product-compliance
Lightning Source LLC
Chambersburg PA
CBHW021659120626
46545CB00004B/1306